Multidimensional Change in Sudan (1989–2011)

Multidimensional Change in Sudan (1989–2011)

Reshaping Livelihoods, Conflicts and Identities

Edited by
Barbara Casciarri, Munzoul A.M. Assal
and François Ireton

berghahn
NEW YORK • OXFORD
www.berghahnbooks.com

First published in 2015 by
Berghahn Books
www.berghahnbooks.com

First paperback edition published in 2020

Library of Congress Cataloging-in-Publication Data

Multidimensional change in the Republic of Sudan (1989–2011) : reshaping livelihoods, conflicts, and identities / edited by Barbara Casciarri, Munzoul A.M. Assal, and Franìois Ireton.
pages cm
Includes bibliographical references.
ISBN 978-1-78238-617-9 (hardback) —
ISBN 978-1-78238-618-6 (ebook)
1. Sudan—Politics and government—1985– 2. Sudan—Economic conditions—1983– 3. Sudan—Social conditions—21st century. 4. Natural resources—Sudan—Management. I. Casciarri, Barbara. II. Assal, Munzoul A. M. III. Ireton, François.
DT157.673.M95 2015
964.4043—dc23

2014033528

British Library Cataloguing in Publication Data

A catalogue record for this book is available from the British Library

Printed on acid-free paper.

ISBN: 978-1-78238-617-9 hardback
ISBN: 978-1-78920-839-9 paperback
ISBN: 978-1-78238-618-6 ebook

Contents

Illustrations

Figures

Tables

Acknowledgements

This volume is the result of a lengthy collective effort. The idea of publishing a collection of work on 'contemporary Sudan' first arose among a loose network of researchers in Khartoum. This network included senior and junior researchers and Sudanese and European scholars. Most of these researchers came to know each other in the course of their fieldwork in Sudan during the first years of the interim period following the Comprehensive Peace Agreement (CPA) in 2005. The Centre d'Etudes et de Documentation Economiques, Juridiques et Sociales (CEDEJ), a French research centre in Khartoum, was then headed by one of the editors (Barbara Casciarri), and in this context it quickly became a central meeting place for these researchers. There the researchers met, swapped ideas on their fieldwork and engaged in broader reflection, whether in the formal framework of research programmes and seminars or in more informal chats and discussions.

In 2007, the renewal of the research agreement between the CEDEJ and the University of Khartoum (with the Department of Sociology and Social Anthropology as the main partner) led to the launch of a three-year joint research programme entitled 'Transformation Processes among Sudanese Rural and Urban Communities: Resources Access and Management in the Context of Globalization.' Within this framework, a group of Sudanese and European scholars was able to create and strengthen academic relationships, coordinate exchanges about their fieldwork and organize debates on topics of common interest. Several master's and Ph.D. students from Sudanese and foreign universities also benefitted from short-term scholarships granted by the CEDEJ and participated in workshops and seminars. Even if most of the researchers shared a background in social anthropology, the range of the disciplinary contributions included history, sociolinguistics, geography, geopolitics, political science and development studies. Although not all of the contributors to this volume participated directly in this programme, and not all of the participants in the programme wrote contributions for this volume, the atmosphere encouraged by this scholarly context was part of the genesis of this edited book.

The three editors were all, in different ways, part of this context. François Ireton has for many years been involved in social research in Sudan, where he started working in the 1980s. He was also involved in creating the CEDEJ branch in Khartoum – the main centre being in Cairo – in the early 1990s, and continued to make a major contribution to its subsequent development until the 2000s. Barbara Casciarri carried out fieldwork in Sudan between the end of the 1980s and the mid-1990s for her doctoral studies. She returned to Sudan in 2006 to head the CEDEJ. Munzoul Assal also had early contacts with French researchers in Sudan as part of the Kassala-Gedaref Programme (1992–95) while undertaking his master's thesis at the University of Khartoum. Following his return to Sudan after completing a Ph.D. in Norway, he was appointed a professor in the University of Khartoum's Department of Anthropology and became the main referee for this international academic exchange. The editors were enthused by this context, which generated valuable discussions between junior and senior researchers from different disciplines and from various nationalities. Some common themes emerged, such as the wish to understand better the major multilevel changes that were affecting Sudan in the 2000s, and the sense that the CPA period was a crucial benchmark for the country. We therefore decided to initiate a collective, interdisciplinary and fieldwork-based book on Sudan. The concept for this volume was first discussed by the editors and most of the contributors during a workshop held at the CEDEJ centre in Khartoum in November 2009, and the first drafts of the chapters were written during 2010. The process of producing the volume was lengthy. During this time, major events in the history of the country occurred: the independence of South Sudan in July 2011 and the dramatic conflicts that followed. As discussed in the introduction, this volume is marked by this wider historical context and its own specific genesis, both in terms of the time span covered by our analysis (the fieldwork was mainly carried out during the interim period in 2006–11) and by the underlying sense that the authors shared at the time of their research and writing of the potential for a 'new (and still united) Sudan'. If this became unrealistic after the south's separation in July 2011, the wish to contribute to a better understanding of the past, present and future of today's Sudans (in the plural) remains an objective of this book.

We are grateful to the institutions (universities or research programmes) that provided academic and financial support for this volume. In Sudan, we would like to thank our colleagues at the University of Khartoum (and especially the Department of Sociology and Social Anthropology and Musa A. Abdul-Jalil, head of the department until 2013) and at the Ahfad

University of Women in Omdurman (particularly the REED extension and its former director, Elsamawal Khalil Makki). We also wish to thank the CEDEJ branch in Khartoum and the researchers of the ANR-DFG Franco-German programme Water Management in Khartoum International Research (WAMAKHAIR) (2008–12) for their assistance. This volume is also the outcome of investigations and meetings that were supported by the French Agence Nationale de la Recherche (ANR) programme Anthropologie du Droit dans les Mondes Musulmans Asiatiques et Africains (ANDROMAQUE) (2011–14); we are grateful to this programme and its academic coordinator, Baudoin Dupret, the director of the Centre Jacques Berque in Rabat, Morocco.

As far as the publication process is concerned, we would like to thank all of the contributors to the book for their patience throughout the revision of their contributions and during the lengthy delay prior to the final publication. This volume owes much to the variety of their disciplinary backgrounds and also to the diversity of their national academic backgrounds (Sudan, France, Italy, Norway, Germany and the United Kingdom). We also have to thank a large group of international scholars for their comments on the initial drafts of the chapters: David Blanchon, Eric Denis, Catherine Miller and Roland Marchal (France); Abdalbasit Saeed and Abdelghaffar M. Ahmed (Sudan); Mauro Van Aken (Italy); Leif Manger and Gunnar Sorbo (Norway); and Justin Willis and Tony J.A. Allen (UK). The manuscript benefitted significantly from the comments of two anonymous readers from Berghahn Books, whose suggestions encouraged us to reframe the volume and to improve the quality of its content. For the editing of the volume into idiomatic English, we are grateful to Françoise and Peter Gillespie (Wordcraft) and more particularly to James Roslington (University of Cambridge). Thanks must also go to Pierre-Vincent Cresceri for his editing of the style of the final manuscript and to Francesco Staro for the index. Thanks are also due to Alice Franck for drawing the 'General Map of Sudan' for this book. A special thank-you goes to Heather J. Sharkey for her precious suggestions about the final framing of the volume.

This volume is dedicated to several individuals who were not involved in its academic or editorial production but who have supported us in different ways during these years. To the memory of those who will not see the outcome of our efforts: Alain Roussillon, the former director of the CEDEJ in Cairo, who died suddenly in 2007, and Othman Mubarak, who left the CEDEJ all too soon in 2010; for nearly fifteen years, he was the CEDEJ's driver and much more besides. To our family and friends, who supported us during (and despite) our frenetic work agendas: little Idir, Kader, Francesca Casciarri and Eirik Aspelund. To all the Sudanese we met during our research in Sudan – the numerous peasants, pastoralists or urban dwellers concerned by the analyses of this volume: in this kind of work, they are all too often reduced to mere 'sources of information', but we have shared with them far more than this, both in our daily lives and in our common desire for a better future rooted in justice and peace for their country and its peoples.

B. Casciarri
M. Assal
F. Ireton
14 February 2014

Notes on the Transliteration of Arabic Terms

The criteria used in this volume for the transliteration of Arabic terms (which are generally written in italics, except for the proper names of places and persons) are the following:

ا	*ā* (*a, i* or *u* at the beginning of the word)	ط	*ṭ*
ب	*b*	ظ	*ẓ*
ت	*t*	ع	ʿ
ث	*th*	غ	*gh*
ج	*j*	ف	*f*
ح	*ḥ*	ق	*g* (dialect); *q* (classical)
خ	*kh*	ك	*k*
د	*d*	ل	*l*
ذ	*dh*	م	*m*
ر	*r*	ن	*n*
ز	*z*	ه	*h*
س	*s*	و	*w, u, ū or ō*
ش	*sh*	ي	*y, ī or ē*
ص	*ṣ*	---ة	*---a*
ض	*ḍ*	ء	ʾ

We normally use the singular form of Arabic words, adding the suffix 's' for the plural (e.g., *farīg*s, 'camps', rather than *furgān*), except in cases in which the plural form expressly refers to a particular phenomenon (e.g., *awlād,* plural of *walad,* 'son', which evokes a kinship group in the Sudanese context). However, for the names of ethnic or tribal groups, the plural form is used (without italics) for the singular (e.g., 'the Aḥāmda' and 'an Aḥāmda leader' rather than 'a ḥāmmedi leader', as it would strictly be in the singular Arabic form of this ethnonym).

In transcribing local terms, we have opted for a transcription based on the pronunciation of the Sudanese standard dialect. Accordingly, the letter ق is transcribed as 'g' (which is close to the vernacular phonetic pronunciation) rather than 'q' (as used in classical Arabic). The same rule applies to the sounds of standard Arabic consonants that are not normally used in the dialect (the letters ث, 'th', and ذ, 'dh', are simplified as 't' and 'd') and for vowels (such as 'o' or 'e') that exist only in dialectal usage. However, we use the standard classical Arabic transliteration for terms mentioned with reference to written sources or official discourse, which in Sudan are not given in dialect.

For cases in which an accepted transliteration is widely used in written texts, we use such forms even though they may differ from the local vernacular (e.g., 'sheikh', without italics, instead of *sheīkh*). We apply the same rationale to personal names (e.g., 'Mahdi', 'Khalifa Abdullahi', instead of Maḥdī, Khalīfa ʿAbdullahi) and toponyms (e.g., 'Khartoum', 'Darfur', instead of Kharṭūm, Dārfūr). The same principle is also adopted for ethnic names that are generally known by a simplified transcription in the literature on Sudan (e.g., 'Baggara', 'Nuba', instead of Baggāra, Nūba).

A translation is given (in parentheses) at the first use of a term in vernacular Arabic in each of the articles. This may be further elaborated with a footnote if the term requires detailed explanation.

Abbreviations

ABC	Abyei Boundaries Commission
AfDB	African Development Bank
AMIS	African Union Mission in Sudan
ANDROMAQUE	Anthropologie du Droit dans les Mondes Musulmans Asiatiques et Africains
ANR	Agence Nationale de la Recherche
BPD	barrels (of oil) per day
CBO	Community Based Organization
CBS	Central Bureau of Statistics
CCMD	Chinese Consortium for the Merowe Dam
CEDEJ	Centre d'Etudes et de Documentation Economiques, Juridiques et Sociales
CMI	Christian Michelsen Institute
CNPC	China National Petroleum Corporation
CPA	Comprehensive Peace Agreement
CPECC	China Petroleum Engineering and Construction Corporation
CWHEC	China Hydraulic and Hydroelectric Construction Group Corporation
CWE	China International Water and Electric Corporation
DIU	Dams Implementation Unit
DUP	Democratic Unionist Party
ECOS	European Coalition on Oil in Sudan
EMDH	Enfants du Monde – Droits de l'Homme
EPRDF	Ethiopian People's Revolutionary Democratic Front
ESIA	environmental and social impact assessment
EU	European Union

EXIM	Export-import
FAR	Fellowship for African Relief
FDI	foreign direct investment
GDP	gross domestic product
GERD	Grand Ethiopian Renaissance Dam
GNPOC	Greater Nile Petroleum Operating Company
GoS	Government of Sudan
GoSS	Government of South Sudan
IAAS	Institute for African and Asian Studies
ICC	International Criminal Court
ICT	information and communication technologies
IDMC	Internal Displacement Monitoring Centre
IDP	internally displaced person
IGAD	Intergovernmental Authority on Development
IFPRI	International Food Policy Research Institute
IMF	International Monetary Fund
INL	Institute of National Language
IPA	International Phonetic Alphabet
IPCC	Intergovernmental Panel on Climate Change
IREMAM	Institut de Recherche et d'Etudes sur le Monde Arabe et Musulman
IRL	Institute of Regional Languages
IWMI	International Water Management Institute
JEM	Justice and Equality Movement
KSWC	Khartoum State Water Corporation
IOM	International Organization for Migration
ISESCO	Islamic Educational, Scientific and Cultural Organization
MDG	Millennium Development Goal
MDTF	Multi-Donor Trust Fund
MOEST	Ministry of Education, Science and Technology
MoFED	Ethiopian Ministry of Finance and Economic Development
MPPPU	Ministry of Physical Planning and Public Utilities
NATO	North Atlantic Treaty Organization
NBI	Nile Basin Initiative
NCCER	National Center for Curriculum and Educational Research
NCP	National Congress Party

NEC	National Electricity Corporation
NGO	nongovernmental organization
NIF	National Islamic Front
NPA	Norwegian People's Aid
OCHA	Office for the Coordination of Humanitarian Affairs
OECD	Organization for Economic Cooperation and Development
OMCT	Organisation Mondiale Contre la Torture
PCA	Permanent Court of Arbitration
PDF	Popular Defence Forces
PPP	public-private partnership
RCC	Revolutionary Command Council
RLC	Report of the Rejaf Language Conference
SAF	Sudan Armed Forces
SAP	structural adjustment plan
SCP	Sudanese Communist Party
SCRN	Sudan Catholic Radio Network
SDG	Sudanese dinar/Sudanese pound
SHHS	Sudan Households Survey
SIL	Summer Institute of Linguistics
SLA/M	Sudan Liberation Army/Movement
SPLA/M	Sudan People's Liberation Army/Movement
SRS	Sudan Radio Service
SUM	Sudan United Mission
UN	United Nations
UNAMID	United Nations–African Union Mission in Darfur
UNDP	United Nations Development Programme
UNESCO	United Nations Educational, Scientific and Cultural Organization
UNICEF	United Nations Children's Fund
UNSC	United Nations Security Council
UP	Umma Party
USAID/OTI	United States Agency for International Development/ Office for Transition Initiatives
WAMAKHAIR	Water Management in Khartoum International Research
WES	Water, Environment and Sanitation
WHO	World Health Organization
WNPOC	White Nile Petroleum Operating Company

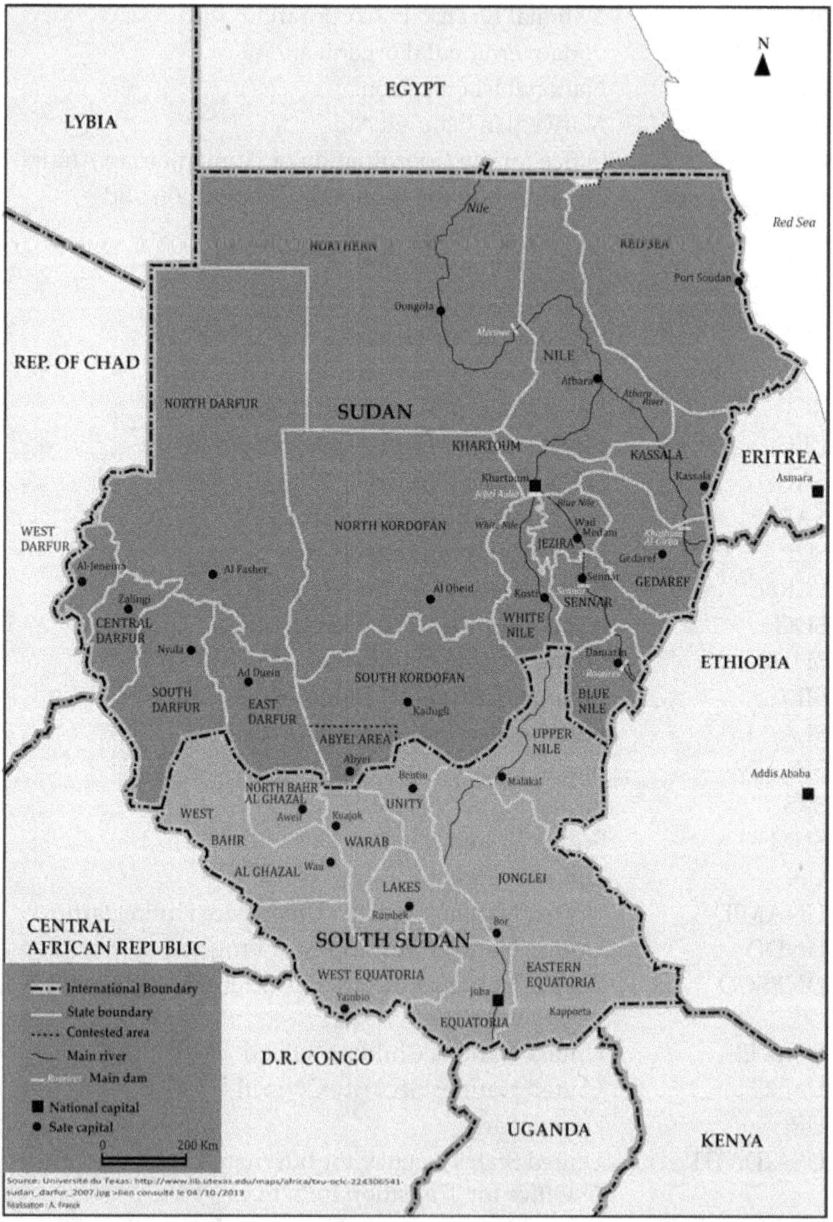

General Map of Sudan

Introduction

Multidimensional Change in Sudan (1989–2011)

Insights from Fieldwork

Barbara Casciarri, Munzoul A.M. Assal and François Ireton

The Comprehensive Peace Agreement (CPA) period (2005–11) witnessed the development and proliferation of research and analysis focused on the former Sudan. For any observer who had previously been familiar with Sudan, it became almost banal to remark on the rapid transformation that affected the country during these years. Important changes were visible at multiple levels: the reshaping of landscapes, rural as well as urban, and the redefinition of their relationships; changes in forms of livelihood and ways of producing and reproducing economic and social life, in terms of new actors and settings, class articulation, and patterns of life and consumption; the growing complexity of the political arena and its subjects, strategies, alliances and legitimating discourses; the rise of 'new' conflicts and the evolution of 'old' conflicts with their local, national and international entanglements; a spiral in identity claims with their shifting boundaries and wider implications; and the simultaneous and growing intervention of outside forces in all their varieties – humanitarian aid, businessmen, 'peace builders' and 'developers'. The perspective shared by the contributors to this volume is located within this particular context: the recent historical conjuncture prior to the separation of South Sudan after the 2011 referendum, an event whose radical impact on both countries is undeniable. This perspective takes into account dynamics that were observed in Sudan during the first decade of the twenty-first century, and is mainly based on fieldwork carried out between 2006 and 2011. In this framework, we talk about 'Sudan' and mainly use the historical present to refer to the context of the late unified Sudan in the period that

Notes for this chapter begin on page 12.

preceded the separation of the two states in July 2011. Given the reconfigurations produced by the two epochal events of 2011 (i.e., the referendum vote in January and the secession in July), the authors of this volume consider it a useful contribution for understanding today's Sudans to take a step backwards. This focuses scholars' attention on the situation that the authors observed during the final years of the former Sudan, with a particular insight into and emphasis on the multilevel changes that marked this period. Put differently, the volume does not seek to address or to follow the development of events in the two countries during the postsecession period.

Too Many Changes in Too Short a Time: How to Grasp Change in the CPA's Sudan?

The multiplication, depth and rapidity of changes in Sudan may be unanimously agreed upon by observers of the country's dynamics. However, once we have agreed on this focus on 'recent changes', a much more difficult task is to retrieve a leitmotiv, a guiding thread with some valuable, updated categories and theoretical approaches, that would allow us to identify a solid link for the explanation of such dynamics and to avoid the risk of perpetuating a fragmented vision of this multifaceted and complex reality. The challenge should thus be to make sense of this conjuncture beyond a simple juxtaposition of the 'striking changes' that are before us. Thus, if we concur with the general statement of some scholars who analyse the relevant dynamics that affect the continent – saying, for example, that 'something big was happening in Africa during the early years of the twenty-first century' (Melber and Southall 2009: xix) – and accept the challenge of interpreting the complex process of change that affected Sudanese society in the past few years, we need to take into account other parallel questions evolving around the notion of change.

The first major difficulty, as we evoke the relevant dynamics of transformation, is to agree on the 'turning point' – if there is one – in this process of change. This would require us to identify more clearly the factors and actors of a possible *before* and *after*. The political (macroscale) dimension is often chosen as the dominant perspective in establishing periods and turning points, even if this approach may be misleading. From the perspective of national political events, 1989 seems to emerge as a turning point, as the beginning of a new regime. This regime, labelled Islamic and authoritarian, worked for the restructuring of the state and its forms of governance, and (despite the initial prophecies of a short life) represented the longest period of stability for independent Sudan. Moreover, this temporal marker may also echo the international turn of the so-called 'new world order' after the end of the Cold War. The dominant macropolitical perspective would later overwhelm other processes and *longue durée* approaches by assuming 2005 (the end of the civil war between north and south) as another 'starting point' and too hastily claiming the entry of Sudan into a postconflict era. However, this emphasis on the political dimension – and actually on its *événementiel* aspect – hinders the aim of properly identifying the levels and processes of change.[1] Thus, although it is important, the political domain should be comprehended at a multiscale level and in connection with other spheres of a more complex social reality (including economic, sociocultural and ideological realities), according to the variety of its rhythms and dynamics. Furthermore, changes would be better analysed and understood in terms of processes, and by enquiry into the deep past roots of the present, rather than as a clear-cut beginning of the 'new'. The same could be said of the aftermath of the outcome of the 2011 referendum and the independence of South Sudan. Undoubtedly this event was a radical change, but if we are to gain an understanding of the contemporary and future social configurations of the two countries, we will need to shed light on the dynamics of the 'many Sudans' (Ryle and Willis 2011) that existed before, transversally and independently from the formal political and territorial separation sealed by the vote of 9 January 2011. Regardless of the disciplinary backgrounds of its contributors, this volume asserts the importance of a basic political approach to social dynamics, but it refuses a conception of 'politics' that is limited to its macropolitical and *événementiel* dimensions.

A second element that risks muddling our efforts to understand recent changes in Sudan and their links and roots is the widespread use of the label 'globalization'. This term, which is presumably attractive as a resource for fixing the idea of a multilevel and planetary change in a single dense and powerful word, has become a blanket notion. Yet the word is misleading, given the ambiguous use often made of it without better defining the crucial elements that it covers in different times, spaces and contexts. The polarization of scholarly (and political) debate between, on the one hand, advocates who exalt the coming and generalization of a new era of democracy, civil society empowerment, poverty eradication and world cultural homogenization and, on the other hand, naysayers who deny every relevant change in the early dynamics of (uneven) North-South relations,[2] increasing exploitation, developing injustice and exclusion, and persistent underdevelopment has sometimes blocked the progress of an analysis of contemporary global and local transformations and has nurtured the unclear and overly widespread use of the globalization paradigm. Some approaches have tried to balance these two poles, for example, by referring to theories of dependency or uneven exchange. They attempt to capture the 'new' character of the socioeconomic configurations of recent decades but without identifying an absolute turning point and preferring to talk of the '*development of* globalization' (Amin 1995). They argue that 'globalization is not new' and should be conceived of as a process intrinsically linked to the expansion of a world capitalist system from its first centuries onwards (Wallerstein 2002). This view does not imply an absence of novelties, at the quantitative as well as the qualitative level, in what is regarded as the late and most contemporary phase of globalization. Others have widened the perspective to the shifting international relations of force in what has been labelled 'subaltern globalization' (Marchal 2008). This approach stresses the role of the political and economic actors of the South, such as China. Other researchers have preferred to talk about 'globalizations' (Perrot and Malaquais 2009) to underline the plurality of dynamics that the North-focused attention directed at this notion often fails to appreciate. In any case, for those who refuse the optimistic (and in some degree ideologically driven) vision of globalization as a new age of planetary interdependence and integration (Friedman 2000), the idea of contemporary Southern exclusion and subordination has to be conceived as an ambivalent one (Duffield 2001).

We feel that we cannot simply ignore the dilemma in relation to the total rejection or the cautious adoption of the notion of globalization as a tool able to provide a useful framework for the analysis of contemporary transformations for the Sudanese context as well as for others. This intellectual uneasiness can be relieved, albeit not solved, if we resort to categories that, in the aftermath of the post–Cold War criticism of 'grand theories' and the supremacy of a neoliberal *pensée unique,* have been stigmatized as unfashionable. So, could an enquiry into the forms and effects of (global) capitalist penetration in Africa, freed from every form of dogmatic orthodoxy,[3] be a valuable 'guiding perspective' for understanding contemporary multiple transformations in contemporary Sudan? If we assume as a basic quality of 'millennial capitalism' (a capitalism whose 'second coming' could be neutrally and euphemistically defined as globalization) the capacity of a neoliberal triumphant economy to reshape at the planetary level access to wealth and power, patterns of social exclusion and inclusion, and identities and ideologies 'in ways both strange and familiar' (Comaroff and Comaroff 2000), we may obtain a general framework to analyse some of the dynamics of change (and their interconnections). To accept the coexistence of strangeness (the 'new' forms and categories) with familiarity (the 'old' forms and categories) can allow us to interrogate the specific forms of present processes and their interrelationships without rejecting entirely and uncritically – as would be the case in postmodernist thought, in tune with the ideology of globalization – some basic lines of analysis drawn from previous paradigms. These paradigms have focused on the complex product of relations of domination (*between* North and South as well as *within* the South itself). Although the notion is far from uncontested, recent works evoking a 'new scramble' for Africa (Olutayo and Omobowale 2007; Southall and Melber 2009) lead us to envisage that the puzzling multiplicity of present processes of change cannot be fully understood, whatever our ideological or theoretical approach, without a basic assumption. The assumption is that, even if in much more articulated and reshaped forms than in previous decades, the processes of capital penetration and multilevel exploitation have remained up to the present day a relevant framework for reading situations of conflict and subordination in peripheral countries like Sudan. The task is particularly tough, as a sort of unexpected convergence seems to be at work between the visions of the 'architects of neoliberalism' and of the allegedly 'alternative' theorists, resulting in a shared 'normalization of inequality' (Gledhill 2005) and 'depoliticization of poverty' (Manji 2008) in the analysis of the social processes of change. In such a perspective, we believe that: first, it is crucial to retrieve a critical approach based on the social sciences that places at its core the issue of contradictions and inequalities through an insight going beyond the fragmentation of social processes (and knowledge); and second, it is important to root this reflection in deep, field-based and localized research, allowing us, in the passage from the local to the global, to rethink categories, to reveal marks of perpetuity and of discontinuity, and to recover at least a part of this sense that remains hidden when we are lost in the multiplicity of the contemporary mutations. Although social science analysis in recent decades has 'often appeared to take neoliberalism's premises for granted as they celebrated global "flows", fragmentation, the "indigenous" grass-root organization and cultural difference' (Edelman and Haugerud 2005: 22), the issue at stake is to shift the focus again from 'interdependence' to 'dependence' processes at work in the context of globalization. Sudan in the first decade of the twenty-first century appears to be an appropriate laboratory to test the validity of this approach and to refine tools of analysis, to find a sense of the ongoing 'great transformation' and its linkages with global capitalism and neoliberalization in Africa (Satgar 2009) as well as with a 'global governance' system where international financial institutions, private companies, donor governments, UN agencies, NGOs and development organizations coexist and interact as essential actors in the dynamics of local change (Duffield 2001).

A third issue might be raised, building on the themes discussed above: the question of what could be defined as the 'domains' and 'scales' of the processes of transformation. Without denying the articulation of social totality in various domains (and the disciplinary specialization of researchers that often fosters it), we feel that one of the most problematic obstacles to a critical grasp of social reality (especially when faced with the complexity of changing contexts) is the separation of what appear to be specific spheres with their relative processes and categories. Thus, political phenomena are viewed in a dominant politically based approach – and, as we said, mainly focusing on macropolitics, formal political institutions and short-term events as markers – while national and international strategic interests reinforce the prior role of politics as an explanatory perspective for the whole. The same could be said concerning the alleged autonomy of the economic sphere (and also, as above, the reasons supporting its claim to be a dominant perspective), which, with the power of its figures coupled with the implicit support of mainstream liberal discourse on the momentous transformations brought by globalization, tends to make invisible or marginal noneconomic relations and processes. Finally, even if it is possible to find links between the two previous domains, the analysis of what is imperfectly labelled the 'sociocultural' domain is even more inadequate. This domain is sometimes seen as 'all the rest' – that which is neither politics nor economics – a categorization that surely fosters the current depoliticization of a wide range of social phenomena. Similar observations should be made concerning the separation of scales, which means the trend of choosing to focus either on large-scale units and actors or on small-scale phenomena and communities.[4] Once again, if each scale certainly needs specific insights, when we pass to a higher level of understanding, the macroscale (whether international or national) cannot be properly grasped without enquiring into the microlevel parallel dynamics that in turn need to be rooted in a wider context. We would like to go beyond such a doubly fragmented vision of social reality, at the level of scales and domains of social totality, and identify how they intertwine, with the aim of achieving a critical minimalist but also global grasp of the processes of change in Sudan.[5] The ambition of this book and the assumption of its editors and contributors converge in stating that social dynamics and social totality need a holistic approach that stresses the interplay of the various levels of phenomena. Although all of the contributors, depending on their disciplinary background and empirical data, focus on specific actors and factors of this multilevel change in the Sudanese society of the late twentieth century and early twenty-first century, we wish to propose a transversal reading of the chapters, aiming to reveal a final recomposition and interlocking of the various scales and domains of such transformational processes.

The Structure of the Volume and Its Contributions

The chapters in this volume are an attempt to provide insight into the patterns of change affecting Sudan in the framework of the global complexity outlined above. It argues for a general dynamic, interdisciplinary and empirically based approach. All of the chapters are based on recent fieldwork on various topics and in different regional contexts in the country. We want to insist on the importance of the accurate and original ethnographic work that is at the base of each individual contribution, inasmuch as we believe that the rethinking of categories and of theoretical approaches – particularly in rapidly changing contexts – can be supported only by a sound underlying and contextualized set of empirical data. Disciplinary variety (anthropology, sociology, geography, geopolitics, politics, history, linguistics and development studies) has also been a major objective of this work, based on the idea that disciplinary fragmentation is a hindrance to the wider understanding of processes of change. At the same time, the variety of scales, ranging from the microanalysis of small communities up to the meso- or macroscales of national and international dynamics, is conceived as a necessary perspective to reach, if not a total, at least a better understanding of actual phenomena. Although each article has a certain autonomy in terms of its disciplinary approach, regional case study and topic (and the authors do not claim a unique theoretical reference), our common aim is to contribute to the clarification of the deeper roots of the past in present processes and of the significant links between apparently local and isolated realities. A common underlying link is the attention paid by each contribution, from its specific perspective, to the general issue of resources access and management,[6] conceiving resources in a wider sense as natural and social, material and immaterial. Without aspiring to offer an exhaustive panorama of the dynamics of Sudanese society on the eve of the independence of South Sudan, this work has two aims. First, it is intended to put at the reader's disposal recent and original empirical data on a variety of domains (as captured by a plurality of disciplinary approaches) concerning social dynamics that were visible in the analysis of Sudan in the context of the CPA. Second, the volume seeks to provide a modest contribution for escaping mainstream ideological approaches, which at best push the acceptance of a vision of the present as a completely new configuration (whose fragmentation and individualization have to be accepted as dogma). At worst, such approaches ignore the deep sense of apparent contradictions and conceive them merely as a sign of the chaotic, ungovernable situation of African countries that can be rescued only by the promises of the 'new world order'. Like social dynamics, this written work also has its own history; its value has thus to be grasped within the dimension that we mentioned at the beginning of the introduction, as an effort towards the understanding of social phenomena at large that interlocked in the recent history of Sudan before the radical breaking point of the separation of 2011. If readers will not find 'current news' about the most recent situation of the two Sudans in this volume, we believe in the need to root the present in the *longue durée* of processes, and we hope that they will appreciate the crosscut of suggestions stemming from these contributions for a better contextualization of the present. The issues raised in the chapters do not claim to be exhaustive, either in terms of the disciplinary approaches or of the selected regional cases and themes. Nonetheless, we think that the effort of reading transversally, across a variety of contributions, and the emergence of common questions could be a support for widening the understanding of some aspects of the processes of transformation in the contemporary Sudans.

The volume is articulated in four parts. Although a common aim is to underline the interconnection of specific topics and domains and to favour transversal reading, we have gathered in each part the contributions dealing with the same dominant issue. The first part focuses on land issues. Recent dynamics show that access to land, whether for productive or nonproductive uses, remains a crucial element for understanding socioeconomic and political configurations in Sudan at the present time. Still the main source of labour and subsistence for most Sudanese communities, land appropriation is seriously affected by ongoing transformations, becoming the focus of growing competition (between local groups, with the state and vis-à-vis private actors) and contributing to the reshaping of territories, uses, users and their rights. In the present Sudanese context, following its accelerated demographic and economic expansion, Greater Khartoum has become a privileged place to observe the dynamics of land grabbing and the results of the encounter between 'old-timers' and 'newcomers'. This is particularly true in some areas at the former edges of the capital, where new middle classes looking for land face the claims of older local groups who dexterously mix tribal identity and state representation to assert their dominant role (Assal). In the real geographical centre of the capital, Tuti Island and Abū Seʿīd, the definition of 'urban' and 'rural' spaces is also questioned by the persistent presence of land devoted to agricultural uses, whose status is increasingly threatened by the impact of oil incomes and the interests of a developing bourgeoisie (Franck). The situation of some periurban areas of Greater Khartoum underlines the unaccomplished 'modernization' of peripheral quarters, and the strategies of new migrants coping with a precarious socioeconomic environment and forced to replace missing 'ethnotribal' solidarities with newly built networks illustrate the complexity of such recent reconfigurations of space in the capital city (Ireton). Finally, the link between land issues, ethnicity, competition over scarce resources and state policies needs to be further questioned regarding its role in the alleged 'tribal' conflicts ravaging some peripheral areas like Darfur (Abdal-Kareem and Abdul-Jalil).

The second part gathers contributions about another crucial resource: water. A historical insight into the hydropolitics of the Nile Valley is fundamental to understanding at the macropolitical level the role played by the main water resource of the country in its relationship with state policies and other African neighbours as well as with internal political dimensions, including the forms of local resistance by populations affected by renewed policies of 'great hydroprojects' (Verhoeven). An insight into a central popular quarter of the capital, Deim, allows us to raise questions on the different forms of social cohesion, and the role that water can play as a 'social medium' in an urban environment where the framework is quite different from the rural context. Thus, the popular multiethnic composition of the quarter suggests the presence of strong links of solidarity and forms of implicit resilience to privatization that challenge the assumption of dominant individual practices in urban settlements (Arango). More focused on empirical quantitative data, a case study of some North Kordofan villages illustrates how small-scale rural communities cope with water scarcity in one of the most disadvantaged regions in terms of natural resources and the supply of modern services (Makki). Concluding this review of 'water issues', the situation of pastoral groups (a persistent component of Sudanese society despite attempts to dismantle their socio-economic systems) shows that the communal management of water can function as a pivot of social cohesion and as a palliative to poverty and stratification. In a period when global capitalism and the neoliberal restructuring of the state covet this primary resource, the reaction of local communities may be a sign of 'resistance', and of the embeddedness of the economy in a society in which water is a core element (Casciarri).

The third part focuses on what can be conceived as some new actors (resources, social groups or institutions) whose presence has played a significant role in reshaping livelihoods, forms and conflicts during the span of time that is the focus of the volume. Primary attention is devoted to oil, an old resource whose full exploitation has been possible only with the ending of the civil war. The turmoil in and growth of the national economy, the redefinition of the country's geopolitical status in international settings, the appearance of new foreign investors and their competition, the reshaping of a Sudanese bourgeoisie and territorial conflicts compete for attention with the increasing presence in Sudan of China and India. It is interesting to cover in more precise detail the economic role of these powerful actors from the South, which is sometimes older than would normally be thought (Panozzo). Yet the issue of oil causes us to shift from the macroeconomic dimension to the microscale of the local people whose livelihood has recently been severely affected by the competition over this crucial resource. The situation of pastoral groups, namely, the Dinka and the Missiriya, in the transitional area of South Kordofan can be grasped only by this interlocking of past relations and new conflicts (Saeed). Understanding the present socioeconomic configuration is not only achieved through focusing on new resources and new economic actors; it is also essential to look at some of the social groups whose presence has been progressively consolidated during recent decades. The ill-defined category of IDP raises more and more questions. The confrontation between an increased number of displaced people in the capital, growing competition on (urban) land and the ambiguity of state policies opens up an analysis of the strategies of this population and the spaces accessible to them to assure their livelihood (de Geoffroy). Finally, an original critical insight into the Darfur crisis, a 'new' Sudanese conflict of the 2000s that has been the issue most covered by the (Western) media in recent years as far as Sudan is concerned, concludes this part by unveiling the political and electoral interests that underlay the intervention by international diplomacy and the great powers in the management of this crisis and the modes of construction in the United States and Europe of a dubious large-scale mobilization to 'save Darfur' (Gabrielsen Jumbert).

The fourth and final part focuses on various manifestations of identity and ideology within these transformations. In relation to this second term, which risks masking the complexity of reality, we stress the relevance of discourses that various actors (social groups, the state, political parties, education systems and international public opinion) build in order to cope with the changing global environment. In the period covered by this volume (1989–2011), religion played a crucial role in the reshaping of ideological constructions. The analysis of the changing strategies of the Islamic movement gives an essential insight into the political influence of religion during the last two decades of Sudan's history (Musso). The issue of religious identity has been historically (and ambiguously) linked to ethnic identity in Sudan. From early times the question of linguistic policies has been fundamental to the Sudanese multiethnic nation. In particular, after the peace agreement, and given the continuing implications of the issue of Arabization, a review of recent decades is needed to understand other levels of the country's political dynamics during the CPA period (Abdelhay, Abu Manga and Miller). The Nuba Mountains, situated in a 'transitional area' that was emerging from decades of armed conflict during the relatively short peaceful period before 2011, are an ideal place to discover how vernacular languages can be used as a political resource by local people in transition. The manipulation of ethnic identities by means of linguistic affiliation is clearly shown to be a major space for (re)building solidarities but also for fuelling sentiments and divisions (Manfredi). In addition to language, the education system is another important tool for enforcing state (or dominant group) ideology. This role can be analysed by looking at the latest changes within the Sudanese school system and focusing on the teaching of disciplines whose ideological content is particularly relevant. An analysis of the notions of 'colonialism' and 'globalization' in school texts allows us to uncover some of the interesting issues at stake (Seri-Hersch). Finally, rather than merely reiterating a synthesis of the sixteen chapters, the epilogue concluding this volume provides a thorough analysis of state dynamics (namely, the evolution of the Islamists and the NCP) from the beginning of the Inqādh regime up to the recent events that have shaken the country, stressing the crisis and the failures of the project that began in 1989 (Marchal).

This volume has been issued at a moment when, once again, crucial political national events (mainly the 2011 separation of the country into two states and its continuing dramatic effects) risk overwhelming other, wider perspectives of analysis. Instead of reducing the complex reality of Sudan and following the focus imposed by (state) national and international debates, this work is intended to be a contribution to an integrated, contemporary but deep-rooted analysis of the interrelated dynamics that have developed in Sudan in recent years within the international context, but with constant reference to microscale, fieldwork-grounded materials. There is no doubt that defining the span covered in this volume with the term 'contemporary' would risk being to a certain degree ambiguous and questionable. Yet we stress again that most of the fieldwork data and general trend in our analysis converge in considering the period between the very end of the 1980s and the first decades of this century as a period of striking, deep and wide-ranging transformations to which we might have applied the category of 'contemporary' had it not been for the radical events of 2011 and their introduction of new dynamics of change. In addition, if the lack of contributions specifically focusing on South Sudan might suggest (especially in light of the 2011 secession) that the volume is a book on 'North Sudan' – in other words, today's Republic of the Sudan – we nevertheless believe that many of its contributions illustrate the interconnection of dynamics and processes that concern both of the present-day countries, which confirms the unavoidable need to deal with the formerly unified Sudan to understand the past and present of both current states regardless of their recently created state boundaries. Finally, all of the contributors to the volume have been marked by the fact of carrying out their research and writing their analysis during the CPA period, and thus sharing an implicit hope that this phase could have led to a 'new (and still unified) Sudan'. If the present situation reminds us dramatically of the flimsiness of such hopes, we may nonetheless hold on to the wish to present through these analyses a modest contribution for the better understanding and imagination of the past and future of Sudan.

Notes

1. In this regard, we may note the multiplication between 2005 and 2011 of research and/or intervention projects displaying in their title the label 'postconflict (Sudan)'. Even if there is no doubt that the 2005 peace agreements were a highly relevant event, often a deep critical view was absent. A critical approach would have investigated such processes from a long-term historical perspective and raised the question of whether Sudanese society had really left conflict behind merely because of the signature of the CPA. This problem was visible well before the events of 2011, that is, the separation of South Sudan and the subsequent resurgence of armed conflict. Largely conditioned by the flow of funds linked to international strategic interests that too hastily adopted the idea of a postconflict Sudan after 2005, this trend was also supported by the emphasis on an exclusively macropolitical short-term approach to (Sudanese) society and its processes of change.
2. Even if we agree with some authors that the regionalization and polarization of the global economy have recast the boundaries of the areas formerly defined as 'North' and 'South' (Duffield 1997), we still feel the need to use these two terms, given the lack of new expressions that could better and more clearly cover the same realities. Nevertheless, we admit that the current context adds to these realities a connotation that is no longer purely geographical but is also social (Duffield 2001: 5), as some spaces characterized as part of the South are territorially included within the North and vice versa.
3. We refer here to a certain impasse of Marxist thought – which, after its hegemonic status in the social sciences in the 1970s and 1980s, has been largely rejected since the 1990s – that represents a hindrance to the contemporary reprisal of some of its useful tools of analysis of social processes of exploitation and subordination at the local as well as the global level and that paved the way for postmodernist critiques and assessments of the existence of a fragmented social world (Ulin 1991).
4. This separation is erroneously justified as linked to the mentioned disciplinary or domain peculiarities, with social anthropologists usually considered as working on a sort of isolated 'traditional' microlevel reality, and economists or political scientists as assigned to the macrolevel dimension.
5. In general terms, we agree with the perspective of a critical anthropology inspired by approaches taken from political economy, which states that 'the fragmentation of social world is not … intrinsic to the nature of contemporary social relations and modes of knowledge but rather is part of their appearance or mystification' (Ulin 1991: 75).
6. This is also due to the fact that most of the contributors had the occasion to exchange their views and research experiences during a former research programme led by the CEDEJ of Khartoum in partnership with the University of Khartoum between 2007 and 2009, whose focus was on resource access and management in Sudan in the context of globalization.

Part I

Land Issues and Livelihoods in the Capital Region and Rural Areas

Chapter 1

Old-Timers and Newcomers in Al-Ṣālḥa

Dynamics of Land Allocation in an Urban Periphery

Munzoul A.M. Assal

As a new residential area in the peripheries of Khartoum, Al-Ṣālḥa represents an interesting case of the conversion of otherwise barren lands into high-value areas that attract a variety of land users, including residents, investors and real estate speculators.[1] Such conversion invites fraudulent practices related to transactions over land including, but not limited to, multiple sales and the falsification of documents. Attracting different people to the area resulted in many dynamics that will be adumbrated in the chapter and include local governance, services and, importantly, the dynamics of interaction between original inhabitants (old-timers) and new residents to the area (newcomers). Apart from what is happening in Al-Ṣālḥa as an interesting and perhaps unique case, there is a real demand for urban land, particularly for residential purposes. This demand is fuelled by fast urbanization in Sudan. Population figures show that already by 2005, almost 40 per cent of Sudan's population lived in urban areas. Khartoum's population grew from 250,000 on the eve of independence in 1956 to 2,831,000 in 1993 – a year when Sudan was said to be 25 per cent urbanized. The 2008 population census shows that Khartoum's population stands at 5.27 million (CBS 2009).

Much of Khartoum's population is made up of migrants, and the bulk of these migrants are internally displaced persons (IDPs). In 2004, it was estimated that around 1.8 million IDPs lived in Khartoum (Assal 2004), living either in officially designated camps or in peripheral areas, with relatives or independently, as squatters. Most residential neighbourhoods in

Notes for this chapter begin on page 30.

Khartoum developed as a result of the planning of former squatter settlements. The pattern of urban planning is predictable: the government plans for and upgrades squatter settlements into officially recognized residential areas, especially third-class areas (S. Bannaga 2010). In other instances, the authorities plan residential areas prior to the arrival of inhabitants. This is often the case with first- and second-class residential areas like Amarat in Khartoum, but also sometimes third-class residential areas like Al-Shaʿabiya in Khartoum North (M. Bannaga 1987).[2] In any case, urban planning in Sudan does not follow a unified regime apart from classifying residential areas as to whether they are first, second, third (and sometimes fourth) class, which distinguishes whether an area is to be considered a town neighbourhood or a village.[3] The existence of villages within larger towns highlights the ambiguity in classification practices in the categorization and allocation of residential land. Needless to say, such ambiguity is responsible for many of the fraudulent practices that characterize land transactions, as will be shown later. Questions related to land are sensitive in Sudan. Despite the fact that as far back as 1970 the government amended the law in such a way that all unregistered lands would be considered government land, that law has not been enforced with respect to communal lands, especially among ethnic groups. Land, whether urban or rural, is the cause of conflicts of varying scale, but also subject to competing individual interests and communal claims that are the very basis of identity politics in present-day Sudan. Such conflicts, as this chapter will show, are sometimes between old-timers who claim ownership based on precedence and newcomers who invoke government ownership based on the 1970 law.

Patterns of land ownership are no less ambiguous than related issues of categorization. In Sudan generally, two regimes of land ownership are recognized: freehold and leasehold. The former indicates permanent ownership that is not subject to appropriation without just compensation for the title holder, while the latter is a system whereby the government leases lands for specific periods of time, after which the authorities may reappropriate such lands for other purposes without recourse to compensate the leaseholder (El Mahdi 1979). These different types of land titles have implications for land uses and the transaction value for the purchase and sale of land. Needless to say, freehold ownership is more valuable economically and socially and, hence, preferred over leasehold.

This chapter presents an ethnographic study of Al-Ṣālḥa, an area southwest of Omdurman on the west bank of the White Nile. The chapter studies the ethnographic present, although the time frame analysed begins with the end of the 1990s. While the chapter provides an ethnographic snapshot of the area, the main focus is on issues that structure relationships between so-called old-timers and newcomers – between the Jamūʿiya ethnic group who have inhabited the area for almost two hundred years and claim ownership by right of anteriority and a heterogeneous population of newcomers who began settling in the area in the late 1990s. The ethnography of Al-Ṣālḥa is then used to analyse local dynamics and the centrality of land for old-timers. The situation in Al-Ṣālḥa is mediated by three aspects that are central to this analysis, including processes of land allocation, the role of 'popular committees' and social interactions between old-timers and newcomers. Rapid population growth in the capital is putting pressure on land, creating competition between old-timers and newcomers and creating hybrid governance structures that are both traditional and modern. As it stands today, Al-Ṣālḥa is a suburb in the making with a future that will be largely determined by public investments in the area: a new bridge and the new international airport.

Al-Ṣālḥa: An Ethnographic Snapshot

Located about thirteen kilometres southwest of Khartoum and on the west bank of the White Nile, Al-Ṣālḥa appeared during the late 1990s as a middle-class residential area accessible to public-sector salaried employees. Residential areas in Khartoum are created either expressly as a result of an urban planning process, or spontaneously as extensions of older residential areas resulting from the increase in urban population. Al-Ṣālḥa appeared neither as a result of urban planning nor as a natural extension. It is an amalgam of scattered villages that were far from each but shared an ethnic identity. As we shall see, however, Al-Ṣālḥa is much more than a concretion of overgrown village centres, but an amalgam of villages connected through and incorporated in the residential projects of newcomers of differing ethnic and socioeconomic backgrounds who managed to penetrate the area and constitute its present-day social system.

As described by an old-timer, the life of old-timers in the area looked simple, as it represented typical village life where people practiced rainfed and irrigated agriculture and animal husbandry. Old-timers in Al-Ṣālḥa belong to the Jamūʿiya group, a branch of the Jaʿāliyn of north-central Sudan. The Jamūʿiya are scattered along the west bank of the White Nile, from Abū Seʿīd to Jebel Awlia. They inhabit sixty-four villages, among which Al-Ṣālḥa is best known.[4] Traditional authority is still present and relevant in Al-Ṣālḥa and is combined with a system of governance by popular committee (*lajna shaʿabīa*).[5] Traditional authority rests with the Jamūʿiya, whereby each of the old villages would have a sheikh and the entire area would have an *ʿomda,* currently the head of the Jādaīn-area popular committee. A delicate balance between traditional authorities and modern ways is ensured at the level of the popular committee.[6]

According to the *ʿomda,* the Jamūʿiya arrived in Al-Ṣālḥa from northern Omdurman in search of grazing lands some 175 years ago. The Jamūʿiya combined animal husbandry with the cultivation of sorghum and millet and the cultivation of vegetables along the banks of the White Nile. The agrarian practices continued well into the 1980s, by which time the area had been deforested for charcoal. Deforestation made the area unsuitable for livestock and it became increasingly urbanized and residential, with more than 120,000 inhabitants according to local estimates.[7] The Jamūʿiya continue to garden along the west bank of the White Nile, and they continue to cultivate the land for cash crops. With time, as we shall see later, new opportunities appeared with the influx of newcomers and the prospect of the international airport in the area. These new developments provided new avenues for property investment, but also led to property speculation and tensions in the area.

Al-Ṣālḥa villages are administratively part of the Omdurman Southern Rural Council and what was historically called *niṭāg al-rīf al-janūbī.*[8] At present, Al-Ṣālḥa is part of Abū Seʿīd Locality (*maḥalliya*). To the northwest of Al-Ṣālḥa is Umbadda Locality. The villages are located close to the White Nile and extend from north to south. Ṣaryo, Al-Ushara, Al-Giya, Jādaīn, Ḥejleja and Al-Ṣālḥa are the main villages. Of all these villages, Al-Ṣālḥa is the most famous, as a result of its history.

Local topography is flat, permeated by small streams and gently sloping towards the Nile. The soil is sandy in the west and rocky and muddy towards the east and approaching the White Nile. The area climate is characterized as semidesert and is typical of North Kordofan.

According to old-timers, the area was given the name Al-Ṣālḥa by a Sufi leader, Sheikh Abdelmajid Al-Jamūʿiy of Abū Seʿīd, who came to the area while it was still forested. The original village of Al-Ṣālḥa lay at the centre of a large area comprised of sixty-four scattered villages. Because of the centrality of the village and the positive connotations of the village name, the name has been extended by popular usage to cover the greater area.[9]

Some of the original villages in the area retain their traditional structures in terms of ethnic composition and social interaction, but Al-Ṣālḥa[10] has been affected by an influx of newcomers and has thus been the focus of property development to the point where newcomers outnumber old-timers.[11] Newcomers are ethnically, economically and politically heterogeneous, both in terms of livelihood strategies and opportunities – some are government employees, others work in the private sector – but also in terms of lifestyles and residential patterns. Some occupy houses built with permanent materials while others continue to live in traditional mud houses. There are also many vacant residential plots whose owners are either unable to build or would like to keep them as an investment.

Due to the rapid population influx into the area, many old villages disappeared.[12] One observation worth noting is that Al-Ṣālḥa's community is eclectic and young, with the majority of Al-Ṣālḥa's inhabitants falling within a category loosely described as 'youth', especially the newcomers. These newcomers bought residential land plots from old-timers, the Jamūʿiya, who are becoming a homogeneous minority amid a culturally, politically and socially heterogeneous community. According to one newcomer, 'the old-timers are encapsulated in their own social systems and their way of life. They are not willing to put up with the changes that have taken place in the area, even though they are affected. Some old-timers did not like the new situation and moved further west to the far periphery of the area.'[13] Social interactions are somewhere along the primary-secondary relationship continuum. Neighbourliness is what links people, particularly among the newcomers: 'we know each other as neighbours only, and even this is the case with very close neighbours', as one respondent noted. Social relationships and interactions between old-timers and newcomers are at best ambiguous, since the newcomers are perceived by the old-timers as 'foreigners' or *ajānib*: '[T]hese people are foreigners. They are bringing bad habits to our area. They are getting in the way of our village relationships. We do not know them and we do not like them.'[14] The tensions between the old-timers and the newcomers reached a peak in Al-Ṣālḥa East (formerly Ṣaryo village) when the newcomers wanted to extend electricity to the area. The old-timers refused to pay the fees and argued: '[L]et these foreigners pay the fees.'[15]

The Provision of Services

Being part of the Village Organization Administration (see the next section) has implications for the provision of services. Provision of water, for instance, requires that access be organized and that roads be clearly marked and maintained, conditions that are not always present in most of Al-Ṣālḥa. Despite efforts of those who arrived early in the area (older newcomers), Al-Ṣālḥa looks conspicuously disorganized. Roads and alleys are narrow, something that renders movement in the area less easy. For this reason, the Khartoum State Water Corporation delayed extending water pipes to homes in Al-Ṣālḥa until the planning process had been substantially completed. Even so, in March 2010, some popular committees in planned areas (Al-Giya East, Hejeriya and Sharom) succeeded in convincing the Khartoum State Water Corporation to extend services into their neighbourhoods. These areas, however, represented only 5 per cent of Al-Ṣālḥa.[16] Town planning and the provision of public services continue apace even if during fieldwork planning marks were observed on walls throughout the district. Water is a perennial problem in Al-Ṣālḥa, since the majority of residents purchase water from vendors with donkey carts for a price-per-barrel ranging between SDG 5 to 8.[17] Ironically, the lack of public water supply provides an opportunity for poor families within the old-timer community to generate income, especially since almost all donkey cart owners are old-timers.

Despite the fact that the planning process is not yet completed, electricity is widely available and was extended to the area in 1999. Power lines may be seen even in areas where roads are rough and narrow.[18] Electricity was extended to the area through popular efforts coordinated by the popular committees, in collaboration with the National Electricity Corporation and financed by the people and a private company.[19] All residents paid instalments, an arrangement considered inconvenient by some: '[H]onestly, the instalments were too much for us. We agreed because we used to have electricity before coming here and it is difficult to live in a house without power.'[20] The fact that most newcomer residents are government employees greatly facilitated the extension of electricity to the area. For the most part, electrification has been perceived as necessary and desirable and without serious objection.

The outlook for public health, however, is rather dim. There is only one hospital in the entire area, from Omdurman Islamic University to Jebel Awlia, a distance of fifty-two kilometres, and the hospital is located in Jebel Al-Tina village, which is forty kilometres away from Al-Ṣālḥa. There are several first aid centres along the main asphalt road that divides Al-Ṣālḥa into east and west. There are also a number of scattered private or commercial pharmacies. For the most part, the citizens of Al-Ṣālḥa depend on hospitals in Omdurman and Abū Seʿīd for health care, while for more serious matters they go to Khartoum or to Omdurman emergency care facilities.

Al-Ṣālḥa has two main markets. The first one is called Al-Ṣālḥa Market and is located along the asphalt road that links Al-Ṣālḥa with Abū Seʿīd to the north and Jebel Awlia to the south. The market is composed of different types of retail shops, restaurants, two pharmacies and a number of building materials shops. All these shops are in fact private homes facing onto the asphalt road. There are also butcheries, bakeries, small canteens that sell various items and a gas station. The other market is located in the western extension of Al-Ṣālḥa and is called Ḥejleja Market. Like the first one, it is composed of a number of small grocers, canteens, workshops and butcheries and is located in the middle of area. There are many tea-selling women in this market, and there are also many places where people smoke hookah (*shisha*). During the evenings, the market provides entertainment opportunities, as there are clubs where people watch satellite TV and engage in other entertainment activities.

Al-Ṣālḥa is relatively well connected in terms of transport facilities. The area is linked to Omdurman and other parts of the national capital through the Abū Seʿīd road that traverses the area from north to south, connecting Omdurman with Jebel Awlia to the south of Khartoum. There are two main transport lines that serve Al-Ṣālḥa: the first links Al-Ṣālḥa with Abū Seʿīd and the second with Suq Al-Shaʿabi in Omdurman. Within Al-Ṣālḥa, people use donkey carts and rickshaws as public transport. The area is well covered with telecom services, and there are many telecom towers in different parts of Al-Ṣālḥa.

Despite its size and population of over 120,000 individuals, there are only five public primary schools (for both genders) and one public high school for girls. There is no high school for boys. Primary schools are overcrowded, with 120 pupils per class. The gap is filled through recourse to private schools, which represent lucrative investments. But people are sceptic about private schools: '[T]hese schools are weak. They do not operate in healthy environment and often located in small spaces, and no one knows the capacities of teachers.'[21] Interestingly, the authorities, while acknowledging that a problem exists, have made investment in new public education facilities contingent upon implementing a physical planning programme for the area. Private education is expensive and out of reach for most workers, notably old-timers. On the other hand, newcomers, who are mostly public sector employees, enrol their children in private schools: '[W]e do not have options. I would rather pay a lot of money and enrol my children in a private school than place them in a public school where there are more than 120 pupils in one class', argues an accountant who is a newcomer to Al-Ṣālḥa. Old-timers are sceptical about the feasibility of education and would rather have their children engage in income-generation activities such as casual work.

In terms of security, there are no serious incidents. Traditional leaders (sheikhs and *ʿomdas*) solve problems and mediate between contending parties. Different types of disputes are resolved through the traditional mechanism of *jūdiya*,[22] and despite the dramatic increase in the number of inhabitants, there are no serious incidents reported to the police except for a few insignificant quarrels between people and incidents of theft.

Land Allocation in Al-Ṣālḥa: An Ambiguous Land Grab

Al-Ṣālḥa is part of the so-called Village Organization Administration. This is a system whereby an area is considered a village and therefore does not undergo the normal planning process. In normal planning, people are provided with residential plots on the basis of certain criteria and upon filing application forms obtained from the Ministry of Physical Planning and Public Utilities. Pantulliano et al. (2011: 19–23) discusses at length the different aspects related to the allocation of residential land in Khartoum, including eligibility criteria, the cost of a residential plot and the difficulties encountered in navigating a cumbersome, costly and entirely opaque application process through official channels. There is much confusion surrounding financial charges and eligibility criteria.

The Village Organization Administration does not follow the normal planning process. Here the eligibility criteria are different, and there is limited government involvement. The process is engaged when a village or group of villages, through their representatives – often popular committee (*lajna shaʿabīa*) members (see below) – approach the Ministry of Physical Planning and Public Utilities with a request for 'planning authority'. The Ministry of Physical Planning and Public Utilities then designates a surveying commission to lay out the village, creating in the process a residential grid with standard plots averaging between five hundred and six hundred square metres. Plots may vary in size depending on the applicant's effective occupancy of a particular plot, such that planning authorities may at times simply confirm an existing occupant's effective homestead. Such deviations from the standard plot size are especially common where plot attributions do not conflict with public service servitudes. Confirmation of ownership is accomplished either through physical presence, that is, the owner is present and inhabits the parcel at the time of subdivision, or the claimant's effective occupation is confirmed by a reliable village source (e.g., the local popular committee or other traditional village authority). This is the process as it happened in the Al-Ṣālḥa village. How land is obtained in such village areas is complex and requires further explanation. Before we attempt such an explanation, we should first consider the nature and role of the popular committee (*lajna shaʿabīa*).

Popular committees have existed in Sudan for a long time. Their presence goes back to the May regime (1969–1985), when local committees were created to marshal support for the ruling party, the Sudan Socialist Union. Part of their function was also to oversee the distribution of subsidized food rations (basically, sugar). Following the 1989 military coup, the nature and roles of the popular committees changed: henceforth they would be used by the government to mobilize people to support the government in its war in southern Sudan and as a means of social control. The instrumentalization of the popular committee as an agency of state security introduced an element of popular mistrust, even if these committees continued to work for their constituencies, providing and maintaining public services as described in this chapter.

If in theory popular committees are elected, in practice they are more or less government-appointed and reflect the ruling party's political line. It is rare to find a committee whose members are not also members of the ruling party. In Al-Ṣālḥa, for instance, the head of the popular committee is a member of the ruling National Congress Party and a member of parliament. Apart from a more or less explicit political role, the popular committee serves the local community in a variety of ways as described in this chapter.

As mentioned earlier, Al-Ṣālḥa is in a way an amalgamation of older Jamūʿiya villages assembled as a result of development pressures mediated by the arrival of newcomers, who are mostly government employees able to afford a plot of land in the area. The newcomers buy land from the Jamūʿiya old-timers, who are considered the owners of the land. The price for a plot of land (of between five hundred and six hundred square metres) rose from about SDG 1,000 during the early 1990s to SDG 40,000–60,000 at the present time. The prices are even higher in areas already subdivided with municipal services (e.g., the eastern parts of Al-Ṣālḥa), where prices range between SDG 70,000 and 100,000.[23] The popular committee plays a central role in land transactions in Al-Ṣālḥa. When a person buys a piece of land, they must obtain a certificate of assignment from the popular committee. The committee issues a certificate, to whomever it may concern, confirming that a plot belongs to someone or is currently inhabited by a known person. The Department of Rural Planning, which is part of the Village Organization Administration, stamps the certificate, validating it as a legal document. The cost of obtaining such a certificate is not fixed, and there is considerable ambiguity surrounding it. With a popular committee certificate, lawyers may produce an act of sale. Also, based on such contracts, new owners may transfer the land title through the Ministry of Physical Planning and Public Utilities and through the Land Registration Authority, which is an agency of the judiciary. The local administrative unit in Al-Ṣālḥa is responsible for approving the activities of the popular committee as well as the sale of land.[24] Corruption in the process of title transfers appeared as early as 2001, when authorities first detected duplicate land sales in Al-Ṣālḥa, resulting in an order to halt the process of land allocation (Pantulliano et al. 2011: 21).

According to the administrative unit in Al-Ṣālḥa, as of June 2010 there was a backlog of five thousand cases of land transactions pending approval, an indication of how people are scrambling for property in Al-Ṣālḥa.[25] Organizing an area that is categorized as falling within the Village Organization Administration is problematic, as it involves disagreements between the inhabitants. An example is the village of Ṣaryo mentioned previously, where there was a problem between the newcomers and old-timers over who should pay the fees for extending electricity to the area.

It should be noted that large sections of land belong to the government. The Ministry of Physical Planning and Public Utilities set aside vast areas for government use. The locality that manages this land may use it for a variety of purposes, but mainly as a source of revenue. The head of the administrative unit in Al-Ṣālḥa maintains that the unit rents out and/or leases land as marketplaces and for manufacturers and investors. Using land as a source of revenue is a practice that is not confined to Al-Ṣālḥa, but extends to other areas in Khartoum and the country at large. Assal (2009) alluded to the appropriation of land not only by and for the government, but also for foreign investors either as exploration leases among oil companies or for large-scale agricultural schemes that affect small producers and pastoralists.

The Jamūʿiya ethnic group, the old-timers, claim ownership of the area through customary laws and hence talk about the right to subdivide their own land. In fact, newcomers who bought land in Al-Ṣālḥa did that through the consent of the Jamūʿiya, who were actually the sellers. Of course, it was not long before the newcomers themselves began trading land among themselves and with others. At first, there were no difficulties with ordinary residential land transactions. However, when the government decided to build a new international airport in the Al-Ṣālḥa area, the Jamūʿiya formally claimed the land and demanded compensation. As a result of these developments, Al-Ṣālḥa came to be considered premium property and prices went up accordingly. The government agreed to negotiate with the Jamūʿiya and finally agreed to compensation, the payment of which, according to local authorities, began in 2007 and continues.[26] By agreeing to pay compensation, the government in effect acknowledged that it misappropriated lands traditionally belonging to ethnic groups. Compensation of the Jamūʿiya is cast against a background of serious misappropriations elsewhere, most notably of government expropriations for development projects, for example, for the Merowe Dam, where people felt that they had not been properly or justly compensated.

Socioeconomic Dynamics and the Centrality of Land

Al-Ṣālḥa is, by any standard, a suburb in the making. It is experiencing conspicuous horizontal population mobility, and the influx of newcomers is so great that it is not possible to get an exact population count. For analytical purposes and according to usage, inhabitants classify themselves as old-timers (*aṣḥāb al-arḍ*)[27] and newcomers (*wāfidīn*).[28] The latter categorization is indicative of the centrality of land for old-timers. The Jamūʿiya consider themselves rightful owners by right of antecedence, having been the first to settle and develop the area for livestock grazing and breeding and for cultivating the land, practices that were sustained until such time as these activities became untenable. For them, land has both symbolic and financial value: 'Without land we are nothing. Land means a lot to us. We have been here for hundreds of years through the presence of our forefathers. While I was young, land meant cultivation and grazing, but now I realize how important the land is. At the present time, land is money. If you have land, you are rich.'[29] It is no wonder that when the government decided to build an international airport in the area, the Jamūʿiya successfully lobbied the authorities for compensation. We will shortly discuss how the Jamūʿiya succeeded in privatizing ownership that historically had been communal. Before we do so, however, we will take a closer look at the *wāfidīn*, or the newcomers.

The *wāfidīn* began settling in the area out of necessity in the 1990s, driven by the demographic pressures operating in Khartoum. Constant rural–urban migration and, beginning in the late 1980s, increased settlement (Assal 2011) drove residential land prices and rents up in an inflationary spiral. Rents in the old residential areas in the three cities that constitute the national capital (Khartoum, Khartoum North and Omdurman) became increasingly unaffordable for low-income employees.[30] In addition to high rents, there are problems related to the ownership and transmission of land as inheritance. While these problems have constituted push factors in moving urban populations towards Al-Ṣālḥa, the district does have a number of attractive features, principal among these being larger plot sizes (between five hundred and six hundred square metres) and reasonable prices compared to other areas in Greater Khartoum. The area was attractive long before the decision to build the new international airport there was made, and the establishment of new modern neighbourhoods on the west bank of the White Nile contributed to raising the clout of Al-Ṣālḥa. These new neighbourhoods extend from Al-Inqādh Bridge in the north to Al-Dabbasin Bridge in the south, which connects Al-Ṣālḥa with Al-Azozab in Khartoum. The planned Al-Azozab Bridge is to be completed with the new international airport in Al-Ṣālḥa and is expected to directly link Al-Ṣālḥa with Khartoum.

The newcomers originate in different parts of the country even though they share a socioeconomic profile as salaried employees in the public and private sectors. Some of the newcomers are retired people who have used their end-of-service benefits to purchase a home in Al-Ṣālḥa, while others have been able to purchase homes in Al-Ṣālḥa as a result of personal inheritance.

A recent significant transformation with regard to land ownership has been a change from community ownership to private ownership, a transition supported by the arrival of newcomers who, anxious to acquire land, provided a ready market for old-timers' lands. Historically, old-timers depended on land for agriculture and animal grazing. As a result of the loss of tree cover, however, the area became barren and the soil eroded. All that remained for cultivation was a narrow strip along the banks of the White Nile, where land is generally owned in freehold *(milk ḥurr)* by a very small number of individuals who cultivate vegetables and cereals. Communal lands no longer suitable for grazing or agriculture were thus distributed in the form of *ḥiyāza*s (holdings) to ethnic Jamūʿiya males who could trace their lineage through the paternal line. The distribution was overseen by village sheikhs, with distributions made to families within the immediate area as well as to nearby Jamūʿiya families.

The process provided a quick source of income for the Jamūʿiya. By transforming communal land to family ownership, the Jamūʿiya were able to capitalize on a substantial investment programme affecting their communal lands. Ownership of Jamūʿiya communal lands was not contested, and the government seemed to have assigned a strategic value to the area, the site of a planned international airport and transit infrastructure.[31] In addition, it could be argued that by encouraging the Jamūʿiya to distribute land, the government was expecting to gain their loyalty and support, an argument that is not far-fetched given the government's similar strategies in other parts of the national capital.[32]

The change in the value of land among the Jamūʿiya indicates an ideational change. From being of nominal value until recently, land for the Jamūʿiya not only represented an obvious economic value, but also an identity issue to the extent that the distribution only targeted those who could prove that they belonged to the Jamūʿiya through the male line. Families then sold land to the newcomers. However, many of the old-timers think they did not benefit from this, since at the beginning land prices were low. For that reason, they believe their livelihoods were not changed, not even their old residential patterns. Some actually complain that due to the increase in the number of newcomers, they feel that they are becoming strangers.

At present Al-Ṣālḥa is an active real estate market reflecting demand for land and the attractiveness of investment in the area. As mentioned earlier, however, this real estate bonanza introduced a number of problems, including fraudulent land transactions, falsified title documents and fraudulent multiple sales schemes. Informants tell stories about selling a single empty land plot multiple times, with problems appearing when one of the buyers begins construction. In most cases such disputes are settled by court ruling, often giving possession to the first buyer. Subsequent titleholders simply forfeit their equity, especially as the courts are not always able to establish responsibility for the fraudulent sales.

The governance system is a contributory factor to the fraudulent practices described above. Historically, villages were governed by traditional social structures, supervised by sheikhs and *ʿomda*s. In this system, villages represent extended, homogenous families. With the newcomers, Al-Ṣālḥa was transformed from a social group defined by family ties to a loosely defined and heterogeneous community governed by a popular committee presided over by an *ʿomda*. While the *ʿomda* and sheikh continue to be relevant, their personal responsibility is no longer engaged, and their authority is circumscribed by the popular committee. These changes took place in the 1990s with the influx of newcomers. The old-timers came to view themselves as having the right to govern without regard to newcomer demands,[33] while newcomers argued that they were entitled to representation and insisted that the planning process go forward with its promise of improved services to an extended area. The conflict was resolved amicably by conceding the presidency of the popular committee to an old-timer in exchange for newcomer representation on the popular committee, even if the old-timers remained numerically dominant.

To the extent that most of the newcomers are educated young employees of government institutions or the private sector, they often surpass the head of the popular committee when it comes to the question of providing services to the area. They exploit their vertical connections in the state apparatus. Educated and young popular committee members contributed significantly in enumerating residents, giving residential numbers to inhabitants, opening roads and building schools. There is an obvious contrast, then, if not an overt conflict, between old-timers and newcomers. In any case, compared to many other similar and new townships, Al-Ṣālḥa developed in a relatively short time and is on its way to becoming a full-fledged town, even if the authorities still look at it, officially, as a village, something that reflects the awkwardness of urbanization and urban planning in Khartoum.

The material in this chapter gives some sense of the complexity of the land question in Sudan. As mentioned in the introduction, in 1970 the government proclaimed that all hitherto unregistered lands in Sudan would become government property. The proclamation was never enforced, a failure that has proved dysfunctional and created problems for territorial management. Enforcing land laws would produce catastrophic results and is largely proscribed as a course of action. This is the case with all lands, residential and otherwise. It should be mentioned that in the African context generally, land is a sensitive issue and hardly amenable to the application of law, especially when such application might conceivably result in the denial of a basic right to land.

Conclusion

Al-Ṣālḥa is no longer a village, even if it is still part of the Village Organization Administration. Old-timer authority and ethnic family identities are giving way to a heterogeneous population of government bureaucrats and lower-echelon white-collar workers. The territory is dynamic in terms of local development; land for residential use is in high demand, and public infrastructure projects are transforming the area from a collection of scattered villages to an area of 120,000 inhabitants. Electrification in 1999 and the completion of the north-south asphalt road in 2000–2001 attracted many newcomers even though municipal services are not universally available in the district. But given newcomer zeal and government connections, the planning process is well underway and likely to be completed soon.

Al-Ṣālḥa is an example of an ethnic group being able to capture government attention and assert its ownership of land. When Al-Ṣālḥa began attracting newcomers, the Jamūʿiya group took the initiative of distributing community land to families considered original to the area whose members could prove that they were indeed Jamūʿiya. By not challenging this move, the state approved it, setting a precedent that will likely lead other ethnic groups to claim lands. This precedent was confirmed when the government agreed to compensate the Jamūʿiya for the land that was appropriated for the new international airport. The Jamūʿiya were satisfied with the compensation to the extent that they deemed it generous and just. By standing vis-à-vis the newcomers, the old-timers are in a way asserting an identity that they think is threatened by the newcomers. The struggle to assert such an identity may look like an uphill struggle, especially in that the area is the object of public investment projects, including a new bridge and an international airport. Indeed, the old-timers have already sold much of the land to the newcomers. What remains are the residential plots in which they have the same rights and status as newcomers. Nonetheless, the story of Al-Ṣālḥa is about more than the emergence of a new residential district in the national capital. It is about land claims and the assertion of ethnic rights. In Sudan, entanglements over property rights are well-known, especially in rural areas where ethnic groups have their homelands, or *dārs*. Ethnic claims on urban land are a recent development, however, and mostly instigated by the government's policy for revitalizing traditional systems in urban areas. This was spearheaded in 1995 when the government convened the Native System Conference. What happened in Al-Ṣālḥa might encourage other ethnic groups to claim land ownership in other urban peripheries, either in the national capital or other cities in Sudan.

Changes are happening fast in Al-Ṣālḥa. Most of the different scattered villages have already been incorporated into Al-Ṣālḥa, and some of these villages lost their names and have completely disappeared. Some, like Ḥejleja, retained their names only to become neighbourhoods in a larger area. Al-Ṣālḥa is a typical example of a rural area being incorporated into an urban system and yet another instance of rural land grabbing by an expanding urban system. While it is fast growing, the available services (especially health and education) do not match the growing need. The number of schools is far below the demand, and there is only one high school for girls in the area. Inhabitants are keen to extend services to the area, and their connections will help achieve that, judging from their success in electrification and efforts underway to extend water service.

As Al-Ṣālḥa is a suburb in the making, its features are not yet well defined. The area is located just north of the new international airport, a facility that will dramatically alter land uses and livelihoods in the area. Such developments, however, may also produce negative consequences, including the misappropriation of public lands, a practice that has already been documented. One aspect that requires further study is the legal dimension of land transfers in Al-Ṣālḥa. Asserting individual rights over communal lands and providing compensation for expropriated lands that were never registered and by law belong to the state is a research area that requires further investigation. The dual nature of urban planning (normal urban planning and the Village Organization Administration) opens the door for many problems, including fraudulent registration of land transactions. An area where the residential plots range between five hundred and six hundred square metres should be considered a first-class area in normal urban planning schemes, yet this is not the case when an area is considered to fall under the Village Organization Administration. Judging by plot sizes, Al-Ṣālḥa should be considered first class, but it is nothing of the sort.

The appearance and development of Al-Ṣālḥa can be seen as a response to the increase in the number of inhabitants in Khartoum. Beneath the apparent relation of cause and effect lie a number of issues that are proper to Sudanese resource conflicts. The ethnography of the area shows clear evidence of conflict between old-timers and newcomers and the interweaving of traditional and modern systems of authority. In this way traditional authority is co-opted as part of the popular committee system of governance, itself a part of a decentralized federal system. Traditional ethnic authorities retain their traditional roles, at the same time acquiring new status as members of a popular committee. Old-timers 'acquire' such status on the basis of a claim of land ownership in the area. In a sense, they successfully leverage their position to convert economic resources into political power. The competition over urban land is likely to grow not least in the context of increasing migration to the national capital. It is also bound to grow in that migration into the national capital is proving to be increasingly sedentary, with temporary migrants becoming permanent city residents.

Notes

1. The fieldwork on which this chapter is based was carried out during different periods in 2008 and 2010. My assistant, Adil Awad Al-Sid, started the work in 2008 through ethnographic fieldwork and initial contacts with informants and officials in Al-Sālḥa. I did additional fieldwork in 2010, when additional informants, including government officials, were interviewed.
2. The classification of residential areas into first-, second-, third- and sometimes fourth-class areas is based on such criteria as size of plot, location and fees paid for obtaining a plot. For instance, in terms of size, first-class areas range between five hundred and six hundred square metres. Second- and third-class plots measure four hundred and three hundred square metres, respectively. First- and second-class residential areas are, for the most part, reserved for the wealthy and include such neighbourhoods as Riyad, Tayef, Amarat and El-Manshiya in Khartoum.
3. As we shall discuss shortly, the Ministry of Physical Planning and Public Utilities maintains a service, the Village Organization Administration, or *idārāt tanẓīm al-qurā*. Old neighbourhoods such as Beit Al-Mal, Abu Rof and Hai Al-Arab in Omdurman are all part of the Village Organization Administration, and organization of the space, size of plots and entitlement to land do not follow the standard system applicable in urban planning. The term 'village' in the urban context has no other connotations than administrative. Such villages are like other neighbourhoods in the city; they are no less developed than other neighbourhoods.
4. Interview, *ʿomda* of Al-Sālḥa village, October 2008.
5. The area has three popular committees: Jādaīn, Al-Sālḥa and Ḥejleja.
6. For instance, the head of the Jādaīn Popular Committee held the position for a very long time and was, in fact, a member of the Khartoum State Legislative Assembly. Many of his relatives are members of other popular committees. In addition to being a political leader, he is also considered a *khalīfa,* a Sufi religious leader.
7. June 2010 interview with Nizar Abdul Hamid, director of the Al-Sālḥa Administrative Unit. The exact number is difficult to get, as the area receives a steady influx of newcomers. As an example, when we started the fieldwork in Al-Sālḥa the first time in 2008, the

authorities estimated the total number of Al-Sālḥa inhabitants to be a little more than fifty thousand individuals. If the current figures are correct, the population has doubled in only two years.

8. This translates into 'southern rural area' (*al-rīf al-janūbī*), which in a way is an amalgamation of the villages south of Omdurman. There is also the 'northern rural area' (*al-rīf al-shimālī*). These names do not have any administrative connotations and they do not represent administrative organs, especially at the present time, when only localities and administrative units are formally recognized as administrative organs.
9. Literally, Al-Sālḥa means 'the pious woman'.
10. The name 'Al-Sālḥa' in this article generally refers to the 'village', not to the area as a whole
11. Interview, executive director, Al-Sālḥa Administrative Unit, October 2008.
12. People spoke about 1998 as the beginning of a conspicuous influx of newcomers to Al-Sālḥa. Since then, the influx of people has continued, as Al-Sālḥa is valued as a residential area for its proximity to the centre of Khartoum, and also due to the fact that land prices are to some extent affordable compared to other areas in the national capital.
13. Interview, popular committee member and newcomer, June 2010.
14. Interview, 65-year-old man from the old Al-Sālḥa village. He has a donkey cart and works in the local market. Interestingly, he is happy working in the market, as his earnings are good: 'Sometimes I make 30–40 pounds [SDG] per day.'
15. Ibid.
16. Interview, representative of the Al-Sālḥa Administrative Unit, June 2010.
17. During 2008–10, SDG 1 = USD 0.4.
18. An official at the local administrative unit argues that approximately 50 per cent of inhabitants in Al-Sālḥa have electricity.
19. The company is called Al-Adiyati Sobhan.
20. Interview, government employee and resident, Al-Sālḥa, October 2008.
21. Interview, head of Education Office, Al-Sālḥa Administrative Unit, June 2010.
22. *Jūdiya* is a traditional arbitration mechanism in which traditional leaders mediate between conflicting parties. The judgement of these leaders is accepted by both parties. The *jūdiya* is a well-known conflict resolution mechanism practiced in different parts of Sudan under different names (El-Amin 2004).
23. Interview, representative of the Al-Sālḥa Administrative Unit, June 2010.
24. This is the smallest administrative unit that is part of Abū Seʿīd Locality, of which Al-Sālḥa is a part.
25. Interestingly, during fieldwork, many informants advised the author to buy a plot of land in Al-Sālḥa. One informant thus laments: 'I think you should really buy a land plot here. I can help if you are interested. Prices are going up, so you better buy now.'
26. The head of the Al-Sālḥa Administrative Unit would not provide compensation figures, even though he mentioned that the last payment he is aware of took place in March 2010. He thought people were paid a lot of money and that the compensation was fair. This confirms findings from earlier studies that showed that residents in Al-Sālḥa considered the compensation they were offered for land expropriated for the new airport generous, although the process of receiving money from the Airport Compensation Committee was delayed (Pantulliano et al. 2011: 21).
27. Meaning 'owners of the land'.
28. Meaning 'migrants'.
29. Interview, sheikh of Ḥejleja, Al-Sālḥa, June 2010 and January 2011.
30. For instance, in third-class residential areas like Al-Sahafa in Khartoum, Banat in Omdurman and Al-Shaʿabiya in Khartoum North, the average rent for a three-room house is SDG 500–700 per month. This is far above the minimum wage and precludes access

for many families who cannot afford high rents. Rents in first- and second-class residential areas are exorbitant.

31. Nonetheless, one informant mentioned that there was a conflict between the Jamūʿiya and the Hawāwīr in a place called Al-Shibeilat, but that conflict was resolved in a short time.
32. For instance, to win the hearts of IDPs around the capital the government embarked on a process of reorganization camps for IDPs during 2003–5. This was done almost fifteen years after the relocation of IDPs to these camps. For more details, see Assal (2008: 148–49).
33. It should be noted that this claim is not far-fetched in the Sudanese context. An ethnic group that has ownership of a piece of land automatically assumes political power in the area. While other resident groups may share that power, the landowners are the ultimate wielders of political power. For more on this, see Harir (1994) and Abdul-Jalil (2009b).

Chapter 2

Urban Agriculture Facing Land Pressure in Greater Khartoum

The Case of New Real Estate Projects in Tuti and Abū Seʿīd

Alice Franck

Introduction: Intense Urban Renewal in Khartoum, an Uncertain Future for Farmland

The starting point for a deep transformation that has taken place within the capital of Sudan between 2000 and 2010 was the oil export terminal commissioned in Port Sudan in 1999. The peace agreements between north and south Sudan were signed in January 2005, reinforcing the role of the land and real estate sector in Khartoum, which had become the major focus of the petrodollar market driving the recent strong growth until the secession of South Sudan on 9 July 2011.[1] The lucrative oil market has not only reinforced the hegemonic role of the capital – as the unique economic pole of the country – but has equally underwritten the conurbation's attractiveness without redressing deep regional discrepancies (Denis 2006). The creation of South Sudan as an independent state clearly affects the situation. Conflicts for resources have been recurrent since Sudanese independence and continue to grow in the border region between the two separated countries. The Republic of the Sudan has lost part of its control over oil resources in the region, but it is still too early to measure the impact of that on urban investments.

The real estate sector is booming and the whole city is being revamped. The morphology of Khartoum has radically changed. Skyscrapers have recently appeared in the city and are designed in the style of modern architectural buildings. These initially model designs in the city centre have

Notes for this chapter begin on page 50.

now been built in adjacent districts stretching towards the outskirts of the city. Thus, this residential architectural model is proliferating throughout the city, and increasingly the construction of skyscrapers is no longer exclusively reserved for hotels and office buildings. Noteworthy urban projects have been quickly implemented, and Khartoum has been rapidly transformed into a huge construction site, wherein businessmen hailing from a diverse array of countries (Sudanese, Arabs, Asians and Europeans) take an active part. The frenzied increase in transport infrastructure construction bears witness to the urban dynamism that has characterized Khartoum in the last few years. Three new bridges have been built between 2005 and 2009, on the confluence of the Blue and the White Niles, with a fourth moving towards completion. Hundreds of kilometres of roads have been asphalted and now connect the different parts of the city centre to the extremities in the outskirts. In the space of less than five years the airport road, formerly full of pot holes, became a brand-new road with four lanes in both directions. The current redesign of Greater Khartoum reveals the sudden openness of the country to the market economy and globalization. This contrasts with the situation since independence and especially during the 1980s, when public works activities were extremely limited. The propagation of prestige urban projects has become the new trend that marks the current era (Choplin and Franck 2010).

My initial research into this location of intense speculation examined the future of the central areas that remained under agricultural activity and how they were gradually being transformed into urban areas (Franck 2007). The approach adopted analysed the resistance of agriculture and farmers to the spread of real estate and the pressure of competition over land ownership. Five years later, the action in favour of urban plan renewal has been drastically intensified and the capacity for resistance severely diminished; three of the five market gardening areas (Tuti, Shambat, Abū Seʿīd, Abu Rof and Mogran) observed during fieldwork in 2001–5 are subject to huge real estate projects (Mogran, Abū Seʿīd and Tuti; see figure 2.1). In this chapter, I focus my analysis on how landowners and the entire agricultural sector can both adapt to and confront the transformation.

The first objective of this chapter is to examine how landowners react differently to the new active interest in their land, the implementation of prestigious real estate projects and the end of agricultural activity. Two case studies are used, at Tuti and Abū Seʿīd. Based on data from fieldwork in 2001–5 and an enquiry carried out in a shorter but more recent period of fieldwork in January 2009 related to the pressing land issue,[2] I will trace the genesis of these new real estate projects. My analysis is based on the premise that land that is allocated agricultural status is of special interest for speculative transactions. Various projects are presented and their key actors are identified.

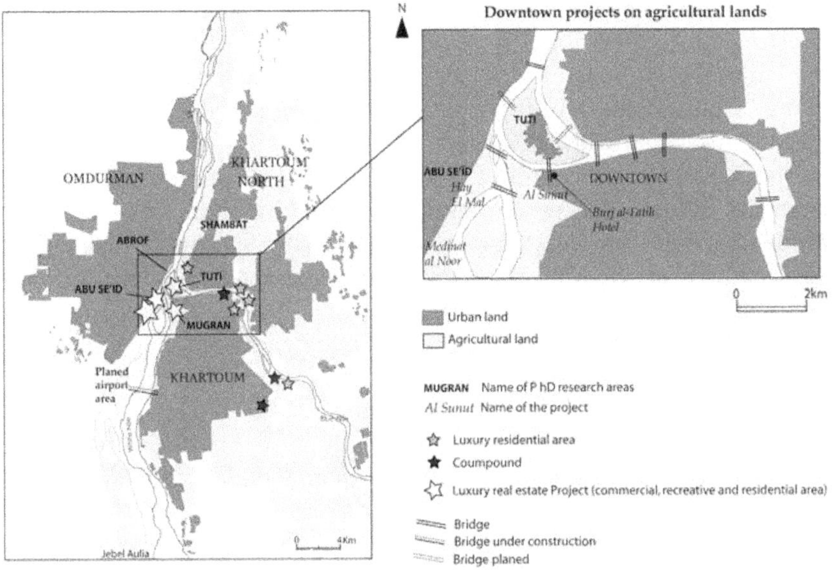

Figure 2.1. Real Estate Projects Affecting Agricultural Land in the Centre of Greater Khartoum

In the second part of this chapter, I examine how Tuti, a genuine rural island in the heart of the city centre, is being transformed. Tuti was chosen because, on the one hand, it has been the site of a symbolic resistance to urbanization for years; on the other hand, currently the majority of the inhabitants have been inclined to initiate or participate in the real estate projects on the island. I extend the analysis to a current land dispute to highlight the ferocity of the ongoing transformations, using Abū Seᶜīd as an example.

Finally, using a comparative approach, I stress the importance of land issues in Khartoum: between Khartoum State, the Sudanese state, foreign and local investors, builders and traditional property owners. The land affected by the new real estate orientations has been appropriated by occupiers over a long period of time. Their identities and social biographies are thus firmly etched on this land. Although they are equally the object of a new urban agenda driven by other actors, two different strategies emerge.

The Specific Attractiveness of Agricultural Lands: The Cases of Tuti and Abū Seᶜīd

The propensity of the Nile to overflow its banks has previously been an impediment to urban development, but with new financial resources the

Sudanese state has now been able to counter this problem. In 2002, the construction of an embankment on the banks of the White Nile, in the agricultural zone around Mogran, heralded the potential of such investments in the capital and highlighted the future potential of the central areas of Abū Seʿīd and Tuti as part of this process (figure 2.1).

Nature no longer contributes to the protection of cultivation zones from the frenzied real estate development. In this new context, market gardening areas epitomize the possibility of the development of tourist and commercial activities, and offer a picturesque and aesthetically pleasing image.

A triple bridge started in 2004 will eventually link Tuti to the three cities that form Greater Khartoum. In addition, a new transportation link between Khartoum and Tuti was completed in 2009, and at the same time excavation works for construction were begun in Abū Seʿīd. Such construction work is evidence of the implementation of agricultural land transformation. The land that lies at the heart of the conurbation, and hosts no construction, is particularly attractive to investors and urban planners. In such locations, investors are planning real estate complexes inspired by the model of functional architecture mixing residential areas (villas, luxury apartments), shopping malls with offices and recreational open spaces.

The Al Sunut Project in Mogran, 630 hectares for mixed-use commercial, residential and leisure including office space, 1,100 villas, 6,700 apartments, a marina and a golf course, was already considered to be oversized in relation to the Sudanese capital. Fifty thousand employees were expected to work on-site.[3] Ironically, the scale of this project is now overshadowed by two larger urban projects. On the opposite bank of the White Nile, in the Abū Seʿīd area, two other waterfront projects are under construction: Medinat Al-Noor[4] and Hay Al-Mal.[5] These projects represent 150,000 square metres for residential and business uses. Furthermore, Medinat Al-Noor will eventually be expanded to 120 million square metres, extending all the way to Jebel Awlia.

Such huge and turnkey urban projects are common within the Arab world (Elsheshtawy 2006; Barthel 2010). These projects draw inspiration from prestige urban planning, in which waterfronts, marinas, zoos and golf courses signify notions of luxury lifestyle and modernity in general. These projects are also singular and differ from others through their deployment of websites and futuristic images as marketing supports. These master plans and Internet sites portray a fixed, ideal and simplistic image of these iconic projects. The Tuti Project, which includes neither an embankment nor a marina, is the least impressive. Even so, with a budget of five billion dollars, the project website[6] uses videos and master plans

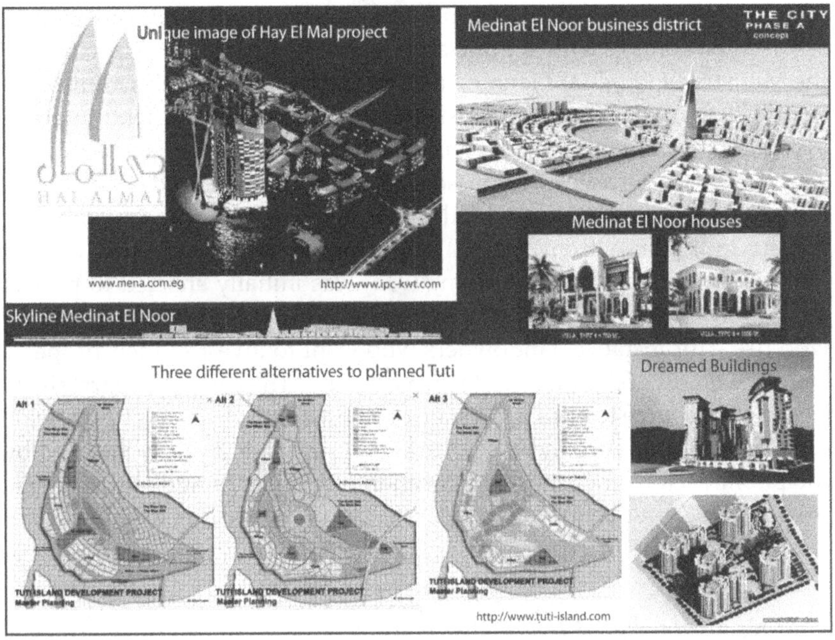

***Figure* 2.2.** Images of the Three Projects

promote huge transformations for the island. This rural island at the heart of the Sudanese capital is destined to become a fantastic crossroads surrounded by luxury residential and commercial areas.

The central location of Tuti and Abū Seʿīd obviously contributes to the interest of public and private investors. The location is all the more special because these lands fall into the category of *sagīa*[7] lands (irrigated high lands on the banks of the Nile). Since the Unregistered Land Act of 1970, any unregistered land is the property of the Sudanese government, and land bought by private individuals holds only a right of usufruct (*milk ḥikr*), and for a duration determined in advance. The special case of market gardening areas on the banks of the Nile appropriated in accordance with freehold principles (*milk ḥurr*) before the act needs to be stressed (El Mahdi 1979).

The agricultural status of these lands needs to be considered within the context of the speculative processes in progress. Agricultural land is measured in *feddan* (0.42 hectares), whereas habitable land is measured in square metres. These measures naturally enhance the possibility of larger benefits from the resale of such agricultural land. For this reason, the annals of land registry in urban localities specify the status of land pertaining to land estate, as well as its permitted use for agricultural, residential or investment purposes (Gordon 1986: 147). Any modification in land status must comply with specific administrative procedures (specified by the Ministry of Physical Planning and Public Utilities, and the Ministry of Agriculture). Moreover, the transformation of agricultural land into residential land is highly taxed, since the state is entitled to accrue 75 per cent of the land's value or to possess 75 per cent of the land surface area. It becomes comprehensible why the state benefits significantly more than private individuals from speculation in agricultural land. This Law of Land Regulation and Registration (1925) was initially enacted to protect agricultural fields, since it restrains private initiatives towards a change of land use – for instance, landowners who want to invest in their property could lose most of their land value (75 per cent). The law has progressively become a resource to enrich the state of Khartoum, however, as real estate development pressure increases, especially through projects initiated by the public sector, since the compensation of the loss of agricultural lands is based on 25 per cent of their existing use value, easily payable in kind (residential plot).

Tuti: Negotiable Law Enforcement?

For private individuals, speculation constitutes an advantage only if the profit generated from real estate land offsets the costs incurred during the procedures that allow reclassification of the land. Alternatively, advantages can be obtained if the conditions for such modifications remain open to negotiation. The originator of the Tuti Project, the Tuti Island Investment Company, seems to have bet on this. According to Mohamed O., a member of the company, prices will be extremely high on the island after the completion of the bridge. This alone justifies the setting up of the project. He affirms his opposition to the compensation payments provided for by the Law of Land Regulation and Registration of 1925 (compensation payable to the state for the transformation of agricultural lands caused by the project). He has confidence in his chances to attain an exemption from such payments due to his connections with the government as well as the overall attractiveness of the project.[8] Such attitudes characterize the status of Tuti elite within the various governments and parties leading Sudan, showing that the community of Tuti is not one of marginalized farmers.

A newspaper article of 2010 also refers to the drastic rise in real estate land values in Tuti. It describes the general manager of Tuti Project 'dreaming of one day selling back a square metre on Tuti for more than 1,600 dollars' (*Middle East Online* 2008). Considering incomes in Khartoum, these prices appear excessively high. Most of the inhabitants of Khartoum would not be able to afford to purchase land at such prices (A. Ahmad 2002).

The actual terms of land status transformation in Tuti led by the company remain obscure at this stage of research. But it is relevant to use this example to underline the distinct and unique aspect of this case. Private investors, particularly landowners, implemented such a momentous project on their agricultural lands without the explicit interference of the state. Thus, the first objective of this case study is to expose the negotiable aspect of the law on land use, given that a few actors have already benefitted from it.

The advertising posters for the project visible from Nile Avenue focus on this aspect: 'It's not a dream … We have the land … We have the vision.' The attachment to land and to landed estates is markedly tenacious in Tuti. Land is a powerful idiom for individual and collective identity; it constitutes the guideline for any analysis of the previous site, and underwrites the tangible elements of the evolution that the ongoing project has gone through.

Abū Seᶜīd: The Struggle within the Frame of Law

The projects at Abū Seᶜīd illustrate the receptiveness of the country to both foreign capital and urban planning strategies widely promoted by Khartoum State. In this regard, the state of Khartoum had originally reclaimed the land on which the projects that are to be resold have been implemented in the name of the greater good. The land at Hay Al-Mal belongs to Mena, an Egyptian real estate company, while that of Medinat Al-Noor belongs to the Kuwaiti Grand Real Estate Company. This increasing interest of the state in land tenure creates novel forms of public-private partnerships.

Capital gains enjoyed by Khartoum State are significant in these projects. In fact, the value of compensation for expropriated agricultural land is determined according to the terms of the modification of its status, that is, 25 per cent of the surface area or of its (fiscal) value. In addition, the compensation is generally made through the provision of habitable land, a benefit in kind, at negligible cost to the state compared to the scale of its landowning in the country. The expropriation processes and the amount of compensation due are the key areas of contention within the conflict, which pits Abū Seᶜīd landowners and the state of Khartoum against each other.

Various Reactions to Real Estate Projects in Two Different Contexts in the Centre of Khartoum

Is Tuti Giving Up?

How is Tuti, the 'rural haven' of Khartoum since its origins and the ultimate symbol of resistance to prolific urbanization for many years (Lobban

1982), to accept the changes taking place in the urban landscape without demonstrating any opposition? At present it almost seems that Tuti has accepted becoming a mere 'roundabout' located at the heart of the conurbation.

Nonetheless, the commissioning of a bridge in 2009 providing vehicle access to the island remains the subject of animated debate among the island's inhabitants. Articles in the local newspapers present the project as mainly well received among the population: 'Most of the 15,000 islanders are pleased, although some people, particularly the elderly, have their doubts at the prospect of a flyover and three more bridges – one connecting Tuti to Omdurman and two others to Bahri' (*Middle East Online* 2008). Of course, most islanders are no longer farmers but work in Khartoum and until recently took the ferry twice a day. There is certainly some resistance among the older generation from people who are nostalgic for the bucolic quality of the island and its unique character. A recently published photography book on the island before the construction of the bridge testifies to some inhabitants' concerns (Hag Mussa 2010). The idea to build a bridge connecting Khartoum to the island is not new. An article written in 1991 had predicted this development as follows: 'Tuti's dilemma is expressed in the debate over a bridge to the island from Khartoum' (Ibrahim and Davies 1991: 119).

Long before the project was carried out, Tuti was the object of greed among public institutions and investors. However, contrary to the predictions of those who were worried about the scope and the speed of Tuti's potential urbanization to the detriment of its heritage as an agricultural zone (Worall 1958), transformations of the landscape were extremely limited until the twenty-first century.

The insular characteristics of the district has largely contributed to its geographical and socioethnical particularity. Human settlement of Tuti dates back to the fifteenth and sixteenth centuries. The island was chosen by the Maḥass tribe from Nubia because of its defensive location at the heart of the river confluence. By and large the inhabitants of Tuti have tried to cultivate and protect their strong identity, which stands distinct from that of the rest of the city. This has reinforced their efforts in resisting the pressure entailed in the processes of land acquisition. Furthermore, the community of Tuti is intricately bound together. The expression 'people of Tuti' (*nās Tūti* or *Tawāta*) is commonly used by both Khartoumese and the islanders themselves and prevails over all other identity references.

According to Richard Lobban, these extremely strong community ties are central to an understanding of Tuti's continued resistance to urban planning:

> By reason of Tuti Island's unique position in the three towns' conurbation it has been able to preserve or reconstruct a stable community which might be projected as typical of the more rural past. This is achieved in opposition to many prevailing trends and forces in the urbanization process. Monopolization of top positions, ethnic encapsulation using highly endogamous marriage preferences, maintenance of a continuous relationship with productive agricultural land, and an avid thirst for education distinguish Tuti Island from neighbouring communities. These features combine to give a remarkable degree of access to social mobility and permit a perpetuation of the strong social network which is at the basis of community life. … In this respect the social patterns of Tuti Island seem to be more of an exception than a rule. (1982: 72)

The ties and interactions that Lobban describes (see also Franck 2007) between the resistance to urban pressure and the maintenance of a relationship with productive agricultural life are important. Significantly, it is the imbrications of an attachment to agricultural land on the one hand and its management on the other hand that is now emerging as a subject of controversy within Greater Khartoum. Tuti is an exemplary case study.

This phenomenon needs to be considered in conjunction with the inevitable division of land into smaller units arising from the precepts of Islamic inheritance. Such patterns of distribution push younger generations to seek jobs in more attractive sectors. As education improves and job opportunities increase, the management of agricultural land is no longer systematically the lot of the eldest son in a given family. Today, it is generally the children who remain unemployed who receive the management of the land as an inheritance.

The whole process that took place during the land and speculation explosion in the capital has led landowners to reconsider their property as a land resource, not just an agricultural resource. Market gardening activity, which in the past paved the way for both economic and social integration with the main body of the city, is gradually losing its hold. Mohamed O.'s words illustrate this:

> The history of Tuti is obviously agricultural, but today landowners are not farmers anymore. All of them employ farmers. Moreover, agriculture is less lucrative than a few years ago. It will soon cease to be a future investment. After the construction of the bridges, the prices obtained for the sale of land will be superior to those of land that is currently agricultural. … Each individual has his own way of relating to financial matters. If someone owns one thousand square metres on the island, I think he would rather sell, and have two houses in Riyad [first-class neighbourhood in Khartoum] in exchange. Another person might well choose to stay and agree to the construction of a skyscraper on his land and eventually ensure his full ownership of two floors. The most crucial element is to build soon given the marked increase of habitation on the island.

> Soon, the project will become obsolete given that there will be no plots of land available.[9]

The feature that has helped to preserve the island's identity for years is its relative insularity. This is now a central theme in the conflict between agricultural lands and construction projects on the island. Tuti has an area of eight square kilometres; due to the natural increase of the population,[10] the original village is now too small to host the construction of new houses. Consequently, there is more construction taking place on land that has traditionally been reserved for agriculture (figure 2.3). In addition to demographic growth, living and habitation standards have changed on the island. The most recently constructed houses in Tuti – smart villas of several floors – bear more resemblance to those within luxurious residential areas located in the capital than to the traditional Sudanese houses. Nevertheless, the one-storey house with a yard was still the predominant architectural model on the island until quite recently. New generations driven by more ambition than their parents before them strive to move out of Tuti in order to achieve a lifestyle available in the more fashionable districts of the capital.

Economic opening up towards the urban sector and wider exposure to the larger society have had significant effects on the social differentiation within the community of Tuti. Muntassir M., a small landowner on the island, describes the transitions taking place in Tuti:

> The land of Tuti is sought after, because many private companies are ready to invest on the island. Twenty years ago, it was impossible to sell one square metre of land. Today, a committee of twenty-five notables has been created in order to prevent the sales. They offer money to landowners who are having financial difficulties to dissuade them from selling their land. But the only solution is to establish a compromise between investors and Tuti's citizens. The land has to stay in the hands of people who live on the island, but we can find an agreement to manage its common use.[11]

In the eyes of the community, the Tuti Island Investment Company, founded by Tuti's inhabitants, appears to have reached a satisfactory compromise. Indeed, this trade-off is consistent with the inhabitants' property objectives. By referring to the ancient interdiction to sell a single square metre of land, Muntassir implicitly refers to the strategies applied by Tuti's old families to maintain land ownership within the community. This interdiction concerns the sale of land to 'foreigners', a term that applies to any individual who does not belong to Tuti's ancient lineages. Even individuals from families established decades ago do not have access to land. Although more accurate information about the 'committee of twenty-five

***Figure* 2.3.** The Front of Urbanization in Tuti

notables' mentioned by Muntassir is lacking, it seems to work towards the same objective of land conservation.

Speeches covering the implementation of the project clearly stress the need to manage feasible arrangements with the foreign firms interested in investing in the island. For instance, the main idea is to provide business leases for thirty-five to forty years. These allow the conservation of bare ownership and establish the possibility of recovering the freehold at the lease redemption date. However, at this stage of research, it appears there are some significant indications that seriously question the seeming approval for the project.

Consultation of Tuti's agricultural lands on the cadastral register and the inventory of Tuti Investment Company dealings since 1998 (the date of the first land purchase) reveals two elements. First, the area of land that has been purchased is particularly small, rarely exceeding half a *feddan*. Second, these plots of land are dispersed throughout the island. This phenomenon shows how the fragmentation of agricultural land is an important component despite the strategies initiated by the community to reduce its impact.

Patterns of land allocation equally identify the controversial aspects of the project. Even where family arrangements exist for the management of agricultural land, these arrangements would be complicated if the land was to be sold as part of a speculation operation. Furthermore, the registry cites the Tuti Investment Company's bills of resale – mainly since 2006–7 – to private firms (such as banking institutions). Hence, there exist adequate grounds to support the thesis of possible conflict within the community.

Given these circumstances, it is appropriate to question who really believes in the advantages of the three proposed plans by the Tuti Project (figure 2.2). These plans obscure both the historical land legacy of the island and how land transaction works in practice. The village has been completely obliterated in the website video imagery, and the agricultural plots of land are invisible. Represented as part of a sanitized and unproblematic process, these projects seem to bear no relation to the complicated realities of land possession. What we see is an 'aterritorial' project (Choplin and Franck 2010). However, this may explain why people did not oppose the implementation of the project or launch a protest. One could say that the Tuti Project is largely an object of fantasy.

The success of such a project presumes that Tuti's inhabitants reach a collective agreement about land. It seems unlikely that a private company could overcome this challenge, whether controlled by inhabitants of the island or supported by the urban authorities. By 2012, the project had made no significant progress, and neither the works in the residential area nor the building of the two planned bridges had started. Negotiations had barely commenced, and the question of who would represent the interests of Tuti's landowners was yet to be resolved. Three local committees[12] (the popular committee, the village committee and the mysterious 'committee of wise men') were involved, each claiming the highest legitimacy. According to one member of the 'committee of wise men':

> The issue which remains pending is who will represent the state and the village in the project. The community refuses to be represented by the popular committee, insofar as the latter already took on the conditions of the state without the consent of the communities. Moreover, the village committee claims that the popular committee election is bogus. On the other hand, the state does not want the popular committee to be absent from negotiations for the project. From our side [the committee of wise men], we proposed the creation of an ad hoc committee with five persons, one from the popular committee, two from the committee of wise men and three from the village committee. But the members of the village committee rejected our proposal, and are against any representation of the popular committee. It is, however, impossible to meet with the governor of Khartoum State without any representative of the popular committee.[13]

The competition between the different committees illustrates the contradictions of local governance in the Sudanese capital. This is certainly worth further research. It also highlights the fact that the Tuti community maintains a hold over the implementation of the project through collective control on the process of land cession.

A Focus on Abū Seᶜīd's Realities

In contrast to the situation described in Tuti, in Abū Seᶜīd, the beginning of construction work on Medinat Al-Noor and Hay Al-Mal, in mid-January 2009, provoked tangible discontent among former landowners. The district is located on the west bank of the White Nile not far from the confluence. It backs onto the district of Fitaḥāb and stretches out to the Omdurman Islamic University. The agricultural landowners in the district are mostly originally from ethnic groups that have historically settled in the area, such as the Fitaḥāb (a subgroup of Jamūᶜiya) and the Zanarkha (especially in the south of the area). Although there are many common characteristics between Tuti and Abū Seᶜīd, notably historical farming traditions in Khartoum, there are two key differences. Unlike Tuti, the central location and attractiveness of Abū Seᶜīd are recent and coincide with the commissioning of a second bridge linking Khartoum and Omdurman in 2000. Furthermore, the community within Abū Seᶜīd does not benefit from the same social capital, such as education, political networks and financial skills, as their Tuti counterparts.

In January 2009 a scandal related to the use of land was revealed at Medinat Al-Noor. The national newspaper *Al-Watan* dedicated two front pages to this topic (*Al-Watan* 2009a, 2009b). The dispossessed landowners were appalled by the manner in which the authorities acted. They were meeting project deadlines by selling plots of land to a Kuwaiti company in 2006, construction work was authorized before previous owners had been compensated and grievances taken to court had not been addressed.

Start of fieldwork in January 2009 coincided with the emergence of the protest, and the conflict remained unresolved in February 2009. However, this specific crisis over land issues and the transformation of agricultural land emphasizes the complications of the expropriation process. I first describe the claims, grievances and demands of landowners; then, I deal with the nature of the social environment, where a pattern of tensions prevails within the community.

Before the beginning of construction work on the contested land, a few landowners were already in conflict with the state of Khartoum. According to the investigations in Abū Seᶜīd, five landowners out of sixty (i.e., five families of landowners) brought lawsuits as a result of the expropriation of their land. Abdel Muneim F. is one such landowner. His complaint dates from 2004 and was, in the beginning, confined to the project of Hay Al-Mal.[14] He reproaches the state of Khartoum for ignoring all the legal requirements. From his perspective, Khartoum State acted neither in accordance with the general interest nor according to the 1930 Law of Expropriation and Transformation of Agricultural Land.

> In our case, all of their actions were not in conformity; to the terms of the law referring to the information for landowners, the announcement of the intentions of the project, and the negotiation of compensation. They decided to expropriate my land in 2002, but I was only informed in 2004 and even then by chance when I went to the office of land registration, because I needed a copy of the my title deed certificate. It was then that they informed me about the decision and told me that my land had been expropriated two years ago. Personally, I could have read it on the government's published listing of acts and laws since I can read and therefore have access to such information, but the illiterate would never have the opportunity to become well informed on the nature of the project.[15]

Although it is true that a certain surface area is required to build either a hospital or a pumping station, this is not an important enough argument to justify the appropriation of the land in question. In the past, the requirement for such measures was to show worthy public action that would support expropriation. Furthermore, the evolution and shifting aspects of the project (the idea of building a pumping station has already been annulled) begs the question of any notion of general interest, which is still legally unclear. After a series of legal actions against Khartoum State, Abdel Muneim F. finally won his case, particularly because of the lack of negotiated compensation. Nonetheless, Khartoum State lodged several appeals. While the verdict on the last case brought by the state was being delivered, a presidential decision was proclaimed in 2007. According to the *Gazette*, the terms of the presidential decision (no. 355, dated 6 January 2008) implied the requisitioning of all *sagīa* land in Abū Seᶜīd.[16].

Hence, for Abdel Muneim F., the possibility of contesting the definitions of general interest was reduced as a result of the presidential decision, given that the definition of general interest falls within the competence of public institutions: 'If the lawsuit was set in a logical way, and abided by the rule of law, nothing like that would have happened to me. ... But here, political decisions will always encroach on the attainment of justice.'[17]

However, presidential decision no. 355 specifies that Khartoum State is obliged to compensate former landowners equitably in the process of disposing fully of the land. It is precisely in response to this issue that landowners launched their protest in January 2009. The start of excavation work provoked an intense shock among the population of Abū Seᶜīd. Landowners, even those who had signed contracts of compensation, now understood that the lands had been sold before the end of the compensation process and in spite of the decision stating that Khartoum State must provide adequate compensation. In addition, the amount of expected compensation remained a mystery. The landowners showed that both payment and the amount of compensation were clearly required by law, so such omissions were in direct contradiction to the legal frameworks of the state. This complaint widely reverberated among Zanarkha landowners, living in the south of Abū Seᶜīd in the Al Rīf Al-Janūbī district, who are equally affected by the Medinat Al-Noor project and the new international airport. Thus, Al Rīf Al-Janūbī landowners vigorously joined the protest.[18] Together, the demonstrators occupied the construction site from 1 February 2009, aiming to pressure the authorities to create an ad hoc parliamentary committee to facilitate and ensure that negotiations and payment of compensation ran smoothly. Two elements are central to the discussions: the first relates to the acreage of habitable plots given as compensation against an expropriated agricultural *feddan*; the other deals with negotiations for the location of this plot.

The negotiable aspect of the law covering change of land use is still an important element with regard to the surface area of these habitable lands. Abdel Muneim F. clarifies the legal situation:

> According to the law, 75 per cent of the land belongs to the state and 25 per cent to the landowners. If I possess a *feddan* of, say, 4,200 square metres, I will get

> 1,050 square metres of land, i.e., one-quarter as stated by the law. In reality, 40 per cent of the 25 per cent of habitable land is dedicated to services. Thus, only 630 square metres of habitable land remains. It is precisely on these terms that the compensation contracts are based in Abū Seʿīd. However, in a few cases when the government has been put under pressure, landowners and the state are sharing – half and half – the land that is not reserved for services. These arrangements were developed in Burri, Jereif and Manshiya [other districts on the banks of the Blue Nile.

Yet, within the district of Abū Seʿīd, the heterogeneity of compensation proposals is notable. Some are made on the basis of 1 *feddan* = 630 square metres of habitable land, while others were allocated an extra 370 square metres. The case-by-case character of the procedures being applied in Abū Seʿīd is significantly different from the process ongoing in Tuti.

The location of the habitable lands also causes problems, as all landowners prefer to acquire lands within Abū Seʿīd's projects rather than land located further away on the banks of the Nile, or even on the periphery and far from the river. Another landowner, Tayeb, adds that the rehousing method employed is arbitrary and unfair.

As in Tuti, younger generations are personally less attached to the land than their forebears (Franck 2007). Thus, on the whole the renovation project of the district is generally well received. It is the forced relinquishment of their land that generally upsets the inhabitants. However, the disappearance of agricultural land in favour of urban development does not constitute a justification for a fight. One person who intervened during a meeting said:

> We have been violated because construction work began even before our problem was resolved. Recognition of our ownership and of our title deed has been flouted. Once again, all we want to know is what does our right of possession entail and how we can exercise it. We want to take an active part in the renovation project of this district. … We disapprove neither of the government nor of modernity, but we want to take an active part in the project and in the talks to resolve the conflict.

The conflict serves to depict the social differentiation process taking place in the district. I attended various extremely lively and tense mobilization meetings: inhabitants insinuated problems of corruption and made accusations against representatives of the district, especially against the *ʿomda* (traditional local authority), who they claimed stood to profit personally from the current state of affairs. In addition, inhabitants called for solidarity, for a common purpose and for the well-planned organization of their objectives in order to improve the quality of negotiations: 'We have to take our own responsibility seriously. If someone gets a fair compensation, it has to be applied to every landowner's case. We have to be brave, which means not accepting secret compensation deals.'[19] Various interviews conducted in Abū Seʿīd refer to a few people both from the district or elsewhere who had previously bought areas of agricultural land under advantageous terms in order to benefit from the prospect of future compensation deals. Consultation of the land register to draw up an inventory of sales in Abū Seʿīd would be essential to determine the actors who gained the most from real estate development in the district.

Conclusion

This chapter has sought to describe, as an initial stage of more exhaustive research, both the differences and similarities of the projects in Tuti and Abū Seʿīd as examples that reveal the same process of land speculation. On the whole, it highlights power struggles, social differentiation processes and the terms of the real application of the law, which are all central themes that emerge in this type of conflict. In Abū Seʿīd, the outcome of the protest by landowners, the report issued by the parliamentary committee and the use of habitable lots given as compensation remain to be analysed. Equally, in Tuti, the progress of the Tuti Project, the collective land negotiations and the decline in agricultural production need further study. However, the initial analysis on the transformation of agricultural lands on the Nile has underlined what is at stake and exposed key issues of such projects within the particular speculative context of Khartoum. Central market gardening areas, which were historically at the margin of the city, are at present a focal point of financial greed. In this area of Khartoum, urban planners, investors and landowners are competing for such a valuable asset. Henceforth, access to land and the fight for land rights will be central topics in Greater Khartoum's public policies.

Speculation is common to both, but the examples of Tuti and Abū Seʿīd typify two different coping strategies. The elites of Tuti strive to control their integration into the project dynamics, while the landowners in Abū Seʿīd engage in a direct confrontation with state policies.

Replanning the city became a very profitable venture for authorities, since the real estate sector is the main target for both foreign and Sudanese investors, including a new type of affluent upper-middle class who are sufficiently motivated to take part in these new urban trends. In this context, agricultural land is particularly attractive for the authorities on account of the legal status that in the past protected it. Nevertheless, even if the three impressive projects near the confluence of the Nile are effectively in progress, only a few buildings have been completed. The projects fall well short of the elaborate videos used in marketing campaigns to promote them. If the projects are eventually completed, Khartoum's city centre will host two zoos, two golf courses, two marinas, three waterfront developments on the Nile and much more. The threshold of profitability of these urban dreams is very high, and we wonder if these projects have been designed with the objective of being achieved. This analysis of Khartoum concurs with other urban studies that investigate the growing ties between financial markets and the contemporary urban fabric (David and Halbert 2010).

Notes

I wish to thank Claire Poursin and Azza Yacoub for the English translation of this chapter.

1. Most of the data exposed in this chapter were gathered before the separation of north and south Sudan, that is to say, at the peak of the country's economic growth and real estate investments.
2. During the course of my Ph.D. project, I conducted fieldwork in Khartoum in the period 2001–5. The data from this period is used in this chapter to underline the evolution concerning the use of land and the attachment of landowners to agricultural land. However, another period of fieldwork in January 2009 focused on land conflict issues related to the agricultural status of land. This latter enquiry provides information about the conflict in Abū Seʿīd and launches another investigation on land administration and land registration. Since 2010, I have carried out regular fieldwork in Khartoum that allowed me to complete some data, in particular in the case of Tuti. Qualitative methods are used leading to a first sociological analysis of the new real estate projects.
3. http://www.alsunut.sd/amir/ (accessed 14 February 2013).
4. http://www.grandq8.com/ (accessed 19 June 2013).
5. http://www.mena.com.eg/en/types.php?cid=3 (accessed 19 June 2013).
6. http://www.tuti-island.com/media.html (accessed 19 June 2013).
7. *Sagīa* (waterwheel) is a thousand-year-old technique of irrigation in the Nile valley. The term designates by extension the highest lands where irrigation is used, unlike *jaref* lands, which are lower and are cultivated mostly as the waters subside after the annual flood (Ohtsuka 1996).
8. Author's interview with Mohamed O. at the Sailing Club of Khartoum, February 2001: 'Currently the square metre costs SDG 6,000 [about USD 23], but after the completion of the bridge, the price will be comparable to one square metre on Nile Avenue: USD 200 per square metre. The prices are going to rise to the extent that they will rival those of Paris or New York. … It is inconceivable to give the major part of the lands to the government. We will solve this problem because the vice president [at the time of the interview, Ali Osman Taha] is also a member of the parliament of Tuti. We plan to invert the rate setting: 75 per cent from the deals would belong to people from Tuti, and 25 per cent to the government. But, actually, we believe that we can manage so that the government won't tax anything. … The government will obviously benefit from the project of the bridge since it will get investment tax.'

9. Author's interview with Mohamed O. at the Sailing Club of Khartoum, February 2001.
10. According to the 2008 census, Tuti Island's population amounts to approximately 20,000 people, whereas in 1988 they were only 6,480 (Ibrahim and Davies 1991).
11. Author's interview with Muntassir M., Tuti, February 2002.
12. Popular committees are a central institution of the current government. Established in 1989, they have the primary function to act as a bridge between the population and higher institutional levels. For their role in the political and social control at the level of the neighbourhood, see M. Abdalla (2008). The village committee likely refers to an authority made up of traditional leaders, similar to those that can be found in other parts of the capital and whose institutional legitimacy remains ambiguous in spite of the Local Governance Act of 2003. The 'committee of wise men' is, according to my research, an arbitration entity consisting of people originally from Tuti but who no longer live on the island.
13. Author's interview with Yunis Elamin, University of Khartoum, August 2012.
14. The Hay Al-Mal project corresponds to the *sagīa* 1 to 7 of Abū Seᶜīd. The Medina Al Noor project extends from the *sagīa* 8 to 97 in Abū Seᶜīd; it spreads across the administrative boundaries of the district and extends further, comprising the *sagīa* 1 to 181 of Al Rīf Al-Janūbī (on the land of the Zanarkha) as well.
15. Author's interview with Abdel Muneim F., Fitaḥāb, January 2009.
16. *Gazette,* issue no. 1752
17. Op. cit.
18. The meeting on 25 January 2009, which took place at Nadi El Nujum, was devoted to the establishment of consensus among all landowners affected by expropriation (Abū Seᶜīd and Zanarkha). It was very successful, bringing two hundred people together.
19. Extracted from the words of a speaker at the Nadi El Nujum meeting on 25 January 2009.

Chapter 3

Access Strategies to Economic and Social Resources among Recent Migrants on the Outskirts of Khartoum

The Example of Bawga Al-Sharīg

François Ireton

Almost all the studies about migrants who settled in Khartoum and its outskirts concern those known as internally displaced persons (IDPs), whose displacement was caused by droughts that hit, particularly since the 1980s, in different parts of the country or as a result of insecurity related to the resumption of hostilities between north and south Sudan in 1983 and the conflict in Darfur since 2003. In contrast, there have been few studies concerning the many voluntary economic migrants who find their way to Khartoum seeking employment and better wages or describing migrant strategies in settling in Khartoum, accessing basic resources, the economic activities of their households or the pursuit of professional interests. Furthermore, studies on migrants to Khartoum, whether 'voluntary' or 'involuntary', generally insist on the fact that they pursue these strategies by mobilizing tribal and 'traditional' lineage support groups, especially when state institutions do not exist or have failed and are dysfunctional. It seems that such studies overlook the fact that there are many 'atomized' migrants, individuals who leave their homes individually, have difficulty maintaining links with their lineage groups and families of origin, and who finally settle in peripheral areas of Khartoum inhabited by migrants from all regions of Sudan only to find themselves stigmatized because their ethnic or tribal affiliations are held in low esteem in the capital (Al-Battahani et al. 1998).

Notes for this chapter begin on page 67.

How do such 'atomized' migrants cope with the search for a livelihood when they have only just arrived from small villages and towns of the outlying *wilāyas* (federal states) and they must settle precariously in the 'rural desert' that surrounds Khartoum and is devoid of community facilities or public infrastructure? The interrogation is only exacerbated when one realizes that such migrants must cope without kinship or tribal affiliation and support networks and without recourse to governmental or nongovernmental organizations. This is the theme on which this contribution on 'economic ethnography' will attempt to shed some light, in particular based on fieldwork conducted in a quasi-experimental situation in which migrants were able to rely on themselves in securing income to buy a plot of land, build a home and access basic services (energy and water). After a brief overview of the peripheral areas in which such migrants settle and of their socioeconomic characteristics and migration trajectories, I will examine how these migrants implement different strategies to access these material and financial resources and goods and, in so doing, how they produce social 'nontraditional' links and networks.[1] This chapter raises some issues that recur in several chapters of this book, such as the role of popular committees, land sales and the rights of established groups.

All social and microeconomic data presented in this chapter were collected by the author during three one-week stays in the field between 2009 and 2010. The data were collected by means of thirty prestructured and in-depth interviews with men encountered among the public spaces of the Bawga Al-Sharīg neighbourhood and who agreed to be interviewed, either outdoors or, more often, at home. Interviewees were not preselected and they do not form a representative sample of the local population living in the area. They are, however, broadly representative of very common situations among the 'atomized' voluntary migrants of Khartoum's outskirts.

Bawga Al-Sharīg, a 'Protourban' Settlement on the Outskirts of Khartoum

The survey was conducted in a small settlement named Bawga Al-Sharīg, which has existed for only five years and is one of the three settlements constituting the *idārā shaʿabīa* of ʿAllujāb.[2] The municipality of ʿAllujāb is part of an area of adjoining municipalities consisting of more than thirty settlements and a total of twenty-five thousand inhabitants in 2008. This area is known by the inhabitants of Khartoum under the generic name of ʿIdd Bābiker. Although located in the immediate periphery of the city of

Khartoum North, this area is classified as rural and administratively belongs to the rural *maḥalliya* of Sharg Al-Nil. A newly asphalted road originating in Khartoum North (twenty-five minutes away by public transport) crosses ʿIdd Bābiker from west to east.

Settlements in the area are located on a sandy, nonirrigated and therefore noncultivated steppe. These lands are the traditional tribal territory (*dār*) of the Baṭāḥīn, an Arabic tribe (*gabīla*) of nomadic pastoralists. Most inhabitants of ʿIdd Bābiker are members of the Baṭāḥīn tribe, settled beginning in the 1950s around a few wells now abandoned, which explains settlement morphologies resembling rural villages. The municipality of ʿAllujāb is a rectangular area almost three kilometres long from west to east and one kilometre from north to south. It is bordered to the north by the asphalted road to Khartoum North and to the south by large agricultural schemes irrigated by the waters of the Blue Nile. Its territory is crossed by a grid of small streets. The regularity of the grid and the density of housing decreases as one travels from the west to the east. In contrast to other parts of ʿIdd Bābiker, the territorial organization of ʿAllujāb resembles that of the peripheral urban extensions of the capital. The extension of the housing in the municipal territory progressed gradually from west to east, in three stages.

The settlement of ʿAllujāb began in the 1950s and was mostly populated by Baṭāḥīn. In 1999 there arrived a group of migrants from Bawga, a large village of the Nile valley in the region of Atbara. These migrants, from the Jaʿāliyn tribe and of peasant origin, were eager to get close to Khartoum and knew that they could purchase inexpensive plots of land east of ʿAllujāb. The migrant families immediately named their settlement Bawga Al-Jadīd (New Bawga). Like ʿAllujāb, the settlement of Bawga Al-Jadīd is now served by the electrical and potable water networks (it has its own well and tank for drinking water) and has its own primary school and a small minibus station.

In a third phase, beginning in 2005, the ʿAllujāb municipality received an influx of settlers from all over Sudan, but especially from Darfur and Kordofan. These populations settled east of Bawga Al-Jadīd, amid the chaotic, stony and sandy terrain of an abandoned building materials quarry pocked with pools of stagnant water collected during the rainy season. In this third 'protourban' settlement, the housing is not clearly aligned as in the areas inhabited during the two previous phases of settlement; it is discontinuous and often seems 'sited' at random, avoiding only the ditches. At the end of 2010, there were in this settlement a thousand people distributed among about three hundred *ḥōsh* (built plots), among them a hundred houses made of red bricks and surrounded by walls, but the vast majority being made of mud bricks, composed of one room and located on plots without walls. One also sees a few huts constructed of sorghum stalks, metal sheets and cardboard. This settlement was gradually identified by the residents as Bawga Al-Sharīg or sometimes Bawga Fōg (East Bawga or Bawga Top). This neighbourhood continues to develop without the benefit of public infrastructure, equipment or public services. The area offers four small grocery stores. While the settlements of ʿAllujāb and Bawga Al-Jadīd are populated mainly by nuclear families, Bawga Al-Sharīg includes many men, married and unmarried, living alone or sharing living quarters and whose families remain in the provinces. Bawga Al-Sharīg is thus distinguished by a number of markers of social marginality, which can be summarized by material deprivation, 'underintegration' (lack of infrastructure and public services) and the absence of a core founding population.

Migration Trajectories, Employment and Socioeconomic Stratification

The majority of migrants who settled in Bawga Al-Sharīg[3] previously resided in rural communities, but some come from small and medium-sized towns. Their migrations were motivated by economic reasons, that is, to find in Khartoum a better-paid job than in their place of origin or obtain a personal income, which they did not have previously. Structurally, two types of trajectories can be distinguished: the first, simple migration (SM), is infrequent and extremely recent, leads directly from the migrant's place of origin to Bawga Al-Sharīg and assumes some prior information about the existence of the settlement as a destination provided by a member of the family or in the village of origin. The second might be characterized as complex migration (CM). It is the most frequent, in which the migrant is first led from his place of origin to Khartoum and then to Bawga Al-Sharīg. Among those who made a first journey to Khartoum, there are two cases. In the first (CM_1), migrants arrived in Khartoum hoping to find a job without having a social network there and without knowing where to stay on arrival; they left by train, truck or bus and often encountered during the trip other migrants with whom they exchanged information about job opportunities in the capital. The vast majority first found jobs as casual day labourers, 'solving' the lodging problem, since labourers generally live on-site while working before moving on. Most have lived in this manner for many years, sometimes finding collective rental housing in Greater Khartoum before organizing a reunion in the capital of their spouses and children from the provinces. Such migrants often began the search for a plot of land that they might afford (using the modest savings made possible by a very frugal life), at which point they learned of the Bawga Al-Sharīg 'wasteland'. In the second case of the complex migration trajectory (CM_2), the migrant knew someone, perhaps an uncle, a cousin or an older brother, already installed in Ḥājj Yūsif (an urban extension very near ʿIdd Bābiker) or in another extension of Khartoum North. Having resided with him for a few years, sometimes for rent or in an exchange of services, the migrant chose or was obliged to move on. Having heard about cheap land in Bawga Al-Sharīg, the migrant bought a plot in this area, perhaps aided by a loan from a family member. Migrants of the CM_2 type have generally been helped by relations, in Ḥājj Yūsif or elsewhere, to find a job in a small shop or a craft workshop, somewhat less precarious than that of a day labourer in construction. The CM_2 migrant would generally have accumulated savings with greater facility than the CM_1 migrant. In addition, and unlike the CM_1 migrant, who initially had no social network, the CM_2 migrant benefitted from the support and relationships of the person who first offered hospitality. The presence of a social network continues to sustain the individual once installed in Bawga Al-Sharīg.

The social position of migrants in the socioeconomic hierarchy of Bawga Al-Sharīg (whose spectrum is of rather low amplitude) is closely linked with their migration trajectory and employment status, and is reflected in their homes (of different kind and quality) and in the respective plot sizes. At the bottom of the social ladder (the first stratum, S_1), we find the newly arrived migrant, with an SM migratory career, who has no house for himself, lives with the man who first hosted him and works precariously as a casual labourer. Next comes the second stratum, S_2, in which we find migrants with a CM_1 migratory career, often casual day labourers with only minimal economic and social capital, but at least also a small plot (of two hundred square metres) and an embryonic house (often a single room) generally made of mud bricks. In the third stratum (S_3), we find migrants with a CM_2 migratory career, with slightly better economic and social capital. These work for fixed and regular wages, usually as vendors, shop clerks or craftsmen in Ḥājj Yūsif or in some other extension and, very rarely, as minor officials in Khartoum. This group is likely to own a plot of two hundred to three hundred square metres and a one- or two-room house, often constructed in red bricks. Finally, in the fourth layer (S_4), we find a sampling of small merchants and independent artisans who have followed a CM_2 trajectory and families who have migrated from another district in the metropolitan area (where they are established and operate a trade or craft workshop with at least one employee). Such families move to Bawga Al-Sharīg because their existing homes are too small and because they are able to afford a large plot (three hundred to five hundred square metres) and build a redbrick house with several rooms, often equipped with a selection of modern devices like refrigerator and television, assuming, of course, they can obtain an 'informal' public utility connection.[4]

This socioeconomic hierarchy is based largely – but not only – on monetary income.[5] We can engage in some approximations, as far as casual day labourers are concerned, based on the average remuneration of a workday and the average number of days worked during the few weeks preceding the interview. The population of Bawga Al-Sharīg engaged in the workforce is almost exclusively male: none of the wives of the men interviewed does paid work, even at home. The men of Bawga Al-Sharīg belonging to S_1 and S_2 are the vast majority of the working population of the settlement and are seen as 'poor' by all those interviewed. The main feature of their work is its irregularity. Their work is piecemeal and they are hired day by day. Piecework labourers perform any task that presents itself, whatever the duration (sometimes only a few hours) and whatever the type of payment (in cash, in kind, in exchange for services). Such work includes, for example, helping to unload material for the construction of a neighbour's house or minding a shop while the owner is absent for a few hours. A regular source of daily paid labour may be found to a limited extent in the seasonally irrigated areas south of the ʿAllujāb municipality and among the construction sites of Khartoum.

Most of the men classified in either of these strata are unskilled and are employed as menial labourers, diggers, brick moulders or mason's assistants. They are constantly on the lookout for opportunities to work for a day, several days or even, in the most favourable cases, for several weeks. Information regarding job availability mainly circulates by word of mouth among neighbours and members of the informal social networks of men who are regularly employed at the sites. When opportunities through these channels are lacking, workers will go early in the morning, with or without their own tools, to various public places that are daily work markets attended by small entrepreneurs, various job brokers or individuals using the services of daily labourers or pieceworkers to perform work at home. The nearest of these markets is located in Ḥājj Yūsif. This practice is described as risky, because there is a cost associated with transport that may not be recovered if the worker is not hired. When a worker fails to find work in the morning, it is still possible for him to try to be recruited in a nearby market. Finally, and in the best of cases, men whose work may have been noted by former employers develop referral networks and may be contacted on their cell phones at any time. Of course, this strategy assumes access to a mobile telephone, a costly purchase that almost all respondents have made and that is often their only 'modern' asset. Those who are regularly solicited by an employer enjoy a kind of specialized, on-the-job training and are usually best placed for future work and ultimately fixed employment with slightly better pay. These workers move from one site to another on behalf of the same contractor. We have here an example of early upward social mobility and sustainable integration into the labour force. Before this happens, however, any work opportunity is welcome and menial and day labour assignments are combined daily and weekly. Three days of work per week constitute the average, and full-time work for one week or even two is considered a blessing. It was not uncommon among respondents to report not having worked during the previous ten or fifteen days. In desperation, those who find themselves unemployed occupy themselves building their own homes, helping a neighbour with his home (an exchange of working days) or building a wall if they were able to make a minimum investment in raw materials and tools (the earth required to manufacture mud bricks has to be bought; it is difficult to find amid the rocky soil of Bawga Al-Sharīg, and its extraction is otherwise illegal).

Concerning respondents belonging to the S_1 and S_2 categories, in late 2010 the full working day on a construction site was paid between SDG 7 and 10 from which deduction must be made of at least SDG 1 for public transportation (minibus).[6] An average week (three working days) thus brings in a maximum income of SDG 30, which we can bring to SDG 40 with the addition of occasional piecework and odd jobs, that is, between USD 15 and USD 25 per week in purchasing power parity. This maximum amount, spread over the seven days of the week, corresponds to USD 3.6 per day in purchasing power parity. If we take, for purely indicative and comparative use, the poverty lines of the World Bank (USD 2 per capita per day in purchasing power parity for the poverty line and USD 1.3 per capita per day in purchasing power parity for the 'deep poverty' line), one finds that a single man would not be considered 'poor', whereas a couple falls under the poverty line (with USD 1.8 per capita per day in purchasing power parity) and a family of three would be considered 'very poor' (with USD 1.2 per capita per day in purchasing power parity). Faced with this situation, a few casual day labourers surveyed said they relied on donations from Islamic charities (*jamaʿīa khayrīa islāmīa*), from NGOs (there are no NGOs active in the municipality of ʿAllujāb, however) or from other family members (although only a few say they borrow from family members). Finally, some married men make remittances to their wives and children in the provinces, especially when they are able to return to their regions of origin. Most men seem eager to help their 'extended' families, but are often unable to do so for lack of sufficient income. This is sometimes a source of 'shame', with negative consequences for their long-term relations with their families.

Those residents of Bawga Al-Sharīg belonging to category S_3 are mostly, as I have said, clerical employees in retail shops, small businesses and workshops. Their average daily income is no more than that of the first two strata, but they work regularly and full time for five or six days a week. Such employees generally receive monthly salaries of between SDG 150 and 250. If we add earnings from piecework (around SDG 50 per month), the total income of the households of this stratum with one active member (the vast majority of such households) therefore oscillates between SDG 200 and 300 (that is between USD 130 and USD 195 in purchasing power parity). Families of three or four persons enjoying the highest income of this stratum live with, respectively, USD 2.2 and USD 1.6 per capita per day in purchasing power parity; the members of families of this stratum with four or more persons are thus 'poor' (considering the poverty line of the World Bank). Members of families of three persons earning the lowest income of this stratum are considered 'poor', and those of families with four or more persons are considered 'extremely poor' (with USD 1 or less per capita per day in purchasing power parity). In terms of the monetary measure of poverty by international standards, the people of Bawga Al-Sharīg are almost all 'poor' and many are 'extremely poor'. A few families, however, have joined the fourth stratum. According to respondents, only those of category S_4 live 'decently'.

Acquiring Land and Becoming a Home Owner

As we have seen, migrants are attracted to Bawga Al-Sharīg by the relatively inexpensive land prices. In 2011 the price of a standard small plot of two hundred square metres, by far the most widespread, was approximately SDG 2,000. A plot of three hundred square metres cost SDG 3,000 and a plot of five hundred square metres cost SDG 5,000, with prices increasing according to the proximity of the asphalt road.

The mode of acquisition is generally as follows: the potential buyer visits the site, examines it, evaluates its capacity to support an intended new construction and enquires among residents of nearby built plots about purchasing conditions of the plot he will buy. He notes the names of these people and goes to Ḥājj Yūsif to see a *muḥāmī* (lawyer), whose name and address were given him by his future neighbours and who also acts as a broker.[7] The *muḥāmī* knows the members of Baṭāḥīn lineages who presumably own the plot.[8] He enquires about their willingness to sell at the expected price. The buyer must pay cash to the lawyer. He receives in exchange a certificate (*shahāda*) stating the names of the seller and the buyer, the surface area of the plot, its price, its approximate location and the names of the owners of the surrounding plots. The sale requires the agreement of the *idārā shaʿabīa* and of the *maḥalliya* administration. Certificate holders are aware that, if the certificate grants title and immunity from arbitrary expulsion in the event of a public planning operation (*takhṭīt*), it does not constitute a guarantee against encroachment in the event of *tanẓīm* (normalization) operations, such as street alignments.[9]

The purchase price for a plot of two hundred square metres, a minimum of SDG 2,000, is the equivalent of one year's income for a casual day labourer of the S_2 stratum, calculated on the basis of an average income of SDG 40 per week. This casual day labourer will spend years accumulating enough savings to afford the purchase price of the plot, borrowing occasionally from friends and family to complete the purchase price, but only rarely from professional lenders, who generally require collateral.

After the plot is thus acquired with great difficulty, building a simple room takes a long time for lack of money, especially since the search for minimal privacy implies the construction, around the plot, of a wall of mud bricks as a priority, given the fact that domestic life – including sleeping in the hot season – takes place in large part out of doors. In Bawga Al-Sharīg it is not uncommon to see an enclosed or partially enclosed plot with a *rakūba* (shelter made of wood and sorghum stalks). The house will be built gradually by adding parts, according to availability of funds. Self-construction is widely practiced, especially by casual day labourers, who call upon colleagues for help and to whom they will one day repay the service. The acquisition of materials and services for carpentry and roofing go no faster. It is only when the walls around the plot and at least one room of the house have been built that a married man can ask his wife and children to join him.

Socioeconomic Reproduction: Accessing Water and Other Resources

Migration in pursuit of improved income and access to decent housing are the two basic motors of the 'life project' of the migrants interviewed. For such a project to become reality it is necessary to ensure domestic reproduction, and for that, access to basic resources is considered essential. In designing the survey used in interviews, it was decided to focus on three basic resources: drinking water – on which this section will mainly focus – lighting and cooking means (CBS 2006).

Access to Water

The Water Distribution System in Bawga Al-Jadīd and Bawga Al-Sharīg

Potable water as water pumped from the Nile, treated and distributed through the urban network supplies a little more than one-third of the inhabitants of Greater Khartoum (Denis 2005, 2006). The network, in fact, essentially supplies the oldest areas of the capital and only the wealthier of the newly urbanized areas. Nearly four million people live in the capital's peripheral extensions (people essentially displaced by successive droughts and civil wars, but also 'economic migrants' from all the provinces) (Pantulliano et al. 2011). Very few of these urban extensions are connected to the municipal drinking water network, and most rely on alternative systems of water extraction and distribution.

The most common system (available in ʿAllujāb and Bawga Al-Jadīd but not in Bawga Al-Sharīg) is a tube well (*bayāra*) drilled at various depths equipped with a pump driven either electrically or by an internal combustion engine, which raises the water into a large metal tank (*khazzān* or *siḥirīj*) located about ten metres above the ground (Nègre 2004). The tube well in Bawga Al-Jadīd, built in 2006, constitutes a 'local public good'[10] and is managed by the settlement's services committee (*lajna al-khadamāt*), which also has the responsibility for a primary school and is composed of seven elected members (including a president, a secretary and a treasurer) and employs the caretaker of the well (*ghafīr*) and a technician.[11]

Concerning the distribution of water, two methods are present in Bawga Al-Jadīd: a mininetwork and the *karro* system (water tanks on wheels pulled by donkeys providing house-to-house water service). In Bawga Al-Sharīg, only the *karro* system is available. From the Bawga Al-Jadīd tank, pressurized water goes down through a pipe, which is then divided into two pipes. The first, equipped with a great tap, is used to fill the *karro*. The second, equipped with two big taps, provision two mininetworks (*shabaka*). These are composed of metal pipes of small diameter buried at a shallow depth in the streets delivering gravity-fed water by tap access to household reservoirs generally located in the courtyards. Home owners access the water by opening and closing a tap. One such mininetwork is opened in the morning and the other in the afternoon in order to maintain sufficient pressure. These mininetworks, built by a small entrepreneur, cover almost the entire territory of the agglomeration of Bawga Al-Jadīd but serve only half of the houses, those willing or able to pay the connection charges, SDG 200 by *ḥōsh* and a monthly flat consumption fee of SDG 15.[12]

The inhabitants of Bawga Al-Sharīg and those in Bawga Al-Jadīd whose houses are not connected to the mininetworks depend upon the water distribution system by *karro*.[13] A *karro* is generally owned by an individual, who drives it or who hires someone else (often a child) and is not necessarily the owner of the donkey. A *karro* driver is attached to a particular well where he must fetch water, because he has an account with the *lajna al-khadamāt* that supports it. Among the forty *karro* drivers attached to the wells of Bawga Al-Jadīd, thirty work daily, serving also the inhabitants of Bawga Al-Sharīg, located on average a mile from the well; this settlement is also served by *karro* attached to the closest wells of the settlement of Ta'awīḍāt (outside ʿAllujāb, but still a part of ʿIdd Bābiker) which sometimes creates conflicts between *karro* drivers. Some of them live in Bawga Al-Sharīg. The job of *karro* driver is quite popular because it is more profitable than that of casual day labourer: first, it is permanent, and second, it can yield a gross income of SDG 30 per day.[14]

The Share of Water Expense in the Household Income as a Poverty Marker

If we now consider the cost of household water consumption as a percentage of the household income among the different socioeconomic strata, it is clear that this percentage is considerable. There are few households whose domestic consumption is less than one *barmīl* per day (250 litres).[15] Household water needs include not only cooking, cleaning and miscellaneous household usages, but often the watering of poultry, a sheep, goats, a garden with vegetables and even one or two fruit trees (to the outsider these uses may appear a luxury, but they are in fact of great practical value.) One- and two-person households consume one *barmīl* every other day. For a household of three or more persons in the S_2 stratum, with an income equivalent to that of a day labourer[16] (total weekly income of SDG 40), the weekly expenditure for water amounts to SDG 14 or a full third (35 per cent) of its income (based on daily consumption of one *barmīl* per day at SDG 2 per *barmīl*). For a household of three or more persons of the S_3 stratum, with a minimum monthly income corresponding to this social stratum (approximately SDG 200), the same daily water consumption represents less than one-third (30 per cent) of income, while, for households of the same stratum with the highest income (around SDG 300), the consumption of one *barmīl* per day amounts to about one-fifth of the household income. Even households of the S_4 stratum, which give no indication of their income, complain about the high share of the cost of water in their household income. The inhabitants of Bawga Al-Sharīg are aware that a monthly fee of SDG 15, similar to the service fee paid by the inhabitants of Bawga Al-Jadīd connected to the mininetwork, would seriously reduce their household water budgets, reducing these to approximately 9 per cent of S_2 household income, 7.5 per cent of the lowest S_3 household income and 5 per cent of the highest S_3 household income (versus 35, 30 and 20 per cent, respectively, in the case of supply by *karro*).

In developing countries food expenditures often occupy more than two-thirds of household income for households classified as 'poor'. In the case of migrants inhabiting Bawga Al-Sharīg and deprived of access through a water distribution network, the cost of water alone – which people spontaneously agree is the primary element of life, a gift of God, a 'natural right' and that it is wrong to pay anything more than a token fee – can amount to one-third of family income. Although this calculation is not formally done by the residents of Bawga Al-Sharīg, the very high proportion of household income devoted to access this basic good is for the vast majority of the people very symbolic of their poverty (Ahmed and Al-Battahani 1995; M. Abdalla 2008) and of the harshness of their lives.

From Water Networking to Social Networking

Faced with this situation, a group of men, following the lead of a small furniture retailer working in North Khartoum, living in Bawga Al-Sharīg and belonging to the S_4 stratum, decided in early 2009 to implement a non yet existing informal *lajna al-khadamāt* for their own settlement. This informal committee of seven, including one woman, was elected by the heads of families living in the neighbourhood. After the project initiators (the project leader and instigator of the meeting became president of the *lajna al-khadamāt*) convened a meeting of the general population, the committee established the priorities of building a well and the establishment of a mininetwork. Without public or NGO funding, the members expected that they would have to 'rely on their own forces' (*juhūd dhātīa*). Given the lack of domestic savings, the committee sought to leverage external means, financial and material (equipment), to drill a well, instal a tank and acquire a motor pump. The search for sponsors (Baillard and Haenni 1997) led to an agreement with a contractor ready to practice for the occasion some *a'māl khayrīa* (charitable actions); his company has drilling equipment, one of which was loaned for fifteen days, hoping that this time would be sufficient to complete the well to a depth sufficient to ensure an adequate flow of drinking water and begin the process of supplying the thousands of underserved residents of Bawga Al-Sharīg. The well was dug, its flow is sufficient and the water quality is good.

The *lajna al-khadamāt* then launched a search for sheet metal from which to construct the tank and the finances to purchase a motorized pump and pay for the welders and technicians necessary to assemble the proposed water tower.[17] The committee is also considering the creation of a water distribution mininetwork, which would enable residents to significantly lower water expenses as a percentage of household income. The committee is placing a bold bet on self-financing through savings: local consumption based on one *barmīl* per day per household (a cost of SDG 2) costs households SDG 730 per year for water delivered by *karro*. Alternatively, a flat monthly fee of SDG 15 per household would cost SDG 180 annually and generate savings of SDG 550 per connected household. This amount, multiplied by the number of households in Bawga Al-Sharīg (three hundred), would generate, in savings to the community, twice the total cost of installing a mininetwork (savings for households consuming one *barmīl* every other day would still amount to SDG 185). The leader of the committee, who is in the habit of making such economic calculations, recognizes that these savings are potential and that they will be difficult to sustain among poor households burdened with urgent and unexpected expenses. Nevertheless, the project leader encourages the committee members, as 'local development activists', to promote saving behaviours for the common good as well as to mobilize collective efforts, in a spirit of *juhūd dhātīa* (personal efforts), to create a real 'community' in Bawga Al-Sharīg in the context of weak solidarity among its inhabitants, a product of the heterogeneous character of the inhabitants and the absence of extended family and lineage networks. *Juhūd dhātīa* together with sponsorship and private charity should be combined, as one resident said:

> You know, there are in this country many people who have made fortunes, often with support from dignitaries of the regime that governs us by methods that religion condemns, yet these people have grown older and care about their future after death. Those must be addressed as a priority, because they have much to be forgiven by Allah, if they want to go to heaven; and they are often very generous. But there are also 'good people' who are rich and want to do good for the poor, one must also know these people and interact with them because they make their own donations to the neighbourhoods that they know and often, these good people want to remain anonymous and request not to say how much they gave. … Others, the 'new rich', like their generosity to be known and visible, but never mind, if they are willing to donate money or materials, or lend equipment, well, they are welcome … and Allah knows best.

In Bawga Al-Sharīg, social integration is low[18] and it is impossible to mobilize 'traditional' social networks as a result of the extreme heterogeneity of the original population. A few residents in Bawga Al-Sharīg took the initiative to create the *lajna al-khadamāt,* assembling heads of families to create an institution representative of the population. Despite the fact that many people in Bawga Al-Sharīg remain sceptical or do not believe that a well – let alone a mininetwork – will ever be implemented in their settlement, this pioneering initiative won the support of a significant portion of the population, who participated in the first group meetings. This can be explained by the importance of the issue of access to cheaper water than the delivery system by *karro* allows, by the personality and the good reputation of the initiators and by the fact that other water and services committees have been established in other settlements of the same peripheral areas and have achieved their goals. This local networking (i.e., the creation of the committee) was indispensable for the establishment of external support networking, which is to say, to connect with charitable institutions, sponsor organizations and so forth. This vital task was performed by the committee president, relying on his social status and relational capital and on persuasive skills developed professionally, a combination that gained him acceptance among his professional peers and allowed him to be 'taken seriously' by the various institutions and donor organizations upon which the project depended.

Lighting and Cooking Means

In the western part of Bawga Al-Sharīg, a few columns of cement stand without electric cables, reminders of a National Electricity Corporation (NEC) project to extend existing lines from Bawga Al-Jadīd into Bawga Al-Sharīg. The majority of people use oil lamps as lighting devices. However, as it is for water distribution in Bawga Al-Jadīd, informal mininetworks serving individual dwellings have been installed in the form of electrical wires running in the streets or along the walls and connected to the service boxes (*'elba*) of some houses situated east of Bawga Al-Jadīd, themselves connected to the NEC public grid. But unlike water in Bawga Al-Jadīd, for which the amount payable by the houses connected to the semi-informal mininetwork is fixed as a lump sum (SDG 15), regardless of household consumption, the grid subscriber and owner of a service box must pay the NEC fees that are proportional to his consumption.[19] The subscriber, before allowing another resident to be relayed from his own *'elba,* must evaluate by himself the estimated consumption of this resident. This generally entails a house visit in which the number of light bulbs and any electrical appliances are inventoried, for which the NEC subscriber sets a price (generally not less than SDG 40 per month for the consumption equivalent of a few light bulbs), considered higher to what would be the estimated cost of that consumption paid directly to the NEC, amounts that are often the subject of litigation.

The majority of people in Bawga Al-Sharīg (and almost all of those belonging to the S_2 stratum) utilize charcoal to cook their food, buying it daily from retail stores in small bags. Anyone using this energy source complains about its high price (SDG 1 per bag used at a rate of two bags per day) and dreams of being able to purchase a refillable gas cylinder. One gas cylinder itself (the empty container) costs SDG 100 and most people in the S_2 and S_3 stratum say they are not able to spare such an amount (representing, respectively, one-half and one-third of their monthly income). Charcoal, on the other hand, will cost the household annually approximately SDG 730 (SDG 2 multiplied by 365 days), as much as the annual cost of water. The acquisition of a gas cylinder and a refill every two months (about SDG 20) would cost the home owner SDG 220 over the first year, producing savings in the first year of SDG 500 and SDG 600 per year in subsequent years. The purchase price of the cylinder represents only one-fifth of the savings to be realized by such an investment, an amount that could easily be repaid in a few months. The inability to accumulate and spare an amount of SDG 100 hinders the acquisition of a simple good that could significantly decrease household expenses. The immediate cause of this difficulty is poverty and insufficient income, which lead in turn to continued poverty and stress on the household budget. The only apparent solution to this self-perpetuating cycle of poverty lies in access to a microfinance network, a social tool that is nonexistent in the municipality of ʿAllujāb.

This example is repeated across the board, the purchase of microquantities of basic goods producing considerable increases in current expenditures. As an example, a mother will send a child to buy a few centilitres of oil to complete a *fūl* (beans dish) for the *faṭūr* (midmorning) meal. The local grocer places a few centilitres in a tiny plastic bag and charges three to four times the unit cost than if the child had purchased a bottle of oil in the same grocery store.

Conclusion

In this chapter, I attempted to describe and analyse, on the basis of field research conducted on the outskirts of Khartoum in an underserved community lacking in public facilities and infrastructure, various aspects of the social trajectories of voluntary economic migrants deprived of any of three types of initial endowments: material means, professional qualifications and pre-existing social networks, 'traditional networks' (kinship, ethnic or tribal networks), which can be mobilized to access resources and goods necessary for everyday subsistence. Without the benefit of any of these three supports, these 'atomized' migrants deploy alternative strategies for accessing income sources (trying to find a job as casual day labourers they can attempt to transform into regular and permanent work), land and house ownership (buying, with small savings gained little by little, a cheap plot located in a far, remote area on the outskirts of Khartoum, and building their house step-by-step, often by themselves and through an exchange of services) and basic services such as water and energy.

These strategies involve the establishment of social ties between individuals and the construction of larger social networks: (a) social ties with other migrants who know the job market and opportunities in Khartoum, with employers likely to recruit them when there are job opportunities, with other people of the settlement to find a plot and help each other to build a house and with people already connected to various grids – water and electricity in particular – for informal access; (b) 'internal' social networking between inhabitants of the settlement to implement a collective project of drilling wells or establishing a water distribution mininetwork; and (c) 'external' networking with institutions and donors. Such activities produce social networking and linkages that constitute an important strategy for dealing with poverty, a problem confronted by all immigrants to Bawga Al-Sharīg and confirmed by the summary attempt to measure monetary income by economic stratum and relate water expense as a percentage of the household income. Networking strategies do not in themselves 'win' the struggle against poverty, but they are part of a complex larger picture involving collective strategies and external social actors.

Difficulties encountered in setting up a semi-informal mininetwork for water distribution and the lack of microcredit facilities impose upon the poor an unnecessarily high level of expenditure for basic services – water by *karro*, electricity by relay – making it impossible for the poor to manage their limited resources to best advantage (the purchase of a gas cylinder or connection to a water mininetwork would produce combined economies of SDG 1,000 per year, the equivalent of five months' income for a casual day labourer). In both cases, the lack of efficient networking and microcredit facilities dramatically reinforces the poverty trap faced by economic migrants who are thus maintained in the so-called vicious circle of poverty (M. Ahmed 2008; World Bank 2009).

Notes

1. This chapter is written based on data collected during a survey in the frame of a Franco-German research programme (WAMAKHAIR) on water management in Khartoum.
2. *Idārā shaʿabīa* means 'popular administration'. It is the territorial administrative unit of the lowest level and the equivalent of a municipality. An *idārā shaʿabīa* can be composed of several settlements (villages or hamlets) and is headed by a *lajna shaʿabīa*, a 'popular committee'. Several *idārā shaʿabīa* are regrouped into *wiḥda idārīa* (equivalent of a district), then *maḥalliya* (locality, equivalent to a county), then *wilāya* (federal state). ʿAllujāb is the name of one subgroup of the Baṭāḥīn tribe, considered to be 'first-comers' in ʿIdd Bābiker.
3. The migrants interviewed are men under forty-five, who most often attended school for only a few years (some are illiterate) and are from very diverse geographical origins, but mainly from the western states (Darfur, Kordofan).
4. The socioeconomic stratification given here is fairly static, but there are forms of modest social mobility, resulting in the expansion, modification and improvement of home comforts.

5. It is very difficult to ask questions about income. The less poor have an idea of their income value but are reluctant to talk about it. The 'poor' do not calculate it, and their incomes are highly irregular and variable over time.
6. At the exchange rate of June 2011, SDG 1 = USD 0.37.
7. The description of sales transactions and of the legal status of the sold plot is the subject of often contradictory information; a deeper investigation is warranted. Here I limit myself to a description of the practices reported by respondents.
8. The status of the 'tribal lands' is far from clear; according to the rules of the Native Administration (abolished in 1970, the administration is experiencing a comeback at present), the land was given to tribes in collective and permanent usufruct by the state. In some areas coveted for construction, members of these tribes have individually appropriated the land and are selling it in violation of tribal regulations.
9. It is for this reason that many people build their house in the middle of the plot.
10. The KSWC collects some fees for the registration of the well and for periodic analysis of water quality.
11. The *lajna al-khadamāt* is not an official body but can be recognized by the authorities of the municipality in which it operates (this is the case for the *lajna al-khadamāt* of Bawga Al-Jadīd).
12. There are also totally informal mininetworks made of flexible plastic pipes running through the streets and connected to the metal pipes of houses connected to the mininetwork; such mininetworks bring running water to houses that are not connected to the public mininetwork.
13. The tank of a *karro* is composed of one or two *barmīls*, which is the Arabic name of a barrel of oil or diesel of 250 litres. A tank made of a single *barmīl* is called a *farda,* and a tank made of two is a *dabol* (a word coming from the English 'double'); in the latter case the *barmīl* lids have been removed and the *barmīls* welded together.
14. In one day a driver may complete up to a dozen trips to the well. For a double *barmīl,* the drivers pays SDG 0.7 to the *lajna al-khadamāt* and sells it to the customer for SDG 4, the earnings per round being SDG 3.3.
15. Is interesting to note that the WHO norm for the minimum amount a person should ideally consume is twenty-five litres per day.
16. It should be recalled that casual day labourers are of social stratum S_1 and generally live with other family members.
17. At the time of my last stay in the field (November 2010), the means to acquire those elements essential to the project had not yet been obtained.
18. I often asked neighbours about an individual or family living in the same lane. More often than not, respondents were unable to provide information about the named person or family, who were unknown to them.
19. The NEC introduced in the 2000s prepaid electricity meters allowing subscribers to purchase electricity in advance.

Chapter 4

Contested Land Rights and Ethnic Conflict in Mornei (West Darfur)

Scarcity of Resources or Crises of Governance?

Zahir M. Abdal-Kareem and Musa A. Abdul-Jalil

Despite the fact that there have been wide global discussions on issues of grassroots conflicts over natural resources, particularly since the 1980s, a number of researchers argue that these studies 'remain fragmented between disciplinary boundaries, which produce conflicting and often mutually exclusive theories. Most importantly, there is a disturbing lack of integrative knowledge on the subject' (Porto 2002: 1). When it comes to the situation in Africa, many scholars have emphasized that natural resource issues, particularly land, have occupied a central place in the recent literature tackling the conflict question on the continent. One author argues that '[t]he access to and control of valuable natural resources, including minerals, oil, timber, productive pastures and farming land, have been crucial factors in the occurrence of violent conflicts across the continent' (Porto 2002: 2). As regards the situation in Sudan, a number of anthropologists have also highlighted the role played by competition over natural resources in the onset of recent conflicts in different parts of the country (Mohamed 2000; Abdul-Jalil 2009a; Babiker 2009; Assal 2006a).

With reference to Darfur, we find that different arguments are adopted by the scholars working in the region to illustrate the nature of grassroots conflicts. For example, some scholars (Mohamed et al. 2003) argue that lack of development is among the main causes behind the eruption of conflicts in the region. Accordingly, they remind us to pay more attention to the negative role played by the successive Sudanese states. Similarly, de

Notes for this chapter begin on page 84.

Waal (2007) ascribes Darfur's conflict to what he identifies as the 'crisis of governance' in Sudan. He suggests that '[t]he war in Darfur should compel us to attend more closely to the ways in which identity conflicts are, in significant ways, a by-product of the political structure of the Sudanese polity' (de Waal 2007: 3). Likewise, Tubiana (2007: 90) argues that

> Khartoum has used land not only to mobilize proxies among landless Arabs who saw an opportunity to renegotiate the terms of their access to tenure, but also to rekindle standing local conflicts from which it stood to gain. At the same time, the rebel groups played on the fears non-Arabs had about their land in order to attract support from those communities. This explains the new fracture that has appeared between landless Arabs, who want new land, and non-Arabs, who fear losing theirs.

Mohamed (2000) concludes that land scarcity in Darfur, together with the negative role played by the Sudanese state, are the major source of Darfur's grassroots conflicts.

From an anthropological point of view, although grassroots-level analysis – which investigates the role played by local actors – is a crucial factor for understanding the conflict phenomena, the role of the state needs to be investigated more carefully. Here it is argued that to fully comprehend the conflict in African communities we need to put more emphasis on the state and on the concept of 'governance'. 'This suggests a need to look at people's use of, and control over, resources at many different levels, thus permitting a consideration of processes of power and authority' (Manger 2005: 135). For the purposes of this chapter, Manger's perspective will be expanded. Thus, the position adopted by this chapter could be stated as follows: apart from focusing on issues of natural resources management, in this case land, equivalent attention should be paid to the issue of conflict management. In other words, this chapter argues that land-based conflicts cannot be explained solely through environmental and economic factors; rather, issues of governance and politics are equally prominent.

The present chapter[1] is based on fieldwork conducted in 2008 in Mornei, West Darfur, a rural community that lies eighty-seven kilometres to the southwest of Al-Jeneīna (the capital of West Darfur State). More detailed information about Mornei will be provided later in a separate section. However, we think it is useful to mention that the existence of massive fertile agricultural lands and pastures, together with the passage of the main water courses through western Darfur, have attracted different pastoralist groups to this area. This makes it an 'ideal' place for studying issues that connect contested land rights and ethnic conflicts.

Theoretical Perspectives Regarding Conflict Issues: Some Important Clarifications

Many social scientists have observed that since the end of the Cold War in 1989 a number of theoretical perspectives concerning the analysis of conflict phenomenon have been developed (Richards 2005). Two approaches have become the most dominant. These approaches are the 'resource-based conflict model' and the 'ethnic-based conflict model'. Without going into a deep theoretical debate, we agree with Sisk that these approaches 'are not mutually exclusive and can in fact be describing different sides of the same coin' (Sisk 1996: 13).

As regards the resource-based conflict model, one notices that a wide range of variables, basically economic in nature, are used as analytical units to investigate the causes behind the conflict. These variables include, although not exclusively, economic growth rate, per capita income, lack of development, greed, scarcity of natural resources and so forth. Among all of these variables, this chapter will mostly concentrate on the role played by scarcity of resources and land in particular, a prime trigger of violence in Mornei in particular and Dār Masālīt[2] in general (figure 4.1). Taking land scarcity as a starting point of our analysis in this chapter stems from the fact that the areas that lie within the boundaries of what is currently known as West and South Darfur have become the main target of different migrating groups. These groups include the camel herders of northern Darfur and Chad as well as the cattle herders of the Central African Republic. A vast majority of the population, consisting of farmers and pastoralists, fundamentally depend on land as a crucial component for their livelihood.

In the ethnic-based conflict model, the main attention is placed upon issues such as ethnicity, identity and/or identification. Since the 1980s, ethnic-based conflicts all across the globe have begun to attract greater attention among social scientists (Fenton 2010; Schlee 2010; Eriksen 2002; Banks 1996; Barth 1969; Hutchinson and Smith 1996). Ethnicity has mostly been addressed through the primordialists' and structuralists' perspectives. Primordialists consider ethnicity as 'primordial or inherited group characteristics' (Porto 2002: 7), whereas structuralists argue that 'categorical ethnic distinctions do not depend on the absence of mobility, contact and information, but do entail social processes of exclusion and incorporation whereby discrete categories are maintained despite changing participation and membership in the course of individual life histories' (Barth 1969: 9). This assumption conceptualizes ethnic identity as 'an instrument, a contextual, fluid and negotiable aspect of identity' (Porto 2002: 7).

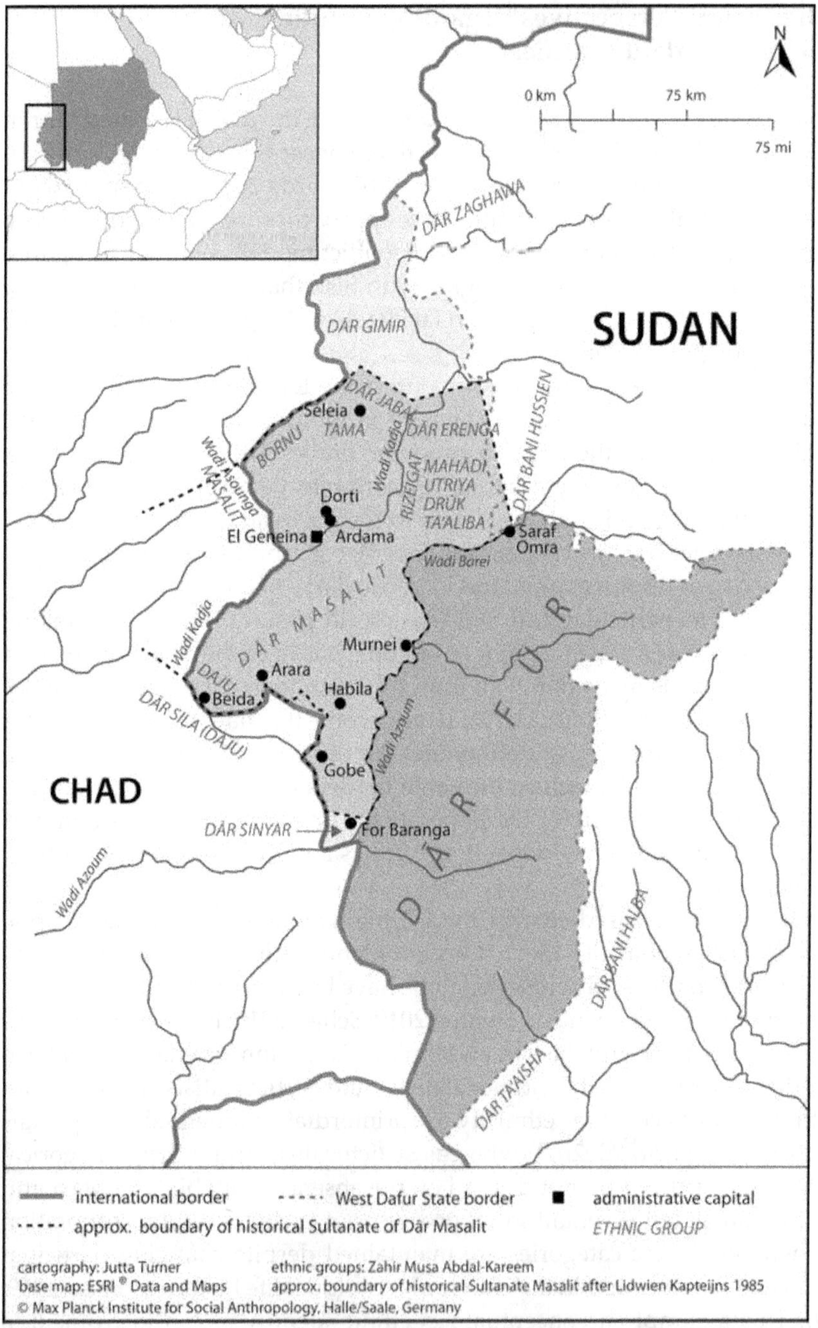

Figure 4.1. Boundaries of Historical Dār Masālīt and Its Main Ethnic Groups

The theoretical perspective adopted by this chapter concurs with Jabri's notion that conflict is 'a multi-causal phenomenon, where different causal sequences may apply to different conflict situations' (Jabri 1996: 65). It follows that the general claim that resource scarcity alone is the prime cause behind conflicts must be in doubt. Other factors, mostly related to the ethnic conflict model, must be considered. In other words, we argue that without denying the role played by economic and environmental factors in the onset of grassroots conflicts in the Darfur region, we need to 'attend closely to the ways in which identity conflicts are, in significant ways, a byproduct of the political structure of the Sudanese polity' (de Waal 2007: 3). To link the theoretical perspective adopted by this chapter with the main subject of the study, the next section will deal with the issue of land in Darfur and its economical, cultural, legal and political importance.

Economic and Social Dimensions of the Land Issue in Darfur

In many parts of Sudan, as in Africa as a whole, land is considered to be the most vital resource for rural communities. It is the main factor upon which they depend for their livelihoods and survival. It is also a measure of sociopolitical identity for the bulk of the population living in rural communities in Sudan (Komey 2008; Abdul-Jalil 2006). This has been the case for centuries in Darfur. So it could be reasonably concluded that apart from its economic importance, land embodies an important symbolic value in the Darfur region. Many scholars have emphasized that, for centuries, land has been the main source of group identification and political authority in the region (Abdul-Jalil 2006; O'Fahey 1980). Settled communities are considered owners of the territory that they occupy, and the land is referred to by their name. Therefore, homeland (or territory) has commonly been acknowledged to be one of the key criteria of group identification in the Darfur region. Moreover, maintaining a tribal homeland and/or territory in Darfur indicates upholding customary judicial rights in the different types of tribal disputes that take place within the territory.

Conceptually, anthropologists and other researchers have considered territoriality an important aspect that made tribes formidable political units in much of African societies for a long time. Tribal identity and solidarity depend first and foremost on some sort of association between the history and geography of the group. In Darfur, land has even played an important role both in the formation and progress of the state itself (see O'Fahey 1980). Historically, tribes in Darfur have continued to function as territorial groups whose solidarity depended on the successful management of the natural resources contained within their homeland (known locally as *dār* or *ḥakūra*). In addition, judicial rights, which are dependent on the tribal homeland, have acted as a local system of conflict management and served to consolidate the status of the tribes as formidable political organizations. However, population mobility has always existed despite the known pattern of territorial distribution of ethnic groups. Groups originally associated with a given territory (old-timers) have political as well as judicial advantages, and they expect that to continue.

In the past mobility was managed by allowing newcomers to join established territories under the political leadership of an indigenous group. Newcomers to such a territory are invariably subjected to the political authority of the original group, which held a monopoly over the rights to manage the territory. Population mobility has always existed. The heterogeneous distribution of groups among territorial units attests to that. People who move out of their territory face the risk of losing some of their political rights. A sizeable minority can be allowed to establish a lower-level native administrative unit like village headship or *'omodiya* (sectional chieftainship). Any ambition for higher positions of leadership is subsequently fiercely resisted by the political elite of the indigenous group. So it can be safely stated that many local conflicts are in fact generated by a mixture of competition over natural resources and/or access to political office.

Mornei: A Background of the Area and Its People

Mornei is located about eighty-seven kilometres to the southeast of Al-Jeneīna, the capital of West Darfur State. It is named after a large mountain that lies in the northern part of the area. It borders Zallingi Locality in the east, Al-Jeneīna in the west, Um Shālāya in the north and the Azūm valley in the south. Historically, Mornei was regarded as one of the main local administrative units (*furushiyāt,* sing. *furushiya*)[3] of the Dār Masālīt sultanate. This area has been subject to the recurrent administrative changes that took place at both national and local levels. For instance, Mornei was transferred to a local council during the early 1970s. This formed part of the introduction of the 'regional governance system' established by the government of Jaʿafar Nimeiri, who ruled Sudan from May 1969 to April 1985. According to the available statistics taken from the locality office of Mornei, the total population was estimated at six thousand inhabitants before the outbreak of the war in Darfur in 2003. The main villages that made up the Mornei area at that time were Sariri, Tomi Foca, Fufo, Aishbara and Bobaya. These villages are located along the western bank of the Madary valley, which divides the area into two parts, west and east settlements.

In the northern parts of Mornei are villages such as Nori and Gandarni. These villages are located in the western side of the Nori valley. According to local sources, the Fukujung, a subclan of the Masālīt tribe, were the first people to establish a settlement in the area in the first quarter of the nineteenth century.

It could easily be observed that this area is ethnically diverse. However, during fieldwork the majority of the interviewed people classified themselves as either belonging to an Arab or non-Arab tribe. The Arabs are commonly portrayed as animal herders. On the other hand, the non-Arabs are generally considered settled cultivators. Such classification tends to obscure the obvious mixed characteristics (physical, economic and cultural) of these ethnic groups. Following Barth (1969), we accept self-ascription used by a particular group as valid, since it gives information on their practical behaviour. Our observations in Mornei indicate that the settled cultivators mostly classify themselves as non-Arabs. Although the Masālīt and the Fur are the dominant tribal groups among this category, there are other cultivators who also classify themselves within this category. These groups include the Daju, who mainly inhabit the western side of Mornei. In addition, other groups such as the Gimir, the Tama and the Missiriya Jabal live in the northern parts of Mornei. A cluster of other groups, including the Zaghawa, the Marāsi, the Barnu and the Berti are spread over different locations in the area.

The Arabs can be classified into two groups. The first group, which we refer to as 'old-timers', includes some families from the Mahādi, the Bani Ḥalba and the Tarjām, who are found in different parts of Mornei. However, the bulk of these families inhabit the northern neighbourhoods. According to local informants, these groups have lived in Mornei since the first quarter of the twentieth century. Cattle herding is said to have been their main economic activity. Over time it has been observed that most of these groups have settled and begun to depend on farming activities. For this reason, classifications such as farmers and pastoralists are flexible. The second group within the Arabs is what we call the 'newcomers'. In the past the members of this group used to visit Mornei after the end of the harvest season in February. They are both cattle- and camel-herding pastoralists. The camel-herding groups (locally known as *abbāla*) are the largest group. They include Awlād Junūb, Awlād Zaiyd, Awlād Rashīd, Al-Najaʿa and Awlād Raḥama. All of these groups are essentially found in northern Darfur, where they are mostly known as the Northern Rizeīgāt (locally known as al-Rizeīgāt al-Shimāliya). However, they form part of a broad belt that extends from northern Darfur westwards across the Sudanese/Chadian borders to incorporate the camel-herding nomadic groups in northern Chad, Niger and Mali. As regards the cattle-herding groups (known locally as *baggāra*), they consist of the Salamāt, the Nawaiyba, and the Bani Ḥalba. According to local Masālīt informants in Mornei, the Bani Ḥalba families have migrated from their traditional homeland in South Darfur, which is called 'Idd al-Fursān. Conversely, the Salamāt families in Mornei, who have strong relations to the Taʿaiysha of South Darfur, are said by local informants to have migrated from southern Chad.

As for natural resources, an observer could easily notice that Mornei is among the richest areas in the Darfur region, with plentiful fertile lands and watercourses. Its topography is composed of different types of soils. These include vast stretches of black clay soil that cover more than half of the total area. This type of soil is known locally as *gardūd.* It lies some distance away from the banks of watercourses in the area. The main crops that are regularly cultivated in this type of soil are sorghum, okra and sesame. The area also includes a considerable amount of stabilized sand dunes. This type of soil is locally known as *qoz.* The main crops cultivated in this type of land are millet, scarlet runner and watermelons. There are also vast areas of lands that extend alongside and around the watercourses (*wādīs*). These areas are covered by a yellow fertile soil with a dense vegetation cover. This type of land is locally known as *tartūra.* It is mostly found in the eastern parts of Mornei. Finally, there are some scattered small areas of hard clay soil (known locally as *naga'a*). This type of soil is not suitable for cultivation. Such areas have been used as dry season grazing reserves for the animal herder groups who visit the area after the harvest season.

As regards the arable agricultural activities, we observed that there are two different, although complementary, types of farming activities practiced in this area, small-scale rain-fed farming and irrigated horticulture. For many decades rain-fed cultivation has been the major economic activity pursued by the bulk of the sedentary population. It is mainly found in the small farms that lie closer to the residential areas (villages). It is called locally *ziraʿa al-bildāt* (the local expression for small-scale farming). One of the main objectives of this kind of cultivation is to meet the subsistence needs of the local households. Sorghum and millet are the main products produced by this type of farming. Groundnut, sesame and watermelon are also cultivated. All members of the household are expected to participate in this type of cultivation. However, our interviewees emphasized that women usually bear the biggest burden of the work.

Women start the initial phases of this small-scale cultivation by cleaning the farms and digging small holes in the ground, which are subsequently filled by crop seeds. This stage usually starts in May or June. After that they wait until the beginning of the rainy season, normally in June or July. Two months after the rainy season, they begin weeding and removal of invasive grasses. Local informants stressed the important role played by women, younger sons and daughters at this stage. Harvesting normally starts in December. At this time, men as well as the elder sons carry out the major part of the work. Small-scale rain-fed cultivation agriculture usually ends in January. However, in some years, cultivators are forced to delay the harvest until February. This is the case when the rainy seasons start later than their regular time or when rains are especially heavy. Cases of conflicts between farmers and pastoralists can be expected during such periods. After the harvest pastoralist groups are traditionally allowed to enter the farms with their animals, who feed on the remains. According to local informants, cases of conflict are predictable when pastoralists enter the area before being informed that harvesting operations have been totally completed. Frequently livestock enter the fields before the harvest is concluded, damaging crops as a result. This is the conventional example of how conflicts erupt between farmers and pastoralists in Darfur. However, it would be very naïve to analyse Darfur's conflicts based on such a simple argument.

As regards irrigated horticulture, it is said by informants that this activity is carried out in winter and in the areas that lie closer to the watercourses. The main products produced by this type of agriculture include onions, okra, scarlet runner, coriander and humus. Recently, a cash crop, tobacco (known locally as *tumbāk*), has begun to be cultivated in Mornei. Traditional tools such as axe and hoe are among the main tools used for carrying out the digging operations in this kind of cultivation. A small rounded wooden container, the *jugulāya,* is used to draw water from wells in the course of the irrigation process. However, according to local informants, people have begun to utilize some forms of modern technology since the beginnings of the 1990s. The use of diesel-powered pumps as well as tractors, locally known as *ziraʿa al-bawābir,*[4] exemplifies this new technology. The introduction of this new type of cultivation knowledge represents an attempt to establish small-scale mechanized farming in Mornei. It was initiated by small groups made up of government employees, local merchants and some local administration leaders. The 1990s has seen a remarkable increase in irrigated horticulture all over Mornei. This has increased the demand for agricultural land. As a result, farming activities have begun to increase at the expense of open areas that used to be allocated to herder groups as dry season grazing reserves during their seasonal migrations to the area. At the same time, informants stated that changes were not only confined to arable agriculture. Animal breeding activities practiced by farmers have been intensified as well.

As mentioned before, inhabitants of Mornei are basically farmers. However, significant animal breeding activities have lately appeared:

cattle, goats and sheep. These are being developed side by side with traditional farming practices. Here, it could be argued that this trend flourished during the 1990s because livestock became more lucrative locally, regionally and nationally. These new developments within the local livelihood systems have reshaped the previous mode of economic reciprocity between sedentary farmers and animal herders in Mornei, with the result that land available for traditional pastoral activities in Mornei have been significantly reduced.

Turning to the nomadic groups in Mornei, it is necessary to distinguish between cattle and camel herders. It should be noted that cattle herders in Mornei practice small-scale farming activities as well, usually cultivating durra and millet. Not surprisingly, cases of settlements among cattle herders have been widely observed. Moreover, a number of families have been fully integrated with the sedentary people. As for the camel herders, there have been no significant changes affecting their livelihood activities as compared to cattle herders. They continue to be mainly confined to camel-herding activities. Both cattle and camel herders satisfy their needs for agricultural products through exchanging and reciprocating their animal products with the sedentary people of Mornei. In addition, both these groups collect firewood from the forests surrounding villages and sell or exchange it with farmers for kind or cash. In the following section we will examine the extent to which these changes in livelihood systems, together with the negative role played by the state, have adversely affected the social relations between farmers and herders in Mornei area since the mid-1990s.

The Trajectory of Conflicts between Farmers and Herders in Mornei

According to local informants, throughout the relatively recent history of relations between farmers and herders in Dār Masālīt and West Darfur, conventional conflicts and/or disputes regularly increase after the harvest season. These conflicts extend on a regular basis from February to May. One of the main causes of these low-level conflicts, in the opinion of local informants, is the damage caused by herders' animals trespassing farms during their seasonal migrations into the homelands of the sedentary people of Mornei. In the past, these clashes used to be minor in nature and consequently easy to control by traditional mechanisms of conflict resolution. But local informants pointed out that cases of conflict between sedentary farmers (such as the Masālīt, the Fur and the Daju) and herders (such as the Northern Rizeīgāt, the Salamāt and the Bani Ḥalba) have conspicuously increased since the mid-1980s. Stories told by local informants clearly show that the cattle-herding Salamāt, who are identified by sedentary farmers as foreigners and/or migrants, have taken part in many disputes occurring in Mornei, particularly against the Masālīt and the Daju around the Azūm and Bāri valleys.

In the same way, camel herders have also engaged in a number of disputes and skirmishes with sedentary farmers in the same period. Like the cattle herders, these conflicts were easy to settle through collaboration between the respective native administration authorities (representing farmers' and herders' communities), who are customarily responsible for conflict management. Nonetheless, our informants stressed that the nature of these conflicts had changed dramatically by the mid-1990s,[5] before reaching a peak with the outbreak of the 2003 war in Darfur. The conflict between the Masālīt and some sections of the camel-herding Northern Rizeīgāt, which broke out in the village of Majmary[6] in 1995, is an obvious example reflecting the shift in the nature of conflicts in Dār Masālīt in particular and West Darfur in general. Awlād Junūb, Al-Najaʿa and Awlād Eid were the main sections of the Northern Rizeīgāt group that engaged in this conflict. According to local informants, cattle herders such as the Salamāt, the Bani Ḥalba and the Tarjām took the Northern Rizeīgāt's side and fought against the Masālīt in that conflict. On the other hand, the Fur and the Daju, also sedentary farmers, chose to support the Masālīt. What was new in that conflict was its brutality, with high numbers of killings among children, women and old people, and with total burning of the village. Given that, even local authorities of native administration in the area were not able to settle it. This had led to the eruption of a more organized and ethnically-based conflict between farmers and herders all over Dār Masālīt in 1997. This has come to be known as the war between the Masālīt and the Arabs in Dār Masālīt and/ or West Darfur.

A further confirmation of the transformation in the patterns of the conflicts between farmers and herders in Mornei is illustrated by an attack carried out by animal herders' groups on some farmers' villages in Mornei in 1997. These villages were Bobāya, Aishbara, Sulma, Traiyfāya and Nuri. Victims of that attack mentioned that all these villages were burned and totally destroyed during the attack, and that their cattle have become one of the main targets during these new conflicts. Other accounts reveal further issues. Cattle herders living in Mornei (especially the Mahādi, the Tarjām and the Hawāra) had been mobilized along ethnic and/or racial lines to fight against the sedentary people of Mornei. For instance, herders were identifying sedentary farmers by their skin colour. This issue was clearly reflected by the extensive use of the term *zurga*.[7] Conversely, animal herders (from Mornei and elsewhere) have begun to be characterized as 'enemies', 'outsiders', 'government allies' and members of the

Arab Gathering.[8] For example, in a group discussion that we conducted with five local sheikhs representing the sedentary groups in Mornei at the time, the same issues (regarding the ethnicization of local conflicts) were observed. Those sheikhs represented the Masālīt, the Fur, the Daju, the Zaghawa and the Barnu. One of the sheikhs stressed that the emergence of this strong trend among sedentary groups in Mornei to define themselves as *zurga* was based on the need to defend their rights over their homelands as well as land ownership. For him, that was a legitimate reaction, because the herders had already been organized under the Arab Gathering organization, strongly supported by the Sudanese government. Another sheikh identified the camel-herding groups as enemies. The same line of reasoning led another sheikh to say that their enemies were not camel herders alone. Rather, he indicated that some cattle herders as well as cultivators, who were considered part of the community in Mornei, had taken the side of the enemy camp. According to him, these included cattle-herding groups like the Salamāt and the Bani Ḥalba as well as cultivating groups like the Gimir, the Tama, and the Bargu. The latter three groups are mostly recognized as non-Arab in the Darfur region.

An in-depth analysis of the informants' narratives and this group discussion suggests that the recent conflicts in Mornei and West Darfur have begun to be heavily couched in ethnic terms. In other words, these conflicts have begun to be interpreted as 'farmers' versus 'herders'; 'indigenous' versus 'newcomers'; 'non-Arabs' versus 'Arabs'; or the *zurga* versus the 'Arab Gathering'. These different levels reflect the extent to which the different parties involved in these conflicts have been polarized across economic, territorial, ethnic and political lines. Informants openly admitted that local politics is heavily subject to ethnic interests. Our interviews show that local elites, for example, primary school teachers, retired officials and members of the local administrative system, have been extensively involved in these processes of polarization. In the next section we aim to show the link between the above-mentioned conflicts and contested land rights.

Contested Land Rights, Changing Livelihood Systems and Conflict in Mornei

Secondary data about grassroots conflicts in Darfur indicate that most conflicts that have erupted in the region since the end of the 1960s onwards (e.g., the Maᶜaliya versus the Rizeīgāt in 1968; the Taᶜaiysha versus the Salamāt in 1980; the Rizeīgāt versus the Zaghawa in 1986) were fought over contested land rights (Tubiana 2007). As regards Dār Masālīt, it should be stated that the owners of homelands or territories in West Darfur, sedentary farmers such as the Masālīt, the Fur and the Daju, have continuously enjoyed accepted customary rights over land tenure and use in this area. However, the profound changes in the traditional livelihood systems in Dār Masālīt put the system of customary land rights to a real test. Here, it could be strongly emphasized that the old system of land tenure had been working efficiently until the mid-1990s. As a result, social relations between farmers and herders were mostly peaceful and complementary.

Informants among pastoralist groups in Al-Jeneīna, however, stated that sedentary farmers in Dār Masālīt have begun to use their customary rights over their homelands to maintain exclusive rights over the land. They said that when sedentary farming groups such as the Masālīt, the Fur and the Daju needed extra land to expand their farming operations as well as animal breeding activities during the 1990s, they found it easy to legitimately utilize the vacant lands that were customarily allocated to livestock grazing by herders who usually migrated to the area after the harvest season. In contrast, local informants in Mornei emphasized that animal herders have begun to claim that Dār Masālīt no longer belongs to the sedentary groups alone. Masālīt informants report that one of the main arguments adopted by these animal herders is that 'land in Darfur is owned by the government now, and not by the tribes. And this is what the laws have clearly stated.' The same Masālīt informants in Mornei report that based on this erroneous interpretation, herders have begun to refuse to abide by the customary land tenure system. Here, the Unregistered Land Act (1970) together with the Emirate Act (1995) are said by local informants to be the key legislation constantly referred to by local elites from herding groups to legitimize their access to land in Dār Masālīt in general.

The Unregistered Land Act of 1970 was introduced by the government of Ja'afar Nimeiri in order to facilitate the acquisition of more land for large-scale commercial farming in the clay plains of central Sudan. Instead of limiting the act to the targeted areas, a universal law was passed that applied to the entire country. Any unregistered land from the relevant date would automatically be considered government land. This meant that people using land under customary tenure would not be entitled to compensation should such land be allocated by government officials to new users. This law later gave reasonable pretext for nonlandowning groups around the country to utilize unallocated land on the assumption that it is government land and hence available for use. Previously such users needed to request permission from traditional authorities to use such land.

The Emirate Act, locally known as *ganūn al-amarāt,* was issued by the governor of West Darfur in 1995 as part of an attempt to upgrade the administrative capacity of native administration institutions for Arab pastoralist groups. As a result, the system of native administration in West Darfur, including Dār Masālīt in particular, was divided between the Masālīt and the Arabs (essentially the Northern Rizeīgāt camel herders). The Masālīt people considered this an unwarranted intervention by the government to abolish their historical customary rights over their homeland, which used to be a separate sultanate, to the advantage of landless groups from the Northern Rizeīgāt (Rabāh 1998).

It becomes clear that the new basis of legitimacy regarding land rights has been indirectly generated by government action that did not introduce safeguards against possible negative repercussions of the new laws. Of course, governments are entitled to review and reform land tenure systems, but when they do it is pertinent that they should consider all factors in the targeted communities. It is rather unfortunate that these two acts have only intensified the conflicts over land and have produced ethnic polarization in Dār Masālīt.

Analysis of the narratives told by local informants clearly shows that there is an association between the changes that affected the livelihood systems and the increase of the formerly traditional conflicts between famers and herders in Mornei. Consequently, it could be argued that the emergence of strong trend towards a market-oriented economy among sedentary farmers in Mornei is among the direct causes behind the emergence of conflicts in the area. Increasing demands for extra land are the direct consequences of this transformation. Given the increasing human and animal migrations to Mornei since the mid-1990s onwards, coupled with the shift towards a market-oriented economy, land has become a scarce resource in Mornei. As a result, fierce competitions over land and pastures, mainly between sedentary farmers and herders (usually camel herders) have taken place. One could safely conclude that one perspective of this conflict is the newly emerging competition between systems of livelihood in the area. This phenomenon is not new, either in Darfur or in Sudan in general. Many researchers in Sudan (Mohamed 2000; Abdul-Jalil 2009a; Babiker 2009) emphasize that competition over land is a common element between most of the grassroots conflicts in Sudan. One researcher has summarized it by simply stating that 'the cause of many conflicts we see today in the Sudan is related to resource access and usage' (Assal 2006a: 102).

Turning our attention to the region as a whole, one would argue that such conflicts are not confined to Sudan. It is no surprise to see similar patterns of conflict documented across the countries in the Horn of Africa. One study from Somalia demonstrates that land and resources alone are not the ultimate sources of conflict in Jubbaland or Somalia. Rather, land and resources are embedded among many other interrelated factors, including conflict to control the state, engagement of third parties, including neighboring governments, ineffectual or missing state institutions, and official policy that curried favour with minority groups through patrimonial favour, but excluded most other groups. (Farah, Hussein and Lind 2002: 349)

In the next section, we consider the issue of governance and its relation to the conflict in Mornei and Dār Masālīt.

The Failure of Governmental Institutions and the Escalation of Conflict in Mornei

The question of governance that we consider in this chapter covers issues that include fragile state institutions, mismanagement, corruption, lack of development, and the inability to distinguish between the state and the ruling party. Issues of corruption and lack of development are extremely important for our analysis. A number of academic contributions about the Darfur region concluded that issues related to governance are among the main causes behind the onset or escalation of grassroots conflicts in the region (Rottenburg 2008; de Waal 2007; Assal 2006a; Mohamed et al. 2003). In West Darfur, an observer could easily notice that there has been a disturbing shortage of educational and basic health services and that the infrastructure in the state is very weak. As an example, our observations indicate that fifty years after the independence of Sudan (1956–2006), not one single paved road was constructed across West Darfur State. Our informants in West Darfur State have repeatedly asserted that lack of development is among the root causes behind their grievances. Similar arguments are used to justify claims advanced by several armed movements in Darfur. Furthermore, it could be strongly argued that almost all grassroots conflicts in Sudan are attributed in some way or another to lack of development.

Similarly, policies endorsed by the central government, such as arming men from specific ethnic groups as a counterinsurgency measure, only worsen the situation, widening conflicts and leading to the polarization of whole communities on the basis of ethnicity. This has been seen in the period from the late 1980s to the 1990s in South Kordofan, where the central government armed the Missiriya cattle nomads in order to stop the infiltration of SPLA fighters northwards. This has led to broad political polarization among the Nuba and Baggara communities at grassroots levels and consequently hindered the establishment of social peace in South

Kordofan, even after the 'implementation' of the CPA, signed in Nivasha in 2005. Intervention by the central government to reorganize local government units and powers in favour of pastoralist groups was initiated in South Kordofan, where the Emirate Act was first introduced. Introduction of the Emirate Act in West Darfur produced the 1997 war between the Masālīt and the Arab pastoralists there. Furthermore, Masālīt youth joined the newly founded rebel movements, probably reacting to the suffering of their people, during fights between Arab pastoralists and sedentary farmers in communities such as those in Mornei. This has further complicated the conflict. By 2003 the central government began to systematically use Arab militias (*janjawīd*) to suppress the emerging armed movements in Darfur instead of using the Sudanese national army. This has led to the present calamity in the embattled region.

Conclusion

Land is the key factor underlying interethnic conflicts in Dār Masālīt in general and Mornei in particular. The increase of human and animal populations in the area coupled with the changes in the subsistence economy of the sedentary groups have created relative scarcity and transformed previously harmonious relations between pastoralist and farming groups into conflictual relations across almost all of Dār Masālīt. One could even claim that identical arguments are relevant to the whole of West Darfur. However, other factors have played important catalytic roles, transforming low-level grassroots conflicts into widespread ethnic strife with an overwhelming basis on ethnic identification. The lack of development, the unwarranted and inadequate land and administrative legislations issued by the government and the absence of efficient conflict resolution mechanisms are the most important of these factors. In other words, this case study illustrates that failing state institutions are part and parcel of the problem.

Notes

1. The research on which this chapter is based was undertaken within the context of the project 'Micro-Macro Processes in Peace-Building in the Sudan'. The authors gratefully acknowledge the generous financial and academic support provided by the Christian Michelsen Institute (CMI) of Bergen, Norway, which funded the project. We should,

however, clarify that part of the fieldwork for this chapter was conducted for the purposes of completion of the master's thesis of one of the authors at the Department of Sociology and Social Anthropology, University of Khartoum (Abdal-Kareem 2010). In this regard, it is important to highlight that our fieldwork was carried out in different periods between 2007 and 2009. This was before the independence of South Sudan in 9 July 2011. Therefore, the new political realities that surfaced in Sudan after this date have not been directly incorporated within our analysis in this chapter.

2. What is recognized today as Dār Masālīt, 'homeland of the Masālīt', is part of the conventional areas of the Dār Masālīt sultanate established in the last quarter of the nineteenth century. It is one of the sultanates that emerged in the most western parts of present-day Sudan. However, it is important to state that the traditional authority of the sultanate covers vast settlements and/or locations that extend across both western Sudan and eastern Chad. According to our informants, Al-Jeneīna and its surrounding locations are considered the historical lands of the Masālīt people. This does not mean that the Masālīt maintain exclusive rights over land tenure and use in the area. Nonetheless, it does mean that all the tribes and/or ethnic groups living in this area are subject to the jurisdiction of the Masālīt local administrative system. According to our interviewees, the Masālīt people occupy approximately two-thirds of the entire area of their homelands. A wide spectrum of the settled groups of the Darfur region can be found in the area as well. Some groups of cattle and camel herders also live in or regularly visit the region.
3. According to the local administrative traditions of Dār Masālīt, the term *furushiya* denotes a form of local administrative unit through which a number of villages are governed by a representative of the *sulṭān* (paramount chief) of Dār Masālīt. The *sulṭān* of Dār Masālīt has the authority to appoint or dismiss the head of these administrative units (*furushiyāt*). These leaders are known locally as *furāsh* (sing. *fursha*). The *furāsh* constitute the council of the *sulṭān* of Dār Masālīt.
4. This expression refers to the use of engines and/or tractors in agricultural activities.
5. It was emphasized by the narratives of the informants that the conflicts that emerged during the later periods have become more severe and have begun to be couched along ethnic lines. In addition, the numbers of killings and injuries have begun to multiply and increase significantly. Increasingly, the settlement of these conflicts is beyond the capacity of traditional means of conflict resolution.
6. Majmary is one of the villages of the Masālīt that lies in the northeastern part of Mornei. Although the Masālīt are the majority, considerable numbers of Fur and Daju live in the village as well. Our Masālīt informants refer to Majmary as the site of one of the most brutal and severe attacks carried out by the Arabs in Mornei.
7. *Zurga* ('black' in Arabic, sing. *azrag*) is a term that has been used since the mid-1980s (and especially during the 1990s and after 2003) to refer to the 'African' indigenous tribes of Darfur who speak different African languages as their mother tongue, and in particular the Fur, the Zaghawa, and the Masālīt. It is worth mentioning that other 'African' groups who speak Arabic as a mother tongue (like the Berti and the Tunjur) are also classified as *zurga*. According to Mohamed (2000), animal herders had first used this term to refer to the indigenous 'non-Arab' farmers who occupy the central part of the region. Later on, those indigenous sedentary farmers adopted the term and applied it to distinguish themselves from their adversaries. According to Mohamed and Badri (2005), this term appeared for the first time in the mid-1980s as a result of competition over leadership positions between the Zaghawa and the Northern Rizeīgāt in South Darfur. That period of time witnessed an intense ethnic polarization that spread over almost the entire region and South Darfur in particular.
8. The term 'Arab Gathering' (*Al-Tajammᶜu Al-'Arabi* as called locally) denotes 'a militantly racist and pan-Arabist organization which stressed the "Arab" character of the [Darfur]

region' (Prunier 2005: 45). According to Mohamed and Badri (2005), this term appeared for the first time in 1987, when a group of educated Arab elites from the Darfur region issued a memorandum to then prime minister Sadiq Al-Mahdi claiming that the Arabs represent about 40 per cent of the population of the region. They demanded that they should share in the power structure according to that proportion.

Part II

Water Resources at the Core of Local and Global Interactions

Chapter 5

Sudan's Hydropolitics

Regional Chess Games, National Hegemony and Local Resistance

Harry Verhoeven

Water in the Nile basin has always been profoundly political, and the control over this 'blue gold' has been contested for centuries. In recent years, the saliency of water as a political issue in Sudan has increased once more because of rapid developments on the regional, national and local level. The Horn of Africa, despite the 1999 Nile Basin Initiative (NBI), has witnessed a dangerous rise in tensions between upstream countries, led by Ethiopia, and Egypt, backed by Sudan, triggering an escalating war of words and blocking regional integration attempts that would enable the Horn to be better placed to meet the economic, social and ecological challenges of the future. Parallel to the complex international picture, Sudan's military-Islamist Inqādh regime has embarked on a Dam Programme that is both regionally and domestically controversial. For Khartoum, the 'hydro-agricultural mission' of building dams and reviving agriculture is of vital importance as it tries to recalibrate northern Sudan's political economy and to survive the postoil era. Billions of dollars are being poured into dams in River Nile State and Northern State and along the Blue Nile to generate power and irrigate fertile land, but also to tighten the regime's long-term grip on power. At the local level, however, this is generating blowback as resistance committees, disgruntled youth and intellectuals are opposing another round of what they see as marginalization of the peripheries. Despite the pro-poor rhetoric, these actors argue that the benefits of the hydroagricultural mission accrue to the Khartoum elite and their local allies, with the costs borne by already impoverished communities.

Notes for this chapter begin on page 107.

This chapter provides an overview of Sudan's hydropolitics on various levels of analysis. After situating it in the broader debate about environmental conflict,[1] the chapter outlines the regional 'game of chess', sketching the Nile's politico-legal framework and the perspectives adopted by Egypt and Ethiopia. Subsequently, the focus shifts to the national level to analyse the impact of the end of the Comprehensive Peace Agreement (CPA) and the secession of South Sudan: it explores how the Sudan People's Liberation Army/Movement (SPLA/M) will try to harness water resources for building the economic foundations of the new state as it navigates a tricky regional context. In the next section I engage with Khartoum's hydro-agricultural mission and the main drivers underpinning Sudan's Dam Programme and Agricultural Revival Programme. Finally, this chapter demonstrates how the Inqādh regime's national 'Breadbasket' dreams are generating strong local opposition. It concludes by underlining the necessity of moving from a zero-sum logic of power to one of benefit sharing and sustainability.

'Water Wars' in the Nile Basin?

It has become conventional wisdom that the 'wars of the next century will be about water' (Serageldin,[2] in Crossette 1995). Neo-Malthusian ideas linking environment, development and conflict have once again surged up the global agenda. Narratives of environmental crises in the Global South – particularly when related to climate change and water scarcity – have proliferated and are increasingly linked to political instability and civil war (Verhoeven 2014). The securitization of the environment is embodied by the following statement from the EU's highest decision-making body: 'Climate Change is a threat multiplier which threatens to overburden states and regions which are already fragile and conflict prone' (Council of the EU 2008).

Despite a lack of evidence (Gleditsch, Hegre and Wollebaek Toset 2007: 62) to link violent conflict and 'water scarcity' – or, more generally, conflict and 'climate change' (Buhaug 2010; Gleditsch 2012) – reports abound on how decreasing availability of resources will cause increasing antagonisms, ultimately spilling over into violence within or between countries. The Jordan, Indus and Nile are named as basins where 'water wars' could break out, while the Sahelian drylands are the supposed archetypal example of domestic scarcity leading to interminable clashes between pastoralists and cultivators over a shrinking resource base. As demonstrated elsewhere (Verhoeven 2011b), Sudan in particular has long been imagined to be at the centre of such Malthusian collapses – Darfur as a 'climate change conflict' (UK Special Representative for Climate Change John Ashton, in Mazo 2010: 73) is but one example – and possible regional confrontations over water usage.

While it is true that tensions in the Nile basin have been increasing in recent years, this has little to do with growing water scarcity as such. Ecological changes *are* occurring and affecting livelihoods of pastoralist communities and agricultural producers, but the fundamental cause of conflict remains political – Egypt's, Sudan's and Ethiopia's inability to redesign the politico-legal framework governing Nile waters in ways that encourage equitable usage and sustainable development. 'If there is a conflict over water, then that conflict is the result of a failure of politics to negotiate a settlement over the shared use of water' (J. Barnett 2000: 276). In the climate change age, it is vital to allocate every drop of water where it can be used most efficiently from a basin-wide perspective, so that countries can jointly meet challenges of food security, job creation and service delivery. Yet as will be shown, such a regional vision is unlikely to become political reality soon.

The View from Cairo: The Survival Imperative

For centuries, Egyptian rulers have considered the Nile to be their key national security interest. Its waters are seen as the bedrock on which Egyptian civilization was built, and since independence there has been unanimous agreement among elites on ensuring continued regional hydro-hegemony: a centralized grip over water allocation – and associated zero-sum policy vis-à-vis possible competitors in the Nile basin – is essential to resurrecting Egyptian greatness. Napoleon's corps of scientists and engineers introduced several key ideas of the French Revolution when invading Egypt in 1798, a coercive, universalizing logic that was adopted by successive nineteenth-century Cairo regimes, starting with Muhammad Ali Pasha: rational planning, a powerful centralized state, human supremacy over nature and 'progress', and a duty for the rulers to stamp out backwardness at all costs.

Egypt's Pharaonic past was reimagined as a time when these principles – and their application on the Nile through top-down irrigation systems, a new 'hydraulic civilization' (Wittfogel 1957) – had constituted the basis of regional ascendancy. The recipe for Muhammad Ali's attempted economic revolution, intended to catapult Egypt back to greatness, consisted of the same ingredients of monopolizing political and economic power; big infrastructure projects; cheap labour (including slavery); and total control over the Nile (T. Mitchell 1989). The latter two motivated the 1821 invasion of Sudan, which asserted Egyptian control over the basin and started a bloody occupation that was inherited by the British, with the British Empire increasingly involved in internal and external Egyptian affairs. Britain made Cairo's objective her own – warding off French, Ethiopian or Belgian encroachment on the Nile and her sources – as Egypt became a vital node in the imperial chain. The British Empire's early twentieth-century Jezira project in Sudan was a classic case of the high-modernist thinking about the Nile, political power and economic development that Napoleon, Muhammad Ali and later Gamal Abdel Nasser all shared (T. Barnett 1977).

As the end of Empire beckoned, Cairo was keen to lock in its 'hydro-hegemony' through the 1929 and 1959 Nile Waters Agreements (Zeitoun and Warner 2006). The 1929 document was signed between Egypt and Britain on behalf of Sudan and British East Africa and allocated 48 billion cubic metres of Nile water to Egypt compared to a paltry 4 billion cubic metres allocated to Sudan (reflecting Egypt's political-economic importance to London and the underdeveloped agricultural potential in the other territories). The 1959 treaty updated this and divided the 84 billion cubic metres of White and Blue Nile waters that reach Egypt every year into 55.5 billion cubic metres for Cairo and 18.5 billion cubic metres for Sudan, with 10 billion cubic metres estimated to evaporate at the Pharaonic project being built at Aswan. Just like in 1929, imperial Ethiopia was kept out of the negotiations (Collins 1990: 247–71).

The roots of Ethiopian-Egyptian rivalry are centuries old (including the late nineteenth-century decade-long military occupation of eastern Ethiopia by the khedive's envoys), but the 1929 and 1959 treaties prioritized an Egyptian national security frame and Egyptian development interests, sowing the seeds of today's enmity (Waterbury 1979). Successive governments have argued that Egypt has historically established user rights and that this pattern of water consumption cannot be dismantled without major socioeconomic upheaval, regardless of discussions about past grievances. Cairo emphasizes that, just like in the last five thousand years, it suffers from an extraordinary dependence on irrigated agriculture due to climatological reasons. Of Egypt's renewable water resources, 97 per cent spring from the Nile, while Ethiopia has plenty of rainfall for its crops (IWMI 2008). While Ethiopia doesn't really need the water to raise agricultural productivity, the Nile is a matter of life and death for Egypt. 'Bellicose' upstream demands to alter the status quo are therefore understood as questioning the very basis of the Egyptian state, whether led by left-wing nationalists (Nasser), pro-market reformers (Sadat), status quo centrists (Mubarak) or the Muslim Brotherhood (Morsi).

One area of frontal confrontation between Egypt and Ethiopia has been the question of dam building on the Nile. Gamal Abdel Nasser's Aswan Dam, also known as the High Dam, was the trigger for the updating of the 1929 treaty and enables year-round irrigation for Egyptian agriculture. The nationalization of the Suez Canal and the construction of the Aswan Dam were to provide Egypt with the material power to give it economic independence but also to reclaim a prominent role for Cairo in international politics (Waterbury 1983: 64–66). Suez and Aswan signalled Egypt taking its destiny back into its own hands: the Aswan Dam connected Nasser's regional aspirations with the imagined glorious past and with the future, as an exponent of high modernism and technical excellence intended to impress domestic and Third World audiences.

However, the dam rested on a crucial geopolitical contradiction (Waterbury 1979). On the one hand, Aswan boosted Nasser's claims as the Arab world's leader and, together with the 1959 treaty, it assuaged fears in the Egyptian security establishment about the possibility of being taken hostage by upstream countries that might tamper with the flow of the Nile. Yet on the other hand, this assertion of Cairo's sovereignty and hegemony eroded Egypt's position vis-à-vis its African regional partners and set them on a confrontational course, making Nasser's security nightmares actually more – and not less – realistic. Sudanese public opinion was displeased about the tens of thousands of Sudanese Nubians who were forcibly displaced due to Aswan, with promises of irrigated agriculture in New Halfa never compensating the loss of fertile ancestral lands and an entire culture. Nevertheless, the Khartoum military regime of General Ibrahim Abboud swallowed the 'Nubian price' and signed the 1959 text with its Egyptian big brother, entrenching a (hydro)political alliance that remained strong until the early 1990s.

If an army dictator was able to rally Sudanese official support for the Egyptian plans, no such appeasement of the other upstream countries proved possible. Ethiopia especially made the destruction of the Nile Waters Agreement a key objective of its foreign policy for the next half a century. This has meant that Egypt has been continuously on the defensive and felt compelled to continuously intervene in Sudanese politics, fearing that its grip on the Nile would be weakened should a more pro-Ethiopian ruler in Khartoum weaken the historical alliance with his or her Egyptian counterpart. This security obsession contextualizes Sadat's repeated warnings that Cairo would go to war to safeguard its present access to Nile water, threatening to bomb any dams built in Uganda or Ethiopia (Dinar 2007: 23); Wikileaks unearthed similar threats uttered by the Mubarak regime in its dying days vis-à-vis the Ethiopian government's plans for hydro-infrastructure on the Blue Nile. It also explains Egypt's long-standing policy to counter demands in southern Sudan for self-determination: the creation of a new state risked shifting the balance of power in favour of the upstream riparian countries.

The economic background for Cairo's inflexible stance is Egypt's prolonged stagnation in past decades; the liberalized economy has not delivered for many Egyptians, inequality has increased and crony capitalism is rampant. A demographic transition, moreover, means that the working-age population has expanded dramatically in recent years, but jobs in both the countryside and the overcrowded cities are sorely lacking (World Bank 2012). Youth unemployment and rising food prices were already major worries before the Egyptian Revolution, and the ancien régime did everything it could not to rock the boat; however, it could not fend off the 2011 Arab Spring, which was propelled by grievances about democratic freedoms but also by rising economic discontent. The idea of Egypt ceding part of its share of the Nile is almost unthinkable, as this would put further short-term pressures on an already struggling agricultural sector. Despite a change in rhetoric following the overthrow of Hosni Mubarak, a fundamental rethinking of Egyptian Nile policy is yet to happen. While Mohammed Morsi and his Muslim Brotherhood–led government tried to redeploy diplomatic energies to Africa – and Ethiopia in particular – by promising a new era of engagement, many fear that the coup of July 2013 by General Abdul Fatah Al-Sisi and the armed forces will take foreign policy back to the future. Egypt's infamous Mukhabarat (the General Intelligence Directorate) continues to disproportionately influence Nile basin policies and prioritize a zero-sum security perspective, leading to persisting tensions with Ethiopia and an overbearing stance vis-à-vis Sudan.

The View from Addis Ababa: Africa's Water Tower without Water?

Egypt's uncompromising security obsession has caused great frustration for many decades. Being presented in 1929 and 1959 with a fait accompli by the Egyptians infuriated Haile Selassie's Ethiopia, not least because circa two-thirds of all Nile waters come from the Blue Nile, the source of which, Lake Tana, lies in the Ethiopian heartland. Fully aware of the strategic importance of Khartoum for the balance of power, Addis Ababa and Cairo found themselves supporting opposite sides in Sudan's civil wars, with Ethiopia backing the Anyanya rebels and the SPLA/M in their struggles against the central government (Johnson 2003). Addis Ababa has historically been reluctant to back southern Sudanese secessionism – perhaps the quickest route to weakening Egypt – for fear of encouraging separatism inside Ethiopia, but hoped for the removal of successive 'pro-Arab' regimes in Khartoum, who always sided with Egypt on the Nile issue.

Ethiopia has long yearned to exploit its water resources, not least given the immense development challenges it faces. Despite progress made by the ruling Ethiopian People's Revolutionary Democratic Front (EPRDF) since 1991, per capita income of more than 88 million Ethiopians is circa USD 300 per annum, an average of less than one dollar per day. With 85 per cent of the population living in the countryside, poverty in Ethiopia is predominantly rural, and low agricultural productivity remains the key reason for why millions of Ethiopians still need food assistance every year to survive (Ayelew and Dercon 2007). Rapid population growth, 3 per cent per year, puts pressure on scarce resources, while the state already struggles to provide food, land and/or jobs for the hundreds of thousands of youngsters entering the workforce annually. More irrigated agriculture could improve productivity and would generate dependable annual production in the face of strong weather variability and associated uncertainty in the rain-fed sector. There is thus a sound economic rationale to do whatever is possible to increase crop production (World Bank 2008), only further underscored by the realities of climate change, which is already imperilling pastoralist and cultivator communities, particularly in eastern and southern Ethiopia (Deressa and Hassan 2009). According to most climate models, extreme rainfall and extreme drought will become more frequent *and* more intense in future decades in the region (IPCC 2007). This is putting livelihoods, already battered by historical government neglect and bad policies, under heavy pressure where subsistence production remains the norm, outside central Ethiopia. Dramatic transformations of water systems are compounding the structural crisis in which Ethiopia's peripheries find themselves. This has led international nongovernmental organizations to warn of deepened marginalization, forced displacement and local conflicts in years to come (Oxfam International 2009).

Exploiting the Nile waters and prioritizing rural areas has an important political dimension. The EPRDF's inner core consists of former Tigrayan guerrillas who for fifteen years fought in the countryside and still believe in the revolutionary role of the peasantry.[3] The EPRDF, for ideological and self-interested reasons, has always been sceptical of urbanization and, as shown in the 2005 electoral results and subsequent violence, is far less popular in cities than it is in the rural heartlands (Gudina 2011). This is why its 'Agricultural Development Led Industrialisation' – now the Growth and Transformation Plan – foresees a key role for Ethiopia's dams, which are to improve the country's irrigation potential and provide electricity as part of the EPRDF's popular service delivery agenda in rural communities (MoFED 2010); currently, only about 1 per cent of Ethiopian energy needs are met by electricity. While irrigation infrastructure is in part meant to draw in foreign investors who will help modernize Ethiopian agriculture, it was the vision of the late prime minister Meles Zenawi and his advisers that expanding and improving the power supply in rural Ethiopia would help keep the government's political base close to its leadership. The post-Meles regime has very much stuck to this trajectory under the new premier, Hailemariam Desalegn (Verhoeven 2013a).

Ethiopia's frustration with the status quo in the Nile basin (Cascão 2008) has been especially strong because most technocrats and academics across the region agree that dam building in Ethiopia is far more sensible than dams in Egypt and Sudan. While Aswan, Merowe and Roseires have enormous evaporation rates and accumulate huge quantities of sediment – leading to rapid dam capacity loss (S. Abdalla 2007) – Ethiopian dams on the Blue Nile would cause less displacement, make more environmental sense and could generate thousands of megawatts of electricity that could be exported cheaply to neighbouring countries. The Grand Ethiopian Renaissance Dam (GERD) on the Blue Nile, on which construction began in April 2011 in the wake of the Egyptian Revolution, is intended as a project of regional integration: it will be cheaper and logistically easier to export its electricity to Sudan than to take it to Addis Ababa. In spring 2013, China committed more than a billion dollars to build transmission lines from the dam to the Ethiopian national grid while lobbying for additional contracts that may cover links to Sudan.

Long known as Africa's water tower, with its potential for hydropower – estimated at forty to forty-five thousand megawatts – dwarfing that of any other country in the region, Ethiopia is thus adamant that its dam programme is not only its inalienable right as the most important upstream country, but also the best way forward for the entire basin from a sustainable development perspective. Throughout the entire country, nineteen dams are either already built, under construction or in the advanced planning stages; the GERD is undoubtedly the most eye-catching and controversial project. Former prime minister Meles Zenawi clearly stated that he will no longer accept Cairo dictating upstream riparian states: 'The Egyptians have yet to make up their minds as to whether they want to live in the twenty-first or the nineteenth century' (Malone 2010).

Addis Ababa questions Egyptian-Sudanese arguments about established user rights and claims that the independence of South Sudan creates a new treaty state, meaning that the 1959 Nile Waters Agreement has to be renegotiated. In light of South Sudan's January 2011 referendum, Ethiopian policy makers let it be understood that they had two fundamental (and for Ethiopia interrelated) goals: peace between the Republic of Sudan and South Sudan and a new institutional architecture for the Nile basin. Because currently only a fraction of arable Ethiopian land is irrigated (IWMI 2008: 21–22), Ethiopia wants its right to build dams on the

Blue Nile recognized and to claim a fair share of the waters for irrigation – an estimated four to five billion cubic metres of Nile water in the most ambitious scenario, according to Ethiopian technocrats. Above all, Ethiopia hopes to emerge as a regional leader from the secession of South Sudan, which it facilitated through its role in the negotiations on post-referendum arrangements[4] between Khartoum and the SPLA/M; American and African Union diplomats have emphasized that without Ethiopian mediation, the old nemeses would probably have gone back to open war. The EPRDF government believes in the transformative power of energy diplomacy, tying its neighbours in the long term closer to it through exporting power to both Sudans, Kenya, Uganda, and (why not?) Egypt and Eritrea (Verhoeven 2011a). But whether such a transformational vision becomes reality strongly depends on the strategic choices made in South Sudan in the next couple of years.

The View from Juba: The Right to Develop

South Sudan's struggle for autonomy has long been at the heart of the region's hydropolitics. As part of the Cairo-Khartoum alliance, Jaʿafar Nimeiri pushed for the construction of the Jonglei Canal to bypass the southern swamps of Sudan, the Sudd. Since 1900 there have been clamours for the 360-kilometre-long canal to free up water for irrigated agriculture in Egypt by bypassing the marshes – the White Nile loses half of its annual flow in the Sudd (Howell, Lock and Cobb 1988). For people in southern Sudan, however, this was yet another example that Nimeiri was not reforming Sudan's political economy, as promised in the 1972 Addis Ababa Agreement, but channelling benefits to his cronies and foreign allies through a white elephant at their expense: the canal's ecological cost and the expected mass displacement of communities were part of the trigger that set off the SPLA/M liberation struggle (Collins 1990: 391–93).

The Jonglei Canal was never built; the planned mechanized irrigation schemes never materialized; and Jonglei State – then part of Upper Nile region – became a major recruiting ground for SPLA/M fighters. Egypt understood that an SPLA/M-held Khartoum or an independent South Sudan would threaten its dominance in the Nile basin and supported all incumbent regimes (Johnson 2003: 176). Even when the Mubarak regime had its falling out with the Inqādh regime following the Gulf War and the 1995 assassination attempt against Hosni Mubarak, Egypt could not bring itself to throw its full weight behind the SPLA/M. As momentum gathered for regime change in Khartoum through the American-aided alliance of Eritrea, Ethiopia and Uganda, Egypt, fearful of the hydropolitical consequences of a takeover by John Garang, got cold feet and ceased its earlier assistance of the opposition. Egypt was all too happy to reconcile with Omar Al-Bashir and Ali Osman Taha when in 1999–2000 they finally removed the reviled Hassan Al-Turabi and opted for a more pragmatic foreign policy (Verhoeven 2013b).

Because of the civil war, southern Sudan's hydro-potential was neutralized for decades, but since independence South Sudan has cautiously begun to explore its options. The South sees much higher precipitation than in the north and is the rendezvous location of many rivers, some of which have hydro-electric potential. South Sudan's natural comparative advantage is agriculture – both rain-fed and irrigated – and could, theoretically, become a regional breadbasket (Yongo-Bure 2007). Development plans are still in their early stages, but given that Juba will go from overdependence on oil (more than 90 per cent of today's government budget) to rapidly dwindling reserves – South Sudan's oil reserves could very well run dry in not much longer than ten to fifteen years (IMF 2010) – the SPLA/M has to start thinking about the post-oil era. Given the lack of other economic assets, labour-intensive agriculture seems to be the only way to provide (some) food and jobs for South Sudan's bulging youth population. Most increases in production should come from rain-fed cultivation, but South Sudanese politicians assert their right to increase output and productivity further via irrigated schemes.[5] This is likely to trigger Egyptian and Sudanese discontent – dividing Sudan's share of Nile water is one of the tricky post-referendum arrangements the Inqādh regime and the SPLA/M are struggling to resolve – but there is not necessarily much the downstream countries can do about it. Luckily for Egypt, what has so far held back progress on Juba's development agenda are two years of a militarized standoff with Khartoum and domestic insurgencies in South Sudan that have sapped the plans of the Salva Kiir government and bogged it down in day-to-day survival mode.

South Sudan's birth pangs have been painful and early promises of peace and prosperity have failed to materialize, but the overall geopolitical trend is nevertheless clear. Momentum in the Nile basin is unmistakably shifting in favour of the upstream countries (Cascão 2009), and South Sudanese independence is a qualitative leap forward, though still short of what Ethiopia hopes for. Egypt, for all its political interference, military threats and American backing, was not able to prevent the recognition of South Sudan's right to self-determination in the CPA. Unassailable under Nasser and Sadat, Egypt's regional weight was gravely diminished under Mubarak and its influence in Khartoum has declined since the coup in 1989. Cairo can still count on Sudanese support because of reasons of self-interest but has been forced to engage in delaying tactics within the Nile Basin Initiative[6] framework. Founded in 1999 as an intergovernmental mechanism to 'achieve sustainable socio-economic development through equitable utilisation of, and benefit from, the common Nile Basin water resources' (NBI 2011), the NBI stimulates regional cooperation and is the negotiating platform for discussions related to the Nile. This multilateral attempt at developing an alternative regime to the 1959 treaty has been stalled as the Egypt-Sudan alliance faces eight upstream countries demanding a greater share of the water, with South Sudan a crucial fence-sitter (Al-Mufti 2010). This impasse has led Ethiopia, Rwanda, Tanzania and Uganda to sign the Nile River Basin Cooperative Framework Agreement in May 2010, later joined by Kenya and Burundi, intending to redraw the hydropolitical landscape. Though force cannot resolve Egypt's – or Ethiopia's – fundamental problems, tensions are rising as Juba enters the debate. The war of words between Cairo and Addis Ababa in late 2010 underscored the explosive potential of continuing disagreements once more, with Meles Zenawi accusing Mubarak of support for Ethiopian rebel movements to thwart increasingly assertive demands for renegotiating the 1959 Nile Waters Agreement.

The SPLA/M has so far neatly balanced different interests as it has been carving out an autonomous South Sudanese hydropolitical position. On the one hand, it is keen to harness its water resources for agricultural development and to side with the states that supported its long liberation struggle – Kenya, Uganda and Ethiopia. It has strong interests in good relations with these neighbours and wishes to import electricity from Ethiopian dams. On the other hand, its most important bilateral relationship is still with Khartoum, and Juba is wary of provoking Egypt and Sudan over the water issue by demanding immediate, drastic water reallocation. Moreover, the United States – a close partner of Cairo, Addis Ababa and Juba – has emphasized that it wants no further regional instability, least of all over a life-or-death matter like the Nile. Therefore, South Sudan is likely to side with the upstream riparian states in demanding a substantial but gradual revision of the 1959 Nile Waters Agreement and to become a supporter of consensus-based regional integration schemes that would play into its comparative advantage in agriculture and help provide electricity and money for development of its impoverished population (Verhoeven 2011a). Not rocking the boat but supporting incremental change seems to be the best strategy for the foreseeable future.

The View from Khartoum: The Inqādh Regime's Hydropolitical Long Game

Sudan has long operated in Egypt's shadow but has since 2000 stealthily become a riverine power of its own, with an assertive but controversial

Nile policy. Plans for harnessing Sudan's water resources date back to Anglo-Egyptian imperialism: the Jezira scheme was mentioned earlier, and plans also included the ambitious 'Century Storage' plan to balance low Nile flow years with high ones through year-over-year storage in a series of dam reservoirs (Collins 1990: 198–202). Sudan, after Egypt, currently has the second-largest irrigated area in Africa, even without tapping into South Sudan's potential. After independence, Khartoum erected Khashum Al-Girba and Roseires Dams in the 1960s to generate power, but, in spite of great enthusiasm to erect more hydro-infrastructure, most other dam proposals turned out to be too expensive to be implemented. This had important consequences for the nature of the expansion of Sudanese agriculture: Nimeiri's breadbasket vision relied almost entirely on mechanized rain-fed agriculture to feed Sudan's regional partners, which contributed to the strategy's failure (IFPRI 2006).

Since the millennium, Sudan's Inqādh (Salvation) regime has launched a so-called 'hydro-agricultural mission' (Verhoeven 2011b) spearheaded by its Dam Programme and the Agricultural Revival Programme. In many ways, this marks a return to the love affair of Sudanese elites – regardless of their ideological background – with hydro-infrastructure. Islamists and generals came to power in 1989 promising political transformation, an Islamic renaissance and economic rescue, but as the war in southern, central and eastern Sudan intensified, the Islamic revolution lost much support. *Jihād* discredited the regime at home and abroad, where a broad coalition emerged to support the SPLA/M struggle, threatening to topple the Inqādh regime. As the revolution risked being consumed by its own flames, a power struggle split the Islamic Movement but led to a way out of the impasse: following the victory of President Omar Al-Bashir and Vice President Ali Osman Taha over Hassan Al-Turabi – the incarnation of Islamist evil in the eyes of outsiders – Egypt and the Gulf Arabs were eager to reconcile with Khartoum, easing the pressure as the war with the SPLA/M sank into a stalemate. The split coincided with Sudan's emergence as an oil exporter in 1999, giving the Inqādh regime the petrodollars it needed to finally scale up its grand political-economic transformation efforts: breaking the Ansar and Khatmiyya networks;[7] expanding patronage systems; and initiating the Dam Programme, Khartoum's developmental top priority.

While much of the literature has focused on the immaterial 'Islamic' aspects of the revolution and the wars the Inqādh regime has waged, there has been less emphasis on its equally important economic agenda. From the Economic Salvation Programme of the early 1990s to the contemporary prioritization of the Agricultural Revival Programme and dams, the military-Islamist rulers have always seen the material transformation of Sudan as essential to their political hegemony (de Waal and Abdel Salam

2004). Akin to Meles Zenawi's analysis of the conditions for continued EPRDF rule, the post–Al-Turabi elites believe that they need to deliver public goods to a critical portion of the population to entrench themselves in power for another generation (de Waal 2010: 16–18). Sudan's new generation of dams, built by the Dam Implementation Unit (DIU) / Ministry of Dams and Electricity headed by the Inqādh regime's rising star, Usama Abdallah, targets fast nonoil growth through the twin goals of enabling more irrigation – Sudan has never used up the entire 18.5 billion cubic metres the 1959 treaty allocates to it – and expanding power supply. With demand for electricity increasing at 10 per cent annually and Sudan's huge areas of fertile but unirrigated land, there can be little question that, as general objectives of government policy, dams could make sense.

The Inqādh regime's ambitions are far reaching. The hydro-infrastructure projects at Merowe, Kajbar, Siteit, Roseires (dam heightening) and Dal are part of a strategy that sees dams as the catalyst for development in carefully selected regions. As underlined by regime strategist Abdelrahim Hamdi, the hydro-agricultural mission is about fundamentally reconfiguring the political economy of northern Sudan – and the 'Hamdi Triangle',[8] Dongola-Kordofan-Sennar, in particular (Hamdi 2005) – especially after South Sudan's secession and with the postoil era drawing closer. The DIU builds dams but also undertakes a whole range of interventions – constructing hospitals, paving roads, initiating agricultural schemes – sometimes hundreds of kilometres from where the actual dam is built. The billions of dollars spent on the Dam Programme underline its political importance and the regime's determination to deliver to key constituencies, whether in the (security-controlled) construction sector or in the core Jaʿāliyn and Shāigīa areas along the Nile.

Sudan's Dam Programme is not just about domestic political economy, much as that is the primary driving factor for the fusion of self-interest and high modernism that underpins the hydro-agricultural mission. There is also an important external dimension to the DIU's unprecedented push to erect new infrastructure. China buys Sudanese oil and sells weapons to Khartoum, while Sinohydro, the world's number one dam company, is the main contractor for Merowe, Kajbar and Roseires (Verhoeven 2011c). These flows of money, hardware and software deepen Sino-Sudanese ties and keep Beijing close to Khartoum, which continues to be isolated by the West despite the changes the regime has undergone since the Inqādh regime broke into two factions. Sudan's Gulf Arab partners are equally critical to the hydro-agricultural mission, as Khartoum is trying to sell itself once more as the regional breadbasket (*Sudan Tribune* 2009b), an appetizing prospect as global food prices soar and Gulf Arab countries phase out their own wasteful wheat production. Gulf Arab funds are expected to drive the Agricultural Revival Programme, and Kuwait, Saudi Arabia and others are also the main creditors for Sudan's dams (DIU 2010), which, particularly in the case of Roseires, are supposed to result in extra irrigation that will help feed Gulf Arab populations.[9] The Kenana Sugar Company, owned by the Sudanese regime and by four Arab states, symbolizes the merger of personal elite interests, food security agendas and regional hydropolitics. Its company philosophy expounds the new breadbasket rhetoric of a cornucopia in the desert; the world's biggest sugar-producing scheme feeds off the White Nile and is trumpeted as the investment model of the future. Less is said about the fact that while extensive government subsidies and major questions about environmental sustainability remain, sugar costs the ordinary Sudanese far more than the world market price, which suggests a case of classic rent seeking rather than agroindustry-led sustainable development.

The wave of dam building and proposed new investment in agriculture is controversial at the local level as well as regionally. Sudan's Dam Programme depended on Egyptian approval, which was intimately connected to the politics of the Inqādh regime's split in 1999–2000, with Cairo subsequently helping to bring the post–Al-Turabi Sudan closer to the Gulf Arabs, with whom it had fallen out after the Gulf War. Evaporation at Merowe and irrigation via Roseires imply that Egypt can no longer use the four billion cubic metres of unused 'Sudanese' Nile water that flowed north, but Sudan's dams bring other benefits to Cairo. Merowe, Kajbar and Shreik will ease the sedimentation problem that is eroding Aswan's capacity in Egypt and in turn face capacity losses due to alluvial sediment (S. Abdalla 2007). Strategically, Cairo knows that Sudan fully utilizing its treaty share gives it a stronger stake in defending the 1959 agreement, locking in the Egyptian-Sudanese alliance. Khartoum is in no position to cede much ground, either to upstream states generally or to South Sudan specifically, when it has just spent billions of dollars on dams hailed by the powerful minister of oil Awad Al-Jaz as 'the greatest developmental project in Sudan's modern history' (DIU 2011). While the Inqādh regime has grudgingly begun to pay more than lip service to the idea of regional integration, its perceived interests and high sunk costs have made it reluctant to enter into detailed discussions on the subject, despite the support of many Sudanese technocrats for such a cooperative 'reset' of Nile basin relations.

The View from the Northern Peripheries: Violence and Marginalization

The Inqādh regime ascribes spellbinding powers to the Dam Programme. The message is that the regime's dams represent wholesale transformation (*inqilāb*), with tangible services like electricity delivered to populations all around Sudan, as well as a multitude of other development projects that the DIU implements parallel to the dam construction. These associated projects are not afterthoughts but an integral part of the logic of the hydro-agricultural mission, as Hamdi, the DIU and other government voices stress (DIU 2008). The Dam Programme is central to the Islamist state-building project and identity after the split between Hassan Al-Turabi and many of his former lieutenants (Verhoeven 2013b).

The rhetoric celebrates sustainability, inclusivity and 'civilization', yet the hydro-agricultural mission is generating blowback in some of the very communities that it claims to be developing. Vociferous voices are contesting the modus operandi of the DIU, the specificities of particular projects and, occasionally, the Dam Programme as such. Allegations target the DIU's extraordinary secrecy – responsible only to the president himself and, despite a public relations offensive, hardly sharing any information with colleagues, consultants or outside observers – and the lack of consultation of local communities for either dam building or the development projects against a background of historical marginalization (Verhoeven 2011b).

Sudan's Dam Programme focuses on Northern State and River Nile State, where the Merowe Dam was completed and Kajbar, Shreik, Siteit/Upper Atbara and Dal are being constructed/planned. These are close to the areas where the three riverine groups live that have historically dominated Sudan's political economy – the Jaʿāliyn (Al-Bashir), the Shāigīa (Taha, UsamaAbdallah) and the Danāgla (late vice president Zubeir and Nimeiri) – and that, according to local activists, are also the main beneficiaries of the DIU projects. While the Hamdab/Merowe Dam led to the forced relocation of over fifty thousand Nubians of the Amri, Ḥamdāb and Manāṣīr communities, the power generated is mainly sent to the urban centres (and regime strongholds) of Dongola, Port Sudan, North Kordofan, Shendi and Khartoum; the displaced people are not foreseen to participate in any of the planned irrigation schemes (which, by 2012, already appeared largely defunct after a very slow start). The DIU claims it is offering people net improvements in their lives – from 'Stone-Age conditions to modern accommodation', in Hamdi's words[10] – but community activists claim that the relocation sites in New Hamdab (Multaqa), New Manasir, Makabrab and Kaheela East are nothing but villages in the desert with no future for bored youngsters or the older generations who are struggling to adapt. The worry of Nubian communities was always that the calamitous displacement of tens of thousands due to the Aswan Dam to New Halfa would be repeated; opponents of Merowe argue that this is precisely what is happening, with possibly the same long-term consequences – destruction of irreplaceable livelihoods, political invisibility and the dismantling of the cultural fabric of Nubian civilization, as in the case of the Ḥalfawīn (Schmidinger 2009).

This is the context for the explosive claims of some anti-dam committees that Sudan's Dam Programme is a cultural genocide, a plot by the *awlād al-baḥar* elite to annihilate Nubian culture; the dams, from this viewpoint, drown places of great sociocultural and archaeological significance and speed up assimilation through urbanization as new generations are forced to look for menial jobs in Khartoum and substitute their rich heritage for deformed Arabism (Committee of Anti Dal-Kajbar Dams 2011). In their eyes, the Inqādh regime is selling out to Cairo by inviting hundreds of thousands of Egyptian farmers to cultivate Nubian ancestral land under the 2005 Four Freedoms Agreement; it is also committing structural violence – 'demographic engineering' (Hashim 2009) – against people whose diversity its Arab-Islamist core cannot tolerate. The disaster of Merowe is about to be repeated with the Dal (second cataract), Kajbar (third cataract) and Shreik (fifth cataract) dams: once again, tens of thousands will be relocated to uncertain futures and without adequate consultation or compensation, to make way for electricity production for metropolitan centres and the Inqādh regime's tribal heartlands.

While there is little evidence to sustain the hypothesis of 'demographic engineering' in northern Sudan – where are the Egyptian farmers, for instance? – the DIU has undeniably taken a heavy-handed approach to the protests the dam construction has triggered (OMCT 2007). Hundreds of people have been killed, wounded or detained over a decade by the police and a separate DIU security force, and few attempts have been made to address the Aswan-inspired fears of the Nubian population as regime officials call those who question the hydro-agricultural mission 'ungrateful'. Moreover, the case of Nadir Awad, a top civil servant who opposed the Merowe Dam on environmental and social grounds and was intimidated and removed within twenty-four hours of his protest, exemplifies the lack of accountability with which the DIU operates and the fear it instils in rival bureaucracies. Awad's refusal to sign a blank cheque for Merowe's environmental and social impact assessment (ESIA) was remedied when Lahmeyer International – a multinational company convicted of corruption regarding dams in Lesotho (World Bank 2006) – was brought in to undertake an ESIA that was more acceptable to the DIU, despite grave worries expressed by several of Sudan's leading scientists[11] and an independent assessment that demonstrated major social and environmental problems (Teodoru, Wuest and Wehrli 2006).

If Merowe's 1,250 megawatts doubled Sudan's energy output (while nevertheless generating less electricity than initially promised), the heightening of the 1965 Roseires Dam (finished in 2012) was mainly about the irrigation of an extra 1.5–2 million *feddan* of fertile land. Yet just as with Merowe and Kajbar, the feeling among many local communities is that the benefits of the dam heightening are for a few – more power for upstream consumption and irrigation water for (foreign) investors in Sennar State – while the costs are borne by those who have already suffered heavily in wartime.[12] Blue Nile State was on the front lines during the Khartoum-SPLA/M confrontation (James 2007), and dislocation due to mechanized farming under Nimeiri caused serious grievances vis-à-vis Khartoum among pastoralists and cultivators alike. It was singled out by (then Al-Turabi's deputy) Ali Osman Taha for the 'Dawa' campaign of the 1990s, with Islamization pushed through social, economic and military means across the region. The dam heightening has displaced around 10 per cent of Blue Nile's population and is for many only the latest assault in a long series of centre-periphery confrontations. The anger against Islamist Khartoum and Taha himself was evident when in February 2011 the latter was humiliatingly forced to cancel a public rally in Damazīn, a stone's throw away from the Roseires Dam, at the last minute as public discontent boiled over (*Sudan Tribune* 2011b).

Angry voices in the most northern provinces of Sudan and in Blue Nile have longed claimed that without fundamental changes to the Dam Programme, large-scale violence is likely to erupt in the future. Such threats have been made for years around Merowe and Kajbar, but protesters lack political organization and the support of a foreign patron to militarily challenge Khartoum. The strategic importance – and explosive character – of Blue Nile has always been of a different magnitude, and the violent fallout there has bogged down thousands of Sudanese soldiers in a dirty conflict. When war returned to the region after a seven-year lull in September 2011, the discontent engendered by the DIU and other government agencies was a key reason for the resumption of hostilities between Omar Al-Bashir's Sudan Armed Forces and the SPLA/M of former governor Malik Agar, who controls a parallel military force of thousands of armed youngsters, many of whom are from dam-affected groups (Small Arms Survey 2012). Tens of thousands of people have been displaced, wounded or killed in the past two years, further hardening divisions in a state that was supposed to be transformed by the civilizing effects of development through the hydro-agricultural mission and the peace dividend.

Conclusion: Confrontation or Cooperation?

This chapter has analysed the intensifying hydropolitical confrontations that are taking place around the Sudanese Nile on three levels of analysis:

the regional, the national and the local. It has tried to offer a range of perspectives, explaining how it is that complex histories, geographic realities and contemporary power dynamics intertwine.

The secession of South Sudan and growing resistance unleashed by twenty-two years of war and the CPA are driving factors behind the rising tensions in the Nile basin, the need to reconfigure Sudan's political economy and the increasingly vociferous protests against Khartoum-led 'development'. Many of the old certainties in the Nile basin are giving way to an unpredictable future. Egypt's projection of power in the basin is becoming ever more difficult. In a context of declining influence under Hosni Mubarak and, now, post-revolutionary turmoil, Egypt faces an unprecedented hydropolitical challenge from an assertive Ethiopia, which is determined to end the injustices of the 1959 treaty and emerge as a regional energy powerhouse. Both Sudans are crucial as Egypt plays for time and the upstream countries seize on Juba's independence to redesign the basin's institutional architecture. South Sudan's loyalties cannot be taken for granted, and the SPLA/M is trying to pragmatically build a state with the resources it has and all the outside help it can get.

Meanwhile, military-Islamist Khartoum has gambled that its Dam Programme will become a catalyst for developmental transformation and counter the economic fallout from losing one-third of the country after 9 July 2011. The regime is using partnerships with China and Gulf Arab states for its hydro-agricultural mission, intended to build a 'new' middle class that will underpin continued Islamist hegemony. Yet the agonizing recession of the last two years and the stagnation of Sudanese agriculture and industry show the mirage-like nature of the DIU's promised *inqilāb* and its 'dams are development' rhetoric. Moreover, not only has the new hydro-infrastructure failed to deliver macro-economically and offset the loss of petrodollars, it has deepened resentment in the northern peripheries of Sudan and is not conducive to regional integration.

Environmental, economic and political changes lead to great uncertainty and fears about conflict around the Nile. Yet they also generate momentum for possible fundamental change in the role water has so far played in the basin, regionally, nationally and locally. Sudan, and the region more broadly, are at a crossroads, and hydropolitics is at the very centre of the decisions that will shape the coming years and decades. The regional, national and local choices regarding water management made today could be based on consensus, inclusivity and sustainability, thus helping Sudan and its regional partners meet the growing challenges of climate change and the post-oil era. The alternative is continued confrontation between Egypt, Sudan and Ethiopia, more exclusionary growth projects from Khartoum and another failed agricultural renaissance. This would further complicate already formidable tasks of alleviating poverty, generating jobs and growing more food. It might also reproduce violence, not because water scarcity will trigger 'water wars', but due to the political choice of failing to replace a zero-sum analysis with an attitude that prioritizes cooperation. The consequences would be devastating.

Notes

1. This chapter is deliberately rather brief in its discussion of conceptual thinking about water scarcity, climate change and politics; for a lengthier analysis of useful (and less useful) ways of framing the debate, see Verhoeven (2011a).
2. Ismael Serageldin was then vice president of the World Bank.
3. Interviews with senior members of the EPRDF leadership, May 2010 and December 2012.
4. These negotiations on the modalities of South Sudan's secession began in 2010 in the Tigrayan capital of Mekelle and subsequently continued in Addis Ababa. At the time of writing (2012), they were still ongoing.
5. Interviews with leading SPLA/M politicians, December 2010–March 2011.
6. See the official website of Nile Basin Initiative at http://nilebasin.org/newsite/ (accessed 29 March 2011).
7. The Ansar and Khatmiyya are two religious sects of Sunni Islam that dominated political and economic life for most of Sudan's modern history. The Ansar are followers of the Mahdi dynasty, tracing their roots to the Mahdiyya rebellion against Ottoman colonialism, with traditional strongholds in western and central Sudan. Their political party is the Ḥizb Al-Umma, or Umma Party. The Khatmiyya have traditionally been led by the Mirghani dynasty, are historically closer to Egypt and their power base has always been more urban, in the north and east of the country. The Democratic Unionist Party is their political vehicle.
8. The idea of a critical northern Sudanese power bloc, essential for the Inqādh regime's survival, was first proposed in its current form by Abdelrahim Hamdi at a 2005 NCP party conference. While leading party members were enthusiastic about the political-economic logic underpinning Hamdi's notion of a central axis that the ruling NCP should focus on, critics accused Hamdi and the NCP of racism, referring to the idea as the 'Hamdi Triangle', as the vision is still known today.
9. On why the Agricultural Revival Programme is likely to fail and already collapsing, see Verhoeven (2012).
10. Interview with Abdelrahim Hamdi, February 2011.
11. Several interviews in Khartoum with members of the Sudanese National Academy of Sciences and some top civil servants, April 2010 and December 2010.
12. Interviews in Blue Nile State, September 2009–February 2011.

Chapter 6

Local Management of Urbanized Water

Exchanges among Neighbours, Household Actions and Identity in Deim (Khartoum)

Luisa Arango

The city of Khartoum is a privileged place for observing the transformation trends that have affected African metropolises in past decades. Khartoum was established in the nineteenth century, but was comparatively small and had limited infrastructure until recent times. Reaching a demographic peak during the 1980s, the capital saw significant economic growth (Denis 2005), although it has now undergone an economic stagnation. The accelerated urbanization and the decentralization and neoliberal policies introduced since 1990 have led to significant transformations in access to and management of vital resources. The situation with drinking water epitomizes these transformations: its conception and management have been subject to noteworthy change, such as the extension of the supply network, increased control of resources by the state, the introduction of policies that have led to partial privatization and the commoditization of drinking water introduced by bottled water companies. The aim of this chapter is to look from an anthropological perspective at how these wider social, political and economic transformations in contemporary Sudan affect the 'socialization' of drinking water in the urban context and its particular power and social dynamics. Analysis of the social relations mediated by drinking water represents an innovative approach in Sudanese studies,[1] while a focus on domestic water in a central urban context, where the local management of resources seems to be less autonomous, collective and socialized than it is in rural areas, challenges the classic anthropological case studies used to analyse social water management.[2]

Detailed and extensive ethnography[3] was carried out in the Deim quarter,[4] an ancient popular settlement located in the centre of the capital city.

Notes for this chapter begin on page 123.

The location and ancientness of the neighbourhood make of it an appropriate place to conduct an analysis of the impact of the changes taking place in Khartoum using a long-term approach (Arango 2009). Although water, which has been managed by central government since the 1950s, was once an easily accessible resource, access to it has become difficult in recent decades, and the quantities provided to households have become insufficient, due mainly to urban growth (Salah and Abbas 1991). This has led to differentiated access to water, as illustrated by the unequal quantities used by neighbourhood households and the domestic devices used to obtain water from the mains.[5] This is further reinforced by the ongoing logics of rational, efficient and profitable water management proclaimed by government policies.

Although they may appear to be striking, these processes have not brought about the visible conflict situations that form a privileged viewpoint from which to analyse the impact of global trends on local forms of water management. Similarly, there is neither the explicit community-based management nor the organized collective action against current trends in water access that are generally used to explain the local social embeddedness of water. An absence of collective action has been observed in other urban situations (Swyngedouw 2004), and the scarcity of conflict and collective responses has been explained in other contexts by the low levels of interdependence among users and a lack of water shortages (Mosse 2003). In Deim, however, despite the lack of an explicit and codified local water distribution system and organized action, an everyday, undifferentiated sharing process takes place with no reference to the social status, origin or identity of the sharers. Thus, water-related practices in the neighbourhood, some of which are highly controversial, allow all inhabitants to access water regardless of the dysfunctions and inequalities of the urban supply system. Access to water in Deim is uncontestably efficient, even though, as other authors have already shown, it is less a consequence of technical excellence than it is of the local solidarities that make the system work (Bédoucha 2003).

After providing an overview of the social history of Deim and a description of its water distribution system, I will look at the increase in differentiated and unequal access to water among neighbours. As other authors have done in other urban contexts (Anand 2011), I will then move on from the dualistic perspective of inequalities to show how in spite of an increasing disparity in the ways water is accessed in Deim, the majority of households in the neighbourhood have effective access to it. I will focus on the various exchanges of water among users and on household responses (such as reconnection to the main pipe following a cutoff of water supplies or the accumulation of unpaid bills) that have been classified by some authors as 'individual strategies' or 'private solutions' (Swyngedouw 2004) and thus disqualified because of their individual and private nature. My aim is to argue that although these arrangements take place in the context of a centralized state water management system and a process of water commoditization and they do not look to overthrow it, they allow the population to produce their own places of action for the management of and access to water.

In this study, the urban tap water network is treated as a means whereby government can hold power over the way people access water, although the rationales of this power will not be analysed here; on the contrary, special attention will be paid to autonomous actions and nonorganized exchanges among neighbours, which will be taken to be an example of Foucault's 'transversal struggles', since, as Foucault explains, 'the main objective of these actions is to attack not so much "such or such" an institution of power, or group, or elite, or class but rather a technique, a form of power [that] applies itself to immediate everyday life' (Foucault 1982: 211). This theoretical choice will allow me to demonstrate the ability of autonomous actions and nonorganized sharing to redefine the exclusive and obvious nature of state- and market-based approaches to water. In the third part of the chapter, I will raise two main features that, according to Foucault, are specific to 'transversal struggles', and that are inherent in the water-related practices of the inhabitants of Deim: first, the 'immediateness' in time and place of autonomous responses to water shortages, cuts and privatization policies; and second, the capacity of these practices to call the status of an individual's access to water into question.

An analysis of exchanges among neighbours, household-based negotiations and narratives on access to water is an appropriate way of evaluating the impact of wider transformations at a local level. Deim is a privileged case study of these effects, because tap water forms a strong symbolic and material link between the urban population and the central government, as has been demonstrated in a context where installation of a tap water system has taken place more recently (Jassens and Thill 2013). My analysis also permits an understanding of grassroots morals and the perception of complex local identities to be gained, despite the ephemeral and socially undifferentiated nature of exchanges of water among individuals.

History of Settlement and Access to Water in Deim

An Overview of Local Trajectories and Identities

During the Turco-Egyptian period, Deim was a settlement for slaves and poor urban Sudanese (Arthur 1980; M. Babiker 2003; Sikainga 1996). After the reconstruction of Khartoum in the early twentieth century, the inhabitants were relocated from their former location on two occasions, due to the need for land for settlements for the expatriates and the middle-class population. In 1902, the inhabitants of Deim were moved from their original settlement near the Catholic Cathedral to the borders of the planned city in the Khartoum 3 neighbourhood, and between 1947 and 1953 they were relocated again to the periphery of the colonial town (Sikainga 1996), which became part of the centre of the city with urban expansion between 1960 and 1980.

During the colonial period, a significant number of people migrated to Khartoum, and Deim saw the arrival of ex-slaves, former soldiers and natives of southern Sudan and the Nuba Mountains, as well as immigrants from neighbouring countries; these people made up the bulk of wage labourers in the colonial city (Fawzi 1953; Sikainga 1996). These populations, with their different ethnotribal, linguistic and regional roots, sought to re-create their original communities by forming numerous 'subquarters' within the neighbourhood, which were named after regional, ethnic or tribal groups, personalities from history and professional categories (Sikainga 1996); some of these names are still in use today.[6] Originally from different contexts and arriving in different waves of migration during the twentieth century, the people of Deim are bound together mainly by a common urban history, their shared socioeconomic conditions and repeated decisions by urban planners to relocate the neighbourhood to the outlying areas of the city. Consequently, neighbourhood networks, professional ties and class identity have become crucial for these populations, rather than ethnic, kinship or tribal affiliations.

The identity of the people of Deim is therefore characterized by multiplicity: tribal affiliation is sometimes mentioned by individuals, while a part of the population still refers to a working-class identity that had deep roots in the neighbourhood, with the existence of local communist groups during Nimeiri's mandate. This multiplicity has been extensively theorized, especially in the study of diasporas and travelling cultures (Gilroy 1993; Clifford 1992), and can be useful for acquiring an understanding of the sociality of the inhabitants of Deim based on mobility and diversity of references. It has been shown that this identity exists alongside a persisting capacity to 'make relations' within open, decentred community fabrics (Chivallon 2002). Since the people of Deim claim that their identity is related both to their urban status and to a long tradition of receiving diverse populations, the 'collective scattering', as Chivallon terms it, can be interpreted as a specific way of weaving social ties. This is well explained by an inhabitant of the neighbourhood:

> In general, every tribe from all over Sudan has a quarter where its people live, but in Deim there are several tribes. Certainly, you have people from every part of Sudan living in Deim. That is why people are very open here ... we all are

> Dayāma [literally, 'people from Deim']. People asked us who we were, and we did not give the names of the tribes; we said, 'We are Dayāma.' We were more and more proud of being Dayāma; for me, Deim is the heart of the capital![7]

After the 1960s, the en masse arrival of Ethiopian and Eritrean forced migrants altered the identity of the neighbourhood to such an extent that Deim began to be known as the 'Ethiopian neighbourhood' of Khartoum (Lehouerou 2004; Pérouse de Montclos 2001). Today, with no continuity with previous migration trends, the area is seeing a growing settlement of the middle classes from elsewhere in Khartoum and a few expatriates working in Sudan. Alongside current urban planning policies, the quarter is therefore witnessing the establishment and growth of many new businesses and new houses, and a dismantling of long-standing collective places, such as the local charcoal market (in 2009). These transformations in identity references and the neighbourhood landscape appear to contribute to the diversity of identities that characterizes the inhabitants of Deim.

Water between Households and Government Management

In Old Deim[8], people used common water sources, and a few of the oldest residents still remember the *bi'r al-dongōlawī* (literally, 'Dongola man's well'), a collective well in the charcoal market from which people used to fetch water in the early days of New Deim.[9] However, the colonial government's aim to create a 'decent', modern and efficient working class (Sikainga 1996) was intended to be satisfied, inter alia, by connecting households to the urban water network. As a consequence, very soon after relocation, every house in the neighbourhood was provided with a single domestic tap, for which people are still supposed to pay a monthly flat fee today.

It is the custom in many households to transfer water using buckets or hoses from the main tap, which is located at the entrance of the house, to the places where it is to be used (the kitchen, or where clothes are washed) or to storage containers, and to have a second tap in the toilets (figure 6.1). Water is extensively handled by individuals, and management of it falls within the category of household duties. Beyond the domestic sphere, however, the inhabitants of the neighbourhood do not assume collective responsibility for access to water. In addition, there is no local water system that might be claimed to be community-based, in the sense of a cohesive system in terms of collective rights and duties distributed among domestic units.

The water supply in Deim has long been managed by the central government – colonial and Sudanese – which distributes water by household with a payment system based on a monthly flat fee. This system of urban

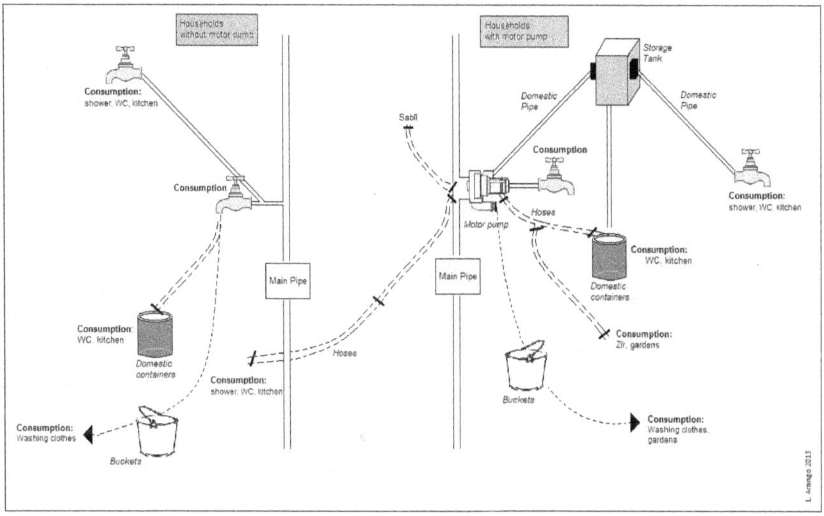

Figure 6.1. The Circulation of Water in the Domestic Sphere

water supply was begun at the time of the final relocation of Deim by the colonial administration, and defines households units for hydrological purposes as a group of people around a tap connected to the mains. This group was supposed to live in a single and defined residence identified by a block and house number. The shift from water management defined by a larger group of people – as was the case with the common wells in Old Deim – to household-based management was based on the implementation of domestic flat fees and the installation of domestic taps. This system produced a household-government connection that became the paradigm of urban water management. Since the adoption of the federal system in the 1990s,[10] urban water management has been under the aegis of the Khartoum State Water Corporation (KSWC).

This long-term access to tap water and the tradition of management by central government mark an important difference from the majority of the city's population, which has no domestic taps and relies on groundwater stored in communal tanks (Njiru and Albu 2004). This difference may be illustrated by the absence of a local authority that controls local water access and resolves related conflicts. While in the rural and peripheral areas of Khartoum popular committees[11] often take charge of drinking water issues (G. Hamid 2000a; Njiru and Albu 2004), in Deim, these local institutions do not have standing to do so, as the head of one of Deim's popular committees states: 'People do not come here to complain about water cuts or high water prices, because these are government decisions. It's not a concern of the *lajna shaʿabīa*; our responsibilities are administrative, and water and electricity are not included – they are a concern of the institutions. In Deim, it is the government that deals with water problems.'[12]

Since the installation of the water network in the early 1950s, water supplies have officially been regulated by a government office located in the neighbourhood, which did not undergo major changes as a result of state-level institutional transformations (the transfer from colonial to Sudanese management, or the institutional decentralization of water management that took place in 1991). However, because it supplies water to one of Khartoum's oldest neighbourhoods and has strong ties to the government apparatus, the water distribution system in Deim is easily affected by other wider urban dynamics, such as a growing demand for drinking water in Khartoum, as well as by transformations at the higher levels of the decision-making process, such as the adoption of neoliberal policies in favour of the privatization of water-related services.

The Production of Differences in Access to Water: Local Practices and KSWC Logics

The water treatment plants on the Nile have become increasingly inadequate for the supply of water to the city of Khartoum due to rapid urban growth and technical dysfunctions in the urban network. In Deim, this means that the flow of tap water is inconsistent, and sometimes nonexistent, and that water is distributed unequally as a function of the intensity of water use throughout the network, proximity to the main pipeline or the height of a building. To cope with these unpredictable variables, individuals show a high degree of flexibility in their water needs and develop creative practices in order to adapt to the irregular schedules in the flow of water, such as keeping very large stocks of water around the main tap and the toilets, keeping the taps permanently open, recycling used water, or waiting for dawn – when water is being used the least in the centre of the city – to fill up their home's containers.

Since the household has emerged as the unit of water management, access to water in the current context of scarcity is achieved by means of technical manipulations at a domestic level (such as putting taps at ground level, using domestic water pumps and reservoirs or increasing the number of taps inside the home) that require a financial investment of a kind that is unaffordable for an important part of Deim's inhabitants. In addition, the use of domestic water dispensers that use bottled water, as well as the growing use of refrigerators, air conditioning and washing machines that require large quantities of water, reinforces differentiation in the amounts of water needed by each household. Hence, the water-related practices, techniques and usage of both new and older inhabitants of Deim produce an increased level of differentiation in water access, which is exemplified by the installation of motorized water pumps, which prevent some neighbours from having access to water while others are using their pumps. Technically, these arrangements aggravate the problem of flow distribution, while socially they underline a changing relationship among neighbours regarding the management of urban water, which is becoming scarce and unequally accessible.

Differentiations in access to water have been ratified by the KSWC in recent decades by means of a series of operating policies and procedures that extend the colonial logics of water management on the one hand, while giving rise to completely new processes on the other. First, the bureaucratization of access to water, which was initiated during the colonial period and facilitated by attributing numbers to houses and blocks, has been reinforced by the creation and use of hydric maps, water bills and detailed lists of water-related debts. This apparatus has strengthened the process of breaking the inhabitants of the neighbourhood down into household units for water management purposes, and has contributed to water-related practices being limited to the domestic sphere. Second, the introduction, starting in 2001, of private Sudanese companies that have gradually replaced the local KSWC offices in the collection of water bills has led to access to water being made more strict in the areas under their responsibility (figure 6.2), due to access to water being cut off for households that accumulate unpaid bills. Third, the accompanying campaign to readjust the monthly fees for each house, which were all paying the same rate until 2001, has normalized the ongoing differentiation within an explicitly legal and economic framework.[13] This shift is well explained by a housewife who lives in the blocks under the responsibility of the private companies: 'If you don't have SDG 16, you don't have water, but I have to. If I don't pay, they'll cut the pipe … in the past, they were very nice, you could tell them that you didn't have enough money, that you couldn't pay, and they allowed you to pay the next month, but now they're hard, they come and cut off the water in one go, just like that!'[14]

According to a senior KSWC official,[15] establishment of these measures is justified by the failure of local KSWC offices to collect payments, by the accumulation of unpaid bills and by misuse of water by individuals.[16] This position is inscribed into the aim of achieving a rational, efficient and accountable use of water, which is specific to neoliberal water management policies (Achterhuis, Boelens and Zwarteveen 2012). The neoliberal policies that began to be introduced in Sudan with the federal administration of resources saw the transfer of water management from a national to a

Figure 6.2. Hydric Map of Deim Showing Blocks and Households

federal level in 1991, and they have been reinforced since the mid-2000s by the introduction of private companies (Beckedorf 2012).

The ongoing transformation of water access in Deim cannot be understood in terms of the dismantling of community management or the dissolution of established grassroots authorities, as has been effectively analysed in rural areas (Bédoucha 1987; Casciarri 2008), because community water management involving individuals beyond the domestic sphere ended in the early 1950s with the disappearance of common water wells. Rather, the ongoing shift is taking place in a much more disguised manner and found its consensus in the rationales of higher decision-making levels and in water access methods and water usage at a local level. This means that a pervasive disparity in water access is produced at both levels, as much by household manipulations and differentiated household needs for water as by the KSWC's water management practices and the diversification of monthly fees or reinforcement of the bill payment system.

Coping with Differentiated Access to Water and Commoditization: Household Practices and Undifferentiated Sharing

In Deim, autonomous actions relating to water access vary from reconnection to the mains after cutoffs, the accumulation of unpaid bills, continuous negotiations with KSWC officials, criticisms lodged with employees of the private companies and the use of domestic water dispensers in ways that were not anticipated by the bottled water producers. These practices, together with narratives from the population and KSWC local officials, illustrate a controversial position vis-à-vis the KSWC's management rationales and the process of water commoditization. In addition, sharing beyond the domestic sphere by passing hoses and buckets between houses and by religious offerings of water to passersby takes place with no reference to the socioeconomic status or identity affiliation of the sharers. These responses, which are frequently performed in urban contexts, have been described by some authors as 'private solutions' or forms of 'individual resistance' that are highly undesirable compared with organized collective action or community management (Swyngedouw 2004: 150). Furthermore, in recent studies, 'water governance', defined as a regulated framework within which 'communities' can articulate their interests and participate in the management of water, is increasingly evoked as a way of overcoming inequalities and individualized access to water (Bakker 2007; Linton 2012).

As a counterpoint to these claims, I will focus on local uses of bottled water, autonomous responses and nonorganized water sharing to address a different issue. I argue that by considering collective action and struggles as the only, or most effective, means of resistance to unequal and individualized water supply methods, scholars are neglecting the immediate power – spatial and temporal[17] – of individual practices to redefine ongoing trends in urban water management and make water access effective for them and their neighbours in their everyday lives. Thus, in the same sense, seeking a formal community of sharers on which to base water management in cases such as that of Deim, where there are no explicit common interests and no collective system of water access, leads to the risk that unsystematic water transactions that constitute a way of evading the dominant managerial urban water order without overthrowing it will not be taken into account.

The use of large water bottles for domestic cooling tanks that dispenses the water is a good example in support of this argument. When people buy the large water bottles they access drinking water from private companies and therefore accept market logics. In addition to cooling the water, these cooling tanks are a symbol of economic status and prestige, even though after the initial purchase, people are accustomed to filling the bottles with tap water. Through this strategy, people reaffirm the merchandizing embodied in the water bottles while reorienting the process by integrating the bottles into the domestic cycle of state tapped water accessed through a monthly flat fee. In addition, household-based arrangements such as individual pumping of water from common pipes, recurrent reconnections to the mains after the water has been cut off or the accumulation of unpaid bills are frequently fiercely explained in narratives that highlight the population's traditional morals of autonomy and self-reliance. These highly controversial actions, which become a structural part of water access, are a means of redefining processes such as the establishment of coercive measures and legal apparatuses or water commoditization while at the same time reiterating these same processes. When people have access to water from taps, they are affirming the power of the urban supply system over their everyday access to water. Hence, local agency, which enjoys visibility as a result of the evasion of water bill payments and the sharing of water for free, challenges the monetary nature attributed to water through the monthly flat fees charged by the KSWC. In addition, by reconnecting to the mains after supply has been cut off, people re-create a space of action for management of the resource within the system, as an inhabitant of Deim lets us understand: 'When we need a new tap, we do ourselves. Everything that is inside the house, if you are able to do, you do by yourself, and if you are not, you bring someone in to do it. There is no need for the government to know this!'[18]

The local KSWC officials also signal their independence from upper management, attributing great significance to the possibility of negotiating with members of the households under their responsibility, unlike the newly introduced private companies. As one of the money collectors claimed: 'I only cut them off if they talk to me rudely. But here the people are poor, and if they are nice I do not disconnect them. It is up to me to decide, not the office.'[19]

As these actions are not proscribed locally, both narratives should be understood in terms of being legitimized by a moral code of necessity that some authors in other contexts have argued can be thought of as a Muslim religious right to be thirsty and to drink (Van Aken 2011: 75). It has been said, however, that these negotiations are 'divisive, inherently conservative, and feed an individualized, fragmented and divided urban political economy based on personal relations, favors and rewards' (Swyngedouw 2004: 151). In contrast to this assumption, I argue that these actions can be seen as local negotiations that allow a large number of people to have domestic water in spite of the dysfunctions of the urban water supply system and the process of monetization of water resources, and thus constitute a real guarantee of access to water, as has been argued for other sectors of Khartoum (Zug 2013).

Furthermore, if we use household narratives and practices to reveal the local social relations articulated through the tap, we see that the transformation in power relations embedded in access to water has operated by eliminating – as a result of the introduction of private companies – close relationships that had been created between households and local government officials over time. Thus, if we disqualify or circumvent individual independent actions and logics of access to water, we will lose an opportunity to shed light on the power relationships in force and to examine the procedures and possibilities for, and effects of, the reappropriation of administrative options by individuals.

As has also been claimed in the area of water rights in indigenous communities in Latin America (Boelens, Getches and Guevara-Gil 2012: 11), the user families in Khartoum are today an important part of the water distribution system. I believe that the nature of everyday sharing among households in Deim is a result of their common history and the long-standing custom of welcoming very diverse populations. In the neighbourhood, those who obtain water – by any means – are supposed to share it free of charge with those who do not, as one inhabitant puts it clearly:

> When we have problems with water, we go to the people who have a motorized pump ... they put a pipe under the door so anybody can take water. You take the water and then you go, you do not have to pay. These people have water while others do not, so you take as much water as you need to be satisfied. You can go and ask anybody, you go where there is water. Everybody can give it to you, you can ask your neighbour: 'Where did you find water?' And your neigh-

bour tells you where, and you go. I give water to those who need it, even if we do not know the person. We do not ask: 'Who are you? Where do you come from?' It is simple: you give water to everyone.[20]

All offers of water fall within the idiom of a religious exchange that may become institutionalized when a person establishes a public place for its distribution, such as a well, a *zīr* (a clay jar used for stocking and cooling drinking water) or a water cooler. These artefacts are called *sabīl* (literally, 'a path') when they are used beyond the domestic space to distribute water in the public sphere. *Sabīl* are mostly installed by relatives in the name of a deceased person to add *ḥasanāt* (good actions) to his account for his access to paradise through the prayers offered by passersby who drink from the *sabīl* (figure 6.3). Coolers and *zīr* may be placed by individuals in mosques, streets, stores, schools and other public places, as well as at the entrances to houses, to provide drinking water to anyone who needs it. Understood as an undifferentiated and religious endowment, water from a *sabīl* is not controlled by the providers, and so it can be used by destitute people, who may or may not be settled in the neighbourhood. While the creation of a *sabīl* is the result of a choice, and there are no means of enforcing its implementation and use, the donor has a religious duty to protect it and to provide clean water.

Although they are not a part of an enunciated, structured and organized system of rights and duties among users, the various exchange networks among neighbours through *sabīl,* hoses or buckets constitute the

Figure 6.3. Types of *Sabīl* (Arango 2009)

main way of accessing water for a significant number of houses in the neighbourhood. The provision of free drinking water does not, however, conflict with the appropriation of larger quantities by some households than by others, and so unequal access and increasing sharing intermingle with no apparent contradiction. This continuity between logics that would appear to be in conflict make the capacity of people's 'transversal struggles' to question the status of the individual quite clear, as Foucault remarks: 'On the one hand, [these struggles] assert the right to be different, and they underline everything which makes individuals truly individual. On the other hand, they attack everything which separates the individual, breaks his links with others [and] splits up community life. ... These struggles are not exactly for or against the "individual" but rather they are struggles against the "government of individualization"' (Foucault 1982: 211).

As a consequence, although it may be achieved by the installation of individual motorized pumps or illegal reconnection to the mains, the negotiation of an increasingly scarce resource also operates through non-organized sharing, which, rather than dividing defined groups of people, minimizes ethnic and religious differences that might be problematic in other situations.[21] The way individual solutions and water sharing are perceived by former inhabitants of Deim is closely associated with the image they have of their own communality – which has been noted in the neighbourhood since colonial times[22] – as including very diverse individuals and being highly autonomous vis-à-vis government (whether colonial or postcolonial). In contrast to contexts where water mediates conflict or hierarchies, in Deim, water links people with differing economic statuses, ethnic identities, or national origins. Nevertheless, the ephemeral, decentralized, inexplicit and anonymous nature of water exchanges makes it harder for them to be understood within a positive framework such as 'community management'.

In this regard, part of the conversation I had with an inhabitant about the presence of *sabīl* in Deim is highly significant:

– I have not seen a lot of *sabīl* in Ḥājj Yūsif, Amarat or Khartoum 2 ...

– I think that it is more in popular neighbourhoods that you will find a lot of *sabīl,* but in the neighbourhoods with a lot of buildings, a lot of big houses, there are no friendly relations between people. That is the reason, I think, why there are not so many *sabīl.*

– But Ḥājj Yūsif is a popular neighbourhood, isn't it?

– It is popular! But it is not an old neighbourhood. In Deim you can find people, the elderly, who have been living here for twenty, thirty or fifty years, Ḥājj Yūsif is a new neighbourhood, there are people who have been living there for just five years. ... There are no strong social relationships among the inhabitants

> of this neighbourhood. In Deim, we have been here for a long time and so we always try to help one another. Deim is a popular quarter with better relationships than in other, new quarters.[23]

Features such as being popular, highly urbanized, settled in the city for a long time and traditionally welcoming diverse people convey a strong feeling of peculiarity that distinguishes the people of Deim from other inhabitants of Khartoum. Water taps confirm this long urban tradition, while undifferentiated water sharing legitimates the incorporation of diverse populations, which appears to be the foundation of the identity of the inhabitants of Deim. An analysis of local water sharing, management and access is therefore an interesting tool for understanding social logics and identities that are not enunciated in any explicit or classical manner.

Conclusion

Water in Deim has long been managed by a centralized government system. The notion of communal water management is limited to the recollections of a few older people who lived in Old Deim or who used common water wells before the installation of domestic taps in New Deim. Long-standing urban roots and a tradition of government management mean that the neighbourhood's water supply system is easily affected by wider transformations in contemporary urban Sudan. Observation of water-related practices and narratives in Deim can therefore offer an illustration of the concrete local transformations that follows urban growth or the neoliberal policies adopted by the state in line with international trends.

The tradition of government management and local history means that a local system of water distribution has not been explained by the inhabitants of Deim in terms of a community of sharers. There is also a lack of organized collective action in response to increasing scarcity and a current trend towards water management privatization supported by neoliberal government rationales. The introduction of new techniques such as motorized water pumps in response to the decline of the water supply system has been interpreted by some authors as a 'private solution' or as 'individual responses'. I wanted to show instead that while negotiations between households and local KSWC officers stand in immediate contrast to current neoliberal trends in water access, undifferentiated sharing among households represents a challenge to increasing differentiation and standardization. Actions of this kind are not specific to contemporary Sudan; they take place in many other urban contexts. If we dismiss or circumvent these actions, therefore, there is the risk that we will fail to analyse a widespread, complex situation where people on one hand affirm their difference and individuality, and on the other stand firmly against any process that might isolate an individual or cut him or her off from the social sphere.

It is only by a detailed analysis of daily water-related practices and narratives at a user level that it becomes possible to understand the social value of water for the urban population and the rooting of sharing practices in social history. By carrying out an analysis such as this, it is possible to decode the seemingly contradictory logics, to reveal the mechanisms that transform water access at the user's level, and to identify the highly political dimension of actions that might at first sight appear to be autonomous and unorganized.

Notes

1. Only a few studies have been conducted on this subject, although within the framework of the WAMAKHAIR project (Water Management in Khartoum International Research, 2009–12), the partners of which were the Universities of Paris X Nanterre and Paris 8 (France), the University of Bayreuth (Germany), Ahfad University for Women (Sudan) and the CEDEJ in Khartoum, various fieldwork was carried out that provides original data in the context of Khartoum.
2. The social dimension of water has frequently been studied by anthropologists; however, most of the fieldwork has been carried out in rural and periurban areas, and it still mainly relates to irrigation systems and only to a marginal degree to domestic consumption and usage (Casciarri and Van Aken 2013).
3. Fieldwork research was carried out between November 2008 and April 2009 in the framework of the WAMAKHAIR project. I would like to thank the different colleagues that participated in this research, especially Barbara Casciarri for her scientific support.
4. Sing. *deim*; pl. *dyūm*. This designation was formerly used during the Turco-Egyptian period. The Dyūm Al-Shargīa (Eastern Deims), where the fieldwork was carried out, is made up of 170 city blocks, with an average of 45 houses of 200 square metres each per block. The area includes approximately 4,800 houses covering a surface area of 26 square metres (see figure 6.2).
5. The field data revealed some extreme cases. For instance, I observed a domestic unit with one tap for nine people, while another had ten taps for five people. The former had no motorized pump and no significant household appliances, while the latter had a motorized pump and a raised cistern for storing water and making domestic devices such as a washing machine and air conditioning units operational.
6. For instance, Deim Banda and Deim Jabal, which were located in Old Deim, took their names from populations from the southwest of the former Sudan and the east of the Central African Republic. In today's Deim, we still have Deim Berti, which is inhabited by a population originally from northern Darfur, Deim Tegali, from the Nuba region, and Deim Jawāmaʿa, which is associated with other ethnic groups (Sikainga 1996).
7. Author's interview with Ibrahim, retired, seventy years of age, April 2009.

8. The term 'Old Deim' refers to the neighborhood when it was situated at the actual quarter of Khartoum 3 while 'New Deim' refers to its present situation. Both terms were used by colonial administrators during the last relocation to differentiate the two places and they are still used by the eldest of the neighborhood.
9. Author's interview with Fatima, housewife, eighty-two years of age, December 2008.
10. For a detailed account of the political genealogy of these institutions, see Nègre (2004), and for an understanding of the ongoing political trends, see Beckedorf (2012).
11. In Arabic, *lajna sha'abīa.* These committees of elected volunteers are responsible for the management of neighbourhood or village concerns. They provide certain services, mobilize the population to accomplish self-help projects, maintain order and enforce the law (G. Hamid 2000a).
12. Author's interview with Samir, head of the *lajna sha'abīa,* from Deim Berti, sixty-eight years of age, February 2009.
13. Rate differentiation was being set up during the fieldwork through a census led by the KSWC local office. It takes into account the presence of siphons and the size of domestic pipes connected to the main pipes as follows: multifloor houses with washing machines or air conditioning and a siphon pay SDG 45 a month if the pipe has a diameter of one inch, or SDG 25 a month if the pipe has a diameter of three-quarters of an inch. The majority of houses still pay SDG 15 a month, as they have no siphon, are less well furnished and are served by a half-inch pipe.
14. Author's interview with Salama, housewife, fifty-six years of age, February 2009.
15. Author's interview with Osman, head of the KSWC's Department of Financial Affairs, fifty years of age, February 2009.
16. There are no public studies showing the efficiency of private companies in Khartoum; nonetheless, it has been proved in similar contexts that the private sector is no more reliable and efficient as far as water management is concerned, as regards either technical performance and connection numbers or even profit levels (Hall and Lobina 2007: 782).
17. In Foucault's terms, these exchanges are spatially immediate, as they respond to the closest process that affects people (access to water) and not to a distant institution, elite or group of decision makers (a government office, a new social class or an elite arriving in the neighbourhood). These exchanges are also temporally immediate, as they do not seek a future solution to the problem of access, but rather one for current everyday life (Foucault 1982: 211).
18. Author's interview with Nuredin, unemployed, fifty-eight years of age, February 2009.
19. Author's interview with El-Amin, employee of the local KSWC office, December 2008.
20. Author's interview with Sara, housewife, forty-eight years of age, January 2009.
21. At the beginning of the fieldwork, I expected to find an influence of religious (Christian/Muslim) or identity (Sudanese/non-Sudanese/ethnotribal and regional) features for the water-sharing network, whereas in fact, the social reality is different, and water is shared with everyone who needs it, whether he or she be a neighbour or just a passerby.
22. 'This depressing picture of the Old Deim is however brightened, especially on the social side. … The Old Deims seemed in many ways to comprise well-integrated communities, sharing certain loyalties, and exchanging certain mutual obligations. … The important point in this respect is the fact that the peoples of the Old Deims seem to have had a certain communal spirit and to have enjoyed certain communal ties' (Fawzi 1980: 516–17).
23. Author's interview with Mona, housewife, fifty-seven years of age, February 2009.

Chapter 7

Domestic Water Supply and Management in North Kordofan Villages

Al-Lowaib as an Example

Elsamawal Khalil Makki

The provision of water in Sudan continues to be a critical problem in both rural and urban areas, especially during the dry months. This problem is particularly acute in North Kordofan State, where the population has limited access to clean potable water facilities. Therefore, domestic water supply and management remains a major concern for different stakeholders, as they strongly believe that water problems hinder the development of North Kordofan, which is located in a semiarid zone where potable water sources are limited. Webb and Iskandarani (1998) suggested that the problems of water insecurity can be grouped under three main headings: availability, access and usage. The issue of access to water extends beyond its mere availability; it also reflects its immediate readiness and the ease of its collection and transportation. Badri (2002) considered the availability of drinkable water for both humans and animals to be one of the most essential services not only for the direct goal of challenging poverty, but also because water is an important requirement that is necessary for sustainable economic and social development. Furthermore, access to water is now recognized as a prerequisite for poverty reduction (Sullivan and Meigh 2003). However, little is known about how an appropriate mix of policies, institutions and market mechanisms can help to achieve household water security in water-stressed environments.

Direct practical benefits from improved access to water have been described in many studies (Moriarty and Butterworth 2003; Ivens 2008;

Notes for this chapter begin on page 138.

UNDP 2006). These studies all focused on improved health conditions, women's empowerment and time savings. However, the potential benefits vary from one beneficiary to the other, and conflicting interests can have a major effect on these benefits.

Water in North Kordofan

In 2009, UNICEF described the water situation in North Kordofan as follows: North Kordofan covers an area of 244,700 square metres and has a total population of 2,479,000 (50 per cent rural, 34 per cent urban and 16 per cent nomadic) with an annual growth rate of 1.45 per cent. Most of the population are agro-pastoralists. Investment in the sector has been quite low due to the long civil war in the country, which has resulted in the deterioration of basic services and increased poverty. Many localities in North Kordofan are frequently affected by drought, and hence there is a shortage of surface and underground water (UNICEF 2009).

According to data from the 2006 Sudan Households Survey (SHHS), 1,313,930 people in North Kordofan (53 per cent), mainly in rural and periurban areas, do not have access to improved drinking water, and 1,777,443 people (72 per cent) do not have access to adequate and safe sanitation. There are 1,345 hand pumps in the state (86 per cent are functioning, serving 16 per cent of the population), 41 motorized pumps (63 per cent are functioning, serving 16 per cent of the population) and 7 large water supply systems (75 per cent are functioning, serving 31 per cent of the population). The main reason for the relatively high number of nonoperational hand pumps is the nonavailability of spare parts and the weak capacity of local communities to manage their water systems. The state is in the process of developing a master plan for the Water, Environment and Sanitation (WES) sector to achieve the UN Millennium Development Goals (MDGs) with the support of UNICEF. The coordination, assessment and implementation of the water, sanitation and hygiene programme has also improved. There is a significant lack of qualified staff, equipment and supplies on the ground, mainly because of inadequate funding, motivation and management systems. Very few NGOs work in this state. Access to improved water sources in North Kordofan is 47 per cent, according to the SHHS. Many localities do not reach this level, and coverage varies between localities.

Water in Al-Lowaib

The village of Al-Lowaib is located seventeen kilometres to the east of the town of El-Obeid in Sheikan Province, North Kordofan.[1] The total population of the village is 473 persons from the Mesallamīa, Jawāmaʿa and Jallāba tribes.[2] Most of the villagers are farmers who mainly depend on traditional rain-fed agriculture using hand tools. The rainy season starts in June and ends in October. In addition to agriculture, some people rear small ruminants and cattle.

The educational level is low in the village, as most of the population have low levels of or no education (41.4 per cent illiterate and 49.4 per cent with primary education). Families are mostly (66.7 per cent) medium in size, having five members and less, while families with six to ten members are 28.4 per cent of the population.

Hand pumps are the main source of domestic water in the area, although sometimes people access boreholes in nearby villages. There are seven hand pumps in the village, but only a single pump is functioning and the rest are in need of repair. The hand pumps were at first mainly installed and operated by NGOs and then managed with the assistance of the local community. Nearby there is an unfinished water pond for the harvesting of rainwater. There is a local water management committee whose main responsibilities are to run and manage water sources in the village, negotiate the development of these sources with donors and other stakeholders and set priorities regarding domestic water issues in the village. The committee was formed with the assistance of the cooperating NGO and the local popular committee (*lajna shaʿabīa*). In theory, the members of this committee should be elected, with the popular committee representative being appointed by its president. The formation and selection of its members is greatly influenced by the popular committee and the interests of the NGO. However, in practical terms, this committee has no function, and only the representative of the popular committee takes actions and decisions. Furthermore, the committee does not meet regularly and is in effect completely absent on the ground. Women play a vital role in water management in the household, as they are most often the collectors, users and managers of water in the household. They are represented on the water management committee, but their role is mostly marginal due to the insignificant role of the committee itself.

Different Western, Islamic and Arab NGOs are involved in the rural water sector in North Kordofan. They all agree on the general intent of their mandate, which is to comply with the MDGs. The main aims of the Islamic Relief Suisse Project (a typical NGO working in the area) are to provide the target population with access to safe water and sanitation facilities through the construction of wells and latrines, and to increase community awareness of health and sanitation issues through an education programme. The long-term goals of the project are to allow households to use more of their time for economically productive activities by decreasing the burden on women and children, who are traditionally responsible for collecting water on a daily basis, and to reinforce the socioeconomic system of the targeted communities, enabling them to meet the demands of combating the chronic imbalance in their economic status.

The main activities of the NGO are: (1) mobilizing the local community to construct and maintain hand-dug wells (one of only two types of water system able to operate in the village given the geological context) to ensure the sustainability of the project; (2) conducting a baseline survey on specific social and economic parameters, community priorities and the potential availability of water to help identify the villages that most require intervention; (3) establishing democratically elected village water committees to act as the community partner implementing project activities; (4) encouraging communities to contribute financially to the cost of the project, thereby building a sense of ownership and ensuring sustainability; and (5) training beneficiaries on health issues and simple management skills through Water and Sanitation Service (WES), a one-week programme supported by UNICEF covering areas such as personal and community hygiene, water and environmental protection and community mobilization.

In general, public roles in the village are constructed around social and to some extent political powers, as is usual in local leadership in many parts of rural Sudan. The *'omda,* who usually inherits this position, is the most influential and powerful individual in the village, followed by his relatives, who acquire this role merely by kinship.[3] The second most powerful group is formed by the sheikhs, who are the leaders of the different tribes in the village. Another powerful group is made up of the 'well-off' community members and educated individuals, who are respected for their education and are accordingly seen as part of the elite. In Al-Lowaib there is one *'omda* and three sheikhs, who head the three main tribes.

Approach, Conceptual Framework and Methodology

This chapter seeks to explore the reasons for the failure of water projects and NGO intervention in the water sector in rural areas in Sudan. This is based on the argument that failure relates to the belief of many planners and engineers that the water supplied to people's homes is solely or primarily used for domestic purposes. Contrary to this belief, large quantities of 'domestic' water supply are used for 'nondomestic' productive purposes. People do not just drink water, or use it to wash or cook. They use it also to grow crops, water livestock, produce goods and provide services in and around the household. Hence, there is potential to make even better use of water in contributing to people's wider well-being and livelihood.

However, the productive use of water creates conflicting and competing interests between the different strata of the community and can result in uneven distribution and access to the benefits of any water scheme. This relates directly to, and is constructed around, dominance and/or social power. Of all the villagers, women's position in this regard can be the worst given their marginalization and lack of empowerment.

Water projects in rural areas do not perform to their design capacity and lack sustainability because planners and decision makers fail to bring together all of the actors in the water sector in the target area. Moreover, the planners and decision makers sometimes lack integrity and view outputs from their own perspective, ignoring how the intended beneficiaries react to and benefit from water projects.

The principal framework for this chapter was the issue of scarcity and accessibility. This supplied the critical approach in this chapter to domestic water consumption and management. This approach was based on a few different assumptions. First, domestic water consumption patterns relate to water availability, family size, the nature of the water source, the person responsible for its collection and power relations in the local society. Second, women play an important role in water management. They are most often the collectors, users and managers of water in the household because they know the location, reliability and quality of local water resources. Many stakeholders emphasize the need for women to become key actors in the water supply and sanitation system (Cunningham 1999). Third, women's involvement in water projects has a related effect on mobilizing finance for gender-based projects, showing that access to water has an effect on gender equality (Ivens 2008). Fourth, traditionally the water and sanitation sector has occupied itself with the small subset of activities described as 'domestic'. The sector's aim has been to supply people with a clean, reliable and safe supply of water with the primary goal of improving their health. More recently, the goal has been extended to include the need to reduce the drudgery involved when people (usually women) have to walk long distances to collect water.

The approach was then broadened to cover 'overlooked' issues. This broadened approach incorporated arguments and evidence from similar research findings globally. It followed the productive water approach described above in seeking to support the contention that 'domestic water' can have an added value and be used for productive activities. The questions raised by E. Bell (2001) were also considered. The approach used by Moriarty and Butterworth (2003) challenged the traditional assumption that water delivered to people's homes is intended for domestic purposes only. It has also been argued that as sources of water develop, its uses are distributed and strategies change (Schouten and Moriarty 2003). Now a broader range of nonhealth benefits have started to be recognized and targeted in an increasing number of studies and reports. Some authors have found that beneficiaries reported a much wider range of benefits for a water project than had been expected or targeted at inception (Bell 2011; Ivens 2008).

Furthermore, the potential benefits were explored, for example, the increased reliability of domestic water supplies, despite the fact that in some cases powerful individuals or elites could make access more difficult by exerting pressure on site infrastructure, for example, by having hand pumps and taps installed closer to their own homes.

The framework then followed Ivens (2008) in arguing that the direct practical benefits from improved access to water supply and sanitation include better health for women and girls due to the improved quality and increased quantity of water. The explicit benefits of women's participation in public decision-making and local community structures are less obvious, despite the prominence of women's participation in international declarations. Moreover, it is far less evident that women's participation in water programmes contributes to strategic benefits such as women's empowerment and gender equality. It becomes clear that it cannot be assumed that increased water access reduces women's workload or strengthens women's empowerment.

As far as methodology is concerned, this chapter adopted a cross-sectional survey design. The data were collected from a simple random sample of eighty-seven households using one type of questionnaire. Additional qualitative data was obtained from group discussions with community members, the water committee and the popular committee. The *'omda* and senior NGO officials were also interviewed. Observation and domain mapping for women were used to provide additional qualitative data.

Domestic Water Collection and Consumption

In Al-Lowaib, domestic water collection is mainly the responsibility of women (68 per cent), either on their own (41.4 per cent) or with assistance from their children (27.6 per cent). Children are fully responsible in more than a quarter (27.6 per cent) of the cases (table 7.1). Women and children's responsibility for water collection is by tradition accepted in rural Kordofan, but this adds more to women's burdens and time budget, especially during the rainy season, when they are supposed to participate in farming activities and manage household demands and duties. Women suffer greatly from this pressing time budget and demand improvements

Table 7.1. Responsibility for Water Collection

Category	Frequency	Percent
Father	3	3.4
Mother	36	41.4
Children	24	27.6
Mother and children	24	27.6
Total	*87*	*100*

Source: Based on questionnaire responses from the field survey.

in the water supply system to reduce the time and effort needed for water collection. However, this seems extremely unrealistic in the current social setting. For children, the responsibility for water collection affects their school performance. When water is needed in the morning (which is mostly the case), they sometimes miss morning classes at school. This theme emerged clearly in group discussions with mothers who were worried about their children's schooling. The same issue was also mentioned by the headmaster of the only basic school in the village. The mothers and the headmaster insisted that if the broken water pumps are not repaired, the pressure on the only working water pump would affect children's attendance at morning classes. They blamed the water committee for this state of affairs. Some mothers claimed that the water committee members were not serious in their attempts to solve this problem because the committee members themselves do not suffer from it.

Water is collected in twenty-litre containers (jerrycans) and transported by hand in the majority of the households (54 per cent), whereas the rest (46 per cent) use donkeys (figure 7.1). Children and women who transport this amount by hand for long distances are subject to the potential health risk factors suggested by Geere, Hunter and Jaglas (2010). Furthermore, this method significantly reduces the amounts collected and consumed, because the number of trips to the hand pump is reduced considerably with distance when water is transported by hand ($\chi^2 = 11.2, p = 0.01$). The households with an alternative means for water transportation consumed comparatively more water. Household water consumption was also dependent on family size ($\chi^2 = 51.4, p = 0.009$). Families had 'limited' capacity for water collection depending on the distance to the water source, the time of water collection and the number of trips to the water source required. Consequently, the daily water collection is set at a certain range, regardless of whether this range is sufficient or not. This reflects an inverse relationship between family size and per capita 'potential' water consumption; hence, smaller families consume more water per capita. The average per capita water consumption is 22.7 litres per day, assuming

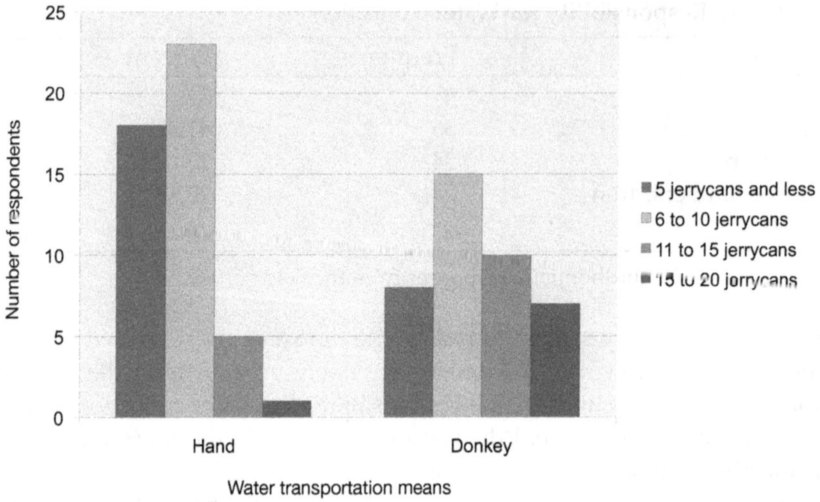

Figure 7.1. Water Consumption as Influenced by Water Transportation Means

that all of the water delivered to the household is used for domestic purposes, which is not always true. This is below the levels recommended by the WHO (between twenty-five and fifty litres). The Pearson correlation coefficient showed a strong inverse relationship between the distance to the water source and per capita water consumption; that is, consumption decreases with increasing distance to the water source ($r = -0.93$, $p = 0.03$). The time of water collection has a significant effect on the quantity of water used by families ($\chi^2 = 19.4$, $p = 0.02$); the cross-tabulation showed a general tendency for lower levels of water collection by families that collect water during morning hours (table 7.2). Reasons for this include the pressure on the only working hand pump and the long time that people need to queue for their turn. The cross-tabulation and chi-square test between water consumption and water collection means (table 7.3) and distance to the water source suggest that the means of water transportation has

Table 7.2. Water Consumption and Time of Collection (in percentage)

	Water consumption (jerrycans per day)			
Time of water collection	≤5	6 to 10	11 to 15	15 to 20
Morning and evening	20.9	46.5	18.6	14
Morning	53.8	42.3	3.8	0
All day	7.1	42.9	35.7	14.3
Midday	50	25	25	0

Source: Based on questionnaire responses from the field survey.

Table 7.3. Water Consumption and Collection Means

	Water collection means			
Water consumption	Hand		Donkey	
(jerrycans per day)	Frequency	Percentage	Frequency	Percentage
≤5	18	69.2	8	30.8
6 to 10	23	60.5	15	39.5
11 to 15	5	33.3	10	66.7
15 to 20	1	12.5	7	87.5

Source: Based on questionnaire responses from the field survey.

greater influence on water consumption ($\chi^2 = 11.84$, $p = 0.008$) than the distance to the water source ($\chi^2 = 49.93$, $p = 0.39$). Accordingly, the location of hand pumps inside the village controlled (indirectly) the quantity of water consumed by the different households. The positioning of the pumps is negotiated by local leaders (i.e., the *'omda* and other elites), who may impose their interests and have pumps installed near their houses. In rural Sudan, the location of houses is based on kinship, and the village leaders live in the same blocks. This is evident on the ground from the distribution of pumps in Al-Lowaib. This successfully supports the argument made by Schouten and Moriarty (2003). Practically all of the hand pumps were located a short distance from the houses of the *'omda* and the sheikhs, leaving the rest of the village without ready access to water. The influence of the productive use of water (i.e., water for livestock) is evident here. Livestock rearing is the main economic activity in the village. The prominent figures in the community own considerable numbers of livestock, whose watering becomes a major concern if water is not readily available. On this basis, the *'omda* and his peers influenced decisions regarding the location of the hand pumps. They saw this as their legitimate right and used all of their powers to achieve a favourable outcome.

The group discussions showed a strong link between people's status and their perceptions of the quantity of water that they should use. Moreover, observations revealed a close relationship between the factors governing water consumption in the village and the factors suggested by Badri (2002) for water entitlements in the neighbouring White Nile State. Badri (2002) linked access to water to different geographical criteria (distance and household origin), economic criteria (occupation and income) and social criteria. He showed an interlocking relationship between the criteria that he called a 'mechanism of factors'. The same trend is clearly observed in Al-Lowaib, suggesting that the quantity of water use and ease of access to water sources relate not only to physical factors, but are also constructed around socioeconomic factors. The factors resulting in reduced water consumption in the village are: (1) the means of water transportation, (2) the time of water collection, (3) the person responsible for water collection, (4) the distance to the water source, (5) the family's size, (6) the family's income, (7) the level of education of the family breadwinner and (8) the social status of the family.

Water Uses

The water usually considered to be 'domestic water' is not used solely for domestic purposes in Al-Lowaib. This validates an approach examining the productive use of water, or at least the diversification of water use beyond drinking and cooking. Only 42.4 per cent of the households use water solely for domestic purposes, whereas the rest (57.6 per cent) use it for domestic purposes and for watering animals. The people in Al-Lowaib raise poultry, small ruminants (such as goats for milk and sheep to be sold in the nearby town of El-Obeid) and donkeys in varying numbers (figure 7.2). The raising of animals can be categorized as a productive activity that can either provide the purchasing power to meet other requirements, or cut the expenditure on such requirements. This takes place either when these animals and/or their products are sold directly in the market, or when these products are consumed in the household and thereby improve the family budget.

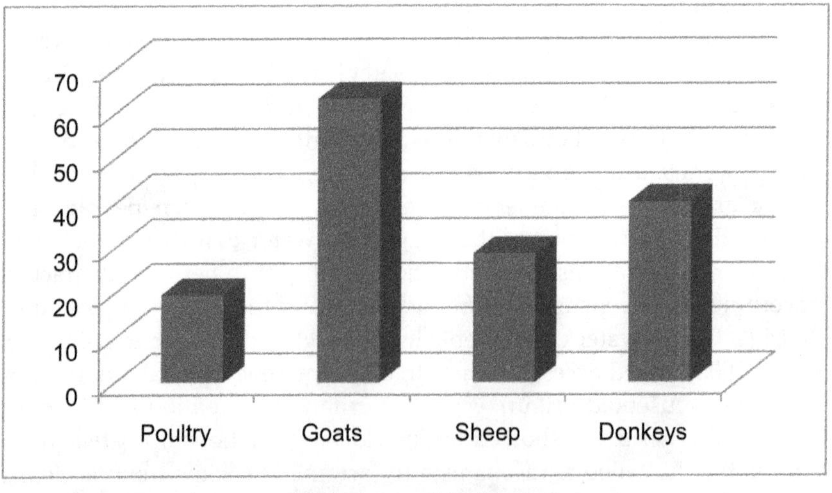

Figure 7.2. Distribution of the Types of Animals Raised

Considerable numbers of these animals are raised by the different households in Al-Lowaib, which suggests that the practice is commercial. The goats are mainly raised for milk and the sheep are fattened to be sold during *'īd* (the main Muslim feast). All of these animals are watered at the household using water collected from the same hand pump. This aggravates the situation for the villagers who are responsible for water collection, and can reduce the amounts used for domestic purposes. The productive use of domestic water generally puts more pressure on the source. This explains the frequent malfunction of the hand pumps, as they are operated for periods exceeding their design capacity. The cross-tabulation between water consumption and the raising of animals (table 7.4) showed that the latter significantly affects water consumption ($\chi^2 = 10.44$, $p = 0.01$) and that the families rearing animals consume less water.

The number of animals raised by the different types of household in the community show that the *'omda* and the sheikhs dominate the sector by raising larger numbers of livestock, thereby bringing their competing and conflicting interests to the fore, in addition to the ordinary pressure exerted on the hand pumps.

Table 7.4. Water Consumption and Animal Raising

		Water consumption (jerrycans per day)				
Raising animals		≤5	6 to 10	11 to 15	15 to 20	*Total*
Yes	Frequency	13	28	14	7	*62*
	%	21.0	45.2	22.6	11.3	*100*
No	Frequency	13	10	1	1	*25*
	%	52.0	40.0	4.0	4.0	*100*
Total	Frequency	*26*	*38*	*15*	*8*	*87*
	%	*29.9*	*43.7*	*17.2*	*9.23*	100

Source: Based on questionnaire responses from the field survey.

Water and Health

The community could not univocally define standards for safe, clean, acceptable or drinkable water. Each household had its own criteria for water quality. Some consider turbidity to be the major concern, others focus on odours and smell, while a third group mentioned taste. However, they all agreed that water is clean from the hand pump and becomes contaminated during transportation or when stored in the household. Water is stored in jerry cans and barrels in all of the households, while drinking water is kept in clay pots known as *zīr* to cool. Nevertheless, this belief in water contamination has not led to better hygienic practices. Water storage and collection utensils were in very bad condition. People's knowledge of waterborne diseases is very low and they are unable to identify protective measures against these diseases.

Despite the claims made regarding the role of the only NGO working in the village in this regard, some of the households lack basic information on these diseases to the extent that they describe vector-borne diseases as waterborne diseases as the NGOs used to refer to. Capacity building is inappropriate and the programmes designed do not match individuals' capabilities. These programmes are mostly carried out through lectures and videos for a community that is mostly illiterate and do not absorb information through formal high educational language. This raises issues regarding how NGOs prepare and design their capacity-building and awareness-raising programmes and how far these programmes can be successful and perform to their full capacity if they do not take into account the characteristics of the community for which they are designed. This has been a major constraint on the sustainability of water projects for decades. As the Water Page (1996) showed,

> capacity building and training programs can be used to bring each aspect of capacity up to the threshold required to sustain a particular technology solution. However, there are limits to both the levels which can be expected to be achieved and the time period required for capacity building, given the educational background of villagers and the time available to them out of their daily routines. Where the thresholds cannot be achieved in any of the different functions, consideration should be given to lowering the level of the technology or the complexity of the development program appropriately.

Water Management

As mentioned previously, there is a water committee in the village whose mandate is to run and develop the existing domestic water source for the well-being of the entire village population. This committee is not elected but is appointed and chaired by the village *'omda*. Women are represented on the committee but without clear duties or roles. In practical terms, the committee is controlled by the *'omda* and his kin, and in some cases can be overruled by him insofar as the other members consent to whatever he decides. The existence of women's representation on the water committee is somewhat misleading and was probably imposed by the partner NGO. Women are neither represented on the popular committee nor in any other committee in the village and are completely ignored in the village's public affairs. Why, then, are they represented on the water committee? Local communities' management of water sources and women's involvement in water issues are strategies proposed and to an extent 'imposed' by the partner NGO, as there is a growing and general acceptance throughout the continent that community-based management of services improves sustainability. This methodology has been supported by senior politicians, officials, NGOs and development agencies throughout the continent (Water Page 1996). Although this principle is generally and widely accepted, its implementation is rarely observed in practice. There is an inevitable time lag between the recognition of a new principle and the creation of institutional and regulatory mechanisms to achieve these new objectives.

Another problem is experience in the field in ensuring that the principle is effectively applied. It is not simple or easy to genuinely achieve community-based management. Most technically trained personnel are inadequately equipped and trained to apply the principle effectively in the field. These problems seem to be the main reasons why the implementation of genuine community-based development is not happening on a large scale in most African countries, and Sudan and North Kordofan are no exception. Furthermore, the community members think that by leaving the management responsibility to the local community, the NGO or the governmental body is shifting the responsibility for the provision of services from themselves to the community level. This is ironic, because it is the correct action for incorrect reasons (Water Page 1996). The problem is that community-based management may not be achieved without the backing of genuine political will, and this holds true for the case of North Kordofan.

Community involvement is a common term, but it still suggests that the community is involved in a process that is primarily being driven from outside. The decisions are being taken outside the community. This is particularly the case in terms of decisions regarding the financing of projects. For women in Al-Lowaib, their low-profile, marginal roles in society and low levels of education were the main barriers to playing a significant role in decision making. In contrast, for men, it was social power and wealth that masked their roles. The water provision and management project did not bring any change to women's lives other than comparatively reducing the distance used to walk to collect water. Even this change did not change women's domains and duties within the village. They still perform the same tasks within the same profile and geographical domain. Poverty and low social status were the main attributes for the lack of participation in public issues generally, in addition to women's existing role in regard to domestic water. The villagers all lack a clear understanding of what 'management' stands for; they mostly refer to safeguarding, fencing and cleaning the pumps as 'management'. They never refer to decision making, because this right is exclusively reserved for the *'omda* and the elites. This includes their notion of water rights. When negotiations start with the NGO or the rural water corporation as the responsible body for water provision at the state level, the *'omda* represents the villagers' interests and decides what is best for them. The institutional relationship of the popular committee with the NGO and the water committee is almost absent, except for the representation of the *'omda* and a few others. Even this relationship is not clearly structured, and this factor probably limited the NGO's role in capacity building and awareness raising. For most of the villagers, the NGO is solely known for having installed hand pumps in Al-Lowaib – 'God bless them', as the villagers say. Furthermore, the lack and in some cases failure to maintain the hand pumps is a direct consequence of the competing and conflicting interests of the *'omda* and the sheikhs. They try to exclude other 'producers' from the market, and because they have the capacity to provide water to their animals (for a short period), they do not act promptly to maintain the existing hand pumps.

Conclusion

The water scheme under discussion here has not been successful, particularly in improving the position of women, because the benefits of water provision are very unevenly distributed. Domestic water consumption and management lags far behind the expectations of the village community. People in Al-Lowaib lack the capacity to effectively participate in water source management, as management is constructed around capacity, social power and education. The role of women is very marginal and will continue to be so for decades to come in the current social setting. The productive role of domestic water is evident, and water entitlements as a governing factor to access to water seem to be prevalent. Wealthier people of higher status reap the greatest benefits from the water project because it allows them to raise livestock for the market. They see this as their legitimate right and use all of their powers to secure this advantage.

Notes

1. The use of the present in this chapter refers to the period of field inquiry in Al-Lowaib (2008–9).

2. The Mesallamīa are an Arabic-speaking group mainly located in Jezira and the White Nile states. The Jawāmaʿa are also an Arabic-speaking group found mostly in western Sudan (Kordofan and Darfur). Despite its local identification with a tribal group, the term 'Jallāba' is more precisely used in Kordofan to refer to the Arab sedentary groups originating in the northern Nile valley (Jaʿāliyn, Shāigīa and Danāgla) who spread across western Sudan in previous centuries for the purposes of trade.
3. In the system of tribal leadership, three levels are represented and hierarchically articulated: at the lower level, the sheikh is the representative of a lineage; at the intermediate level, the *'omda* can be the representative of a group of lineages or a tribe, and is the superior of several sheikhs; and at the upper level, the *nāẓir* is the superior of several *'omda*s and represents a tribe or a cluster of tribes. During the colonial period, the British Native Administration institutionalized this local political system and reinforced the fixed and hereditary parameters for the transmission of leadership. Despite the formal abolition of the Native Administration in 1970, tribal leaderships continue de facto to function, especially in rural areas, and have recently been 'revitalized' by the current government from 1994 onwards.

Chapter 8

Water Management among Sudanese Pastoralists

End of the Commons or 'Silent Resistance' to Commoditization?

Barbara Casciarri

The debate on the management of 'common resources' gives rise to a renewed interest – shared by researchers, national and international planners, and development organizations – in the discourses about the 'globalized' post–Cold War world (Nonini 2007). In Sudan, as well as in other African countries since the structural adjustment plans (SAPs) of the 1980s and 1990s (Ould-Mey 1994; Founou-Tchouigoua 1996), the issue proves particularly crucial for at least two reasons. The first is the hegemony of neoliberal policies during the last decades and their ravaging effects in terms of social costs on local livelihoods. The second is the persistence of groups whose productive systems are based on communal appropriation of resources, although they interact with a dominant market-exchange model.

The consolidation of privatization policies in Sudan since the strengthening of a neoliberal option in the mid-1990s (E. Ahmed 1997; Elhiraika and Ahmed 1998) favoured several processes: the opening to private investment, the withdrawal of the state as the main services provider and a trend toward the expropriation of common resources. In this context, water became a major target of the 'great transformation', which turned this common and socialized good into a commodity. The patterns of water management inspired by liberal conceptions, which have spread in most African countries during the last decades (Jaglin 2005), have progressed also in Sudan (Nègre 2004). Recent research on Sudanese water

Notes for this chapter begin on page 159.

policies (Beckedorf 2012) sheds light on the reform programmes led by the Sudanese federal states' water corporations following three basic neoliberal principles (decentralization, privatization and commercialization). During the first decade of the twenty-first century this restructuring has promoted a radical transformation of water access and use at national and local levels, in line with the global rise of neoliberalism.[1] This model implies a progressive disengagement by the state as a primary supplier of water services (hence the increasing opening to private actors) and a gradual shift from the notion of water as a 'right' or 'good' (free or at low subsidized fares) to one of water as a 'commodity' whose price is increasingly subject to market logics. In such a framework, the citizen becomes a customer, facing the expropriation of his water rights – a process often paralleled by the expropriation of land rights. The rooted forms of local (social) water management – still persisting in rural as well as ill-equipped periurban areas – are more and more undermined by the overreaching control of the state and of private providers of water as a commodity.

The situation is nonetheless far more complex than it may appear in such a rapid assessment. In order to avoid ambiguities, I add some clarifications about the dynamics concerning these alleged opposite poles (community vs. private sector/state) in relation to water management, because neither can be considered a 'perfect model' in its category, whether communal or liberal. The first observation concerns the strategies and practices of the Sudanese state and its interaction with the private sector. If for various sectors a shift in national economic policies towards neoliberal options can be confirmed since the late 1980s, as far as the water sector is concerned one cannot yet speak of an accomplished privatization, which would imply a dominant (exclusive) role for private actors and complete subordination of water access to market logics – 'commoditization' *stricto sensu*. The Sudanese state retains strong control over the distribution and management of water resources in the country, meaning that in various local contexts, the most visible evidence of state presence has been either the assumption of local services not previously under state control or the reinforcement of state oversight for the local water supply's systems. At the same time, recent studies on current dynamics of the water sector reforms in Sudan (Beckedorf 2012) confirm that the trilogy of decentralization, privatization and commercialization has been progressively reshaping the patterns of water management since the 1990s and more strongly after the 2000s. The transformation of federal states' water corporations into 'governmental entities similar to private companies' (Beckedorf 2012: 120), the recruitment of staff from the business world, the outsourcing of tasks to private investors, the shift to cost efficiency and profit maximization in the distribution of water, and the commercially driven mentality required from employees and inspiring recent legislation all confirm that, despite some contradictions in this ongoing restructuring, the process clearly resembles the patterns of market management of water as a commodity. Thus, if the significant state presence in 'water matters' mitigates the characterization of the Sudanese model as purely neoliberal – an ideal typology produced by liberal philosophers – the ambiguous role of the state should be taken into account within the dominant, capitalist trends in Africa, and one can view, as others have (Jaglin 2005), the progressive introduction of market norms in services management and even the so called public-private partnerships (PPP) as an actual particular form of commoditization.

The second observation concerns the ambiguity of the notions of 'commons' and 'community', and their consequences for the issues of 'commoditization' and 'liberalization'. In fact, within this debate some authors have stressed the need to nuance the multiple focuses on the commons and avoid a clear-cut dichotomy of communal versus private actors and practices. As they say, when speaking about communal regimes, one should rather specify different levels that range between open access to common resources, their common management and communal property rights: these levels may operate and combine differently according to context, to such an extent that in some cases even the 'anti-Hardinian' literature lacks detailed definitions of communal regimes opposable to the thesis of the tragedy of the commons (B. Burke 2001). Moreover, the notion of community is sometimes used too undifferentiatedly in discussions about the commons, while, on the contrary, each case study needs to detail the status of the community, the social entity linked to the commons and its relation with other non communal actors. As suggested by Bakker (2008), more than a dual polarization between commons and 'the rest', one should consider the complex interplay between three poles (commons-state-private) whose interactions with respect to water resources range from ownership rights to access, management and decision making. As this chapter will demonstrate, these actors, their rationales and their practices interact in ways that go beyond the simplified vision of 'pure privatization' versus 'pure communality'.

Rather than focus on the macrolevel of national water policies in Sudan, the aim of this chapter is to explore, at a less-known microlevel using a qualitative anthropological method, the forms of local water management among a particular category of people: pastoral groups. From this perspective, I point out some dynamics that shed light on the contemporary breakup of a tradition of water as a socially managed good and the diffusion of new forms of water commoditization as suggested by national and international logics. Following the above specifications, I use the term 'commoditization' to stress that Sudanese state action on water management among pastoralists is not yet an accomplished transformation of water as a purely market-determined commodity. In the same perspective, I use the term 'liberalization' and 'privatization' with the nuances that must be taken into account when talking about state-cum-private patterns of water management in African countries such as Sudan.

General Features of Water Management among Sudanese Pastoralists

Pastoral peoples have been affected by early and constant pressures by the state (colonial and postcolonial) as well as by other economic actors whose aims were to push them to sedentarization in order to achieve political control and to incorporate their production into a market economy (Mohamed Salih 1990b; Casciarri 2002). At the same time, pastoralists have been often ignored by development interventions and constitute throughout the country a marginalized sector of wider society. Despite an unfavourable context and persistent marginalization, a general appraisal (Casciarri and Ahmed 2009; Krätli, El-Dirani and Young 2013) shows that pastoral groups remain an important component in contemporary Sudan, at the demographic level but also for economic production and sociopolitical settings. For our purposes, pastoralists offer a good example for the observation of how water resources may be transformed from a good into a market commodity. Pastoral societies have been affected and upset in a lesser degree by such neoliberal trends in part because of their spatial and socioeconomic marginality, but also as the result of the 'embeddedness'[2] of water in their society (and in sociopolitical patterns that favour collective behaviour). For its particular status as a social medium – interwoven with material production, sociocultural reproduction, political institutions and symbolic values (Mosse 2008) – water among pastoralists offers a privileged domain in which to observe the contradictions between market logic and communal practices.[3]

The forms of appropriation of water resources among Sudanese pastoralists are linked to land appropriation and exploitation and to the specificity of their production system.[4] Water is a critical factor for production and its availability is determinant for people's and herds' movements. Despite the ambiguity of Sudanese land tenure law that, from the earliest colonial codifications, continues to be disadvantageous for pastoral modes of appropriation (M. Babiker 2009), and despite the existence of various forms of private property (livestock, fields and other), water appropriation among Sudanese pastoralists is associated with the appropriation of land for pastoral activities and both share a communal character. In the semiarid zones of central Sudan, water exploitation is carried out mainly by wells and *ḥafirs* (hand-dug reservoirs for rainwater). It is generally the tribal or lineage group that claims a given territory that has the right to dig wells and reservoirs and the duty to defend them against external threats. In this context, even if the right to ask for (and get) water, whether for oneself, one's family or one's livestock, is recognized inasmuch as it is linked to the Islamic principles of piety and solidarity, a 'foreigner', not belonging to the descent group for whom a territory is considered the homeland, could not dig a well or construct a *ḥafir.* Two observations stem from this general feature of water appropriation. First, water resources and the sociotechnical forms of their exploitation challenge the logics of individual property and access – even if, as mentioned previously, private property is not totally absent in pastoral societies. Pastoralists rely on communal logics that permeate multiple spheres (joint work for construction and maintenance, equal access rights and uses, common action for defence, values attributed to water as a free, collective and symbolically marked good). The second observation is that water resources have to be linked to an identified social community, whose borders and criteria of inclusion, exclusion, reproduction and internal articulation are shared by the group claiming communal management. In the pastoral context such a 'socio-political common' forms the basis for a 'natural resource common' and corresponds to what one might consider a 'tribal paradigm', whose basic operational principles are patrilineal (agnatic) descent and segmentation.[5] Although the intervention by colonial administration fostered among pastoral peoples the strict association between tribes and land or water resources – reinforcing, for political reasons, the exclusivity of a relation that would have been more flexible – the principles and practices of communal water management have remained vigorous up to recent times. These, moreover, retained a strong link with a tribal model of social organization, whose vitality persisted in phases of official dismissal by the state (1970–94). For this reason, pastoral societies offer a perspective from which to investigate the mechanisms by which water shifts from its status of social good, managed by a local community, to the status of commodity, subject to dominant market logics and external actors, as well as other goods.

Before going to the core of this chapter, I should make some preliminary remarks. In fact, I am not assuming the existence of a mythical, harmonious, untouched, egalitarian pastoral communal organization preserved from any contact with market forces. First, such societies have recognized the principles of private property in domains other than water, and they have entertained relations with capitalist markets since these were first introduced in Sudan. Second, like all societies, even the most remote, pastoral societies have early established economic, social and political relations with the 'outside world', and they have always been affected by the dynamics of change and adaptation. Third, even if pastoralists stress communal practices and shared values in managing their water supply, in other domains of social life they may show non egalitarian and non communal features. Fourth, the dynamics of 'desocialization' of water management and access can vary from one pastoral society to another, even in timing and modes of practices. These remarks noted, allowing this chapter to avoid a dichotomy between pastoral/collective/egalitarian and state/individual/hierarchical – an approach that masks social processes – I focus on the following point: among pastoralists water often stands as a sort of last rampart against the spreading logic of commoditization. Over the past 'liberalization decades', pastoralists have increasingly faced pressures to surrender their local and communal control of water resources.[6] I give here some examples of how they have coped with this process of 'disembedment'.

Some Fieldwork Cases about Water's 'Great Transformation'

The central issue concerns the relation between water and society as manifested by actual forms of water resource access and management among pastoralists. In a dynamic perspective, I propose an explanation of the processes by which the interweaving of water and society is constructed. I focus on the effects of a broader transformation of pastoral society – as the local expression of socioeconomic change at regional, national and international levels – upon the dismantling of such links, which can be understood as a shift from communal to individual, market-oriented practices and values, from water as a common good to water as a commodity. My approach is inspired by the seminal work of anthropologists who place the interlocking between sociotechnical, political and cultural systems at the core of their analysis of 'water issues' (Bédoucha 1987; Mosse 2003, 2008),[7] and on more recent works stressing the contribution of anthropology to the analysis of 'local waters' in the framework of global affairs (Casciarri and Van Aken 2013). I also refer to the work of Polanyi (1944, 1968) and his suggestions for an economic anthropology approach. Though Polanyi never refers explicitly to water issues, his notion of 'embeddedness' of economy in society, his focus on local institutions for understanding economic processes in non capitalist societies as well as his insight regarding processes of the 'great transformation' in which market logics replace and subordinate complex socioeconomic patterns among local communities have been utilized recently as an analytical framework for understanding the social management of water by a dynamic perspective in a globalized context (Baron 2007; Casciarri 2008).

The situation of some pastoral peoples of central Sudan, where I have conducted anthropological fieldwork over the last twenty years[8] (figure 8.1), provides empirical data to support the analysis of two basic dynamics: on the one hand, the forms of 'embeddedness' or socialization of water among local (pastoral) communities, and on the other, the modes of their recent 'disembedment' or 'desocialization', which parallel the water commoditization process underway in global Sudan as part of a neoliberalization trend.

Deep Ancient Tribal Wells: The Material Evidence for Water-Society Embeddedness

Since early times among pastoral groups of the Butana, the principal means to exploit water resources consisted in digging wells and *ḥafirs*.[9]

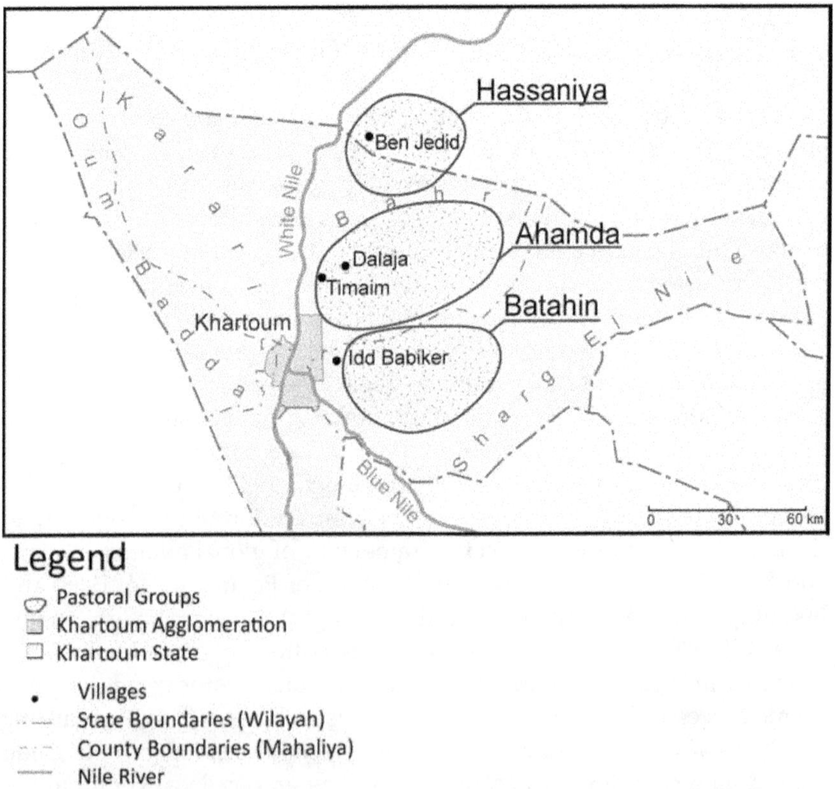

Figure 8.1. Localization of the Three Pastoral Groups in Khartoum State

The former tap into perennial underground water, while the latter function as reservoirs for the collection and storage of rainwater. In rural areas most of these structures have been built and are maintained using local techniques, simple tools and traditional materials, without the intervention of external actors and modern technology. The so-called 'pastoral hydraulics' policies, here as elsewhere in Africa, have been often sporadic and contradictory in their results (Baroin 2003; Casciarri 2013). Whether because of the remoteness of the pastoral territories or a general neglect of 'pastoral development' in policies favouring intensive and commercial agriculture (Mohamed Salih 1990b), interventions by the state for digging modern water structures become visible generally after the 1984 drought and spread gradually in the mid-1990s. For these reasons and from the beginning, pastoralists have been accustomed to manage their domestic and productive water needs in an autonomous way. This explains why water access among these pastoralists is a complex system of sociotechnical relations and norms for resource appropriation and transmission, but also of ancestry and kinship as a basis for social organization, symbolic values of communal use, sharing, reciprocity and solidarity, and ethno-tribal identity. Pastoral wells stand as the living, material and visible expression of the embeddedness of water into wider social dynamics in a context where individual market considerations are not dominant. Drawing on descriptions of three 'well complexes' among the pastoral groups of the region – the Aḥāmda, the Ḥassāniya and the Baṭāḥīn – I try to look at this interlocking of water and society and evaluate its transformation imposed by the contemporary diffusion of liberalization.

'Idd Ad-Dalaja (figure 8.2) is a clear example of how Aḥāmda pastoral society is embodied within a material water structure. 'Idd Ad-Dalaja is neither the oldest nor the deepest well in Aḥāmda territory. Its relevance, however, stems from two factors. First, it is the only well that made all lineages of the tribe gather for its construction – and later for its use – and for this reason it is sometimes defined as 'Idd Al-Aḥāmda par excellence.[10] Second, it is the only well that had not been abandoned by 2013, when all similar wells, which were still functioning in the 1990s, were replaced by alternative modern water supply systems.

'Idd Ad-Dalaja is located approximately fifty kilometres northeast of Khartoum. It is forty-seven *rajil* deep (about eighty metres) and presents a morphology analogous to other traditional desert wells: a wooden superstructure necessary to support a system of pulleys for raising the water to the mouth of the well. A large goatskin, or *delū,* is attached to a long leather rope, or *selaba,* and lowered into the well. The *selaba* is then walked out by a camel that proceeds along one of four paths leading from the well. The water is poured into underground stone culverts, *sabalōka,* where it flows

Figure 8.2. Watering at 'Idd Ad-Dalaja Well (Calias, 2008)

into a series of basins, or *ḥōḍs*, lined with stones and branches, where the watering actually takes place. A perennial source of water, 'Idd Ad-Dalaja is used only in the dry season. When water stored in the *ḥafīrs* during the rainy season has been depleted, the decision to use the deep well is taken collectively by people from the surrounding *farigs* (camps), who are the constant users of this resource (Casciarri 2011).[11]

But the history of the well is more interesting than the forms of its current exploitation for understanding both the strategies of territorial appropriation by pastoral groups and the importance of collective (tribal) management of water resources in a wider context. 'Idd Ad-Dalaja was dug during the final phase of the British colonial period, most probably in 1950. By that time the Aḥāmda had already begun limiting their movements into eastern Butana, spending longer periods in the western part of their territory. Following the 1949 drought various nomadic groups opted to settle near the capital while the Aḥāmda persisted in their pastoral option, even if they were forced to adopt some adaptations. As the western part of their lands, closer to the Nile, begun to be affected by the encroachment of intensive agricultural schemes, they opted to dig a deep well in the desert zone of their *dār damar* – part of the territory occupied during the dry season – comprising one of the tribe's main grazing areas, the Khor Al-Kanjar. The construction of the Dalaja well allowed them to avoid an early sedentarization and the abandonment of pastoral production, permitting them instead to adopt an original form of adaptation, a 'semisedentarization' in desert areas where their pastoral mode of life could continue. The success of this strategy is proved by the persisting pastoral option (both in the productive and social sense) that a fair part of the group has been able to maintain up to recent periods (1990s).[12] The digging of the well – which lasted almost one year – gathered the representatives of various lineages of the Aḥāmda *gabīla* of the time. Despite conflict with neighbouring groups, the Aḥāmda managed to register the well with the colonial authorities. The relevance of the 'social framework' within which the well water management is embedded thus began with the construction of the well. The system of basins and canalizations stands as the spatial translation of the social group's articulation, an articulation that is also manifest in the lasting norms of management: the common defence of the well against foreigner (non-Aḥāmda) intruders, the corvée to provide manpower for maintenance joint work, the inalienability of water rights and the equal access for all members of the Aḥāmda *gabīla,* the collective decision concerning uses and calendar, and the symbolic value of 'free water' and its ritualization through sacrifices performed at the well for its annual opening or for minor occasions.

Despite some differences, the setting of the Ben Jedīd wells, 'communal property' of the Hassānyia pastoralists living east of the Nile at the border between Khartoum State and Nile State, show similar features of interdependence between society and water resources. Unlike other Ḥassāniya of the same region, the thirteen *farīg*s of Ben Jedīd illustrate a configuration of nomadic groups who, even if they have abandoned higher mobility, still give priority to pastoral production, have a weak engagement in wage labour and grant political loyalty to local sheikhs and tribal leaders. Although Khartoum is farther from Ben Jedīd than from 'Idd Ad-Dalaja (eighty kilometres), the proximity of the Jeily oil refinery and of the 'free market zone' developed between 2006 and 2009 represents another case where persistent pastoralists inhabit an area where the dynamics of the centre and the trends to urban incorporation may prevail (Casciarri 2014). At the core of the thirteen *farīg*s are nine shallow wells (figure 8.3) that continue to be used as a principal water resource for domestic and livestock supply. Compared to 'Idd Ad-Dalaja, there are few details on the history and excavation of these wells (oral accounts describe the digging of the wells simply as 'immemorial'). Even so, similar dynamics of sociohydraulic embeddedness can be observed, expressed in daily communal uses and practices. In-as-much as the water table is easily accessible in this area (between five and fifteen metres), the Ḥassāniya did not need the coalition of the whole tribal group to dig and maintain the wells. Nonetheless, the 'abstract appropriation' (Bonte 1981) of land by a joint tribal group is

Figure 8.3. Sheep Flock at One of the Nine Wells of Ben Jedīd (B. Casciarri, 2009)

evoked as a source of legitimization by minor agnatic sections claiming access to the wells. At the same time, even if each *farīg* makes constant use of a specific well among the nine of Ben Jedīd (usually the one that is said to have been dug by a 'grandfather'), there are two significant features of the water-society nexus. First, the link between a *farīg* and 'its' well is quite loose: the wells are close to one another, and it is not uncommon to find people of one *farīg* accessing the wells of another as a matter of water availability or concentration of herds, suggesting that the entire group agrees on a generalized communal management for such crucial resources (including uses but also equal rights, defence and maintenance). Second, tribesmen from all camps share a common discourse stressing the free nature and inalienability of the Ben Jedīd water resources and the founding role of the tribal ancestry, with its agnatic segmentation, as a source of solidarity in asserting the status of the water and the wells as communal, highly socialized goods.

The third example concerns a deep well of the nomadic Baṭāḥīn, another Arabic-speaking group of the Butana. 'Idd Bābiker – named after its builder – was dug around the end of the nineteenth century[13] at a site twenty kilometres east of Khartoum by members of the Baṭāḥīn *gabīla,* mainly of the Butugāb branch. The well, whose morphology resembles the 'Idd Ad-Dalaja of the Aḥāmda, was dug to a depth of twenty-four *rajil* (about forty metres)[14] in a desert area that was rich in pastures and constituted the dry season site of the Baṭāḥīn coming from eastern Butana. The well site is confirmed in the first maps of the region drawn following British colonization. These early maps clearly show that the area at the time was rural, devoid of fixed settlement and far from the first urban core of the Sudanese capital. Much later, following the expansion of Greater Khartoum, this area became very populated both by the expanding urbanization processes and the development of irrigated agriculture schemes and dairy sites. With the expansion of the Ḥājj Yūsif neighbourhood in the 1970s and from the beginning of the 1990s with the influx of new migrant populations coming from the rural exodus and regional conflicts (southern Sudan, the Nuba Mountains, Darfur), the area was transformed into a sort of vast periphery of Khartoum North. Today the toponym 'Idd Bābiker designates an agglomeration of around twenty neighbourhoods with an original population of Baṭāḥīn intermingled with 'newcomers' of different origin. The local denomination of this area as 'Idd Bābiker stands as the memory of the origin of this first settlement but also as an acknowledgement of the Baṭāḥīn status as 'old-timers' and legitimate owners of this 'tribal land'.

The importance of this well and its links with the tribal social group of reference were visible for more than a century after its construction. Throughout the first half of the twentieth century 'Idd Bābiker and its grazing area was a favourite concentration site of the nomad Baṭāḥīn, allowing them to live with their herds during the dry season without negotiating access to the Nile with settled people there. This link became especially critical in the late years of colonization, when following the drastic drought of 1949–50, a number of Baṭāḥīn were forced to abandon the Butana and benefitted from the presence of this 'tribal well' – recognized as such by the British administration – to settle in the area. In this way certain branches of the Baṭāḥīn were able to recover from the disruption brought about by drought and adapt their livelihood patterns, finding a niche where they could establish themselves almost permanently thanks to the well's perennial water supply and seasonal resources represented by *ḥafīrs*. Simultaneously, they took advantage of their proximity to Khartoum and became providers of milk and meat for a growing urban population. In the following years 'Idd Bābiker remained the focal point of a communal (tribal) water management, avoiding the principles of water management typical of other peripheral urban areas. In the name of this collective 'tribal ethos', it continued to attract peoples of the same group, like several households that left the Butana after the 1984–85 drought to settle in the 'Idd Bābiker area thanks to access to land and water granted by their tribesmen. Despite the specificity of this third case, which most notably is not located in a rural area as in the previous examples, and considering that the well was abandoned in the late 1990s with the arrival of modern water systems, the history of 'Idd Bābiker illustrates another configuration of the embeddedness of water management in society, dynamics that are very similar among pastoral tribal groups.

Postnomad Rural Villages and Periurban Quarters: The Gradual 'Disembedment' of Water

In these ethnographic examples we can simultaneously read the social history of a pastoral group and the story of its access to water resources. These three configurations illustrate the dynamics of water-society embeddedness in the phase of its active interlocking. Yet the same dynamics may be observed in situations where the water-society nexus is affected by change – in particular, processes that result in the 'disembedding' or 'desocialization' of water resources. It is not possible to trace schematic borders between the 'ancient' and the 'new' for processes whose times, modes and actors are variable. Nonetheless, to apply this chapter's water-focused analysis in understanding social change, I propose a unique perspective. This insight focuses on situations in which a technical and sociopolitical water management complex undergoes transformation, usually under the effect of private or state actors appropriating the control of water resources according to principles of centralization and commoditization. In my fieldwork I have tried to focus on situations in which the embeddedness of water in society is gradually replaced by its 'disembedment', a process that causes a shift from water as a common socialized good to water as an individually managed commodity. I will now turn to two cases of this process of water 'desocialization' among pastoralists.

The first example concerns the sociohydraulic complex existing today in Timaīm, a settled Aḥāmda village in the rural zone of Khartoum State. This site in Aḥāmda territory is about fifteen kilometres east of the Nile and constituted a place of 'temporary' sedentarization for pastoral households that entered into wage labour earlier than their tribesmen (1970s). Though a fair number of Timaīm inhabitants continued to keep herds and practice seasonal transhumance in the desert, the features of a settled mode of life and the proximity to sedentary poles have produced demographic growth of the village[15] and exposed it to a stronger impact by the central state's and extrapastoral actors' interventions. The influence of these factors has become particularly upsetting during the last decade, when the rapid expansion of Khartoum transformed Timaīm into a quasi-appendix of the larger peripheral area surrounding the national capital (Casciarri 2014).

Up until recent times (1990s), the sociohydraulic context for residents of Timaīm did not differ significantly from the context described for their tribesmen, despite their settlement in a permanent village closer to the Nile. First, as the Aḥāmda of Timaīm still raised livestock (even if they no longer did so as a primary or unique source of livelihood), during seasonal movements they continued to share the use of *ḥafīrs* and deep wells and to be involved in the system of communal rights of access and management. Second, within the village five shallow traditional wells still functioned for domestic water uses, supplemented by a borehole, dug by the state following the 1984–85 drought, whose supply proved unpredictable as a result of an insufficient network and the uncertain availability of fuel. The changes that took place in the early years of the twenty-first century and affected, more generally, social relations and modes of life transformed the patterns of water access within the village. A social and hydraulic fragmentation has been rapidly followed by a degradation of practices and values of communal sharing and autonomous management of water resources. First, the decrease of livestock diminished the engagement of Timaīm's people in managing the *ḥafīrs* and wells of the 'tribal territory'. Second, a growing socioeconomic stratification created a stronger differentiation among households of the same village. Wealthier households with greater access to cash and modern means of transport were able to resort to alternative water supply and pay for water services.[16] The poorest households continued to rely on an uncertain and difficult access: being cut off from the tap network, they were obliged to fetch water by donkey carts (*karro*) and, occasionally, to use the traditional village wells – which were no longer properly maintained, as most villagers refused to take charge of the collective task of their cleaning. The main driver of change, however, was the intervention of the Khartoum State Water Corporation (KSWC), which started in 2009. In the wake of a general policy of liberalization (Beckedorf 2012) applied both in urban and rural areas, the KSWC extended its control over local water management in the village, reappropriating the public pump well (drilled after 1984), ending 'free' access by *karro* and imposing upon every household the connection to the tap network and the payment of a monthly bill with rates like the ones of urban Khartoum. Regardless of the unrest and debate that this raised among villagers – and the dissolution of the local water committee (*lajna al-mōya*), an informal group constituted to autonomously manage local water resources – within only a few months this 'technical' change contributed to rapidly breaking up practices of water sharing based on a communal tribal ethos that had persisted for many years, despite early settlement in

Timaīm. The individuation of water access appears thus as a phenomenon concurrent with the commercialization of the resource. At the same time, for people of a pastoral background, this means the disentanglement of water from the wider social body, its principles and practices.

As a second example I turn again to 'Idd Bābiker, where similar dynamics concerning the processes of water desocialization can be found. 'Idd Bābiker, unlike Timaīm, is a periurban area on the eastern outskirts of Khartoum where the pastoral Baṭāḥīn began the settlement process before the Aḥāmda of Timaīm. For these reasons the change process and the disentanglement of water from society took place earlier. Nonetheless, if one goes back through the history of 'Idd Bābiker, the ancient well that has since the 1950s supported the progressive settlement of the Baṭāḥīn, it can be noted, thanks to oral witness, that as late as the 1970s the diversification of water access due to demographic expansion had not upset the principles of the relations between tribe and water with their corollary of communal practices and values. From the beginning, the multiplication of water sources advanced along the lines of the segmentation of patrilineal groups. Thus, if all the Baṭāḥīn who settled in the region initially relied on the common well source, managing it together, with time each social group stemming from the original core (now also spatially differentiated) undertook to dig a traditional well of its own, meaningfully named after its own lineage (ʿAllujāb, Tabbarāb, Reddāb and so on). Nonetheless, there persisted a general coherence between society and common water access: first, because the original common tribal well, 'Idd Bābiker, remained in activity and was accessible to every group; and second, because the principles of free water, equal access and duties for collective maintenance continued to be the rule for the 'segmented' wells. In 'Idd Bābikir, however, proximity to the urban centre and the expansion of neighbouring quarters (notably Ḥājj Yūsif) lacking in ethnotribal homogeneity produced early disengagement from the traditional processes of autonomous collective responsibility and, along with it, the disembedding of water management from the social fabric.

The drilling of modern wells appeared gradually in the 1970s and spread during the 1990s.[17] Of course, state intervention for establishing wells and dictating their administration functioned according to rationales that did not correspond to the social and tribal boundaries recognized by the Baṭāḥīn, who tended to reproduce locally the water embeddedness of their pastoral background. In this sense, the KSWC's wells generally followed criteria dictated both by the physical characteristics of the resources and the new administrative divisions established after the introduction of the federal system in the early 1990s. Such intervention draws a new framework for the local situation: on the one hand, the users became progressively deprived of autonomy in managing water access norms. On the other hand, the mixing of different ethnic and tribal groups as users of a single water source upset the coherence the Baṭāḥīn had preserved between the social (tribal) group and its common water units. In this process the principles of free water access, communal work, resource sharing and exchange, which had been previously been supported by the underlying tribal background, were progressively weakened.

Tribes and Water: Understanding Pastoralists' Responses to Water Commoditization

The empirical data illustrate the particular relation between water management and social practices among pastoralists at the moment of strong embeddedness and during phases of change and disembedment. I will now develop some observations on the social tribal background, which functions as a basic support of the socialization of water, and local actors' responses to water commoditization, in the relative specific sense given in the introduction to this chapter.

Pastoral societies adhere to a 'tribal paradigm' that appears as a multifunctional, flexible setting for collective-oriented social behaviour (Casciarri 2009a, 2009b). Among Sudanese pastoralists, a tribe is 'a kin structure, a legal system and a political configuration as well as a symbolic device for meaning and value attribution' (Casciarri 2009a: 70). Despite repeated efforts by the central state to dismantle tribes and dynamics of tribal reshaping resulting from processes of 'neotribalism' or 'retribalization', tribal structures as a global framework for action and conceptualization proved persistent and strictly embedded commons' management (Casciarri 2009a: 71), even if they were flexible in adapting to new patterns of change. As the study of pastoral Sudanese groups has shown, in water management matters, tribal networks remain a sound basis for the definition of water rights and uses. Dynamically linked, water and tribe are mutually self-reinforcing and are evidence of a deeper embeddedness of water management (that is more than an economic resource in the terms of Polanyi) into society as a whole.

Looking at the first example, 'Idd Ad-Dalaja, the embeddedness of water and society is immediately apparent through the morphology and functioning of the well. Its articulation with the Aḥāmda tribe and its social components is expressed in a coherent system of access rights, collective tasks for defence or maintenance and conceptions of a tribal ethos inspired by the principles of free access, inalienability and ritualization.[18] Transmission of a detailed narrative of the excavation provides a collective history of the tribe and of its territorial legitimacy. The case of the Ben Jedīd wells presents a different context that lacks an analogous involvement of the entire tribe but shows the same strong reference to a set of practices and values: water is again linked to the tribal dynamics operating within the relation between the Ḥassāniya *farīgs* and their nine common wells. Finally, in the case of the 'Idd Bābiker well, though this common water source has been abandoned and its users have been incorporated into a quasi-urban environment, it is possible to reconstruct a social history of the well that parallels the Baṭāḥīn tribe's history as far as territorial appropriation, agnatic segmentation and symbolic values are concerned. Thus, whatever the specific sociohistorical situation, we can say that among 'persistent pastoralists' and 'postnomads' the tribal paradigm seems to function as a sort of 'sociopolitical common' supporting the existence of a 'natural resource common'. The strong and rooted interconnection of tribal society and socialized water (especially the water from these wells) appears as a strategic buffer in addressing new water-society relations, especially when these lead to the increasing of livelihood precariousness and undermine local solidarity.

The focus on the tribe(s)-water relations during the processes of resource commoditization offers an excellent indicator of the linkages between water and society among pastoral groups. Far from mere material adjustments – as assumed by external stakeholders and planners – technical transformations in water management and access have the potential for disruptions that broadly alter local social relations, practices and values. The examples presented show the simultaneous disruption of social networks and water management for cases in which rooted practices of communal access to a water resource begin to be replaced by modern centralized systems increasingly framed, although in contradictory ways, by liberal individualizing conceptions of water supply as 'technical affairs' to be managed by a new state bureaucracy.

Nonetheless, it would be too hasty to claim that, even in liberalized Sudan, water-focused social transformations bring an automatic and definitive 'end of the commons'. Despite processes intended to disrupt local autonomy and undermine communal criteria of water management, pastoral groups strive to maintain collective forms of water sharing. Without explicitly expressing open protest movements against the privatization of water, a fair part of these pastoralists continue to practice a less visible communal reappropriation of water resources, which coexists with new forms of commoditization and can be read as a 'silent resistance'[19] to the forces of desocialization of water that dominate in global Sudan. Among the Aḥāmda and despite the upsetting changes in the region[20] or the attacks targeting the joint management of land and water resources, a group of persistent pastoralists continues to gather around 'Idd Ad-Dalaja and perpetuate communal practices in water sharing, even going so far as to perform the annual ritual sacrifice commemorating the well as more than a mere resource for material production.[21] By stressing that this historical well is the 'soul of their territory' (*rūḥ al-balad*) and that 'water links the tribe' (*al-mōya tarbiṭ al-gabīla*), their attempt to maintain 'Idd Ad-Dalaja as a basic source of production and reproduction is performed with a parallel wish to oppose the decline of tribal networks of solidarity. In a similar context, the Ḥassāniya of Ben Jedīd were reminded of the importance of tribal autonomy and communal management of traditional wells after witnessing the disastrous effects of privatization and land expropriation among their kinsmen following the establishment of the Jeily oil refinery and the nearby 'free market zone'. Elsewhere, in places where water desocialization processes are more advanced, as in the settled Aḥāmda village of Timaīm, some families decided in 2011 to resume collective maintenance of an abandoned traditional well after they experienced the technical breakdown of the new state supply system and the appearance of numerous microconflicts. Finally, in the more urbanized context of 'Idd Bābiker, where the replacement of the locally managed water system by a modern state network was made even earlier, the Baṭāḥīn have succeeded in 'reembedding' water into sociotribal structures within the interstices of an apparently homogenous, unified and centralized system of water distribution. Towards these ends, the Baṭāḥīn have created informal committees for water management, whose members are chosen on principles of lineage and tribal affiliation, and who apply their own 'social' criteria of water distribution and sharing. This autonomous action functions as a device to reshape the actual modes of water access and circulation according to coherent and meaningful 'social logics', even if it is invisible for the KSWC, whose intervention is limited to collecting monthly fees for the water infrastructure.

Conclusion

In this chapter I have attempted to understand social processes linked to water commoditization, processes that have been spreading rapidly in Sudan since the beginning of the century, in step with global liberalization. These general trends are gradually disrupting local modes of common access by people for whom water is a free, socialized and autonomously managed resource – although I stress some limits and ambiguities based on the diversity of 'communal' practices and the persistent control on the part of the Sudanese state. This chapter's perspective focuses on a specific category of people, populations with a strong pastoral background.

The particular forms of production and social reproduction of these groups make water structures – mainly wells – a complex system for grasping the embeddedness of water management practices and values within broader local society. The underlying bases for this social configuration show the relevance of the 'tribal paradigm' as a multilevel framework for social action and discourse, which proves to be much more dynamic and persistent than its stereotyped notion would assume. The link between 'tribes and water', the parallel history of their making and unmaking, is equally illustrated in situations where water uses are still strictly socialized and backed by the communal logic inscribed in a shared 'tribal paradigm' and in other cases where both domains are affected by disruptive changes that undermine the water-society nexus and subordinate social relations to market logic. Yet the 'end of the commons' wished for by Sudanese policy makers and their international partners encounters forms of 'silent resistance' among pastoral peoples who adopt alternative strategies, reincorporating water use within the wider social organization.

Without a doubt, the forces engaged are uneven, and a general appraisal might lead one to conclude that the complete desocialization of water is the unavoidable outcome for pastoral people. On the one hand, alongside water supply transformations, pastoralists must face a more general process of commoditization: land expropriation, attacks on subsistence-oriented production, the dominance of wage labour, economic stratification, overlapping dynamics of inner differentiation and stronger political hierarchy. On the other hand, there are a number of nonpastoral forces operating somewhat ambiguously in the intervention on local water management. While it may seem that market-oriented water management is the sole purview of global capitalists (private investors and the state), NGOs and other agencies involved in local development, while claiming to solve 'water problems' in the name of common resource preservation, often favour the same individualizing approach (Nègre 2004), failing to criticize the wider liberal option and supporting analogous trends of the individuation of rights and the market rationale as a basis for water use. If water remains a crucial issue for understanding commoditization processes among pastoralists, it is only the final outcome of liberalization trends in Sudan that will show whether pastoralists, and others groups, will succeed in maintaining or reintegrating water as a pivot of social relations free of the threat of capitalist exploitation, with its intrinsic production of uncertainty, poverty and conflict.

Notes

1. The use of the term 'neoliberalism' is preferred to 'liberalism'. While the latter normally evokes the ideology and practices linked to the historical establishment of a capitalist system since the eighteenth century, the former is more widely used to define similar trends that emerged during the last decades of the twentieth century in the phase labelled 'globalization'.
2. I explain later the use of this notion taken from Polanyi (1944, 1968) and applied to the water domain.
3. Elsewhere, I have illustrated (Casciarri 2009a) the criteria of delimitation of such 'communities' as well as their dynamic frontiers, and explained how the relation between 'market logics' and 'communal practice' is not to be conceived as a dichotomy.
4. Apart from texts in natural sciences, engineering or development, social sciences literature on water issues in Sudan is poor: I could mention a work by geographers (Shepherd, Norris and Watson 1987), one about NGO interventions in the Khartoum periphery (Nègre 2004) and a recent one on South Kordofan (Ille 2013). Though useful information about water issues can be found in documents or reports by NGOs and development organizations, a global social approach to water management among Sudanese rural populations is still lacking.
5. The term 'tribe' translates to the vernacular Arabic term *gabīla*. Far from evolutionary and conservative approaches, which brought anthropologists to reject the concept as defined in colonial times, I refer here to the rich debate that since the 1990s (Bonte, Conte and Ould Cheikh 1991; Bonte, Conte and Dresch 2001; Abdul-Jabar and Dawod 2003) has revealed the pertinence of the notion for a huge set of people of the Muslim-Arabic area and redefined it as a useful analytical tool for a dynamic conception of the 'tribal model' (Casciarri and Ahmed 2009: 17–18; Casciarri 2009a, 2009b).
6. Although when the state and/or the private sector impose control on hydraulic resources the 'new' water regime is also a social construction, this 'resocialization' modifies radically the intimate link between community and water and shows new features of hierarchy and dependence.
7. Despite their importance for a global anthropological approach to water issues, these studies concern almost exclusively irrigation systems and peasant societies. Pastoral groups continue to be neglected in the domain of anthropological studies on water issues (Casciarri 2013).
8. I studied the Aḥāmda during my longest period of fieldwork, begun in 1989 for my Ph.D. (Casciarri 1997) and followed by a restudy (2006–13). Between 2009 and 2011 I carried out fieldwork among the settled Baṭāḥīn in Khartoum State, within an international project focused on water (WAMAKHAIR). Finally, I studied the Ḥassāniya over shorter survey periods between 2007 and 2009 (Casciarri 2014).
9. Though historical data on the origin of these techniques is lacking, oral witness suggests that deep wells existed at least since the Turco-Egyptian period. For the Aḥāmda, most wells were dug during the colonial period, and this is said to be linked to changes in nomadization cycles and decreasing mobility.
10. As stated by Mosse (1997), water structures often become 'public institutions' in the sense that they entail extrawater political roles.
11. Local care for water resource preservation functions thanks to the 'tribal ethos' that considered natural resources to be commons. In some cases, the tribe can decide the exceptional opening of the well all year: this happened during the 1984–85 drought, when due to the lack of water in the *ḥafirs*, the Aḥāmda were 'saved', as they say, thanks to the well's supply.
12. This option has some basic features: kind of habitat, communal resources management, priority of extensive livestock raising and rain-fed agriculture (mostly subsistence ori-

ented), minor engagement in wage labour, household division of labour, strong stress on values and practices of mutual aid within the (agnatic) tribal group and affiliation to traditional sheikhs (Casciarri 2009a).

13. The well was probably dug between 1850 and 1870. In fact, oral witness says that it already existed during the Mahdism – a period whose memory is stressed in the Baṭāḥīn's oral history as a result of their persecution by Khalifa Abdullahi. Mentions of the use of slave manpower confirm the construction of this well during the Turco-Egyptian period (1821–85).
14. The ancient 'Idd Bābiker well ceased functioning about twenty-five years ago. The site and what remained of the well could be visited as recently as 2010. Most information about this well is derived from oral witness by elders, who used the well in early times and until the 1990s.
15. While in most cases permanent Aḥāmda villages are similar to former *farīgs* (in dwelling patterns, demography, socioeconomic relations), such continuity does not exist for Timaīm. Even if we can still identify the framework of an agnatic segmented structure, the dimensions of the village – 275 households according to the 2008 census – make it impossible to preserve a social fabric like in smaller villages and *farīgs*.
16. For example, the ones that had frequent relations outside the tribal territory, normally due to wage labour, and benefitted from modern means of transportation could obtain water from people of sedentary villages or towns (for free or by paying the granter). Also, pastoral milk vendors, which collect daily milk from the desert *farīgs* (wealthier groups compared to the simple producers) and go by vans to Khartoum, ask their customers to fill the big tin cans with water after they are empty at the end of the day.
17. To be more precise about the relative urban character of 'Idd Bābiker, I should note that, despite the proximity to the centre, most infrastructure linked to the development of modern water services arrived late in the quarter: for example, electrification only took place in the second half of the 1990s, and the asphalt road to Khartoum was only built in 2006.
18. In-so-far as sacred and ritual aspects are concerned, the annual opening of the well in the dry season is marked by a sacrifice performed by tribesmen at the edge of the well. Nobody can access water before this act is carried out. Also, minor events (births, reconciliations of local conflicts, recovering from illness) can be an occasion for doing a *karāma* (animal sacrifice) at the well.
19. In an article about the Aḥāmda and the Awlād Nūba, a pastoral group from South Kordofan (Casciarri 2009a), I argued that some persisting local institutions (*nafīr, sālif, diya* and *barmaka*) stand as a sort of 'silent resistance' towards the intrusion of market liberal logics as guiding principles of social practices and values.
20. Between 2004 and 2011 important changes (other than effects due to the urban expansion of Khartoum) affected Dalaja area: the erection of a dam on Khor Al-Kanjar, the construction of an asphalt road connecting Khartoum North to the Jeily oil refinery and the development of extraction enterprises exploiting the soil for building materials (Casciarri 2014).
21. Even if the group contesting the dominant individually based new pattern of management is a minority of the tribe and its protest remains within the limits of a nonopen conflict, anthropologists should pay attention to these manifestations as 'weapons of the weak', especially in the context of global liberalization. As remarked in other cases for the peasant society of the global South, the conflicts that crystallize around basic values can be read significantly as 'a struggle over the appropriation of symbols, a struggle over how the past and present shall be understood and labelled, a struggle to identify causes and assess blame, a contentious effort to give partisan meaning to local history' (Scott 1987: xviii).

Part III

New Actors, New Spaces and New Imagination on Conflicts

Chapter 9

Asian Players in Sudan

Social and Economic Impacts of 'New-Old' Actors

Irene Panozzo

Economic reports on Sudan published by various international economic and financial institutions in the late 2000s usually began with descriptions of the good performance of Sudan's economy. According to the World Bank–coordinated Sudan National Multi-Donor Trust Fund's (MDTF) 2009 annual report, 'Over the past decade, Sudan has enjoyed some of the highest economic growth rates in Africa, bolstered by higher oil production, a good harvest, and a continuing boom in construction and services.' (MDTF-N 2010: 2) The introduction to the 2009 World Bank (WB) report entitled *Sudan: The Road toward Sustainable and Broad-Based Growth* was even more eloquent: 'Sudan is in the tenth year of its longest and strongest growth episode since independence, benefiting from the advent of oil in 1999. The size of its economy, measured by nominal gross national product, has grown fivefold – from $10 billion in 1999 to $53 billion in 2008. Per capita income … has increased from $334 to $532 (constant USD2000) over the same time period' (WB 2009: 1).

All that glitters is not gold, of course, and at the beginning of the 2010s the Sudanese economy still suffered from many weaknesses and shortcomings, which became evident after South Sudan's independence and Juba's decision, in January 2012, to stop the new nation's oil production. Yet most commentaries and analyses of Sudan's presecession decade-long economic situation and evolution began with a reference to three interconnected issues: oil, sustained economic growth and better statistics. Though it was not featured in the opening lines, instead usually analysed elsewhere in the reports, some Asian countries, most notably China and India, played a key role in the transformation of Sudan's economy, which

Notes for this chapter begin on page 180.

at the time of South Sudan's independence was one of the highest recipients of direct foreign investment in the continent (MDTF 2010). Starting with huge investments in the oil sector, since the mid-1990s and early 2000s, respectively, China and India have developed a deep and multifaceted partnership with and presence in Sudan, both north and south. Sudan has served as a stage to test both Asian giants' new role in Africa (Goldstein et al. 2006; Broadman et al. 2007; Ravaillon 2008; Brautigam 2009; Strauss and Saavedra 2009; Harneit-Sievers, Marks and Naidu 2010),[1] based mainly on business, with special focus on resource-driven projects. At the same time, improved relations with Asian players have allowed Sudan to break from the international isolation experienced in the early 1990s and to become, prior to South Sudan's secession, sub-Saharan Africa's third-largest oil producer. This chapter will analyse how relations between the presecession Sudan and the two Asian giants developed and how they have helped transform both Sudans' economies.

China and India: Old Friends, New Oil(ed) Partnerships

Neither China nor India is a newcomer to Sudan. India opened a liaison office in Khartoum in March 1955, before Sudan's independence. The next month, Sudan's interim prime minister, Isma'il Al-Azhari, stopped in New Delhi on his way to Bandung, Indonesia, to take part in the first Afro-Asian Relations Conference. India's prime minister, Jawahar Nehru, reciprocated the visit in July 1957 (Embassy of India in Khartoum n.d.). In February 1959, Sudan became the third country in Africa to formally recognize the People's Republic of China, after Nasser's Egypt and Morocco. A few years later, Sudan was among the countries visited by China's premier, Chou En-lai, during his December 1963–January 1964 ten-legged African tour, the first ever official visit by a Chinese leader to the continent (Larkin 1973: 40, 68–69).

The positive diplomatic relations between Khartoum and both Beijing and New Delhi had an economic purpose as well, especially during the first decade of President Nimeiri's rule (1969–1985): while in the 1970s India was Sudan's largest trading partner (Embassy of India in Khartoum n.d.), China inaugurated an aid programme soon after the 1972 Addis Ababa peace agreement and, during the same years, built a grand conference hall on the Blue Nile's western bank in Khartoum, dubbed the Friendship Hall. At that time, however, China's economic relations with Sudan were not particularly relevant to either country (Askouri 2007; Large 2008).

Things changed during the 1990s, when a series of coinciding events and situations served the interests of both Sudan and China. In the aftermath of the 1989 coup that, only a few weeks after Tiananmen Square's dramatic events, brought President Omar Al-Bashir to power and saw Khartoum support Saddam Hussein's Iraq during the 1991 Gulf War, Sudan's foreign relations had changed considerably, especially with regard to the United States. When Washington decided to put Sudan on the 'sponsor of terrorism' blacklist and to adopt unilateral economic sanctions against the country in 1997, China had already entered Sudan's to-be-developed oil sector, deserted by important foreign companies such as Chevron and Total soon after the second north-south civil war had begun in 1983.

As Large (2008) underlines, '[Sudan's] turn to China for oil investment may have been debated within ruling circles, and questioned by some'. But it was necessary, and China's 'competitive political advantage' (Alden 2007), based on the principle of noninterference in domestic affairs,[2] made it a potential and interesting political ally. This met a convergent interest on China's side. When in 1995, during President Al-Bashir's visit to Beijing, the China National Petroleum Corporation (CNPC) signed its first contracts for operations in Sudan's Block 6 (figure 9.1), the People's Republic of China had already become an oil importer, though its government was still unconvinced that conspicuous investment abroad was the right path to follow. The CNPC's acquisition in Sudan was thus decided and implemented without the central government's approval and support in a highly risky move by the company, which later proved to be the right one (International Crisis Group 2008).

After fifteen years of gradually opening to capitalist economy and double-digit growth, China was starting to recognize the need to secure sources of energy and other critical resources, as well as new markets for the commercialization of Chinese manufactured goods. Moreover, steady economic growth had given China a large amount of foreign currency reserves, which could be invested abroad. The CNPC's 1995 acquisitions in Sudan thus anticipated what was later to become the Chinese government's 'go out' policy: with a resource-driven commercial diplomacy, in the late 1990s Beijing began to encourage state companies to invest abroad and assisted them generously through various schemes, such as tax breaks, credit, customs preferences and low-interest loans.

In 1997, the CNPC acquired the majority share (40 per cent) in the newborn Greater Nile Petroleum Operating Company (GNPOC), which won a concession in Blocks 1, 2 and 4. The CNPC's partners were Malaysia's Petronas (30 per cent), the Sudanese national oil company Sudapet (5 per cent) and Canada's Arakis Energy Corporation (25 per cent). While seismic and exploration work was in progress in the oil fields, and in order to produce oil by the deadline of the Salvation Regime's tenth anniversary (30 June 1999), the CNPC's affiliate construction company, China Petro-

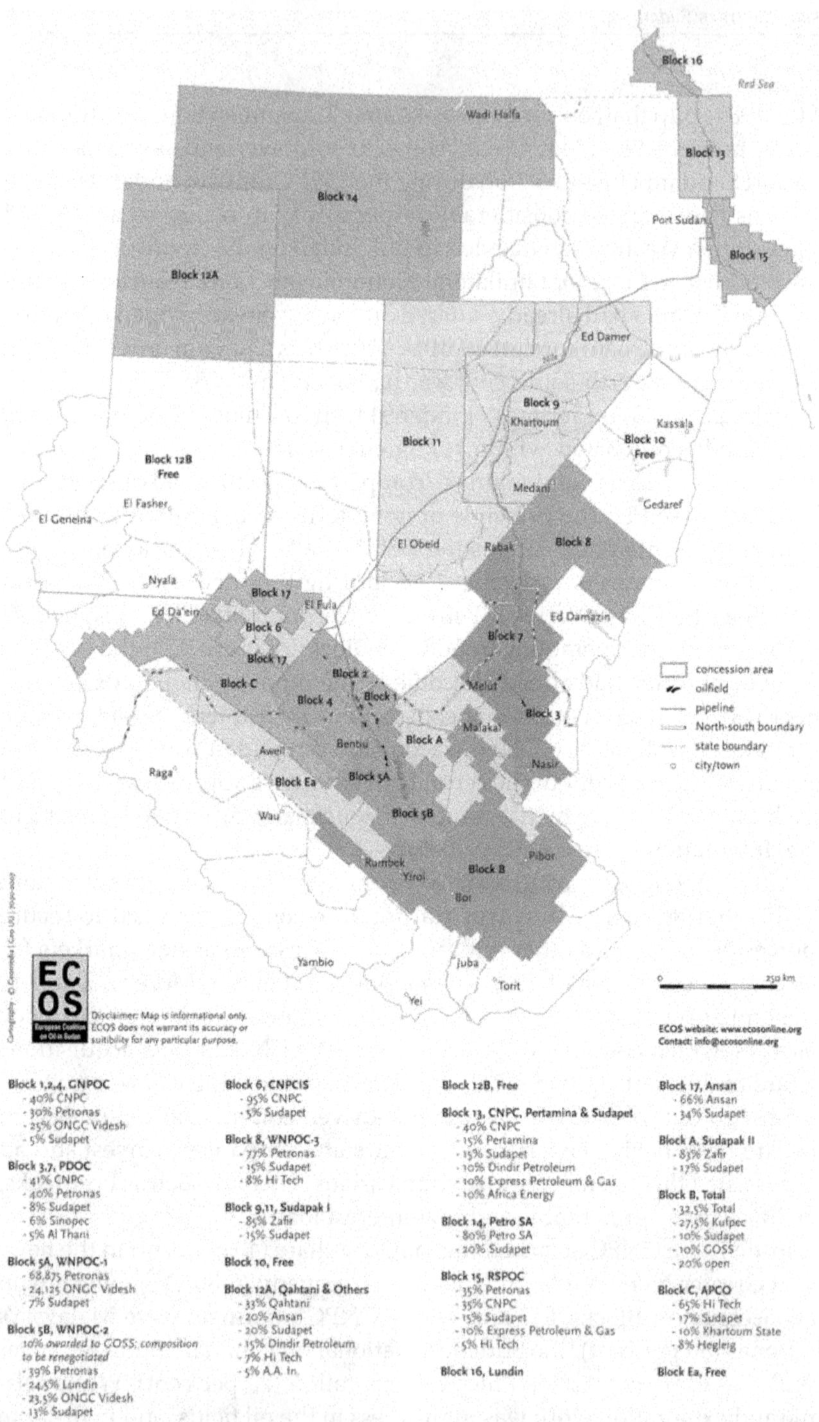

Figure 9.1. Sudan's Oil Blocks Concessions (European Coalition on Oil in Sudan, 2007)

leum Engineering and Construction Corporation (CPECC), brought ten thousand Chinese labourers to assist in building the 1,540-kilometre pipeline linking the consortium's blocks to Port Sudan, which was completed in August 1999. A month later, Sudan became an oil-producing and oil-exporting country (Panozzo 2009; International Crisis Group 2008).

In addition to being a partner in the GNPOC, the CNPC is also the largest stakeholder in Block 3 and 7 (41 per cent), Block 6 (95 per cent) and Block 13 (40 per cent) and has the same share as Petronas in Block 15 (35 per cent). While its role in Sudan's oil sector is very important, the CNPC is just one of the players in the arena. Malaysia's Petronas and, to a lesser extent, India's ONGC Videsh Ltd have invested heavily in Sudan since the mid-1900s and early 2000s. As previously mentioned, Petronas was part of the GNPOC since its inception and later acquired several other stakes in block concessions around the country. ONGC Videsh Ltd entered Sudan later by buying the stakes that Canada's Talisman Energy Inc. (which had acquired Arakis Energy Corporation's stakes in the GNPOC) and Austria's OMV (Österreichische Mineralölverwaltung), with holdings in the southern Block 5A and 5B, were compelled to sell under pressure from powerful human rights campaigns in Europe and North America against their operations in oil fields whose control was a bone of contention between armies, rebel groups and militias fighting on both sides of the north-south civil war. The same happened to the Swedish Lundin Oil when it was forced to sell its stakes in the White Nile Petroleum Operating Company (WNPOC), the consortium operating two southern blocks, to Petronas (ECOS 2010).

Beyond Oil: Trade, Infrastructure and Agriculture

While it is an essential element, oil is not the only factor in the change in Sudan's relations with China and India. China – and India a few years later – viewed Sudan as a testing ground for a new approach to African countries, their resources and their markets. In the 1990s, Sudan had an untapped market potential: the largest country in Africa offered little to no business competition, even though there were investment risks and challenges (Large 2008; Panozzo 2009).

Bilateral trade volumes with China and India grew steadily in the 2000s. Averagely, petroleum and petroleum products had the lion's share in Sudan's trade with both countries,[3] but there were several other items traded between Khartoum and Beijing and Khartoum and New Delhi. China statistics (Maglad 2008) show that, in 1990, Sudan's imports totalled USD 618.5 million, while exports stopped at USD 374.1 million. Sixteen years later, in 2006, imports were at USD 1.68 billion and exports at USD 4.24 billion (Central Bank of Sudan 2006). In 2009 imports from China decreased to USD 1.92 billion from USD 2.16 billion in 2008 (table 9.1), while exports to Beijing rose to USD 8.75 billion in 2008, only to decrease the following year to USD 5.93 billion (table 9.2) as a result of the global economic and financial crisis (Central Bank of Sudan 2008, 2009).

Bilateral trade between India and Sudan totalled USD 621.53 million in 2006, divided between USD 22.5 million in exports, with gum arabic as the largest single item, and USD 599.04 million in imports, an 88 per cent increase over the 2005 figures (Large 2008). The largest portion of imports was made up of petroleum products (USD 226.19 million), followed by manufactured goods (USD 113.01 million) and machinery and equipment (USD 102.8 million; Central Bank of Sudan 2006). In 2009, imports from India decreased to USD 624.5 million from USD 885.80 million in 2008. Petroleum products ranked fifth, totalling USD 18.17 million (see table 9.1). As far as exports to India are concerned, in 2009 they totalled some USD 194.78 million, a little increase from USD 182.98 million in 2008 (Central Bank of Sudan 2008, 2009; see table 9.2).

As a comparison, it may be useful to enlist some data about Sudan's imports and exports to and from industrial countries as a group, that is, the European Union countries plus Switzerland, Norway, the United States, Canada, Australia, New Zealand and Japan (see tables 9.1 and 9.2): in 2009, the total amount of imports from industrial countries was USD 2.4 billion, some USD 100 million less than imports from China and India together, while exports totalled USD 377.4 million, sixteen times less than the exports to China and India registered that same year.

The first general conclusion we can draw from bilateral trade data is that oil and petroleum products are definitely not the only items traded between Sudan and foreign countries. Imports of machinery and equipment, manufactured goods and transport equipment are higher than imports of petroleum products and crude materials. Further analysis shows that China, India and Malaysia are just three among many other countries entertaining trade relations with Sudan.

Nevertheless, oil remains extremely important. Oil exploitation and export drove GDP growth in the 2000s; before South Sudan's independence, Sudan ranked as sub-Saharan Africa's third-largest producer of oil, with 490,000 BPD in production. Moreover, by becoming an oil-exporting country, Sudan has been able to open up its economic sectors to foreign investment. The chapter on Sudan in the 2009 *African Economic Outlook* is very clear about this when it says that 'the exploitation of oil reserves and "the peace dividend" were the main drivers of [Sudan's] economic success. … Most of the new employment opportunities are concentrated

Table 9.1. Imports by Country and Commodity (2009), value in USD

	Tea	Wheat & wheat flour	Other food stuff	Beverages & tobacco	Petroleum products	Crude materials	Chem-icals	Manufac-tured goods	Machinery & equip.	Transport equip.	Textiles	TOTAL
China	85	1	26,100	7,294	309	8,243	97,582	640,926	752,445	232,361	161,590	1,926,936
India	40,901	17	14,725	7,334	18,175	3,197	60,410	137,256	253,689	50,627	38,174	624,509
Malaysia	6	0	39,564	10	1	8,467	10,983	11,938	9,507	571	5,884	86,931
S. Korea	2	0	445	0	1	4,874	11,982	7,806	61,905	11,464	1,918	202,397
Industrial countries (EU, USA, Canada, Australia, New Zealand, Japan)	26,113	451,214	266,062	18,366	32,946	14,967	126,574	421,642	503,299	525,105	5,582	2,391,875
TOTAL	67,107	451,232	346,896	33,004	51,432	39,748	307,531	1,219,568	1,580,845	820,128	213,148	

Source: Central Bank of Sudan, 2010.

Table 9.2. Exports by Country and Commodity (2009), value in USD

	Petroleum & petroleum products	Cotton	Gum arabic	Sesame	Gold	Hides & skins	Other	TOTAL
China	5,893,061	7.059	238	24.401	0	96	10.84	5,935,695
India	138.797	3.53	9.558	0	0	814	42.085	194.784
Malaysia	40.525	0	0	0	0	0	85	40.61
S. Korea	0	0	1.194	3.454	0	0	5.781	10.43
Industrial countries (EU, USA, Canada, Australia, New Zealand, Japan)	208.198	711	16.659	5.536	85.533	509	60.246	377.405

Source: Central Bank of Sudan, 2010.

in the service sector. ... Increased investment, however, in labour-intensive infrastructure and construction projects and trade in services ... provide opportunities for employment generation and broad-based growth' (AfDB/OECD 2009: 717–18).

China and India have played a role in the construction and service sectors' boom, as investments in infrastructure (pipelines and refineries, as well as roads, railways, communications and water- and power-related projects) have been an important part of both countries' new approach to Sudan and, more generally, to Africa since the mid-1990s to early 2000s. 'Aid packages' – usually made up of grant aid, technical assistance, concessional and interest-free loans and debt relief – were part of China's 'go out' policy from the very beginning. More specifically, concessional and interest-free loans, usually granted by China's EXIM Bank or by China Development Bank, were used to fund large-scale infrastructure projects (Davies et al. 2008). On some occasions, financing came from other sources, such as Arab funds and governments, mainly from the Gulf. Such is the case, for example, of the Roseires Dam Heightening Project: in April 2008, a consortium of Chinese companies specializing in dam construction was awarded a contract worth USD 396 million to heighten by ten metres the wall of the Roseires Dam, built in the 1960s on the Blue Nile, but the budget for the project was secured through several Arab funds contributions (DIU 2009).

The Export-Import (EXIM) Bank of India also played an important role in financing Indian exports and investments to Sudan – which, between 1996 and 2005, attracted 'the fourth-largest share ($964 million) of Indian foreign direct investment (FDI)' (Large 2008), mainly used for oil infrastructure (ONGC Videsh Ltd built a USD 200 million oil and gas pipeline between the Khartoum refinery and Port Sudan and completed the construction of a USD 1.2 billion refinery in 2005). India's EXIM Bank extended a line of credit of about USD 50 million on several occasions to finance a package including solar power, railways and other projects. In December 2009, representatives of Sudan's and India's governments signed a deal in Delhi to pave the way for increased oil production and exploration and infrastructure development in the coming years (Stevenson 2009).

United Sudan thus became one of the highest recipients of foreign direct investments (FDIs) in Africa. A very important source of both external financing and foreign exchange, 'net FDI and portfolio inflows hit $3.5 billion in 2006, largely because of foreign entrants in the telecommunications and banking sectors, in addition to FDI supporting foreign operators in the oil sector' (World Bank 2009: 27). After 2006, however, net FDIs declined and, according to the World Bank's report, were 'projected to be $2.4 billion for 2009', one-third less than just three years earlier. Similarly,

China's FDIs to Sudan peaked in the years leading to 2006, when Sudan was the most important recipient of Beijing's official FDIs in Africa (Large 2008). The decrease in recent years was a consequence of the global financial and economic crisis, which was a severe blow to FDI flows worldwide and also, most probably, of the Chinese State Council's decision to remove Sudan, together with Iran and Nigeria, from the list of countries where Chinese companies could invest in oil with the whole package of usual incentives. Brautigam (2009: 88–89) says the move was perceived as politically motivated, particularly because of China's image problems with Sudan.

In any case, FDIs have not gone exclusively to the oil and infrastructure sectors. Sudan has tried to attract private FDIs in agriculture too (AfDB/OECD 2010). In the last decade, Khartoum signed several agreements on farmland and agricultural investments with foreign countries, particularly Middle Eastern and Gulf countries. In 2002, for instance, Sudan and Syria signed a deal that granted the Damascus government a fifty-year lease over a land area of 30,000 *feddan* (about 12,600 hectares) in Jezira State. Similarly, Zad Holding Company, a state-owned firm from Qatar, was reported to consider entering a joint venture to produce food in Sudan for export to Arab markets (Cotula et al. 2009: 33–36). Saudi Arabia's firms have been very active as well (Reuters 2009a, 2009b).

While India does not seem to be interested in farmland acquisitions, though agricultural cooperation is one of the five 'priority sectors' in the government-sponsored investment framework (Large 2008), China is investing in Sudan's land in spite of the 2008 decision by China's National Development and Reform Commission to exclude foreign land acquisitions from a new twenty-year food security strategy adopted by Beijing that year, as reported by Cotula and colleagues (2009: 55). A protocol on agricultural cooperation was signed during Vice President Ali Osman Taha's visit to Beijing in June 2008 (*Sudan Tribune* 2008b), two months after China announced that it had decided to create an agricultural research centre to help Sudan's agriculture sector (Ali 2008). In March 2010, media reported that the Chinese telecommunication company ZTE had received an allocation of approximately ten thousand hectares of land from Sudan's Ministry of Agriculture (*Sudan Tribune* 2010a).

The government's focus on agriculture might be part of an effort to restore balance to the economy. As a matter of fact, several reports by international financial organizations point out that Sudan's oil-dependent boom presents challenges and risks. In a 2009 report (AfDB/OECD 2009), the African Development Bank (AfDB) and the Organization for Economic Cooperation and Development (OECD) warned that 'some symptoms of a "Dutch Disease" *were* unfolding': the Sudanese pound is appreciating and traditional agricultural exports, such as cotton and gum Arabic, are declining, as was the case when Sudan's growth began to be driven by oil exploitation and export. Nevertheless, agriculture still accounts for one-third of GDP and two-thirds of employment, while oil revenues dropped by 21 per cent in 2009 as an effect of the international decline in oil prices since the last quarter of 2008 and in spite of an increase in oil production (AfDB/OECD 2010).

In early January 2011, as southern Sudan went to the polls to vote in the referendum on self-determination and news coming from Juba clearly indicated that the region would choose separation, Sudan's Central Bank and Khartoum's Ministry of Economy and Finance sounded the alarm: soaring inflation must be curbed and an austerity package (*Sudan Tribune* 2011a) must be voted on to avoid possible serious economic challenges in the north, partly caused by uncertainties about future relations between the two regions and the unresolved series of economic and financial post-referendum arrangements between them – such as currency, external debt and a new agreement on southern oil exploitation.[4]

The Merowe Dam

At the time of its construction and inauguration, the Merowe Dam was the biggest hydropower project in Africa since the completion of the Aswan High Dam in the late 1950s. Also known as the Hamdab Dam, the Merowe Dam, which was built on the Nile close to the fourth cataract, 350 kilometres north of Khartoum, is 67 metres high and 9 kilometres long and has created an artificial lake 174 kilometres long. The project was planned to double Sudan's power-generating capacity and cost almost USD 2 billion. USD 520 million was provided by China's EXIM Bank, in three different loans to be repaid within twenty years. Sudan's government provided USD 575 million, while the remaining USD 871 million were given by six different Arab funds or governments, mainly from the Gulf (C. Burke 2007).

China was thus the most generous single foreign investor. Moreover, the Chinese Consortium for the Merowe Dam (CCMD), formed by the China International Water and Electric Corporation (CWE) and the China Hydraulic and Hydroelectric Construction Group Corporation (CWHEC, also known as SinoHydro Group), two of China's biggest hydropower companies, was awarded the USD 660 million contract to build the dam. Therefore, the dam has always been perceived as a Chinese project, although the CCMD developed it under the supervision of the German group Lahmeyer International, while France's Alstom Power and Switzerland's ABB where selected to supply, respectively, the turbines and the transmission lines.

The first two of the ten turbines of the hydropower project were inaugurated on 3 March 2009 by Sudan's President Omar Al-Bashir, just one day before his international indictment by the International Criminal Court (Agence France-Presse 2009). However, the Merowe Dam 'history' had not been trouble-free up to then, not so much in terms of actual technical and construction work, but for its effects on the human and natural environment in the area. What the Chinese official news agency Xinhua presented as 'the pearl of the Nile' (Xinhua 2007) was confronted by the opposition of residents in the affected area, mainly small farmers and nomads who had to relocate to make room for the dam and the artificial basin. As Askouri underlines (2008: 154), 'generally speaking, the affected communities are not opposed to the project'. But the ways and means used by the Chinese consortium and Sudan's authorities fuelled animosities, protests and direct confrontations.[5]

The organized opposition to the project by local civil society was not the only critical voice. In August 2007, the United Nations Special Rapporteur on the Right to Adequate Housing, Miloon Kothari, expressed his deep concerns for the 'situation of the communities affected by the hydroelectric project in the Merowe and Kajbar areas in the northern Nile valley in Sudan which has continued to worsen during the past two years'. He urged Sudan to 'fully comply with international human rights standards' (United Nations 2007).

A similar recommendation, referencing the World Bank's guidelines, had been issued a few years before in a fact-finding mission report by two independent environmental and human rights advocacy organizations, the International Rivers Network and the Corner House (Bosshard and Hildyard 2005). Beyond the social impact caused by the relocation of populations and their access to water and land, the two authors underlined more specifically the serious environmental impact the project was likely to have and the lack of a detailed and credible environmental impact assessment.[6] At the same time, they called upon the international investors and companies involved in the project to respect and implement internationally recognized dam construction standards.[7]

Criticism of the Merowe Dam project did not have a substantial impact on Sudanese citizens' appreciation of China's presence in their country, as Sautman and Hairong (2009) reported following random sample and university-based surveys conducted in Sudan as well as in eight other African countries. In one typical survey, 48.6 per cent of university students responded that they were satisfied and 23.1 per cent of the respondents were very satisfied with Chinese companies working on large projects in their country; 17.1 per cent had 'no opinion', while only 7.2 per cent and 4 per cent answered that they were dissatisfied or very dissatisfied, respectively.

China and Darfur

While there was hope that criticism by civil society would have an impact on China's behaviour as a major investor and builder of infrastructure in Sudan and elsewhere, it was the dynamics of politics and conflict in Sudan that influenced Beijing's attitude towards the country. The first test for China's involvement in Sudan was the war in Darfur. When the conflict in the western Sudanese region started, in early 2003, China had been present in the country's economy for almost a decade, cultivating very good relations with the ruling National Congress Party (NCP). China was thus largely perceived, both inside and outside Sudan, as Khartoum's best friend, and justifiably so, as the partnership between Khartoum and Beijing was probably at its climax in those early years of oil production. Malaysia was already participating in Sudan's oil industry, while India had just entered the scene and was still to develop and enlarge its presence in the country. From the outside, especially as viewed by Western capital cities, the NCP's government appeared to still be at the helm of the country mainly because it could rely on China's political backing and economic investments. China's role was thus highly politicized, and Beijing found itself incorporated, probably against its will, into Sudan's foreign relations defence (Large 2009: 67).

To the outside observer, as well as Darfur rebel movements, China's key position in Sudan's oil sector could and should be used as leverage to convince Khartoum to use some restraint in its western region. But this did not happen, at least in the first years of the conflict. To the contrary, China sternly abstained or threatened to use its veto power to moderate United Nations Security Council (UNSC) resolutions trying to impose economic sanctions against Sudan (Brautigam 2009: 282), in a move widely perceived as an unstated defence of Khartoum's interests. In fact, Beijing's objections to embargoes and sanctions were consistent with its foreign policy tenets. But China's role and action both in Sudan and on the international scene and its apparent unwillingness to take any steps to stop the killings in Darfur ended up being bitterly criticized worldwide and became the main focus of human rights activists. The Darfur issue thus became a thorny testing ground for China's policy towards Africa, while its no-strings-attached economic investments and noninterference tenet were put under scrutiny because of the political and social consequences they might have in African countries such as Sudan.

China's image was further tarnished by the fact that Beijing had been one of the largest arms sellers to Sudan since the late 1980s, during Sadiq Al-Mahdi's rule (1986–89). In the early 2000s, during the last years of the north-south conflict and while the Darfur conflict was developing, China became Sudan's largest weapons seller, in addition to assisting in the construction of weapons factories near Khartoum (Large 2007). Beijing's position thus became uncomfortable when, in 2004, the UNSC voted for Resolution 1556, imposing an embargo on the 'sale and supply' of arms to the three Darfur states. This did not mean that state-to-state arms trade was prohibited. What was prohibited was bringing weapons into the region. In May 2007, a report by Amnesty International accused China and Russia of supplying arms used in Darfur. The report said that 'the irresponsible transfers of arms to Sudan and its neighbours are a significant factor in the massive human rights catastrophe in Darfur and its spread into eastern Chad' (Amnesty International 2007). China's answer was immediate: its arms sales to Africa violated no international law (Associated Press 2007). Although Beijing later pledged that it would try to prevent weapons sold to Sudan from reaching war-torn and embargoed Darfur, a 2009 report by a UN panel of experts found that 'many of the arms and ammunition documented in the Darfur region have been manufactured in China', whose cooperation was therefore sought (UNSC 2009).

China's attitude towards the Darfur issue began to change in 2007. It is difficult to determine what the main reason behind the change was. There were probably several. One reason could be the widespread criticism raised by China's presence in Sudan: with only one year to go before Beijing's Olympic Games, China was probably eager to take the wind out of the critics' sails. Another reason might be the Chadian government's decision to move formal diplomatic relations from Taiwan to mainland China (Large 2008). The Darfur conflict had always had an important and deep-rooted regional dimension; therefore, after establishing relations with N'Djamena and with the prospect of oil investment in Chad, a direct or proxy confrontation between the former French colony and Sudan was not in Beijing's interests. Moreover, in October 2007, the Justice and Equality Movement (JEM), one of Darfur's rebel groups, attacked Chinese oil operations in Diffra, in South Kordofan. A year later, nine Chinese workers were abducted in the same state. Five of them were killed by forces who claimed affiliation to JEM, which was officially denied (Reuters 2008).[8]

China's change of attitude towards the Darfur issue became evident when President Hu Jintao visited Khartoum in February 2007. China's leader stated four principles that, to his mind, were to be the basis for any solution to the Darfur conflict. First of all, Sudan's sovereignty and territorial integrity should be respected. Second, the issue should be solved through dialogue and cooperation. Third, the African Union and the United Nations should have a constructive role in peacekeeping missions in Darfur. Last, improving the situation in Darfur and the living conditions of its locals should be considered imperative (He 2010: 186).

While this was the message expressed in public, the message stated in a private meeting with his Sudanese counterpart was even clearer: 'Darfur is part of Sudan and you have to resolve this problem', Hu reportedly told Al-Bashir (Reuters 2007). Some time later, Beijing appointed Ambassador Liu Guijin as the Chinese government's special representative on Darfur, and Khartoum was forced to agree with the UN proposal to send a joint UN–African Union peacekeeping mission to Darfur (UNAMID). UNAMID replaced the much smaller AMIS, the African Union mission in Sudan, on 31 December 2007, with the participation of a Chinese multifunctional engineering unit, as Ambassador Liu proudly underlined in a speech at London Chatham House in February 2008 (Liu 2008). China's shift, based on continued support for the NCP and pressure upon its senior leaders, was recognized by the Bush administration, in particular by Andrew Natsios, the president's special envoy to Sudan, and also by the International Crisis Group, a Brussels-based international think tank that had been very critical of China's role in Sudan (Brautigam 2009: 282). Defining the new strategy as 'influence without interference', Beijing's leadership avoided breaking the state sovereignty and noninterference tenets at the base of its foreign policy (Large 2009: 70). This was not sufficient for Hollywood stars such as Mia Farrow and George Clooney and for the Save Darfur Coalition activists, who in 2008 launched a boycott campaign against the Olympic Games. It proved unsuccessful but kept China-Sudan relations under scrutiny by Western public opinion.

China and India in Southern Sudan

On 14 October 2010, a *Bloomberg* news article reported on the visit to Juba of a Chinese Communist Party delegation. Less than three months before the referendum in which southern Sudan was to decide whether to remain in or secede from a united Sudan, Chinese officials were in Juba to discuss investment in energy, infrastructure, agriculture and services and tell southern Sudan's ruling party, the Sudan People's Liberation Movement (SPLM), that 'China stands ready to provide help to the south within its capacity, no matter what the changes will be in the situation here' (Boswell 2010). The SPLM's answer was reassuring: 'The largest investment in southern Sudan today is Chinese', explained SPLM Secretary-General Pagam Amun, speaking to journalists. 'They have invested billions of dollars in the oil sector, and have a large number of Chinese workers in the oil fields. We have given assurances ... [we will] protect the Chinese investments ... and are desirous to see more investment in the future' (*Sudan Tribune* 2010b).

The meeting and the words used by both sides on that day in Juba in the presence of journalists were in stark contrast with the opinion expressed by southern Sudanese and their leaders until the mid-2000s with regard to China's presence in the country. During the last ten years of the north-south civil war, China had been considered in the south as the enemy's best friend and financier because of Beijing's investments in Sudan's oil sector, its arms sales to Khartoum and its political backing of the NCP's rule. Moreover, China's foreign policy tenets of state sovereignty, territorial integrity and noninterference in internal affairs had translated into the defence of Khartoum's position against the southern struggle for self-determination and possible independence. In the late 1990s and early 2000s, however, China was rarely called to defend Khartoum and its partnership with Sudan, because the north-south civil war did not attract as much international attention and campaigning as the Darfur conflict was about to attract a few years later (Large 2009: 70).

Things changed when in January 2005 the NCP and the former rebels of the SPLM signed the Comprehensive Peace Agreement (CPA). Its provisions included the creation of a semiautonomous government of South Sudan (GoSS) controlled by the SPLM, a wealth-sharing protocol to split southern oil profits between north and south and the recognition of the south's right to self-determination through a referendum to be held six years after the signing ceremony in Nairobi. The oil-rich area of Abyei was given the right to a parallel consultation, to decide whether it should remain with the north or join the south.

A GoSS created by means of a negotiated peace agreement could thus become a direct partner of Beijing's without obliging China to formally deny its sovereignty and territorial integrity tenets or to alter its warm relations with Khartoum, setting out what Large (2010) defines as a 'dual-track' diplomacy. The SPLM managed to overcome their distrust of the role played by the Chinese in the country during the conflict, and pragmatism on both sides led to the establishment of good relations between Juba and Beijing, which in 2008 evolved to 'quasi-diplomatic' when China opened a consulate in Juba. Since then, Chinese money has arrived in large amounts. As soon as he took office, the new consul general said that Chinese companies were ready to invest in several sectors: from water purification to textile industry and cement factories, from private housing to construction of roads, schools and hospitals, and from hydroelectric power to rice and sugar schemes (Dak 2008). As regards the oil sector,

China has begun to explore the possibility of building a new pipeline from South Sudan to Lamu's new port through Kenya, to allow Juba to become independent from Sudan's oil infrastructure (*Sudan Tribune* 2009a).[9] Yet at the same time, China has extended a grant aid of USD 3 million to Sudan's central government to be used for strengthening north-south unity (*Sudan Tribune* 2008a).

China was not the only 'Khartoum's friend' to establish good relations with Juba. India and Malaysia followed the same path and for the same reasons: most of the oil fields where they have invested so heavily lie within the southern region and, although contracts and concessions had been negotiated with Khartoum, they knew they might need to renegotiate them with an independent government in Juba after the referendum and the end of the CPA in 2011, as eventually happened. Moreover, a region like South Sudan, with a strong need for postconflict reconstruction, presented great opportunities for investment, trade and development. The SPLM's leadership has always been well aware of this. In May 2008, during the party's second convention, Secretary-General Pagan Amun said in his report to the delegates that 'the Secretariat plans to establish relations with the ruling parties in China, India and Malaysia (including opposition in India and Malaysia). … The SPLM needs to engage those countries to ensure efficient development and management of oil resources to the benefit of the Sudanese people' (Amun 2008: para. 65).

In the months preceding the southern referendum, China, India and other foreign investors, such as Japan, Korea and some Arab countries, intensified their contacts and trips to the region (Mayom 2010) and have continued to do so after South Sudan's independence. Although all have promised to continue to keep good relations with both Khartoum and Juba and have so far kept their word, the unresolved tension, if not conflict, between the two Sudans and the uncertainties surrounding their relations remain a cause of worry, especially for China, India and Malaysia, who need to secure their investments in oil production and the safety of their nationals working in the oil fields.[10]

Conclusion

The Sudan we know today has been greatly influenced by its partnerships with emerging Asian players in the last fifteen to twenty years. China has had the greatest impact on Sudan because of the economic trade and investment volumes between the two countries, as well as Beijing's weight in international politics. The CNPC's acquisitions in the late 1990s dramatically changed the pace of Sudan's oil industry development and transformed a quasi-isolated economy into the third-largest oil producer in sub-Saharan Africa, with strong ties to several foreign investors and booming infrastructure, construction and service sectors. Economic growth helped Sudan's ruling elite remain in power, and Beijing's friendship has provided important backing on the international scene, in particular on the UN Security Council, where veto holder China (and Russia, one of the largest arms sellers to Sudan) have strongly defended Khartoum.

Sudan-China relations have had a great impact on Beijing too: in the mid-1990s, Sudan became the testing ground for China's developing new approach to Africa. And it has remained so. The Darfur issue forced Beijing to take into consideration the political dimension and consequences of its own image in Africa in general and in Sudan in particular. On the other hand, Sudan's CPA, by granting autonomy and the right to self-determination to the south, risked putting China's foreign policy tenets under strain; Beijing overcame that difficulty by initiating a 'dual-track' diplomatic policy (Large 2010), allowing the establishment of warm 'quasi-diplomatic' relations with Juba well before the south's independence. Therefore, in recent years China's engagement in the two Sudans has changed: economic partnership, business and resource extraction remain essential to Beijing, and will need to be protected in case of renewed conflict, but China can no longer underestimate the political effects of its actions and role, in both countries as well as on the larger scene of world politics.

India's presence in the Sudans has not drawn the same attention, because the volume of trade and investment between New Delhi and Khartoum has been smaller than between Beijing and Khartoum, and also because India lacks the international weight and status of China. But the patterns of India's economic partnership with both Sudans do not differ very much from China's, and they will probably need to be watched in the same manner, particularly because of their impact on social and environmental security.

South Sudan's independence has not brought drastic changes to the patterns of China's and India's presence in the two separate yet still highly interdependent countries. Asian players, as well as other foreign investors, have maintained good relations with both Khartoum and Juba. Stable and friendly north-south relations would be in their (and the two Sudans') best interest. Two years after South Sudan's independence, several postsecession issues (the final status of Abyei, the demarcation of the new international border and the implementation of the September 2012 agreements) are still outstanding. The crisis that followed South Sudan's decision to stop its oil production in early 2012 greatly affected China, India and Malaysia's huge investments in the sector. They were directly hit, and in spite of their warm relations with both governments, Chinese and Indian governments and oil companies did not seem to be able to play the leverage role they were credited with by many outside observers. Better, more constructive influence on both governments to avoid any kind of conflict, find ways to solve issues peacefully and implement the signed agreements would be a great help to stabilize the border regions, where both Beijing and New Delhi have great interests and investments to defend, and would benefit the relations between the two Sudans.

Notes

1. During the 2000s, China-Africa trade increased by 30 per cent. In 2008 the total trade volume reached USD 106 billion, while China's long-term investments in almost all African countries have remained unchanged despite the international economic and financial crisis. Unlike China, India's presence in Africa is led mainly by private investors. Although India-Africa trade volume is far smaller than that between China and the continent, India is clearly oriented to increasing its presence in African countries.
2. In his address to the first Afro-Asian Relations Conference (also known as the Bandung Conference) in 1955, Chou En-lai reproposed the 'Five Principles of Peaceful Coexistence' adopted the year before in China-India bilateral negotiations. Those principles – mutual respect for each other's territorial integrity and sovereignty; mutual nonaggression; mutual noninterference in each other's internal affairs; equality and mutual benefit; peaceful coexistence – have remained the basis of China's foreign policy (Panozzo 2009).
3. The picture has radically changed after South Sudan's secession. The Central Bank of Sudan's statistics for 2012 show that during that year China and India remained the main importer to Sudan, followed by Saudi Arabia, the United Arab Emirates, Egypt, Australia and Japan. As far as petroleum and petroleum products exports were concerned, however, they dropped dramatically in comparison to presecession years, and China, India and Malaysia got nothing. Petroleum and petroleum-derived products, for a total value of USD 256 million, were sold to Ethiopia, Eritrea and the United Arab Emirates only, while gold, which had barely featured in previous years' export statistics, was exported to the United Arab Emirates and Canada for a total value of USD 2.16 billion (Central Bank of Sudan 2012). Similar statistics for South Sudan were not available at the time of writing.
4. The alarm sounded in early 2011 proved to be right: South Sudan's independence, the difficulties in reaching and implementing agreements and Juba's decision, in January 2012, to stop its oil production have had serious repercussions on Sudan's economic performance. Khartoum's government has thus tried to start diversifying its economy ever since, putting more efforts in the exploration and production of gold.
5. See, for example, *Sudan Tribune* (2005, 2006). Askouri (2008) says the people displaced by the project were more than seventy-five thousand: '[T]he affected communities are the Hamdab, representing eight per cent of the total number of the affected people, Amri, representing twenty-five per cent and the Manasir, representing sixty-seven per cent'.

6. A 'brief presentation' of the '2002 Environmental Assessment Report' is available on the Merowe Dam project's official website (DIU n.d.).
7. The political and economic risks connected to their participation in the project pushed the Swiss company ABB to stop their operations and withdraw from the Merowe Dam project, while the other two European companies involved, France's Alstom and the German Lahmeyer International, remained part of it.
8. Chinese workers were not the only targets of kidnappings: four Indian technicians and their Sudanese driver were abducted in an area adjoining the oil-rich region of Abyei in May 2008 (Agence France-Presse 2008).
9. A similar proposal was made by Japan's Toyota Tshusho Corporation (see also *Sudan Tribune* 2010c). As of late 2013 the possibility of building a new pipeline, either to Lamu or to Djibouti, is still on the Juba government's table, but no final decision has been taken, nor any work begun.
10. Inability to reach an agreement on the post-CPA outstanding issues – Abyei, demarcation of the international border, transportation fees for South Sudan's oil and citizenship among them – led in January 2012 to Juba's retaliatory decision to turn the oil tap off. This move exposed the high dependence on oil exports of both economies, which suffered greatly. Most of the issues were agreed upon and formalized in the Addis Ababa agreements signed on 27 September 2012, but in the following several months implementation has been uneven, if not completely absent.

Chapter 10

Oil Exploration and Conflict in Sudan

The Predicament for Pastoralists in North-South Borderline States

Abdalbasit Saeed

Introduction: The Problem and a Primary Assumption

This chapter calls attention to the predicament increasingly faced by pastoralists as borderline communities that traditionally do not recognize boundaries or borders according to the same modes of settled groups. Their fate is further aggravated by the overall context characterized by built-in government biases in favour of irrigated agriculture, oil interests and foreign oil exploration and production companies in a fractured internal and local political landscape. This reflects the situation of Abyei area (2008–9) during the interim period and prior to the referendum on South Sudan in 2011 (Saeed 2009, 2010). The chapter also draws attention to the neglect by the governing elite of the way in which pastoralists view (and consequently manage) their relations with neighbours, settled farmers and the urban sphere and the people who occupy it. The main actors who influence government policy and the implications of their positions are briefly described and assessed. The issues directly encountered in peace negotiations between the Ngok-Dinka and the Missiriya are summarized and presented as a simplified description of the historical background to the current stalemate in negotiations regarding the persisting crisis in the disputed area of Abyei. The chapter recommends that the two pastoralist communities be secured and their livelihoods protected in their homelands, which are rich in oil and minerals, by developing an area-wide shift in the strategic policy framework for southwest Kordofan.

Notes for this chapter begin on page 200.

Sudan's borderline states (ten) between the north and south cover areas that are home to the country's oil and mineral wealth. Some fourteen million persons live there, mostly as rural settled farmers and mobile pastoralist communities. The oil wealth of the country constitutes a major factor in the problems faced by pastoralists and in the policies that affect them. The relationship of oil wealth to these problems and the conflicts they engender is interpreted in three ways in the literature (Gadkarim 2010: 1). First, the literature claims that the export of oil from 1999 made sizeable revenues available to propel the civil war at a time when the Islamist regime in Khartoum was faced with great internal and external difficulties. During the six-year interim period, which is the time frame for the events and processes considered in this chapter, the two major partners to the Comprehensive Peace Agreement (CPA) used their respective shares to build up lethal weaponry rather than investing in development. Second, it is argued that north-south competition over the distribution of oil revenues is a cause of dispute and conflict. Third, revenues from oil have not only promoted corruption among state officials, but have also aggravated social and economic disparities between rural and urban communities, hence creating greater injustice and denying access to social services for the majority of the population.

The predicament faced by pastoralists is a result of this exclusionary scenario. Poor governance, marginalization, insecurity over community livelihoods and lack of access to education are persistent issues curtailing the ability of pastoralists to adapt and cope with climate change, but also inhibiting their capacity to become an asset for stability and peace in Sudan. Poor, variable and erratic rainfall and reduced sorghum and millet production due to persistent ethnic violence and the high cost of farm inputs, including the high cost of fuel, have precipitated the threat of a food crisis in Kordofan. Desertification and land degradation will also gradually increase risks and vulnerabilities, thus putting more pressure on already overstretched coping strategies, magnifying regional disparity, economic inequity and social inequality.

The research problem emanates from this difficult situation, which encompasses two pastoralist communities, the Missiriya and the Ngok-Dinka of southwest Kordofan, that found themselves caught up in twenty years of conflict and war between contending armies, the Sudan Armed Forces (SAF) and the Sudan People's Liberation Army (SPLA). This chapter has two aims. First, it suggests entry points that address issues and problems related to land and natural resources management, in the context of competition and conflict for surface resources worsened by oil production under government protection. Second, it assesses the status of rights of access to land use and the manner in which such rights are created, sustained and protected. In particular, it analyses situations in which pastoralists are squeezed into narrow livestock routes for seasonal migration. In order to achieve these two aims, the chapter uses a descriptive method of presentation, probing the pastoralists' informal community institutions and customary norms and traditional practices governing dispute resolution, access to land and natural resources.

The primary assumption,[1] therefore, is that as long as the Missiriya and Ngok-Dinka, the identified primary, and beneficiary, stakeholders, do not form partnerships for peaceful coexistence among themselves, they will continue to fall easy prey to the more organized interest groups that influence government policy in a situation of fluid statutory legislation and ill-conceived mechanisms by the governing urban elite, including not only contradictory customary practices upheld by the elite on natural resources management, but also contradictory policies, particularly in the borderline states, in regard to transboundary passage for pastoralists from one state to the next. Such a situation allows for serious gaps and deficiencies in land use that could be used for a possible re-emergence of disputes and conflict, unless such gaps are filled as a matter of priority. The corollary to this statement is that a central focus is needed on land use and natural resources management legislation as an entry point in planning endeavours for poverty alleviation, including sustainable employment-focused approaches and concerted human settlement development accompanied by small-scale enterprises for reducing poverty, including Missiriya and Ngok-Dinka pastoralists.

The Ngok-Dinka of the Abyei area and the Missiriya share pasture and water resources in southwest Kordofan on the basis of interdependency for cooperation, collaboration and mutual benefit as borderline communities between north and south Sudan (Pantulliano 2010; Pantulliano et al. 2009). The two communities are impoverished geographic neighbours living in an area with large oil resources. They were caught for two decades (1985–2005) in the cross fire between north and south Sudan. As pastoralists, however, they have to live side by side and share surface natural resources,[2] notwithstanding the separation of South Sudan from Sudan in July 2011. Their borderline rural economy and society was adversely affected by postseparation dynamics, where conflict transformation, peace building and human development perspectives were strategic policy options for successor states in South Sudan and Sudan, and for the interests of oil exploration and production companies. The data and information contributing to this narrative is therefore limited to the period covered by the CPA, and in particular 2005–9.

Weakly Organized Pastoralists: Easy Prey for Exclusionary Government Policy

Since the nineteenth century, pastoralist livelihoods in the central Nile valley have experienced perpetual crises of production. For historical and political reasons ranging from conquest and colonization to the creation of nation-states, a large proportion of these pastoralists have been dislocated several times and/or displaced and subsequently forced to move southwards, leaving space for government-sponsored agricultural schemes. In the process of venturing into new frontier areas, disputes and conflict with local inhabitants over surface resources became widespread. The issue of the dislocation of pastoralists from lands appropriated for establishing the Jezira scheme for cotton plantations early in the twentieth century (Abbas 1980) is just one example. In the 1960s pastoralists were evicted for the second time in fifty years. They moved further southwards as the government dislocated the pastoralists to establish the Managil extension of the Jezira scheme. In the 1970s the government adopted concurrently the policy of large-scale mechanized farming in Blue Nile and Kordofan and a policy for irrigated sugar cane plantation agriculture on lands hitherto used by pastoralists on the east bank of the White Nile River. Large-scale irrigated sugar cane plantations were created and managed by the Kenana Sugar Company, the Asalaya Sugar Company and the White Nile Sugar Company. Concurrently, during the 1960s and 1970s, pastoralists were also dislocated from traditional grazing domains in order for the government to open new lands and spread mechanized farming into the states of South Kordofan and Blue Nile.

At present the government privatization and liberalization policies, including the expansion of sugar cane schemes to the west bank of the White Nile, generate disputes and conflict over surface resources. More than 425,000 *feddan* (200,000 hectares) have been allocated to the Sabina Sugar Company, and more pastoralists have been dislocated. The same situation can be found in western Sudan (Mohamed Salih 1990a) and in eastern Sudan, with the striking example of the Khashum Al-Girba scheme (Sorbo 1985). These government policies and the institutional failures that accompanied them proved to be the main causal drivers for disputes and conflict as they pushed pastoralists to venture into new frontier areas already inhabited by other farming and herding communities.

In addition, persistent drought and continuing desertification since the 1970s in north Sudan exacerbated this trend and forced both camel nomads and transhumant cattle-raising pastoralists to move southwards. Such dislocations were faced by the gradual expansion of the war from southern Sudan into the north. This was a protracted medium- to high-intensity armed conflict that had expanded from the south from the mid-1980s, encompassing the western, central and eastern parts of the country in the context of conflict and war that ended in 2005. Furthermore, displacement forced by the war in southwest Kordofan was compounded by the displacement of whole communities living in areas where oil exploration was initiated, particularly in the mid-1980s. In addition, environmental damage caused by oil development led to the displacement, dislocation and restricted movement of all groups in the borderline belt, including the Ngok-Dinka and the Missiriya in the oil field areas (Wesselink and Weller 2006). Oil roads cut off water catchments, block seasonal rivers and lower lakes and *ḥafirs* (reservoirs) north and south of the Bahr Al-'Arab River, including Abyei area. This trend has pushed more livestock southwards to find pasture. Oil development is also attracting economic migrants to the producing areas in pursuit of wage work. Finally, pollution by contaminated water has also reportedly killed some animals and caused abortions in an undetermined number of pregnant women.

However, although pastoralists have been affected by (and have had to react to) several transformations, they still show continuity with respect to forms of livelihood, including seasonal movements and livestock breeding practices, custom, norms, lifestyles and their cultural 'world view'. Since political independence in 1956, the pastoralists of Sudan have gradually realized that the nineteenth-century pattern of slave raiding, warfare and 'tribal/ethnic' mediated conflict could no longer bring them a better future. Due to their marginalization by elite groups in the centre, pastoralists have been forced to 'learn' new ways of coexistence with other peoples, through accommodation and living with difference. In the present circumstances, and given the separation of South Sudan, a period of transition must be allowed for pastoralists – and other borderline communities – to smoothly adapt and move from a united country to an acceptance of two successor states. This is particularly pertinent not only because oil produced in areas where pastoralists practice herding livestock has gained increased primacy as a focus of the economic landscape, but primarily because any obstruction to oil production and the refining and transport processes would hurt both of the successor states. By the same logic, and in order not to risk any violent hostilities in the borderline states, the design of reconstruction and development programmes for advancing borderline transformations must preserve and ensure the rights of pastoral peoples in land use and natural resources management development.

Positions of Major Stakeholders as Transformers of Livelihoods

The positions of major stakeholders are summarized below to depict the extent to which they affect not only government policy stances, but also the position of traditional native administrations and the SPLM, particularly in South Kordofan State and the Abyei area. In view of the situation described below, and given the multiplicity of problems and economic forces confronted by pastoralists, a better understanding of their governance institutions and the way in which they act, react or interact with endogenous and exogenous factors and the forces of change requires pastoralists to play a key role in determining their own future and in shaping the future of the region as a whole. In spite of the marginalization of their forms of social organization and the further constraints of illiteracy on access to positions of power, pastoralists' ability to cope with the forces that impinge on them should not be underestimated. Therefore, alternative policies concerning the issue of pastoralism must address the environmental, economic and political problems of the area and identify the real needs specific to each context.

However, in the governmental perspective inherited from the condominium of the colonial era, customary land possession or occupation and/or established use is not recognized as constituting 'ownership'. During the colonial period, all precolonial forms of land rights were subordinated to the colonial system with a concurrent blanket denial of the understanding of land rights by indigenous peoples (M. Babiker 2009). 'Land ownership' as understood under the colonial legal 'tenure' system and inherited at the time of political independence tended to create two principal categories: the so-called Crown/state/government land that may be occupied and used by private persons or communities, a condition falling short of ownership; and private freehold or leasehold by natural or juristic persons. In effect, the colonial paradigm superimposed the status of tenancy on the settled and pastoral communities that had hitherto occupied and used land and natural resources for three centuries. Land that belonged to such communities was thus turned into the property of the Crown/state/government. The introduction of registration of titles to land, mainly in small riverine patches, further distorted and weakened the security of access to land among indigenous peoples. However, the majority of the population in rural areas sustain themselves on simple subsistence agriculture and livestock husbandry through land possession and land use rights granted by village headmen and communal access and use rights governed by tradition and custom, premised on residence in a village or membership in a tribal group. This is seen by magistrates' courts to contradict the government dictum that 'land is the property of the state'. At variance with this official dictum, the NCP-led government of Sudan and the SAF continue to promote among their Missiriya clients the saying that 'the Ngok-Dinka are taking "your land"'. The Missiriya are accordingly incited to wage war on the Ngok-Dinka, often killing scores of them: the ideology works. However, it is unlikely that the Sudanese government would register land in the name of the Missiriya, even if they eradicated the Ngok-Dinka from the disputed territory.

Some leading government civil servants and technocrats still believe that migratory livelihood systems and the accompanying arrangements for land use and access to surface natural resources could hardly be regarded as capable of sustaining an organized, large-scale effort to exploit natural resources through modern techniques for increased food production, nor do they appear to stabilize land use and natural resource use sufficiently to encourage the kind of sustained investment in land resources necessary to achieve that goal. In the same vein, it is also held that mobile basic social services such as mobile basic schools for pastoral nomads and mobile health services are only exceptional arrangements. They cannot be maintained as part of a programme for longer-term sustainable development for pastoral communities. Such positions find justification in the infamous Unregistered Lands Act of 1970 (El-Sammani and Salih 2006: 19–20; Shazali et al. 2006), the first substantive national legislation on national resources, which proved even more regressive than the colonial-era legislation. The 1970 act entitled the government to use force to safeguard 'land'.[3] Its promulgation was virtually concurrent with the abolition of the system of native administration, a measure that resulted in virtual chaos in rural Sudan. With the overthrow of President Nimeiri in 1985, many social and political forces called for the reinstatement of native administrators to redress the chaos, but to no avail. On the one hand, the current NCP government in Khartoum still insists on the basic tenet that land is owned by the state. The SPLM, on the other hand, insists that land belongs to the local community, and that '[i]t must be registered in the name of the community; and that the government may not carry out any investment without the consent of the local community and a just compensation'.[4]

Evidence from Field-Based Consultations with the Authorities and Communities

A few examples from the field may show the complex situation of land issues at the state level. Blue Nile's *wālī* (governor), a member of the NCP, stated in an interview in 2006 that he had serious land problems at hand that would have to be addressed as a most important priority.[5] The commissioner of Damazīn Locality, a top NCP leader at the state level, supported the governor's view and added that unless these problems were addressed within the following three months (July–September 2006), the 'time bomb' would explode. The entry point was, in his view, to establish the National Land Commission as soon as possible. The commissioner of Damazīn also added that, as the eastern and southeastern parts of Blue Nile border Ethiopia, Blue Nile was an entry point for refugees. Substantial assistance would be required to prepare local communities to respond positively to the returnees. As security was restored, including demining in all localities, the population would begin to return and demand on agricultural land would increase. No land-related conflicts were anticipated along ethnic lines. The National Land Commission to which commissioner of Damazīn referred in 2006 did not materialize, as the six-year interim period ended in the separation of South Sudan on 9 July 2011.

Conversely, the *wālī* of South Kordofan (a member of the SPLM in 2006) said that land ownership and resource access issues were the root causes of conflict and war. He added that if the citizens had known and understood the meaning and implications of the unjust land laws of the central government, they would have revolted much earlier than 1985. He went on to say that every citizen in South Kordofan knows his ancestral lands, and would easily return from IDP status, refugee status or upon demobilization from the army and assume possession of his ancestral land. Following in the footsteps of South Kordofan's *wālī*, the paramount chief of the Ngok-Dinka in Abyei area (also from the SPLM) was of the view that each of the nine Ngok-Dinka chiefdoms knows the land of their ancestors. They did not expect any problems regarding the reintegration of returnees (IDPs, refugees and/or demobilized soldiers) whenever they arrived. The most important issue for Abyei area was to establish Abyei special administrative status, first and foremost.

A Dead End for Long-Distance Livestock Herding as Seen by Pastoralists

Land as a Community Asset

As previously mentioned, past government policy resulted in the dislocation of livestock pastoralists to the west bank of the White Nile and camel herders reaching as far as Kadugli in South Kordofan. Pastoralists are faced with frequent closure of access to pasture and watering sites. The situation is even worse in the Blue Nile State, where by 2006 three of the eight major trekking routes had been closed down by large-scale agricultural leasehold owners. For the remaining five nomadic routes, along the east bank of the Blue Nile, continuous threats of confiscation of livestock apprehended in the Dinder National Park have not only posed serious hazards to pastoral peoples, but also have made herders and shepherds realize that they could save their livestock from random confiscation only if they resort to the 'barrel of the gun'. This is a potential threat to peace in the state.

Currently, the transplanted condominium concept of 'land tenure' is not known to the majority of the rural population, particularly among pastoralists. For rural residents, usufruct equates with ownership, a fact not accepted either by magistrates' courts or by local administrators. For the purposes of this discussion, 'land rights' as opposed to 'land ownership' by the communities is seen as more inclusive of multiple forms of land possession or occupation and rights of use, including rights to settlement or residence, grazing, watering, hunting, crop farming, tribal initiation and burial and rights of way and passage. It also accommodates overlapping or shared rights. Land is a 'natural right', presumably arising from the fact of birth to a family household, at a certain location, in association with a particular tribal group. This is the case for the majority of people in the rural areas of Sudan. Customary norms and practices prescribe the types of possession, occupation and use, and patterns of social division of labour at the household level. Access to water points, grazing rights, forest products and wildlife are all resources associated with tribally guaranteed and protected rights and practices. Land characteristics include all reasonably stable environment attributes, including soil types, climate, underlying geology and relief, hydrology and vegetation, and the attendant impact of activities by humans and animals as socioeconomic dimensions. In this context, surface natural resources include agricultural land, free range pasture and grazing and water sources such as seasonal streams, open ponds, open hand-dug wells, artesian wells and boreholes, and artificially excavated ponds to store rainwater for use in the dry season.

Land as an economic asset has been undergoing substantial change since the discovery of petroleum in the 1970s. The movement has been one of a slow pace towards the commoditization of land despite the hitherto prevailing customary norms and traditional practices, that is, a movement away from inclusive land use towards exclusive land use, land occupation and land possession. Concurrently, there has been massive population movement caused by the war in the south and land degradation in the north, where IDPs are seeking jobs as cheap agricultural labour, sharecroppers and daily wage workers on the outskirts of rural towns. In this context, land is being gradually and consistently transformed in rural areas from communal use to private possession.

Policy Makers' Views of Pastoralism

Stereotypes of pastoralist violence must be situated in the context of mutual opposition and exclusion against the backdrop of a struggle for access to resources. Growing population pressure and a declining resource base due to persistent land degradation throughout the past four decades, coupled with increasing environmental pressures such as droughts, have reduced pastoral access to water and other resources that are vital for survival. In a context where access to resources and land ownership are structured by more organized strata, according to individual property rights and privatization policies rather than by regulated communal systems, livelihood-related interactions can easily break down.

Violent conflict in which pastoralists may be involved is often wrongly viewed as a symptom of intertribal conflict over cattle and other common property. This miscomprehension 'gap' has counterproductive implications for government policy (Assal 2009). The second flaw is an assumption by policy makers that pastoralists, because they prefer mobility to settlement, do not have an interest in land possession and/or ownership. The implication for policy is that, first, there is no defined government policy or strategy towards pastoralists (Mohamed Salih 1990a); and second, settled communities wrongly think of pastoralists as persistently landless and 'unwanted neighbours'. The third flaw is a perception that pastoralists are troublemakers with regard to land property rights. At the same time, pastoralists are perceived as having a history of suspicion towards the 'centralized' authority of the state, viewing the central authority as a threat to their distinctive 'nomadic/mobile' lifestyle. Hence, although resource competition plays a fundamental role in exacerbating periodic outbursts of violence, the reality is more complex. Equally important to understanding insecurity as a trigger among pastoral groups is their distant and often oppositional relationship to the 'state' and the 'urban'. As with other peripheral groups in the identified borderline states, pastoralists believe that they have suffered systematic marginalization by central state authorities (Casciarri and Ahmed 2009). From this perception arises the strong tendency among new generations of pastoralists and rural smallholder farmers to constitute a 'striking force' by joining the armed movements that have fought the central government to forcefully overthrow the NCP-led regime. They are inspired by the acute unemployment that they face in the dry season, and by the economic inequity and social inequality that they perceive from the share of oil revenues denied to them by the governing elite in the centre.

Pastoralists' Views of Government Policy

The pastoralists strongly believe that they are often neglected in the allocation of government services. Because formal legal and police services are usually nonexistent in pastoralist communities, the state seldom plays a role in guaranteeing their stability and security. When these communities become an object of state interest, such as during violent conflict, the state often uses top-down intervention aimed at dislocation and/or settlement programmes with some form of coercive effort to make pastoralists conform. Furthermore, in the case of security promotion, state actions tend to be authoritarian and heavy-handed. This strengthens the pastoralist tendency to remain aloof from state authority. Under such conditions, the demand for small arms increases, mediated by preferences for self-defence and attempts at the acquisition of resources.

All in all, pastoralists continue to fall prey to insurmountable circumstances beyond their control, especially in the states of Blue Nile and South Kordofan, where they have become the victims of some of the most damaging aspects of the 'failed development' policy that has aimed at the commercialization of agriculture since the 1960s. For instance, in South Kordofan seasonal migration routes spanned by pastoral communities have been blocked by mechanized schemes and have been permanently lost to agricultural capitalist leaseholders due to the increased expansion of both demarcated and nondemarcated mechanized farming from 300,000 *feddan* in 1969 to 4.5 million in 2008.

To build strategies for cooperation and collaboration between Sudan and South Sudan, particularly given the long-standing dispute between the Missiriya and the Ngok-Dinka at the end of the interim period, Sudan needs to take important steps to consolidate peace through taking land and natural resources as the entry point, including: (a) rectifying the fragmented land laws; (b) recognizing workable land-related norms and customary practices in legal statutes; (c) developing sound, participatory (people-centred) and negotiated policies on the rights of access to land and the use of natural resources; and (d) creating responsive community-based arrangements to ensure not only informed and safe articulation of community issues but also to make access to land and the reintegration of pastoralists a smooth process to reinforce livelihood and security.

An Example of Conflict between the Ngok-Dinka and the Missiriya in Abyei

Historical Background to Community Issues and Geographic Focus

The Ngok-Dinka Nilotic group of Abyei and the Missiriya Arabs are neighbouring cattle-herding pastoralist communities that have been living together for centuries and sharing land, range and pasture, and water and forest resources in the lower segment of the Bahr Al-'Arab River, also locally known in the Ngok-Dinka language as the Kiir River. The Bahr Al-'Arab River basin, which is about 763 kilometres long, is shared by South Kordofan and South Darfur in north Sudan as well as four other states of South Sudan, Unity, Warrap, Northern Bahr Al-Ghazal and Western Bahr Al-Ghazal. Local disputes are common around the Bahr Al-'Arab River basin. Conflicts between the Ngok-Dinka and the Missiriya in southwest Kordofan, which took place in the first decade (1898–1905) of British colonial rule (1898–1956) against the backdrop of the nineteenth-century practice of slavery, prompted the colonial authorities to transfer the Ngok-Dinka in 1905 to be administered jointly with the Missiriya by Kordofan Province.[6] In that year, a tribal meeting was organized by the authorities to encourage the two communities to coexist peacefully. A 'traditional' mechanism for peaceful neighbourliness was created (S. Ibrahim 2004: 3). It was called the Brotherhood Agreement between Missiriya and Ngok-Dinka (1905). Local customary practices arising from the 1905 pact were consolidated between the two communities and, over time, were accepted as Ngok-Dinka/Missiriya 'tradition'. The pact was sustained for sixty years, only to be broken in 1965 when violent conflict erupted, resulting in the loss of lives and precipitating mistrust.

The 1905 Brotherhood Agreement was signed by representatives of the two communities (S. Ibrahim 2004). Its provisions were observed for six decades. In spite of much social interaction and intermingling, suspicion and mistrust between the two communities generated intermittent and protracted disputes and conflict. Limited violent encounters did occur. They augmented and transformed intergroup relations towards ethnic violence, particularly from the mid-1960s, due to factors external to the two neighbouring communities, made worse by two decades (1983–2004) of conflict and war between the SAF and the SPLA. The two communities were entrenched in war-related alliances with the contending armies, premised on an ideology of 'self-defence' generated by the two armies to lure local communities into the conflict. The Ngok-Dinka and the Missiriya were not sufficiently aware of the full dimensions and implications of such alliances and the ideologies of self-defence that they engendered. As a result, Abyei area has become the centre of local, national and international attention. It became one of the 'three transitional areas' during the IGAD-sponsored peace negotiations that resulted in the signing of the CPA in 2005. The Abyei Protocol envisioned in the CPA to resolve the local conflict has not been implemented. In 2008, the two partners to the CPA opted for final and binding arbitration on Abyei area by the Permanent Court of Arbitration (PCA) at The Hague.[7] The PCA's final and binding resolution has also not been honoured, to date, mainly due to NCP intransigence. Therefore, the conflict has been left to fester, with the prospect of a return to war or even the application of Chapter VII of the UN Charter by the UN Security Council if the arbitration award is not honoured.

Responses to the Abyei Arbitration Tribunal Award: The Authorities, the Missiriya and the Ngok-Dinka

The NCP rejected the Abyei Boundaries Commission (ABC) (Petterson et al. 2005) report of 14 July 2005, arguing that the experts of the ABC had exceeded their mandate of 2005. On 7 July 2008, the NCP and the SPLM agreed to submit their dispute for a final and binding decision by the Permanent Court of Arbitration. The Abyei Arbitration Tribunal was fully constituted on 30 October 2008. The final award of the Abyei Arbitration Tribunal at The Hague rendered a final and binding verdict delimiting Abyei area's boundaries on 22 July 2009. By so doing, the PCA ended four years of disagreement between the NCP and the SPLM. As soon as the Abyei Arbitration Tribunal award was announced in The Hague as the final and binding decision, the NCP and the SPLM declared immediately and respectively their unconditional acceptance of the final award. Both the CPA partners pledged to enforce expeditiously and in good faith the verdict of the PCA without delay.

The Ngok-Dinka announced their acceptance of the ruling made by the Abyei Arbitration Tribunal. Two clans of the Missiriya Ḥumr-Ajāira expressed discomfort with the Abyei Arbitration Tribunal award, particularly the Awlād Kāmil and Mazāghna clans, whose usual seasonal transhumant movements with their herds cross from north to south the central part of Abyei. This is sufficient cause for mistrust that could lead to revival of the conflict. Hence, making an immediate internal 'social and political' settlement would be the nearest shortcut to a sustainable peace.

To quote the words of the tribal chief of the Awlād Kāmil and Mazāghna clans, the *amīr* Mukhtar Babu Nimir,

> My land at the Ragaba Az-Zarga (Ngol) has been taken away from me, by the government of Sudan, and has been given to the Ngok-Dinka. I am not going to challenge the verdict of the Abyei Arbitration Tribunal award, as this is a final

> and binding decision on the Sudan government. If there is anything I might say, that reflects the feelings of my people, I will direct my words and the views of my people to the head of state, President Omar Al-Bashir. I know that the president approved compensation for the people in the north who have been adversely impacted by the Merowe Dam, both in cash and in kind. My question is: 'Is the president going to compensate the Missiriya people, or not, for our land that has been given away by the Sudan government to the Ngok-Dinka?' If the president is not going to compensate us, then we will have a different say and approach.

This is a significant digression from earlier Missiriya positions. It articulates demands directly to the head of state. This was the first time that the Missiriya had asked for compensation without making threats to the Ngok-Dinka. There was no public response from government authorities; presumably, the authorities were not interested in any settlement that involved 'compensation'. However, it must be noted that during all stages of the north-south conflict, especially during the first phase of the violence (1962–65), the Missiriya have persistently sided with the central government and the national army in Khartoum, irrespective of whether the governing regime is civilian or military. The Ngok-Dinka, in contrast, have always sided with what they perceived as a social revolution in the south: Anyanya I and Anyanya II (1962–72), and subsequently the SPLA/M (1983–2005).

Missiriya Guest Residency in Abyei as a Peace-Building Initiative

Little, if any, of the Abyei Protocol has been implemented, in spite of the multitude of proposals presented by experts and mediators, including the proposals on guest residency or on the exchange of surface resources. None of these proposals was accepted by the local antagonists. Therefore, failure to implement the CPA is the responsibility of the NCP and the SPLM, as the major partners in the agreement. The proposed offer of guest residency was intended to save the Ngok-Dinka and the Missiriya from the negative implications of these institutional failures by their governments. However, there are two defining questions that help to disentangle the problems with the implementation of the Abyei Protocol. First, should the Abyei problem be regarded as part of the wider politics of Sudan, or are the issues genuinely local problems that are left to fester in Abyei? Second, do the problems stem from the overall agreement and the lack of political will to implement it, or from the manner in which it is being implemented? There are three important aspects required to revitalize the 'spirit' of the Abyei Protocol: it must secure the homeland of the Ngok-Dinka; provide for the unmet requirement of a referendum for the Ngok-

Dinka and other residents of Abyei area; and secure grazing and watering rights for the Missiriya across Abyei area. In addition, building peace requires managing the negative effects of oil development in the area, that is, disrupting the water table, pollution, the displacement of people, the blocking of livestock routes, a more intensive security presence/militarization and greater political interference. The Abyei Protocol also provides financial benefits from oil for the local populations according to their entitlements under the CPA. Last, success depends on how well the Ngok-Dinka and the Missiriya manage the rapid social and economic changes brought about by the return of people and the opening up of their area.

Determining Residency in the Abyei Protocol and Proposing Guest Residency

According to the CPA, the residents of Abyei are '[m]embers of the Ngok-Dinka community and other Sudanese residing in the area'. As the CPA interim period ended with the secession of South Sudan (9 July 2011), with no referendum in sight for the Abyei people, the exact criteria of residence in Abyei area must be assumed to remain undetermined. The issue of who has residency remains undecided as well. Following from this, there can be no final determination of residency in Abyei area except through the agency of consultation, renegotiation and rearbitration to settle this critically contentious issue between the two successor states.

However, according to the Abyei Protocol, residency in Abyei area means that persons (adults aged eighteen years and above) can vote in elections and in the referendum, if held. It also means that they can be members of local government: 'The administration of the Abyei Area shall be representative and inclusive of all the residents of the area' (CPA 2005). Last, residency determines who has primary rights to customary land. Land in the customary system means the sum of near-surface and surface resources such as soil (i.e., farms), water, minerals, forests, swamps and grassland (i.e., pasture). Primary rights in land include individual and family holdings and estates held collectively by a group in undivided shares. Secondary rights, such as grazing rights, are negotiated with the primary rights holders. In Abyei area, these are generally seasonal user rights.

Although the issue of residency is not yet determined, there are some likely parameters. It is not disputed that residency includes the Ngok-Dinka. The other criteria may include people born in the area or may give residency to people with parents born in the area. It is very likely that consultation between the successor states would set a benchmark date that would allow non–Ngok-Dinka people living in the area before that date to claim residency. As mentioned above, the ABC was formed in 2005. It was not mandated to foresee subsequent developments after that date, such as the railway, oil, nomad resettlement, shifting state boundaries and the arrival of other persons who are full-time inhabitants of Abyei.

Guest Residency as an Entry Point for Peace Building

The land area (10,460 square kilometres) identified by the Abyei Arbitration Tribunal in July 2009 belongs to the Ngok-Dinka. Henceforth, the Missiriya cannot claim legal rights to such land as property. Any attempt to settle in this area without the consent of the Ngok-Dinka would be tantamount to forceful occupation by the Missiriya. The Missiriya believe that this piece of land was taken away from them by the Sudanese government and handed over to the Ngok-Dinka as the result of an unfair verdict issued by the PCA in The Hague. They demand compensation from the Sudanese government. The Missiriya also think that they are, as a result, alienated from the dry season water sources at Ragaba Az-Zarga, which they have been frequenting for centuries. They concluded that, on the separation day of 9 July 2011, they would be barred from accessing Ragaba Az-Zarga water sources, in which case it would be a matter of sheer survival. As a result, the Missiriya believe they will be doomed to perennial war with the Ngok-Dinka. This is because the Missiriya always herd their livestock while carrying arms. In contrast, the Ngok-Dinka believe that the presence of arms in the hands of the Missiriya, construed by Ngok-Dinka as 'hand on trigger', is a security threat of the first order to Ngok-Dinka security and survival.

Such being the case, a perennial war of contradictory survival interests would be a suicidal scenario for both communities. The Missiriya, by implication, are deeply concerned that their future livestock survival opportunities will be seriously impaired. The Missiriya also believe that statements made in the Abyei Protocol alluding to the preservation of Missiriya rights to water and grazing pasture cannot be ensured if they herd livestock with 'arms in hand', particularly if the Ngok-Dinka were to join the new state of South Sudan following the secession of the south in July 2011.

The alternative scenario, suggested by some of the Missiriya, would involve the Ngok-Dinka willingly accepting the Missiriya as guests in the Ragaba Az-Zarga watercourse and allowing them guest residency status there. The proposition arose, for those who presented it during the CPA interim period in interviews with the author, as a reciprocal gesture from the Ngok-Dinka against the backdrop of the Missiriya belief that they had received the Ngok-Dinka as guests when they reached this land, presumably in the eighteenth century. The Missiriya also say that they are willing to abandon carrying 'arms in hand' during herding and to unconditionally accept the Abyei Arbitration Tribunal award and the subsequent redrawing of Abyei's boundaries as stipulated in the award, provided that the Ngok-Dinka are willing to reciprocate with guest residency status in the Ragaba Az-Zarga watercourse. In addition to their willingness to disarm themselves while herding livestock or visiting market places, they will also commit never to claim any portion of Abyei area as Missiriya property if the Ngok-Dinka willingly accept and subscribe to Missiriya guest residency in Ragaba Az-Zarga. The area of the portion proposed for Missiriya guest residency status falls within the identified PCA area for Abyei, immediately to the north of the streambed of Ragaba Az-Zarga. It has an estimated total land area of three thousand square kilometres. Guest residency status could continue for fifty years, during which time households are expected to settle, outside Ngok-Dinka land, while livestock could still move.

This peace-building initiative is not only a 'land-for-peace formula', but also aims to transcend the possibility of potential turbulence and unrest and ensure for the Missiriya continuous and unimpeded access to dry season water and grazing. In addition, it seeks to address the perceived potential threat to Ngok-Dinka community security. The NCP did not accept this proposition, as their eyes are fixed solely on 'the oil dividend'. The SPLM also did not accept the proposition, presumably because, following independence for South Sudan, they have their own strategy for addressing the whole issue of the 'Abyei State' that they intend to create for the Ngok-Dinka. The alternative for the successor state in Sudan and South Kordofan was to immediately embark on major water harvesting of seasonal streams falling north of Abyei, so that Missiriya transhumance could be guaranteed water for livestock in order to mitigate conflict.

Conclusion

Three sets of issues have dominated the current debate on resource competition and conflict resolution and continue to be of great relevance in Sudan, particularly in the borderlands between north and south. First, it is important to examine the role of institutions and their capacity to mediate between the anomalies resulting from resource appropriation in the context of an accelerated rate of pastoral commercialization, state withdrawal from provisioning of basic social services and environmental degradation. Second, what is perceived locally as resource competition could originate from global processes that are beyond the control of pastoralists. Pastoral communities are interlocked in an interdependent world in which no human society is immune from its positive or negative consequences. Third, pastoralists are not passive accessories in the relationship between market, state and environment. They interact and react to institutional and developmental interventions in a variety of ways. They may resist or turn away.

To generate change and transform the present situation of the two pastoral communities into a better future, emerging issues and persistent challenges not only require a major strategic shift in rural development planning to streamline rural direct producers and pastoralists in particular, but also the overcoming of factors that curtail the ability of pastoralists to adapt and cope with climate change and face up to the severe constraints inhibiting their capability to become an asset for sustainable stability and peace in Sudan. Government plans, programmes and projects aimed at improving the constrained livelihoods of the pastoralists need to make land and natural resources management the entry point for revitalizing local community aspirations through institutional restructuring and awareness raising among pastoralists of the finite nature of such resources through recognizing and streamlining workable customary norms and practices in statutory propositions for land possession and land use. Furthermore, the prevailing economic policy reforms of the 1990s, including structural adjustment programmes aimed at economic liberalization, the privatization of public assets and decentralized governance need to be recognized as inherently insufficient. They nonetheless constitute the basic principles of the day, within which the overall government policy framework is predetermined.

It is further suggested that redressing the predicament of pastoralists in the first decade following the separation of South Sudan in July 2011, and in particular addressing land rights and access to natural resources, is a central issue for the reintegration of the pastoralists in development plans and projects.

There is a need for institutional change and reforms where global sustainability and pastoralism are concerned. Institutions and instruments (particularly legal ones in areas where peace and order are jeopardized by structural violence) capable of achieving the fair and sustainable distribution of entitlement and power should be created or expanded. Institutional reforms must ensure that the basic driving forces of nonsustainability and conflict are addressed (i.e., through the effective reduction of poverty and insecurity) or neutralized (i.e., through appropriate technological intervention) for increased food production.

Notes

1. The assessment methods and techniques for the collection of data and development information comprised a desktop literature review followed by a field visit. First, one week was spent on reviewing the relevant literature and secondary data and development information on South Kordofan and Abyei area, including recent reports, maps and the text of the CPA. Second, field observation was made possible by air travel and a surface return journey over three weeks covering three thousand kilometres through South Kordofan and Abyei area. Simple 'geographic' observation during the field observation enhanced understanding of the landscape, range, vegetation, forests and tree cover, topography and wildlife, livestock travel routes, the state of rural roads and the distribution of human settlements. Furthermore, unstructured interviews were conducted separately with primary and secondary target groups and beneficiary stakeholders in South Kordofan and Abyei. Meetings and group discussions were held, including with area-based national NGOs, Community Based Organizations (CBOs), youth organizations and smallholder farmers' organizations.
2. Natural resources, for these purposes, include water access points for humans and animals, ponds, rivers and dams for fishing, free-range grazing pastures and seasonal migration routes for the movement of pastoralists in the wet and dry seasons, forests and game reserves, large and medium-scale mechanized farms (both demarcated and nondemarcated) and agropastoralist smallholdings in villages.
3. Article 4(1) of the 1970 Unregistered Lands Act states that 'all land of any kind whether waste, forest, occupied or unoccupied, which is not registered before the commencement of this Act shall, on such commencement, be the property of the Government and shall be deemed to have been registered as such, as if the provisions of the Land Settlement and Registration Act, 1925, have been duly complied with'.
4. Author's interview with the governor of South Kordofan, Maj. Gen. I.K. Jallab, Kadugli, June 2006.
5. Author's interview with the governor of Blue Nile, Mr. Abdal-Rahman Bu-Median, Damazīn, June 2006.
6. 'Kordofan Province' was the administrative designation of the area at the point of British Occupation of Sudan in 1898. The name was used, as such, in the transfer of Abyei area to the jurisdiction of Kordofan. The Condominium authorities began to change names of provinces after 1922 when they started to implement the policy of Indirect Rule in Sudan.
7. On 22 July 2009, the presiding arbitrator stated: 'The Security Council of the United Nations, which recognizes the importance of this Award to peace and reconciliation in Sudan among all of its peoples, has called upon the Government of Sudan and the SPLM/A to treat the Award as binding and to implement it fully. The Parties are so bound by the terms of their Arbitration Agreement and by the force of international law. The Tribunal has produced an Award which resolves the dispute between the Parties over the validity of the ABC Decision and which, in accordance with the Arbitration Agreement, draws a boundary that reflects the facts and law of the matter. The Tribunal has acted scrupulously within its mandate to prepare an award in whose terms and holdings it has every confidence. It is equally confident that the Parties will abide by and implement the Award in good faith' (PCA 2009).

Chapter 11

What Place in Khartoum for the Displaced?

Between State Regulation and Individual Strategies

Agnès de Geoffroy

Conflicts and periods of drought and famine have riven Sudan over recent decades: war in southern Sudan from 1956 to 1972 and from 1983 to 2005, drought and famine in the 1980s, war in the Nuba Mountains in the 1990s, the more recent war in Darfur, conflicts in the east and intertribal conflicts throughout the country. These crises have caused a massive displacement of the civil population. There have been and still are many reasons for displacement. According to the Internal Displacement Monitoring Centre (IDMC), a reference institution for forcible internal displacement,[1] Sudan is the country with the largest number of displaced persons. The IDMC counted 4.9 million displaced persons in Sudan in 2010, (IDMC 2010)[2] which comprised 11.5 per cent of a total population of 42.3 million inhabitants. These figures are unanimously used in the press and reports on Sudan. However, this apparent consensus within international organizations hides a more complex reality.

The massive waves of migration (whether voluntary or forcible) have led to a rapid and massive arrival of migrants in Khartoum over the past three decades that has considerably altered the ethnic composition of the population of the capital. This has undoubtedly been interpreted as a threat by the central power. The purpose of this article is to study the successive policies conducted by the state towards those displaced persons settled in Khartoum. I will show how policy on public space serves security control

Notes for this chapter begin on page 223.

regarding displaced populations and how urban planning measures have enabled the state to determine and control the settlement areas of these populations. The strategy of the Sudanese state towards displaced persons is characterized by the predominance of the spatial approach, and the successive policies set up by the state in Khartoum have focused on a principal question: where should the displaced population live? This leads to several additional questions that relate to the scale of reflection. Which places should or could displaced persons occupy in Greater Khartoum, and according to which criteria? Where would they better serve the political intentions of the various actors: in the north or in the south of the country? Thus, the two main issues of the policies initiated by state-controlled actors in Khartoum are urban planning, which aims to relocate displaced persons in and around the city, and a programme enabling them to return to their original region, which has been set up nationwide and is concentrated in Khartoum. However, these measures are not being applied to passive recipients, and the security control strategy of the state is countered by individual and collective strategies. The purpose of this article is to study the effect of the state's urban planning policies on displaced populations and the individual and collective strategies set up to circumvent, take advantage of or put up with these policies. Moreover, the specific measures taken towards displaced persons should be interpreted in the wider context of the policy put in place by the current regime. The Inqādh regime, which seized power with Omar Al-Bashir in 1989, adopted strict measures of control over the population. This political, security and social control relies on several means: the creation of popular committees (*lajna shaʿabīa*), which are the basic units of political representation in charge of some local matters, and which often become a means of control for the party in power; and a very well-developed security apparatus (police, army and an omnipresent and very powerful national security service). Security control is reinforced for certain populations and places, among which displaced persons occupy a prominent position.

At the most fundamental level, the government's policy is based on its loose and restrictive definition of who is an internally displaced person (IDP) (the first part of this chapter). The state's policy towards displaced persons has long been confined to spatial regulation, by establishing and controlling their location in Khartoum (second part). The policy has recently been evolving towards a longer-term strategy, based on opening up access to private property in the agglomeration of Khartoum for displaced populations (third part).

Forced Displacement and Urban Growth in Khartoum

Defining IDPs: International Norms and National Arrangements

The official definition of IDPs as given in the Guiding Principles on Internal Displacement, which was adopted by the General Assembly of the United Nations in 1997, is:

> [I]nternally displaced persons [IDPs] are persons or groups of persons who have been forced or obliged to flee or to leave their homes or places of habitual residence, in particular as a result of or in order to avoid the effects of armed conflict, situations of generalized violence, violations of human rights or natural or human-made disasters, and who have not crossed an internationally recognized state border.

According to Walter Kälin, the former Representative of the UN Secretary-General on the Human Rights of Internally Displaced Persons, the Guiding Principles 'guide and assist governments, international humanitarian agencies and societies to better discharge their responsibilities in protecting and assisting the men, women and children who have been forcibly displaced in their country' (Kälin 2008). In addition to the challenges of determining which organization should take the lead at the international level, operational difficulties and conceptual debates have arisen concerning internal displacement. Some authors have argued that displaced persons should be categorized according to the cause of their displacement, such as violence, natural or human-made disasters, or development projects (Castles 2005), whereas the international trend has been to include an increasing number of situations within the IDP category as defined in the Guiding Principles. From an operational point of view, it can be hard or even pointless in certain contexts to distinguish between these different causes. For example, when a conflict is combined with underdevelopment, the line between objective and external constraint and voluntary choice is blurred (Turton 2003).

The Guiding Principles, which 'reflect and are consistent with international human rights law and international humanitarian law' (United Nation 1998: Art. 3), are not binding, and the primary responsibility regarding displaced persons lies with the state. This is necessary to preserve the sovereignty of the state in its own territory, but is also a source of weakness in terms of the protection and assistance extended to this population group, namely, displaced people who remain to a large extent subject to internal political interests.

In the Sudanese context, there seems to be no consensus among stakeholders regarding the definition of an IDP. The picture is particularly murky in the context of Khartoum. The different stakeholders (public authorities, civil servants, employees of NGOs and international organizations, and members of local associations) use different criteria (region of origin and/or ethnic affiliation, place of living and social status) to create their own definitions of who is an IDP. The cause of the displacement, which, in the definition of the Guiding Principles, is the founding criterion that justifies the creation of this new category of population, is by and large eluded in the Sudanese context. We shall see that the urban planning policies that have been implemented over the past three decades in Greater Khartoum shed light on the confusions and manipulations surrounding this category of population. For the purposes of this article, we adopt the same loose definition as the different stakeholders in Khartoum. We do not distinguish between the people displaced from the south, from the Darfur region and from other marginal areas of Sudan (e.g., South Kordofan). Most of these people were pushed out because of warfare or drought. In any case, the neglect of the state towards peripheral regions and populations did nothing to prevent it.

Heading to the Capital

A significant proportion of the populations that were forced to relocate or that migrated during the past decades came to live in Khartoum in search of protection and opportunities. For the last decades, the agglomeration of Khartoum has been the receptacle of both voluntary and forced migration, and the urban growth rate has been maintained at a high level[3] (Denis 2005; table 11.1).

Table 11.1. Khartoum Population (in thousands)

	1955	1973	1983	1993	2008
Greater Khartoum (urban districts)	*245*	*784*	*1,343*	*2,920*	*4,273*

Source: Government of Sudan, National Censuses. From de Geoffroy (2009).

This strong urban growth, fed both by forcible and voluntary migration, certainly explains to a large extent the confusion that prevails in Khartoum regarding the displaced population. The difficulty in distinguishing between forced and voluntary migration in a context of recurrent and multiple conflicts, natural hazards, famines and underdevelopment adds to this confusion (G. Hamid 1996; Assal 2006b). The IDMC, mainly based on reports produced by humanitarian actors, estimated the number of displaced persons in Khartoum at nearly two million in 2006, with only

270,000 living in the four official IDP camps (IDMC 2006: 59). This figure was subsequently adjusted to 1.7 million in 2010 following the first return waves of displaced people to their region of origin (IDMC 2010). Tufts University conducted a profile study in Khartoum in 2008 and concluded that 'we get a range of 1,329,300–1,675,500 IDPs in all of Khartoum' (Jacobsen 2008). The government of Sudan carried out its own assessment in 2009, which concluded that 623,667 persons could still be counted as IDPs in the capital, with 1.5 million 'ex-IDPs' having 'been officially allocated land for their ownership'.[4] It is difficult to obtain reliable and accurate figures for the number of displaced people living in Khartoum, and estimations vary over a wide range. Nevertheless, displaced people represent a significant demographic weight in a capital that has 4.3 million inhabitants according to the fifth national census, which was performed in 2008.

Spatial Regulation as a Means of Control

The Creation of Specific Spaces

In the case of Khartoum, state intervention is particularly strong and obvious, which led Marc Lavergne to publish an article entitled 'Violence as a Means of Regulation of Urban Growth: The Case of Khartoum' (Lavergne 1997a). State intervention is indeed a crucial factor in the localization of displaced persons in the city. The settlement of displaced people upon arrival in the city follows certain lines of reasoning, depending on whether they arrive in groups or alone, whether they rely on social networks and solidarity systems or not, and whether they rent, use free housing or simply occupy vacant land. The state therefore has to regulate and rectify practices over which it initially had little control.

In 1982, ninety-six squatter settlement[5] areas were counted. By 1983, over half of the population living in Khartoum consisted of migrants born outside the town. Although the two phenomena, namely, squatter settlements and the arrival of new migrants, do not always go together, the massive and rapid arrival of migrants in Khartoum in the 1980s and 1990s greatly contributed to the development of existing squatter settlements and the creation of new settlements. The National Capital Act was adopted in 1983 together with a programme destined to eradicate squatter settlements within a twenty-five-kilometre radius in the capital city (S. Bannaga 1992: 9). This policy failed because the means deployed by the state was insufficient when faced with the massive arrival of new migrants. In 1987, in a new attempt to control urban growth in Khartoum, 'Dār Al-Salām' schemes were created on the outskirts of the three cities of the capital: ten thousand plots[6] in Khartoum North, thirty thousand plots in Omdurman and ten thousand plots in the south of Khartoum (at Jebel Awlia) (S. Bannaga 1992: 12).

According to S. Bannaga (1992), there was initially resistance to the plans to relocate the squatters from their existing sites to the Dār Al-Salām. However, with the heavy rains and floods that struck Khartoum in 1988, destroying nearly 150,000 houses mainly in the large squatter settlements, relocating people became in many cases a necessity. These Dār Al-Salām, planned 'sites and services' schemes on the fringes of the city, are relocation sites that were conceived as a substitute for illegal settlements. In this context, 'planned' means that the plots are demarcated and levelled. These areas are therefore ready to receive public services and notably network services. In the agglomeration of Khartoum, nonplanned areas are, for instance, not connected to the regular water supply system as long as they have not been regularized. Moreover, in planned areas, the plots are given to households that can become official owners if they accomplish all the necessary administrative procedures to consolidate and legalize their initial right of occupancy to the land. The name of these new areas (Dār Al-Salām means 'house of peace') evokes the context in which they were created and their purpose of welcoming migrants who have recently arrived in Khartoum.

Following the same logic of spatial planning and segregation of different groups of the population, four official camps were created in 1990 for displaced persons. These zones were not planned, as they were intended to temporarily welcome displaced populations. The displaced persons evicted from the city and relegated to camps, therefore, do not have access to land ownership, nor any hope of being connected to the services of the city, as the plots have been neither demarcated nor levelled. This reveals much about the prevailing state of mind of the Sudanese authorities on the issue of forcible displacement. A temporary right of occupancy of the land was granted to the displaced population in certain peripheral neighbourhoods of the agglomeration, prior to their return to their place of origin. They were, in a way, treated like second-class citizens, and had to resettle outside the camps if they wanted to obtain access to land ownership and formal public services. Nevertheless, in many instances, the situation is not better for the larger population of the urban poor living in fourth-class neighbourhoods or squatter settlements.

Figure 11.1 was designed by the Ministry of Physical Planning and Public Utilities (MPPPU)[7] in 1992. When viewed alongside figure 11.2, it offers an opportunity to explain and understand the urban plan subsequently designed by the public authorities. The classification proposed on figure 11.1 was based on the criteria of seniority (i.e., older squatter settlements as opposed to new settlements), the level of structure of the area (i.e., or-

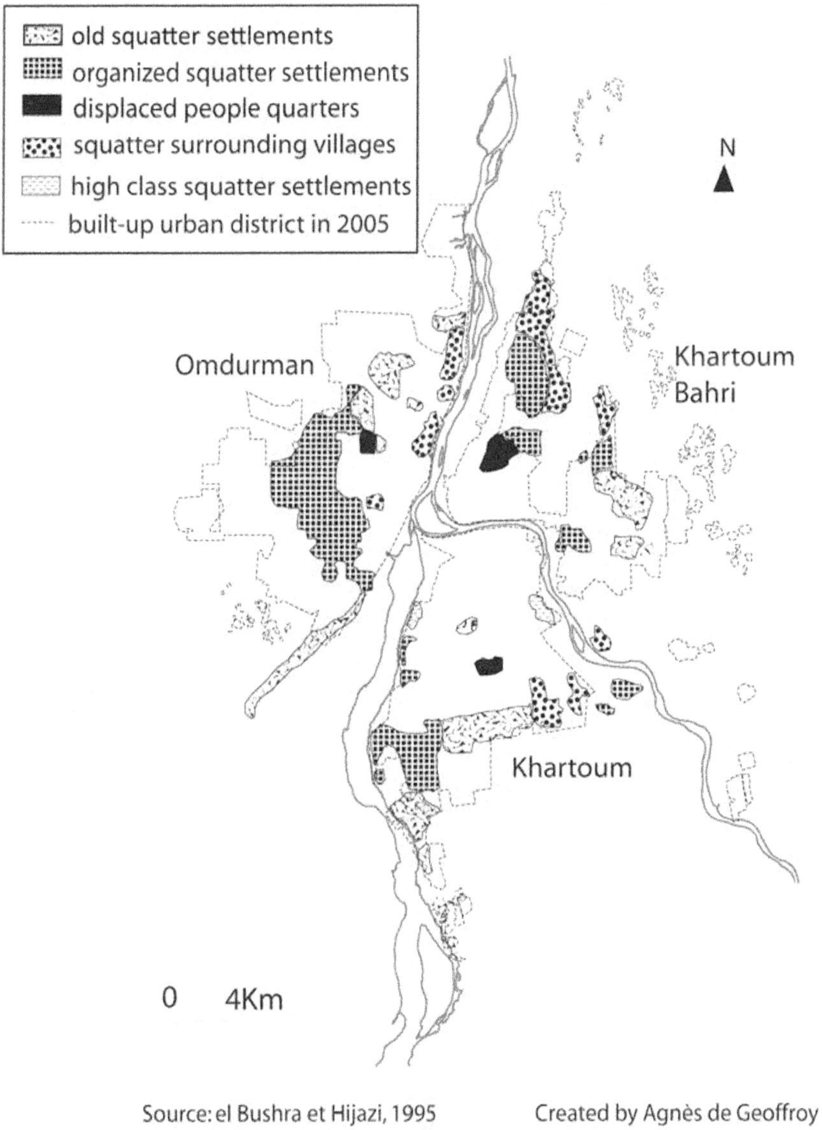

Figure 11.1. Classification of Squatter Areas in 1992 (according to the Ministry of Physical Planning and Public Utilities)

ganized squatter settlements as opposed to unorganized activity) and the type of population living in it, with the displaced population being singled out. Interestingly, on this map, squatter settlements are designated as illegal habitat zones where new migrants and poor urban populations

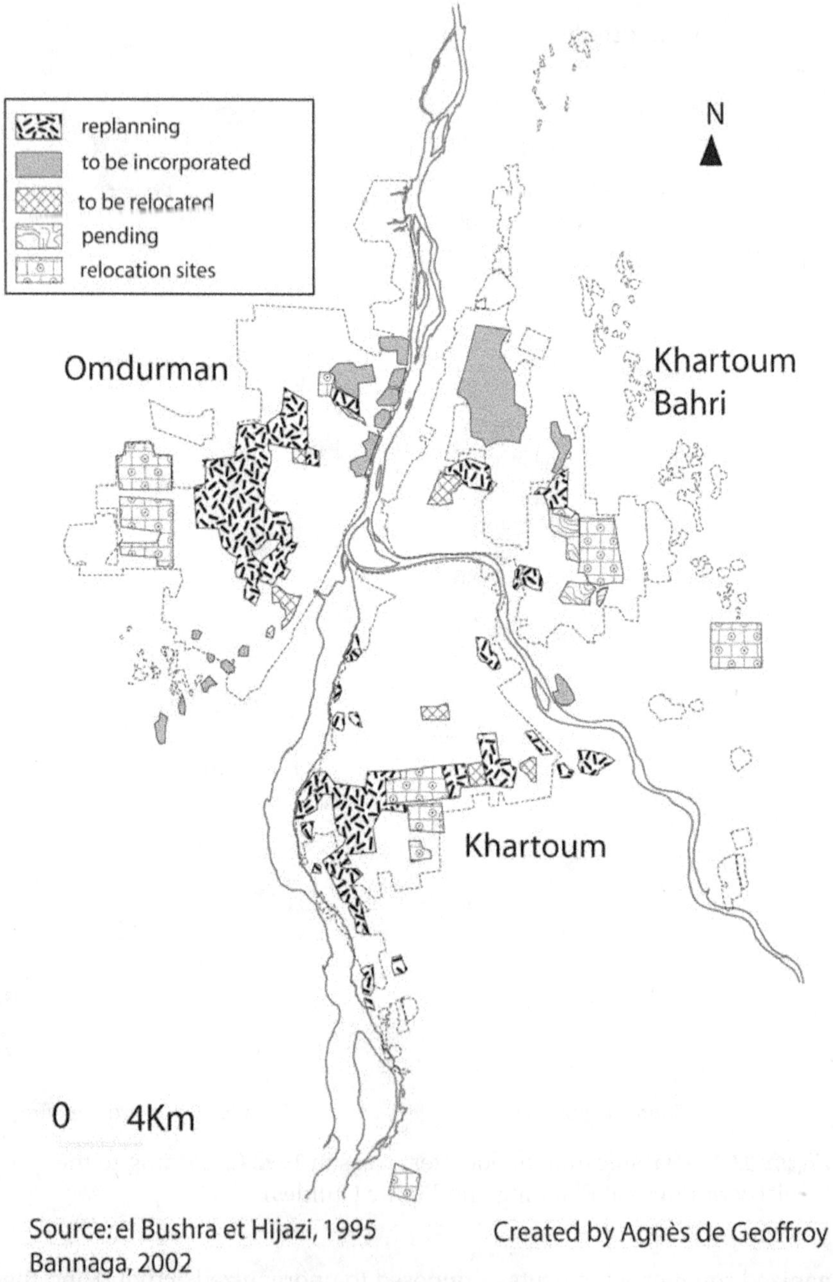

Figure 11.2. Urban Planning Designed to Remove and Treat the Squatter Settlements in Greater Khartoum in the 1990s

live, differing from displaced areas, which were also illegal habitat zones, but where displaced populations lived.

Theoretically, squatting is a way of illegally occupying a place, but in the Sudanese context it came to designate a type of population differentiated from the displaced population. In fact, many displaced persons live outside the official camps or planned areas and also squat on the land. Nevertheless, these two maps designed by the state of Khartoum's MPPPU, before the creation of the official IDP camps, distinguish between squatter and displaced person settlements, probably based on their date of arrival in the city, the region of origin of the population and the capacity they had shown for integration.[8] Behind these two criteria of seniority in the city and level of integration used by the administration, there in fact lies a policy of ethnic and social selection based on urban planning. The areas designated as displaced settlement areas on the first map were all intended to be relocated in the development plan, whereas incorporation and planning measures were proposed for most of the other cases. Incorporation measures have aimed to register existing urban built environment in a land registry (cadastre) with as few changes as possible. These measures generally concern extensions that have developed around villages located on the outskirts of the agglomeration. The planning measures generally consist of demolishing the existing built environment, demarcating roads and plots, levelling them and finally reallocating them to the resident population. As a result of these replanning measures, part of the resident population is evicted and resettled elsewhere, on relocation sites, because the postreplanning demographic density is usually lower than the original density of the neighbourhood.

Figure 11.3 shows the current location of the displaced population, which confirms that much of the development plan has been applied. We can see that relocation sites have indeed been created where intended in 1990, with Dār Al-Salām sites as a kind of relocation site. Likewise, most of the areas intended for replanning and incorporation have indeed been legalized and the urban built area registered.

Violence and Intraurban Forcible Mobility

The urban planning policy developed in the 1990s as outlined above, which consisted of planning for already occupied areas, creating new relocation sites and therefore demolishing existing habitat and relocating part of the resident population, goes hand in hand with extremely common intraurban forcible mobility as well as repeated violence by the state to achieve its objectives. A minority of the displaced population (38.4 per

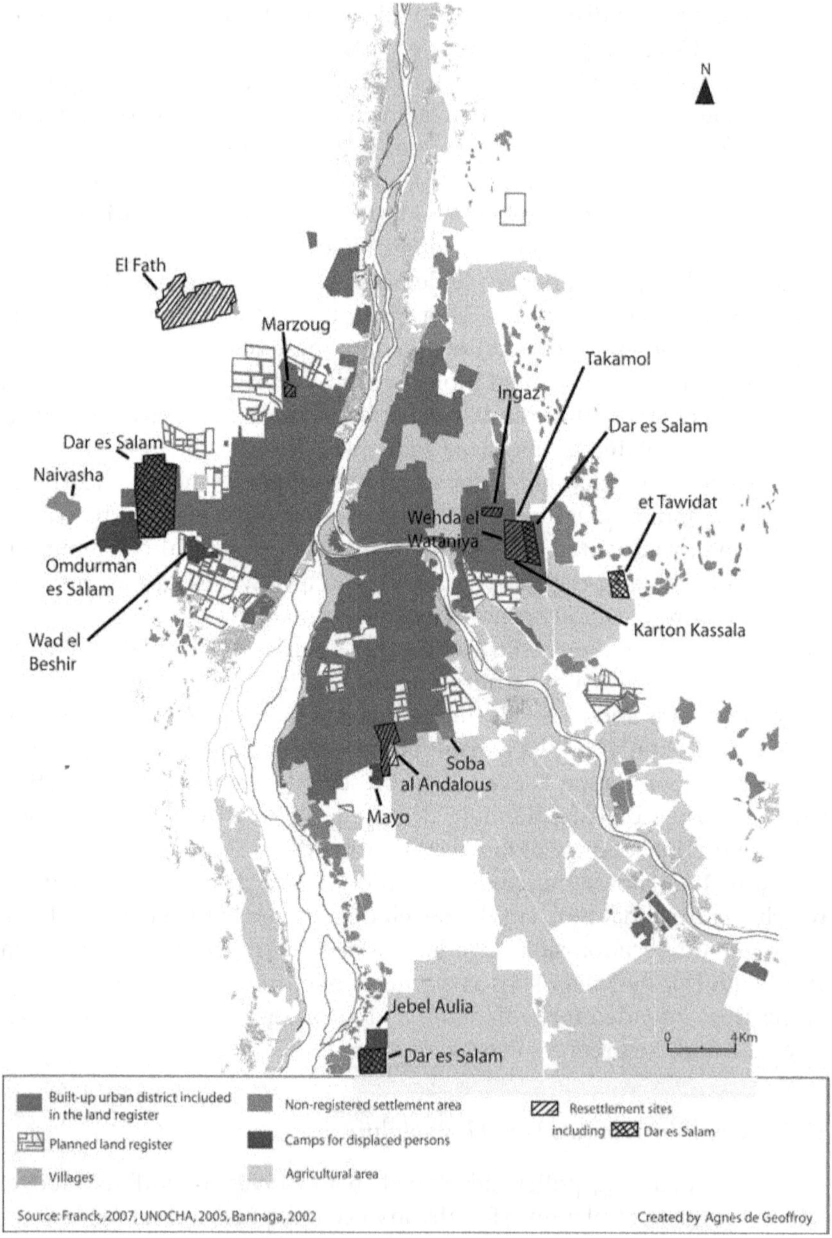

Figure 11.3. IDP Camps, Dār Al-Salām Sites and Relocation Sites in Greater Khartoum Today

cent) has been settled in camps since their arrival in Khartoum. However, the majority (61.6 per cent) of the displaced population living in camps first settled in other places upon arrival, such as in El Gamayer in Omdurman, El Izba, Zagalona, Souk El Markazi, the industrial zone of Khartoum North, Umbadda, Ḥājj Yūsif or outside the state of Khartoum (S. Bannaga 2002: 116). According to S. Bannaga (2002), the percentages are identical for the population living in Dār Al-Salām sites and new planned extensions. The high mobility of these 'newcomers' is not the sole result of market mechanisms and survival strategies of the people.

The 'residential' path of the urban poor and migrants is indeed characterized by forcible intraurban mobility. For several decades, the state has evicted[9] populations living in squatter areas and has relocated them or not to other areas, ousting the more vulnerable and more recent populations to the outskirts of the city. 'In March 1992, 425,000 people had been evicted with such brutality that it had shocked the international public opinion. At the beginning of 1995, the 712,000 displaced that had been censused on the 35 sites in September 1991 had been transferred to temporary camps that had been opened for them. But in April 1995 the entire population of the camps was estimated between 250,000 and 400,000'[10] (Lavergne 1997a: 59). One of the camps located in Omdurman bears the official name of Omdurman Al-Salām, but has been renamed Jabarōna by the displaced, literally meaning 'we were forced'. As Eric Denis has emphasized, 'displacing unwanted populations towards the margins and requalifying the land as the metropolis grows still applies' (2006: 113).

In 2007, a civil servant from the Structural Planning Department estimated that the squatter settlements still represented 10 per cent of the agglomeration. These squatter settlements had represented 40 per cent of the agglomeration in 1985, 60 per cent in 1990 and 20 per cent in 2000. The declared goal of the ongoing structural planning policy was to eradicate these illegal districts from Greater Khartoum before 2010. In addition to the regularization of these last squatter areas, the state had also planned displaced persons camps for several years. The pace of demolitions again intensified for the displaced population, and according to the OCHA over 330,000 displaced persons have seen their homes demolished since 2004.

A case study carried out in Khartoum in 2007 by the Feinstein International Centre from Tufts University in collaboration with the IDMC shows a significant difference between the displaced and nondisplaced populations. The aim of this study, carried out in several districts of the agglomeration, in the three cities (Omdurman, Khartoum North and Khartoum) but not within the displaced person camps, was to study the situation of the displaced population in the city outside the camps. There appears to be discrimination between the displaced and nondisplaced in terms of mobility in the city. Of the nondisplaced population, 53 per cent declare having previously lived elsewhere in Khartoum compared with 62 per cent of the displaced, and 18 per cent of the nondisplaced declare having been forced to move or evicted, compared with 39 per cent of the displaced (Jacobsen 2008: 50). A study concerning Dinka migrants was carried out between 1989 and 1991 in the district of Souk el Markazi, south of Khartoum (Yath 1995). After having been compelled to regroup in Jereif East because of high housing costs and precarious living conditions, these Dinka were displaced from their squatter settlements to a new place, Souk el Markazi, from where they were again displaced in 1990 and 1991 to the camps for displaced persons in Jebel Awlia. At the time, the camp of Jebel Awlia was a mere 1.5-by-1.5-kilometre strip of land in the desert without any connection with the outside world, and was surrounded by police and military checkpoints.

In recent years, the state has again applied the same eviction policy consisting of pushing new arrivals and the most vulnerable members of the population further towards the outskirts of the city. Yesterday's peripheries have gained value thanks to their relative planning and their progressive integration into the urban fabric of the agglomeration. Dār Al-Salām sites and camps for displaced persons have been caught up by dynamic urban development and the growing urban sprawl of the past twenty years. The new main relocation site for people evicted from the city is El Fath, located in Karari Province,[11] about forty kilometres north of Omdurman. Thus, evicted people who have not received offers of resettlement within the urban perimeter of the agglomeration (with seniority as the primary criterion), or do not have the means to pay ownership taxes or possibly the price of the plot, are displaced outside the agglomeration, at El Fath.

These planning measures and the forced removal of part of the population have several aims. The priority of the public authorities, behind the regularization of the neighbourhoods and of property, is of course to ensure an even development of the city in the long run: proper infrastructure, adequate services and legal land tenure. The control of the population and security does not lie very far behind. Nevertheless, if the authorities conduct the first phase of the planning process (i.e., demolition and plot allocation) in a relatively swift manner, in contrast the provisions of services for the newly planned areas for the lower classes takes a long time and is in many instances left to private initiative or to other stakeholders.

As shown in figures 11.4 and 11.5, demolitions leave the resident population in extreme poverty. The inhabitants build precarious shelters on the site or in the place to which they were relegated, using sticks and

Figure 11.4. The IDP Camp of Omdurman As-Salam under Planning: After the Demolition by Bulldozers (A. de Geoffroy, 19 April 2005)

Figure 11.5. The IDP Camp of Omdurman As-Salam: Temporary Shelters (*rakūba*) Built after Demolition, Pending the Plot Allocation Process (A. de Geoffroy, April 2007)

pieces of plastic and cloth. These shelters are consolidated over time. In the poor outskirts of Khartoum, self-made habitats largely prevail. Mud bricks, made locally with soil taken on-site mixed with water and faeces and then dried in the sun, are used for construction. These habitats are fragile and show little resistance to bad weather conditions and bulldozers. Before the planning measures in the camps, the habitat takes on various forms according to the construction techniques used in the region of origin of the displaced population and their economic capacity. Following the planning measures, the reconstructed habitat is much more homogenous and mainly adopts the architectural style of Khartoum, that is, a wall surrounding the plot, an inner courtyard (*ḥōsh*) and one or several rooms built within the premises. Some of the new constructions also use baked brick, which is a sign of social differentiation because baked brick is much more expensive.

Between Reconquering the City and Silent Resistance

The displaced population has adopted strategies to adapt to this new form of violence,[12] and voluntary intraurban mobility echoes the regulatory and segregated violence of the state. A certain porousness has developed between the various types of areas created by the state. In reaction to the evictions and the tragic losses that they generate, the displaced population sometimes chooses to return and squat in the city. They sometimes pursue a twin strategy of 'illegally' reconquering the city and accepting the practices of the state, in order to access land ownership. Resettlement areas are planned and theoretically offer access to land ownership for the people who are brought there. The displaced population then calculates the value that the land will gain in these marginal areas, which are not yet equipped with basic services.[13] Interviews in the resettlement areas of El Fath and Ḥilla Al-Jedīda (Al Manar, Abū Seʿīd Locality, west of Omdurman) have indicated that displaced individuals return to the city after having built a precarious shelter (*rakūba*) in the resettlement area, as this shelter guarantees their land rights there, or that families are split in two and the members who work return to squatter settlements in the city while the rest of the family remains in the resettlement area.

Many movements and departures can be observed early on following the planning and relocation measures, which last as long as the plots have not been allocated. 'In El Fath, many moved and then returned to the city [Greater Khartoum]. They prefer to live poorly in the city than to live in El Fath.'[14] However, it was mentioned several times that this kind of strategy always occurred in the beginning, when the new relocation sites are not serviced and do not offer real survival conditions, and would become blurred over time. The population settles down with the progressive arrival of services (water, health and education) in the relocation area.[15] Thus, in December 2004, the NGO Enfants du Monde – Droits de l'Homme (EMDH) observed demolitions and evictions made by the state in the squatter settlement of Shikān in Omdurman. People were transported to El Fath. However, at the beginning of January 2005, EMDH recorded 650 *rakūbas* erected in the area of Shikān since the demolitions, then 1,750 on January 27 and 915 at the beginning of March (cumulative totals). Those figures show that the eviction policies actually worked after some pendulum movements: the people expelled from Shikān and taken to El Fath first started to reinvest in Shikān in an invasive mode, and then slowly settled in El Fath over time and with the progressive – but still very limited – development of the relocation area.

A second resistance mechanism in response to the regulatory violence of the state is for people to gather by family, tribe or original region. It has been mentioned that when the state demolishes squatter areas, plans them and allocates parcels on-site or further away, it dissolves the groups created by the populations. These networks seem to reemerge progressively after the evictions and resettlements by the state. This dynamic was evident in the case of Omdurman As-Salām. In 2008, 60 per cent of the Omdurman As-Salām camp had already been planned. This planning imposed the intermingling of populations and the mixing of tribes, which is interpreted as a positive element (in that it enables them to meet 'good' people and 'good' neighbours) but also as a negative element (by dissolving bonds of solidarity and making isolated people – such as old people and widows – more vulnerable). However, in the camps, there was discussion of the lack of transparency and possible corruption[16] concerning the mechanisms for plot allocation, which enabled some people to remain grouped together. In fact, interviews conducted in 2005, 2006 and 2007 in the IDP camps under planning revealed great confusion among the population, who were taken by surprise by the planning measures and were ignorant of the procedures for plot allocation. During later interviews conducted from 2008 onwards, the displaced population displayed far more understanding and guile, using a double strategy consisting of waiting for the planning process to take place in their own neighbourhood and applying for a plot before considering returning to their place of origin. Similar reunification phenomena have been noted in the Dār Al-Salām of Ḥājj Yūsif notably since the recent arrival of Darfuri populations as the conflict intensified in the region from 2003. Plots sold by people leaving the area are bought by new arrivals, notably people arriving from Darfur to find members of their family or their tribe who had arrived with a previous wave of migrants.

Access to Land Ownership Is Highly Sought After by Displaced Persons

Economic Development and the Housing Boom in the Capital

The oil boom, economic development and the enormous growth of investment in Khartoum have increased the pressure on land ownership in the Sudanese capital. Since the end of the 1990s, the development of the oil industry has led to a reallocation of national economic resources. 'Oil now accounts for over 80 per cent of the exports, while in 1999, livestock and sorghum exports still accounted for over half of the exports and their revenue barely covered the cost of oil importation' (Denis 2006: 118). Asian countries have invested extensively in the oil sector, whereas Western countries have boycotted the Sudanese economy. Between 1990 and 1999, 61 per cent of all foreign direct investment in the country was invested in the capital. The investment in the economy of the capital translated into a housing boom, which affected the markets for office spaces and luxury residences (Denis 2006: 119). This pressure on property affects the city as constructions rise and modern projects appear, such as the proposed business district of Mogran. The pressure on property can also be felt in the subcentral areas of the capital. The construction market is very dynamic and the entire city seems to be under construction, from luxury residential areas to peripheral areas. A quick overview of the city shows the dynamism of investment in the construction industry.

The mechanical effect of this development is the increased pressure on land ownership at the expense of the more vulnerable populations. This mechanism has already been discussed in relation to the eviction of Dinka from the surroundings of Souk El Markazi at the end of the 1980s. In the opinion of Arwan Yath, the pressure of land speculators and private investors was decisive in the decision of the state to evict displaced persons (Yath 1995: 99). At the present time, because of the value of land in Khartoum, private owners who initially let squatters invade their land now want to recover the use of their property. This phenomenon is particularly problematic in the case of the camps of Mayo Farm and Jebel Awlia. These lands, which are theoretically for agricultural use and where, respectively, 133,000 and 175,000 people[17] have settled, are now claimed by their owners, who require the monetary value of their land. The lands on which the informal settlements of Soba Aradi developed belong to the Faculty of Agriculture of the University of Khartoum and the army. An agreement between these two institutions and the government enabled their conversion to residential land use. The increase in land prices, which was a result of increased market pressure, has created a dynamic of eviction for the poorest populations with which the state has to deal.

State Regulation and Access to Land Ownership

It is in this context that the state has developed urban strategies and policies. Behind area planning, regularizations and parcel allocation is a more complicated game than is initially apparent. In spite of the authoritarian means used, this policy is actually considered to be positive and is desired by most of the population affected, who see it as a means to access land ownership and to secure their presence in the city. During the interviews, inhabitants were on the whole in favour of the planning measures and deplored situations in which the process seemed to be blocked.[18] The population density in the areas prior to the planning process was, however, too high for Sudanese standards, according to which plots allocated to families must measure at least three hundred square metres, with the planned areas having been reclassified to third-class habitat zones.[19]

The difficult and sensitive issue is then to determine who will receive a plot within the area under planning and who will have to be displaced to a relocation area. This right to a plot within the planned area triggers envy and conflicts, and the rules determining this right are subject to numerous pressures. In the case of squatter areas, the right to a plot is defined according to the following criteria (S. Bannaga 1996: 34): (1) being Sudanese (as proved by a birth certificate or military service certificate); (2) having a dependent family (proved by a marriage certificate); (3) living in the area since before 1990 (this date is subject to change over time according to the type of area); (4) earning a living (evidenced by socioeconomic investigation); and (5) not having another place of residence in the state of Khartoum.

To obtain the right to a parcel within the planned area, the absolute prerequisite is to be on the list of people selected by the *lajna shaʿabīa* (in some cases, a specific committee is set up, which is responsible for all matters concerning the area planning). The selection criteria are officially those stated above. However, local management of such important issues favours the emergence of other pressures and corrupt practices. As always in these cases, the more vulnerable populations, with less developed social and economic capital, hardly ever benefit from these situations of pressure and power.

In the case of planning for the IDP camps, interviews revealed quite similar criteria: (1) being Sudanese (proved by a birth certificate or military service certificate); (2) having a dependent family (proved by a marriage certificate); (3) possessing a displaced person card, given by the government in 1997 following the census made in the camps in 1996; and (4) not having another place of residence in the state of Khartoum.

In the case of the camps, once again the *lajna shaʿabīa* selects the IDPs who will be entitled to a plot within the area. These criteria and procedures deserve some attention, as they determine the conditions of access to land ownership and consolidate integration into the city. Displaced persons are disadvantaged in several respects. Obtaining official documents (such as birth, marriage or military service certificates) has a significant cost and is a real challenge for populations from faraway regions where written records and civil registrations did not always exist, particularly during the war years. To overcome this difficulty, doctors in Khartoum deliver certificates estimating the age of the individual based on their physical appearance. Marriage certificates are often very hard to obtain for people who were married in the south following customs that are very different from Muslim marriages, and who do not have any written document as evidence. Some people possess the 1997 displaced person card, but others either never received such a card or have lost it. The first stage, which consists of gathering the required official documents, is already a real obstacle. In the second step, the challenges faced by displaced persons involve evaluation and selection procedures for the plots.[20]

The *lajna shaʿabīa* is very powerful in this stage because government officials refer cases to the committee, which vouches for the good moral character of the inhabitants of the area and their seniority in the area in the event of any doubt.[21] The selection process is characterized by a high level of nepotism and economic corruption. It is therefore impossible to obtain straight answers regarding taxes to be paid in the first stage. The amounts are not set and vary according to people and places without any form of logic behind these variations. In the camp of Omdurman As-Salām, a report written in 2005 by several humanitarian agencies (FAR et al. 2005: 15) described taxes of about EUR 15 to the Survey Department, EUR 30 to the locality (specifically, to the service in charge of allocating the plots) and 'something' for the engineers who measure and demarcate the plots.[22] In some situations it also mentioned a tax given to the *lajna shaʿabīa* to initiate the plot request procedure.[23] More generally, in the camps, a total amount close to EUR 100 has been given for all the taxes to be paid before the allocation of a plot, with a significant increase in these taxes since 2003. In Dār Al-Salām–Ḥājj Yūsif and the Ta'awīḍāt, a relocation area created at the time of the planning of Ḥājj Yūsif, inhabitants confirmed having paid about USD 50.[24] In Soba Aradi, the report mentioned above described taxes ranging between EUR 70 and EUR 500. If the inhabitants do not have the required documents, the taxes are increased. Moreover, it is said that the amount written on the receipt does not match the amount really paid. The demarcation and allocation of the plots are the first step of the planning process. For the selected inhabitants, the payment of the taxes described above gives them the right to stay on the plot that has been allocated to them. Some inhabitants, who cannot carry the procedure any further, leave it at that but remain very vulnerable, as another buyer who goes to the Land Office can acquire ownership of the same plot. The first stage does not entitle them to property titles. They have to start a completely new procedure to obtain the title. In this second stage, the level of the fees varies much more. In 2005, in the camp of Wad Al-Bashīr, EUR 100 was enough to obtain property titles, whereas in the camp of Omdurman As-Salām higher amounts were needed, ranging from EUR 300 to 600. In Ta'awīḍāt, fifteen years ago, these property titles cost about USD 200.

The sums mentioned above correspond to the fees that have to be paid to the different intermediaries intervening in the process, such as public administrations, engineers and lawyers. The government has made a real effort to make land ownership accessible in the IDP camps, in Dār Al-Salām sites and relocation areas, as land is allocated for free. This last point makes the land very attractive and explains the strong speculative pressure in these areas, sometimes diverting the planning process from the primary objective of the government. The total amount of the fees to be paid provides income for a poor, underpaid administration, but in many instances the land is sold at rates well below its commercial value.[25]

When the areas are located on private land, the situation is obviously more complicated. The camp of Jebel Awlia is unique in this respect. The locality sent a letter in 2007 to the *lajna shaʿabīa* of the camp of Jebel Awlia asking it to evaluate the area and set the amount that people should pay for the land. The *lajna shaʿabīa* refused to answer such a request and asked the state how an IDP camp could have been settled on private land. In the case of Soba Aradi (a squatter area), the price to acquire the plot varies widely depending on the date of arrival in the area (as attested by the *lajna shaʿabīa*). According to interviews in the area in 2005, people who arrived before 1993 had to pay about EUR 450, arrivals between 1993 and 1995 had to pay over EUR 1,500 (up to a maximum of over EUR 2,000) and people who arrived after 1995 could not acquire a plot on-site and were displaced to a relocation area. The state gave the buyer the possibility of paying an initial 25 per cent and spreading the remaining 75 per cent over eleven months. Those sums, even if below the market prices, are difficult to gather for IDPs and poor people in general, given their almost inexistent savings capacity. It is thus creating a socioeconomic filter, allowing access to land property only for better off inhabitants.

Land Speculation: Benefit or Prejudice for IDPs?

The already confusing plot allocation procedure has become even more complex because of the widespread land speculation that characterizes the state of Khartoum. In a way, the state subsidizes access to land ownership in these areas, and the possibility of buying land at low cost obviously attracts many people. The issue of people who are not from the area, and who set up a *rakūba* (shelter) shortly before or at the beginning of the planning process, is unanimously considered to be a problem by the various actors questioned.[26] Senior civil servants consider that this practice undermines urban policies and diverts them from their initial aim. IDPs see it as dangerous competition. A displaced person working for an NGO estimated that when planning and demolitions start in an area, 40 per cent more people arrive from the outside to try and obtain a plot. Poor urban populations can develop real strategies to access land ownership. Eric Denis estimates that within the agglomeration of Khartoum, '85 per cent of the housing stock belongs to the third or even fourth category and to illegal habitat. Property insecurity concerns 40 per cent of the habitat' (2006: 96). Access to land ownership is therefore a crucial issue for thousands of poor households. There is also the phenomenon of widespread speculation. In areas that are being planned, people referred several times in interviews to rich people, 'women covered in jewellery', who were not residing in the area, standing in line in front of the *lajna shaʿabīa* office on the day that tokens (called *debaya*), which symbolize the right to a plot, are given out. Sharaf el Din Bannaga energetically disapproves of this practice, saying that '[i]llegal possession of government and private lands as well as land speculation is damaging government reputation and paves the way for corruption and illegal wealth. In addition, they damage the national economy and the moral behaviour of people. This illegal act should be fought by all available means' (2000: 28).

Islam indeed condemns this kind of practice. However, it is profitable because selling the plots acquired in these areas at the market price ensures a substantial increase in value. In the camp of Omdurman As-Salām, a *debaya* (i.e., the token giving the right to a parcel in the area) acquired after having paid a tax of EUR 100[27] is resold for about EUR 375. A property title in the same camp acquired after having paid about EUR 750, (with all procedures included) is resold for between EUR 2,500 and 3,000. Another example was given at Dār Al-Salām–Ḥājj Yūsif, where plots were acquired with the payment of minimal tax fifteen years ago (between EUR 7 and 11). Ahmed, an inhabitant from Geneina (Darfur), bought his unbuilt plot for about EUR 2,100 in 1999 and sold it for about EUR 4,400 in 2007 after having built two rooms on the plot.

The urban planning policy allows sociospatial selection. Only a small minority of IDPs can access full ownership in the agglomeration of Khartoum. The majority, being unable to start the plot request procedure given their precarious situation or to secure land occupancy, stop after obtaining the *debaya*. In contrast, the speculation of land brokers, combined with the profit that displaced persons can make by reselling their *debaya* or their property title, contravene the state's attempt to prevent the illegal occupation of land. A visit to the relocation areas (Al Manar and El Fath) and areas of illegal habitat on the edge of the city and the desert (Naivasha) shows the extent of the phenomenon. The inhabitants of Khartoum bet on the value that the land will gain, even in far-off, isolated land without any basic service provision, by building a *rakūba,* with the more-or-less long-term view that the state will issue plans to develop the land and will allocate plots accordingly.

Conclusion

The massive displacement of the population over recent decades has been fostered by the deeply unbalanced development of the country, leading to a rapid urbanization of Khartoum. The Sudanese authorities were undoubtedly overwhelmed by the scale of this phenomenon, leading to a largely uncontrolled and illegal expansion of the city, which was invaded by undesirable populations. Urban planning was initially used as a means to control this heterogeneous population through spatial and forcible regulation during the 1980s and 1990s. More recently, planning has become a means to encourage the best-integrated members of the population – those surviving economically or who were among the first to arrive in the city – and to evict more precarious and recent arrivals further away to the outskirts of the city. As explained above, property prices are very disparate between the various areas of the agglomeration, thus creating a segregation sieve: the richer and therefore more integrated members of the population can stay, whereas the poorest are forced to leave, driven away by the combined forces of the market and a segregationist state. Nevertheless, IDPs should not be considered only passive victims. On the contrary, many individual interviews reveal that strategies are developed at the micro- or local level to curb such measures and to take advantage of the process when possible.

In conclusion, let us briefly look at the decision mechanisms in terms of urban planning. They show how much urban planning in Khartoum is of particular interest, both for the local political power and the central government. The technical ministry that is theoretically in charge of urban planning and development is in fact stripped of its strategic decision-making powers because the structural development plan for the city was instead elaborated by foreign consulting agencies. Beyond this technical dispossession, another, more political factor has also encouraged the bypassing of this ministry. Decisions are taken by the state governor (*wālī*) and his advisers, with the MPPPU being limited to the execution of orders. Moreover, localities (*maḥalliyas*) reinforce this bypassing by referring directly to the *wālī* and no longer to the MPPPU. The *lajna shaʿabīa,* which is an instrumental actor for urban development policies, is also strongly politicized and draws its strength from its closeness to the party in power.

The functioning of Sudanese political life and its institutions suggest more and more that local decision making is to a large extent subject to the priorities and wishes of national leaders. The containment policy (i.e., settling and control) set up by the government of Khartoum in regard to southern displaced populations during the transitional period stipulated by the Comprehensive Peace Agreement (2005–11) has now been revised in the aftermath of South Sudan's self-determination referendum. The return of displaced persons is strongly encouraged by the governments of South Sudan and Sudan, which is the first sign of an expected hardening of the northern government's policy towards members of the southern population still living in Khartoum.

In fact, the regional origin of the displaced populations has become increasingly important over the past few years, in particular after the secession of South Sudan. This chapter demonstrates the contradictions and uncertainties in the state's policy towards IDPs. Some significant efforts have been made to settle displaced persons and squatters by opening up access to land ownership. Several reasons can be put forward for this policy: an attempt to fix this population in Khartoum, the southerners in particular, to influence the ballot of the referendum and encourage a pro-unity vote; the genuine will to clear the city of squatter settlements to improve urban planning and service provision; and the eviction of poorer members of the population to the benefit of land investors, once those initial settlers had cleared and requalified the land. IDPs and poor settlers can be considered as city clearers to a large extent in the context of Khartoum. Nevertheless, since 2010, when this chapter was first conceived, the policy of the state towards southerners has clearly changed, with the latter becoming foreigners overnight with independence. Since that day, the pressure exerted on southerners has had a direct impact on the land market. Many southerners sold their land before departure, or for fear of being dispossessed by the state, at a price far below its market value. The state cannot be considered a deus ex machina, or an omniscient player. The hazards of history cannot be attributed solely to the state's inconsistency, given that it too is buffeted and driven by contradicting forces and interests.

Notes

1. The IDMC was established in 1998 by the Norwegian Refugee Council, an NGO. It is supported by the UN, which proclaimed it a reference organization for the observation of the phenomenon of forcible internal displacement. The IDMC publishes an annual report on the situation of internal displacement in the world and an annual ranking of countries most affected by this phenomenon. For these countries, the IDMC also publishes an annual country report.
2. Darfur: 2.7 million; Khartoum: 1.7 million; southern Sudan: 390,000; 'transitional areas': 60,000; eastern states: unknown numbers.
3. 1955–65: 6.16 per cent; 1965–73: 6.9 per cent; 1973–83: 5.53 per cent; 1983–93: 8.08 per cent; 1993–2002: 3.29 per cent.
4. The Ministry of Humanitarian Affairs commissioned a study (unfortunately no more available online) from the IDP Centre, a Sudanese public institution, to estimate the number of IDPs in Khartoum and to make an assessment of their living conditions.
5. Squatter settlements are characterized in Khartoum by the illegal occupation of land. Given the specificity of the landed ownership system in Khartoum, these lands often belong to the state and have been left vacant (i.e., unused or for a recreational purpose, such as a football field or town square) or are intended for agricultural use. The squatter settlements are also often characterized by a self-made habitat that its inhabitants consolidate over time according to their socioeconomic capacity. However, sometimes people squat in already planned, but vacant, lands that belong to others.
6. A plot is an area allocated to each household to set up a living space. An area classification system prevails in Khartoum that is determined according to the surface of the plot and the type of habitat (i.e., the construction material used and the characteristics of the habitat). Dār Al-Salām sites are classified as the fourth class, each plot having a surface area of at least two hundred square metres.
7. In the Khartoum State Ministry.
8. S. Bannaga (1992) mentions the difference between economic migrants who have been integrated into the city by finding work and housing in fourth-class (and even illegal) neighbourhoods and displaced persons who are temporary residents and as such have no right to build. Sharaf el Din Bannaga was the Khartoum State minister of physical planning and public utilities in the 1990s and was responsible for the implementation of urban planning policies. He published several books and documents on this issue.
9. Heavy-handed evictions were carried out in Khartoum. The authorities sent bulldozers to the planned areas, the police and the army enjoined the resident population to come out of their houses, and the bulldozers demolished and cleaned the area. The populations usually knew in advance that their area would be planned, but they did not know the date or the time and could not prepare for these demolitions, which therefore involved tragic material loss. Because of the suddenness and violence of the means used, these evictions sometimes took a tragic turn, as was the case in Soba Aradi in May 2005 (de Geoffroy 2005: 38).

10. The United Nations estimate the number of displaced in the four camps at 325,000 in 2006, which represents about 10 per cent of the displaced population living in Khartoum (United Nations and partners 2006: 295).
11. In 1991 Sudan adopted a federal system. The federal state (*wilāya*) is the main power structure at the subnational level. Each federal state consists of provinces (*muḥāfaẓas*) that are in turn made up of localities (*maḥalliyas*). Each *maḥalliya* has a legislative council that elects the executive body. The *maḥalliya* has great responsibility, covering politics, security, economy, finance, education, social affairs, public works and public health, and has to coordinate its activities and decisions with the *wilāya*. The *wilāya* of Khartoum is divided into seven *muḥāfaẓas*: Karari, Umbadda, Omdurman, Khartoum North, Khartoum, Jebel Awlia and Sharg Al-Nil, which in turn are divided into thirty-six *maḥalliyas* (G. Hamid 2000b: 234).
12. Examples of resistance to eviction and demolition are very rare compared with the widespread use of these practices. In any case, the state always has the last word and the resistance cannot last very long. In the case of Soba Aradi, clashes resulted in the deaths of fifteen policemen and military and an unknown number of inhabitants in 2005. The planned demolitions and evictions finally took place, but the planning process stopped at this stage. Inhabitants of the camps of Omdurman Al-Salām and Dār Al-Salām Omdurman also relate incidents at the beginning of the creation of these areas and the 'settlement' of the first inhabitants. The nickname given to the camp of Omdurman Al-Salām, Jabarōna, literally 'we were forced' or 'they forced us', refers to the violence during the creation of the camp.
13. These areas are planned, which means that communication lines have been set up or at least planned, and that the plots are demarcated and allocated as new populations are brought to these places. Services are provided gradually over time with successive arrivals of new populations and the intervention of private stakeholders and associations (patronage, NGOs and international organizations) and in some cases of public actors. A hospital was, for instance, built in El Fath at the beginning of the 2000s by public authorities using foreign funds. During the author's most recent visits to the area in 2007, the hospital was still not functioning due to a lack of human resources.
14. Comments made by the employee of an NGO established in El Fath in 2007.
15. The same strategies were mentioned in relation to the creation of the Wad Al-Bashīr camp at the beginning of the 1990s. Part of the population waited to have access to basic services and the arrival of NGOs before settling definitively in the area. Before that numerous families commuted between the formal city, squatting or living with acquaintances, and the camp.
16. This point will be developed in a further paragraph.
17. Numbers from the International Organization for Migration (IOM).
18. This was the case in 2007 in several places: Mayo Farm, where planning is still at a very early stage (civil servants came to mark the houses concerned by the planning with a white cross, but nothing has happened since); and the camps of Omdurman As-Salām and Wad Al-Bashīr, where a large portion of the camp had already been planned. Soba Aradi is a specific case that we shall study later.
19. The fourth class, which represented a plot of two hundred square metres, was discontinued.
20. Some individuals had a clear understanding of the allocation procedures of the plots and their malfunctioning, but most did not understand much and continued with the process step-by-step when they could afford to.
21. The *lajna shaʿabīa* is theoretically elected but in some instances, as seemed to prevail in IDP camps, the logic of such appointments corresponded to political affiliation rather than to a local representation process.

22. For the convenience of the reader, prices have been converted into euros. The currency used in Sudan changed during the field research period (on 1 July 2007), and the exchange rate of the Sudanese currency experiences significant fluctuations. The value in euros was calculated according to the exchange rate prevailing at the time when each interview was conducted. For these purposes, the exchange rates were taken from the official site of the European Commission (http://ec.europa.eu/budget/inforeuro).
23. An amount varying between USD 4 and 20 was mentioned in Soba Aradi concerning this tax paid to the *lajna sha'abīa.*
24. It must be stressed that at the time the value of the USD was much higher than its current value and the exchange rates with the SDG have been fluctuating strongly.
25. The price of the plot on the official land market would be much higher. The state subsidizes the price of the plots in these areas by allocating them to the initial resident populations, provided that the official procedures are not bypassed or circumvented.
26. I was not able to talk to the civil servants or engineers who actually carried out the urban planning on the sites where I conducted the interviews, the problem being regarded as too delicate and controversial at a local level, and especially for a female foreigner. Nonetheless, I was able to interview engineers in the ministry offices, and cases of land speculation were reported in many instances, both in interviews conducted with IDPs and with civil servants.
27. Conversions based on the exchange rate at the time when the interviews took place.

Chapter 12

Activist Mobilization and the Internationalization of the Darfur Crisis

Maria Gabrielsen Jumbert

The relative silence surrounding Darfur since around 2010 is in stark contrast with the level of international outcry over the conflict a few years earlier. The war in Darfur was one of the most mediatized conflicts of the last decade (2000s), and large amounts of human, financial and political resources were deployed to try and resolve the crisis, and protect and assist the victims of the violence. While the war itself left deep scars on Darfuri society, with the displacement of thousands and the killing of many more, this internationalization of the conflict did not leave the internal political dynamics, not to speak of the conflict resolution mechanisms, untouched. The internationalization of the Darfur crisis is, however, not only the result of external mobilization and manifestations of international solidarity with the victims of a humanitarian crisis. It is also a process that was pushed forward and shaped by the warring parties, and especially by some of the rebels' desire to project their struggle on the international arena in order to gain international support for their cause. Furthermore, it was shaped by the Sudanese government's actions, although the government rather resisted more than sought international involvement in its internal crisis. The focus here will, however, be on the parties proactively seeking internationalization.[1]

When the rebellion in Darfur broke out, the north-south negotiations were moving forward in Naivasha in Kenya. The southern rebels had over the years managed to gather consistent international support for their

Notes for this chapter begin on page 240.

cause and recognition for their claims. The war in Darfur, however, received a different type of international attention, in many regards a louder and more massive mobilization, but less coordinated. In this chapter, I will first look at how international activists became aware and engaged in the cause, and thus how they qualified the issues at stake, before showing how some of the rebels attempted to capitalize on this international mobilization. As we shall see, heavy focus on the humanitarian consequences of the war to the detriment of the deeper causes of the conflict has shaped the international response to the Darfur conflict.

Understanding the Massive International Mobilization for Darfur

The diplomatic engagement for Sudan would probably not have been the same without the massive international activist mobilization, first of all in the United States but also in many European countries such as France, Great Britain and Germany. This massive outcry against the situation in Darfur eventually made it impossible for elected policy makers to ignore the crisis. To understand the conditions that made this internationalization of the Darfur crisis possible, two elements should be studied: the general international context surrounding the outbreak of the conflict and the specific qualifications used to describe it.

From an Unfavourable International Context to a Favourable One

While the civil war in southern Sudan went on for almost twenty years, moving in and out of the international spotlight but remaining mostly out of it, the war in Darfur was in comparison relatively swiftly set on the international agenda. Several contextual factors of the beginning of the Darfur conflict differing from the onset of the civil war in the south contribute to explain this. To begin with, in 2003, as opposed to in 1983, the world was no longer organized in terms of bipolarity. During the Cold War, local conflicts were mainly interpreted as a result of the bipolar rivalry, and the great powers were more interested in supporting friendly regimes against hostile ones than trying to solve these conflicts. The liberal discourse on the need to defend human rights and spread democracy worldwide that developed in the post–Cold War period, although the seeds of this discourse were already planted during early mobilizations around humanitarian crises and antiwar movements in the 1960s, has played an important role in transforming the way local conflicts in Africa are viewed in Western democracies (Wheeler 2000; MacFarlane 2002). Beyond the fall of the Berlin Wall and the beginning of a 'new world order', this evolution should be understood in relation to the development of new information and communication technologies (ICTs).

Although the media's role in shaping public opinions and policy makers' agenda is not a new phenomenon, the way international news is presented in the media has changed in content and in rapidity over the past two to three decades. The immense progresses in ICTs since the 1980s – high-speed Internet, cell phones and satellite TV producing instant reports from far away fields – has changed the way distant and intrastate conflicts are represented in the Western world. Wars and human suffering in Africa more easily, and much more rapidly, become imaged and visible issues for Western audiences. Neil MacFarlane (2002: 50–51), in his study on the changing form and content of post–Cold War interventions, draws on the 'evolving nature of war', leading to an explosion in numbers of civilian casualties, internally displaced persons (IDPs) and refugees, in order to explain the newfound 'interests of major states *vis-à-vis* internal conflicts'. However, he admits, 'many of these phenomena were hardly new', and explains that as human suffering was projected on television 'the result in the developed states was strong pressure on governments from public opinion to assist and protect the victims of these catastrophes'. This reduction of time and space that progress in modern technologies has led to is manifested in the globalization of domestic policy agendas, as issues previously conferred to the sphere of foreign policy is now debated on domestic arenas. The mere production of news has also changed, as, for example, every Darfur activist equipped with a cell phone could become a journalist and contribute to the coverage of the conflict and the mobilization around it, through blogs and social media. However, not all conflicts and humanitarian crises receive the same amount of international attention, and this is where the specific international context plays a role.

Gary Goertz (1994), in his study on the influence of international context on states' behaviour, identifies three different types of contexts: first of all, context as a causal factor for a given outcome; second, context as a barrier, preventing certain outcomes; and third, context as changing the meaning of certain events. These different types of context are useful to make sense of the international context surrounding the emergence on the international arena of the conflict in Darfur. Indeed, the 'timing' of the first alerts may have a significant meaning for the reach the news about a conflict will have. In many ways, when the rebel attacks reached a new scale in Darfur in the first months of 2003, it was 'bad timing'. The context of the Naivasha peace talks in many ways played the role of a 'barrier', since it was neither in the interest of the parties to these talks, nor the international mediators, to open up the process to another rebellion. In addition, it was a difficult time for the talks, as the parties were negotiating the probably most sensitive area of the negotiations: the security arrangements. This moment of the talks required the full attention of the international mediators as well as the parties to the talks, the SPLM and the government of Sudan (GoS).

As for the broader international context of the time, the world was in the first months of 2003 intensely following the escalation towards a US intervention in Iraq. The heated debates within the UN Security Council among the great powers, as well as the massive public demonstrations in Europe and the United States against the intervention, made it difficult for any internal conflict at the time to receive a decent amount of attention. On the other hand, the fact that international spotlights had already been set on Sudan due to the historic negotiations that had started a year earlier certainly made it easier for the Darfur conflict to eventually obtain sustainable international attention. In the spring of 2004, a breakthrough in the peace talks between the GoS and the SPLM helped pave the way for the new focus that was to be given to Darfur. But it was the international context of the ten years' commemoration of the Rwandan genocide that constituted the veritable trigger element for internationalization, the context that changed the meaning of the first alerts to the situation in western Sudan. It started in late March 2004, when Mukesh Kapila, the UN Humanitarian Coordinator in Khartoum, claimed in unusually critical terms for a UN official that what was happening in Darfur was 'more than just a conflict'; according to him, it was 'an organized attempt to do away with a group of people' (*BBC News* 2004). But perhaps more importantly, he told international news channels that the only difference between Rwanda and Darfur were 'the numbers involved' (AllAfrica 2004). Shortly after, on 2 April, Jan Egeland, the UN Under-Secretary-General for Humanitarian Affairs, described the conflict as one of 'ethnic cleansing' (*UN News Centre* 2004) in front of the UN Security Council. The alerts were quickly picked up by journalists, scholars and human rights activists. Samantha Power, a Harvard scholar and author of a much publicized book on 'America and the age of genocide' (2002), wrote in a *New York Times* op-ed[2] on the eve of the official commemorations: 'Remember Rwanda, but take action in Sudan' (Power 2004).

The appeal did not go unnoticed, neither among policy makers nor among public opinion, still remembering the international community's failure to react in time to the genocide in 1994. During the summer months of 2004, a massive activist campaign emerged in the United States under the banner of the Save Darfur Coalition, a network that came to gather more than 180 faith-based, political and human rights organizations committed to 'end the genocide in Darfur'. The fact that this network included Jewish, Christian and Muslim organizations, human rights groups, the Black Caucus and neoconservatives, with the wife of President George W. Bush manifesting a special engagement for Sudan, gave it a unique influence over US domestic politics. As elections approached in the United States, and as the war in Iraq was moving further and further away from a 'mission accomplished', speaking out on Darfur and condemning the violations there became an efficient tool for politicians in search for public support. Darfur was again a central issue in the US presidential campaign in 2008, as well as in the French presidential election in 2007. As we shall see next, the specific context that pushed the Darfur conflict towards international recognition has played an important role in the way the conflict has been understood and qualified.

The Qualifications of the Conflicts Determining the Level of Internationalization

A given qualification may have little importance at one given point in time, but have a much greater resonance at another moment. Some observers indeed attempted to qualify the war in southern Sudan as 'genocide' in the 1990s but received little attention, but as we have just seen, the efforts to label the war in Darfur as 'genocide' at the time of the ten-year commemoration of the Rwandan genocide had a very different impact. However, it was not only the context but also the fact that the discourse was seized and adopted by the activist movement that came to give Darfur its very special place on the international agenda. Finnemore and Sikkink (1998: 908) argue that norms based on relatively simple ideas and 'prohibiting bodily harm to innocent bystanders' are more likely to find transnational support. As such, the more general idea of the need to internationalize internal conflicts generating large-scale human suffering may easily attract support, while more complex ideas of conflict resolution through negotiations may be more difficult to promote. Furthermore, conflicts implying ethnic violence or possibilities of genocide will more easily attract high-level international attention, since they express the occurrence of 'bodily harm to innocent bystanders' in an organized form, where in addition those affected by the violence seem to be targeted not because of what they have *done* but because of what they *are*.

Symbolic images and black-and-white representations of the Darfur conflict have played an important role in the internationalization of the conflict, with the representation of the conflict as a struggle of 'Arabs vs. Africans' as the most notable example. The terms 'Arab', 'non-Arab' or 'African' do refer to realities on the ground: the first is more linked to (claimed) historical origins while the second is more a result of the recent conflicts, a way to distinguish between those who are Arab and those who are not. The usage of these terms largely stem from the Fur-Arab conflict between 1987 and 1989, and the description of the conflict as an ancient struggle between these two groups heavily overshadows the complexities on the ground (Harir 1994; de Waal 2005). Also, while people in Darfur often refer to themselves as 'Arabs' or 'Africans'/'black' (*zurga* in Arabic), these terms might contain a different meaning when reused in human rights reports, for example. Such ethnic terms are indeed instrumentalized by international NGOs and activist groups, since they facilitate the internationalization of the conflict – especially when the very terms refer to identities that are not specific to the region (e.g., 'Arab' and 'African' as opposed to 'Fur' or other specific tribes' names). Hence, the Darfur rebel groups, being the ones most interested in internationalizing their struggle, have been eager to put forward the 'African-Arab' divide, while the government in Khartoum, seeking to hush down the international fuss, has tended to describe the conflict as an 'intertribal' dispute.

This establishment of a clear divide between the groups was also applied to differentiate between the so-called victims and perpetrators in the conflict, a representation often reproduced in human rights and activist reports on Darfur. The description of a conflict in terms of 'victims' and 'perpetrators', however, has the consequence of occulting the political dynamics behind it. As Mahmood Mamdani writes, the general narrative of the Darfur crisis conveyed an image of 'a world populated by villains and victims who never trade places and so can always and easily be told apart' (2007: 6). But not only do some qualifications more easily attract international attention; some are also more closely associated with an international responsibility to intervene. As Scott Straus (2005: 128) argues, two reasons motivated activists and other observers of the crisis in Darfur to insist on the qualification of 'genocide'. First of all, they believed that the situation responded to the criteria of 'genocide', since, as Straus writes, 'the violence targeted an ethnic group for destruction, was systematic and intentional, and was state supported'. Second, they believed it would almost automatically trigger an international intervention to stop the violence. Straus quotes Salih Booker and Ann-Louise Colgan from Africa Action, an advocacy group specializing in Africa-related issues, who wrote in *The Nation*: 'We should have learned from Rwanda that to stop genocide, Washington must first say the word' (Booker and Colgan 2004). This clearly reflects the underlying assumption in the international campaign to 'Save Darfur', and has led some critics to point to the fact that qualifying the crisis as 'genocide' has at times been given more importance than reflections on what to do.

Internationalization from Within: Between Rebels' Strategies and Victims' Testimonies

The rebel groups in Darfur have not been insensitive to this international interest in Darfur, and have actively sought to capitalize on this attention. However, this quest started already before the first large-scale attacks in early 2003 as leaders of the movements tried to garner support from the mediators involved in the peace talks in Naivasha. The lukewarm response they received from the international actors was interpreted as a justification of the need to take up arms, just as the southerners had done for so many years. However, to impose themselves as indispensable partners on the national arena and as the legitimate representatives of the Darfuris on an international level, they needed outside support. And the Darfur rebels have had a structural advantage over the government in Khartoum in terms of mediatization of the recent conflict. Journalists seeking to cover the conflict have had great problems obtaining travel permits from Khartoum, but they have had much less difficulties in accessing the region when they have accepted being accompanied by rebel leaders crossing the border from Chad (Gabrielsen 2007, 2009).

Yet, in terms of internationalization strategies, a difference should be noted between the two main rebel groups who initiated the uprising against the government: the Justice and Equality Movement (JEM) and the Sudan Liberation Army/Movement (SLA/M). The JEM is close to the Islamist ideology, and its leader, Khalil Ibrahim, is an intellectual and former member of the NIF government.[3] Although any link between Hassan Al-Turabi and the JEM has been consistently denied by both sides, many of Al-Turabi's old supporters have joined the ranks of the JEM in recent years. The JEM has first of all had an important support basis in Chad – where it not only planned its attacks on Sudanese government positions, but also recruited Chadian armed mercenaries. Indeed, most of the JEM rebels are of the Zaghawa tribe, an ethnic group whose bases stretch out from western Sudan to eastern Chad and the same group that the Chadian president, Idriss Déby, belongs to. The SLA, however, has not benefitted in the same way from a specific external supporter, but has been known for a much stronger popular support basis in Darfur, notably within the IDP camps and especially within the Fur community. Seemingly seeking to follow in John Garang's footsteps, Abdulwahid Al-Nour has been much more turned towards a Western audience and has put large efforts into portraying himself as the only true voice representing the marginalized people of Darfur. Acquiring external support has been a central part of his strategy, seen as a way to increase the movement's leverage on its adversaries in Khartoum. As a representative of a women's charity organization working in Darfur said: 'Without the media, Abdulwahid cannot do anything. After he called them [the Western journalists], they came to Darfur to see what was happening.'[4]

Responses to External Mobilization: The Rebels Seeking the Right Framing

As Clifford Bob (2005) points out, the movements seeking international support are numerous, and only a few become famous international causes. In order to reach the international agenda, the contenders have to present their cause in the most attractive manner possible. Their discourse should fit with NGO concerns, and their cause should sound like the ultimate protection of 'right' against 'wrong'. If possible, they should also align their political struggle with foreign policy priorities of countries likely to support them. Abdulwahid Al-Nour, a lawyer trained at the University of Khartoum and exiled in Paris from late 2006 to late 2010, has well understood the importance of the right framing, in the right place and at the right time. His discourse on the crisis in Darfur is more aligned with what his European audience is likely to be moved by than marked by specificities in the Darfur context. While the debate on whether the crisis in Darfur has amounted to genocide or not has been the subject of a heated debate internationally, it certainly was in the interest of rebel leaders such as Abdulwahid Al-Nour, but also his sympathizers in Darfur, to adopt this term and insist on its gravity. Deploying the 'genocide' discourse became first of all an efficient tool to discredit their adversaries, while at the same time distracting attention from their lack of a clear political agenda. Second, it was a means to extend their international support basis, in turn compensating for their failure to include a broader political educated elite in Sudan and the diaspora. The result, internationally, was a massive mobilization around what has been seen as the confrontation between one clear group of perpetrators and one clear group of victims. There has, however, been little knowledge beyond expert networks about the root causes of the conflict, that is, the structural problems that need to be resolved in order to put an end to the conflict.

Abdulwahid Al-Nour has, however, gone even further in his attempts to gather international support. When speaking to a Western audience, he frequently compared Darfur to the genocide that has marked European history the most deeply: the Holocaust. He describes the IDP camps as 'concentration camps' and refers to the counterinsurgency campaign led by Khartoum as the government's search for a 'final solution'.[5] To stop this, he for a long time called for a NATO intervention in Darfur, believing that a UN peacekeeping force waiting for the Sudanese government's authorization would never become a reality. As he skilfully expressed it at a press conference in Paris in early 2007: 'If we are not Europeans, we are citizens of the world. Don't we deserve the same fate as the people of Kosovo, where NATO intervened to put an end to the ethnic cleansing?' (Aït-Hatrit 2007). Other public speeches he has voiced have made clear references to the moral imperatives of the Western countries, as, for example, when he praises the opportunity to speak in France, 'a democracy' and 'the country of the human rights', before adding that that is not the case in Sudan.[6] As Jean-François Bayart (2000: 226) writes about the strategy of extraversion, 'the discourse of democracy, is no more than yet another source of economic rents, comparable to earlier discourses such as the denunciation of communism or of imperialism in the time of the Cold War, but better adapted to the spirit of the age'.

Western NGOs and diplomacies, albeit presenting themselves as seeking to protect victims of violations no matter who they are, indeed obey their own strategic agendas in order to promote themselves on the international arena (Duffield 2001). This shows us that the efforts to export the conflict in Darfur onto the international arena are not only autonomous initiatives to alert the foreign public and powerful Western governments, but are also developed in reaction and as a response to the international attention addressed to the crisis. The 'genocide' and 'lack of human rights and democracy' discourses of the human rights organizations is reproduced and reshaped by the rebel leaders and Darfur civil society spokespersons. As their calls for support are related in international media channels, they contribute to legitimate parallel calls for support for Darfur voiced by the international activist movement. However, reproducing the international human rights discourse may have given the rebels more a feeling of spreading the message rather than a true influence on the human rights organizations. In fact, by insisting on the victimization of the Darfuri people to the detriment of credible political claims, this discourse has justified the need for physical protection, while also contributing to the drifting away of a viable political process to solve the problems in Darfur.

Victim Testimonies: Activists and Humanitarians' Preferred Source of Information on Darfur

Despite the international activism of several representatives of the rebel groups, some Western human rights activists deliberately refused to be associated with anyone from these movements, not wanting to be seen as supporting an armed rebellion. Others openly welcomed personalities such as Abdulwahid Al-Nour at their public events organized to raise awareness and mobilize politicians. This has perhaps most of all been the case in France, where various personalities from Urgence Darfour, the French answer to the Save Darfur Coalition, built up a close relationship with the SLA leader. Some dissensions even erupted between the American and the French activists[7] when the latter organized a large gathering in March 2007 and invited both Abdulwahid Al-Nour and an American representative of the Save Darfur Coalition. Indeed, the envoy from the United States did not want to stand on the same stage or shake hands with the rebel leader. But beyond these conceptual disagreements, the calls for international support voiced by rebel leaders or representatives from the civil society in Darfur indirectly justified the raison d'être of the international activist campaign. The rebel leaders, and most notably Abdulwahid Al-Nour, however, failed to become the legitimate spokespersons of the people of Darfur.

Indeed, going through the activists' various calls for action and the support material they have developed with this aim (documentaries, books, reports and briefings, Web-based articles), one can rarely find any trace of the testimonies and appeals for intervention voiced by the rebels. To build their advocacy, the activists and human rights advocates broadly preferred to use victim testimonies and stories told by those displaced by the war. Accounts of civilians suffering, having fled from their villages under attack, often losing family members on the way, seem to better illustrate what the human rights reports want to communicate than a call for military intervention by armed rebel soldiers would. Indeed, what the activists sought to portray was an image of a population in need of protection and assistance, not a population among which you can find armed provocateurs.

The work of the humanitarian aid workers on the ground can be seen as twofold: delivering aid to the people in need and reporting back to their headquarters about the state of the situation. In their interactions, they are naturally in contact first of all with people who have suffered tremendously from the conflict, where most have fled from their home and lost family members on the way. This is the population the humanitarian aid workers are there to assist and give relief to. When it comes to other stakeholders in the conflict, such as the armed rebels or the government-sponsored militias, the humanitarians, in their search for 'neutrality', are naturally inclined to do all they can to avoid being seen as interacting with them. Although 'neutrality' has more often been used as a cover for the NGOs to gain legitimacy, its meaning has changed in recent years, moving towards what is often referred to as the 'new humanitarianism', overtly more politicized and engaged (Gabrielsen Jumbert 2010). However, even the NGOs who openly take sides are generally reluctant to be associated with *armed* actors. Thus, the human rights reports based on information the humanitarians have collected on the ground will generally reflect this reality, with a clear majority of 'testimonies' coming from IDPs – the 'victims' and 'survivors' in humanitarian jargon. These testimonies also contribute to justify the very presence of the humanitarian organizations. According to Jane Blayton (2009), an English literature scholar, 'as a genre, human rights reports provide an exclusive explanatory framework which asserts moral and factual certainty and does not leave room for multiple explanations'. Relating the experiences of other actors, either who have not suffered or who are partly contributing to the violence, has little pertinence for them, as it would blur their narrative of the situation: an inoffensive population of victims.

Furthermore, Blayton (2009) writes, 'the wealth of victim testimony can play some narrative tricks. For example, in some reports, the sheer number of the testimonies gives the impression that the whole story has been told, whereas in fact no testimonies have been provided from the perpetrators' point of view, which would be necessary for a complete picture. The sample has been carefully selected by the researchers and writers.' These reports thus contribute to the impression often held by external observers that the victims are clearly distinguishable from the armed parties. If the point of view of the 'perpetrators' is not taken into account, the rebels' role is also often minimized. Not only does the number of testimonies give the impression that the whole story has been told, but it also gives the impression that the crisis is everywhere in Darfur and that external aid is imperative to avoid the breakdown of the entire region. Ironically, the human rights organizations' selection of victim testimonies to illustrate their reports leads to actually giving a large space to those who are usually referred to as the 'voiceless' victims. However, they are generally presented as having little or no agency of their own and no influence over the future development of the conflict and violence that is unfolding in their own homeland. The armed actors, however, on each side are generally presented as capable of stopping the violence at any time.

The journalists, having gone to the region to see for themselves, have been more willing to use rebel testimonies, although this depends on their access to such sources. Indeed, the journalists obey different logics when they approach a conflict-mined field, as they seek to relate opposing and contrasting testimonies to illustrate their reports. However, access to Darfur has been highly restricted to journalists, and thus most have had to content themselves with speaking with refugees and armed actors on the Chadian side of the border. Others have managed to travel a few kilometres into Darfur, usually with the help of the rebels.[8] This was based on mutual interest, as the rebels were keen to show the foreign journalists around and the journalists needed someone who could conduct them more or less safely across the border (Gabrielsen Jumbert and Lanz 2013). This was the case when the French writer Bernard-Henri Lévy, one of the most active in the Urgence Darfour movement, travelled to Darfur in March 2007. His journey was organized from Paris by Abdulwahid Al-Nour and assisted on the ground by his men from the SLA. Lévy's account from Darfur, published in a two-page article in the French newspaper *Le Monde,* is somewhat exceptional in that he concludes his report by recommending that the international community sponsor and arm the rebels in order to help them win the war (Lévy 2007). Most journalists content themselves with relating the calls for intervention voiced by the rebels, whether in the Western capitals, in the regional capitals or in Darfur. While undeniably giving them a platform on which they could express themselves, the support the rebels sought through their calls for assistance in the media was far from obtained automatically.

Rebels Failing to Become the 'Voice of Darfur' and 'Heroes of Liberation'

One of the important reasons for the southern Sudanese rebel group's success is the late leader John Garang's capacity to eventually unite an internally split movement and to effectively play the role of the charismatic leader internationally. The overthrow of the Mengistu regime in Ethiopia in 1991, which was the strongest supporter of the SPLA in the 1980s, led to an internal split in the rebel movement. For the larger part of the 1990s the SPLA remained divided between the original SPLA ('mainstream'), led by Garang, and SPLA-United, led by Riek Machar, who in 1997 signed an agreement with the government in the north and fought with the Sudan Armed Forces. Yet, although Garang had lost his most important support in former socialist Ethiopia, it did not take him long before he built up a new web of strong international supporters – notably thanks to a peaking interest for southern Sudan and the fate of its Christian population within evangelist circles in the United States. Garang was frequently invited to hold lectures in the United States, at think tank seminars, in front of the Sudanese community or in front of religious communities with a special involvement in southern Sudan. He also travelled across Europe and spoke with academics, members of humanitarian NGOs and church organizations – all the while, crucially, spending most of his efforts in maintaining a popular support basis in the field in southern Sudan. He managed in 2002 to reunite with Machar, who previously had tried to overthrow him, and this was one of the key steps making the peace talks and the following Comprehensive Peace Agreement (CPA) possible. Although critiques existed, he was then, and is still today, referred to as the 'charismatic leader of South Sudan', and many humanitarians working in

South Sudan who came to know him,[9] as well as European and American academics and politicians, developed a close friendship with him.

The SLA rebels in Darfur were from early on inspired by the SPLA. Indeed, it was the southern rebels who from the outset sought to support the Darfuri movement, even before it was really constituted as one. However, as Julie Flint and Alex de Waal (2008: 89) write, Abdulwahid Al-Nour was 'an enthusiastic but not wholly uncritical admirer of John Garang' – critical of his toughness against his own people, yet highly admiring of his vision. Abdulwahid Al-Nour's discourse on a 'new Sudan' and a 'secular and federal Sudan' as exposed to his audience in Paris and beyond is also very close to the late Dr Garang's policy vision for Sudan. However, Abdulwahid never managed to come even close to a 'new Garang' for Darfur, in terms of local support and international recognition, and he has thus not been able to rally support for his political claims. As many from the international diplomatic contingent in Khartoum, as well as humanitarian aid workers, expressed when asked about the political support for the cause of the Darfuris on the international arena: '[T]here is no Garang in Darfur'.[10] The humanitarian aid worker behind this quote continued by saying that 'there is Khalil Ibrahim who has a certain political stature, and there is Abdulwahid who has a certain political vision for Darfur as well'. But again, no Garang. Others are much more severe when it comes to judging Abdulwahid's credentials. As an international official in Khartoum said: 'We have phone and SMS contact with Abdulwahid, encouraging him to return to the negotiations after the failure in Abuja in 2006, which he left without signing the peace agreement, but he's not interested. He requires certain things that won't be implemented until after an agreement. … I don't think he has any strategy. But he wants to be vice president of Sudan.'[11]

A northern Sudanese independent consultant related some of the rumours circulating about Abdulwahid Al-Nour in Sudan, putting into question the seriousness of his lobby activities in Paris, where he was rather seen as living a comfortable and easy life. Yet, he admits, 'when he speaks, he speaks on national problems and not just as a Darfurian. He's addressing the real problems.'[12] The SLA leader is thus not devoid of a political strategy and vision for Darfur, but this part of his discourse has received less echo internationally than his efforts to portray the crisis in Darfur as a 'genocide'. When it comes to his reluctance to return to the negotiating table, the Khartoum-based consultant also points to Abdulwahid's personal ambitions: 'Abdulwahid is intelligent, he doesn't want to be one among twelve others, he wants to be the one.'[13] Along with his long exile abroad, Abdulwahid Al-Nour has indeed come to be seen as detached from his people and those he is supposed to represent in the negotiations. A lieutenant colonel from the US Army, working as an observer with the African Union mission in Darfur, summarized Abdulwahid's position well: 'He was a hotel rebel' (Wallace-Wells 2009).

Initially, however, the rebel groups did gain tacit support from the international community – not an openly voiced support, but a sort of implicit support given as a reaction to their adversary's conduct in the war relying on scorched earth tactics. Jan Pronk, the former Special Representative of the UN Secretary-General for Sudan, said in December 2004 in the *New York Times* that the rebels 'had a lot of sympathy in the international community' (Sengupta 2004), which he deemed they were losing after they had conducted several surprise attacks. In comparison with the SPLA in southern Sudan during the 1980s and 1990s, it should be noted that the existence of satellite phones and the possibilities for extensive and almost instant media coverage have not been only beneficial to the Darfur rebels. While the SPLA factions were responsible for at least or as many violent attacks causing civilian casualties in large parts of the south, this was before the era of satellite phones and journalists had little access to southern Sudan, except when 'embedded' with the rebels themselves. Despite a continued restriction of access for journalists into Darfur, the presence of humanitarians and observers from the African Union and later the UN have largely facilitated access to information in Darfur. New technologies and a continued demand for news on Darfur have thus contributed to regular coverage of the violence committed on each side of the conflict. The rebels of the SLA, the JEM and the other smaller factions have thus been much more exposed to the international media spotlight, in turn providing the international community with more grounds for scepticism and critique.

As argued in an article cowritten by this author and David Lanz, the internationalization of the conflict indeed had ambiguous effects on the rebellion. On the one hand, it solidified the rebels' cause and consequently constrained the room of manoeuvre for the Sudanese government. At the same time, however, it encouraged the rebel leaders to make maximalist demands at the expense of addressing the broader root causes of the conflict (Gabrielsen Jumbert and Lanz 2013). Indeed, the fact that the rebel leaders failed to gather the different factions in one broad movement, or at least behind a set of common policy objectives for the region, contributed to their failure to become seen as 'heroes of liberation', or even simply as the legitimate representatives of the Darfuri population. The political stances voiced by the different rebel leaders speaking with international media have become lost amid reports on attacks carried out by their troops and the indictment of three rebel commanders by the International Criminal Court (ICC).

Conclusion

With their strategies of internationalization, the rebel movements of Darfur have fed and contributed to the larger international activist outcry destined to 'Save Darfur'. However, they have not become the exclusive 'voices from Darfur'; on the contrary, the 'voiceless victims' have been the privileged witnesses that international activists and NGOs have referred to when they have sought to alert a Western audience to the situation in Darfur. Indeed, what could be read as an international response to the rebels' calls for international support, from the activists campaigning to the numerous human rights reports published on the conflict, has in fact developed rather independently from the internal calls for support.

The rebels, however, seem to have largely interpreted the massive international campaign, strongly condemning Khartoum's handling of the crisis, as direct support of their struggle. This may have led them to believe that international support was on their side, something they did not need to work much for to keep (Gabrielsen Jumbert and Lanz 2013). Human rights reports, quoting civilians exclusively on their experiences as victims and never armed actors on the political reasons for their struggle, have served as a primary source of information on Darfur for many activists, journalists and last but not least the ICC. All in all, this has contributed to the broader criminalization and, more importantly, the depoliticization of the international understanding of the conflict, justifying the intervention of the ICC as the most appropriate instance to help find a solution to the conflict. Despite the Darfur Peace Agreement of 2006 and the Doha Document for Peace in Darfur signed in 2011, both signed only by one rebel group out of several, the image of the conflict in Darfur remains one of a largely unsolved conflict. Since the start of 2013, there have been regular surges in fighting leading to new flows of refugees and new reports of dire humanitarian conditions. There is, however, much less international attention on Darfur today, whether from the media, activist groups or human rights organizations, with correspondingly little political push to respond to the evolutions on the ground.

Notes

1. The findings presented here are based on fieldwork realized in the context of my doctoral research, with interviews carried out in France, the United States and Sudan. A special thanks in this regard to the CEDEJ branch in Khartoum, for its logistical and sci-

entific support during my journeys in Sudan, in 2007 and 2009, and to its coordinator at the time, Barbara Casciarri. A grant from the Alliance Program at Columbia University in New York also enabled me to carry out fieldwork in the United States.

2. Referring to the page opposite the editorial page in a newspaper, usually including commentary by journalists or external writers.
3. The National Islamic Front (NIF) is the political organization of Hassan Al-Turabi, who acceeded to power in 1989, ruling through the National Congress Party (NCP), led by President Omar Al-Bashir.
4. Interview with Ahlam Mahdi, Chair of Ahlam Charity Organization for Women Empowerment and Child Care (South Darfur), Khartoum, 26 March 2009.
5. Interview with Abdulwahid Al-Nour, Paris, 14 March 2007.
6. Abdulwahid Al-Nour speaking at a public meeting organized to launch a special issue of the journal *Outre Terre* dedicated to Darfur, Hotel de Ville du Vème arrondissement, Paris, 21 October 2008.
7. The two are not institutionally linked in any way, but as networks working towards the same goal, they have had frequent contacts.
8. Interview with member of Darfur rebel group, Khartoum, 24 March 2009.
9. Very few humanitarian NGOs had direct contact with the SPLM in the south during the war, with the exception of the Norwegian People's Aid (NPA) and World Vision International.
10. Interview with official from French NGO, Khartoum, 14 November 2007.
11. Interview with international official, Khartoum, 17 November 2007.
12. Interview with independent consultant, Khartoum, 21 November 2007.
13. Ibid.

Part IV

Reshaping Languages, Identities and Ideologies

Chapter 13

The Islamic Movement and Power in Sudan

From Revolution to Absorption into the State

Giorgio Musso

This chapter analyses the evolution of the Sudanese Islamic movement from social movement to political party, and from acting as an opposition party to becoming the main pillar of the regime that has ruled Sudan since 1989. By focusing exclusively on the external activism of the Sudanese Islamist regime, most outside observers have failed to understand the roots of its power system and the endogenous reasons for its resilience. The Islamist project has deeply evolved in terms of ideology, institutions, resource exploitation, dynamics of social control and legitimacy. Its ability to adapt to changes on the domestic and external fronts is precisely the reason explaining the longevity of the regime. At the same time, Islamism has lost much of its revolutionary appeal along the way, failing to establish an alternative model of governance and development, reverting instead to a common pattern of authoritarian rule. This analysis tries to shed light on the dialectical relationship between Islamist ideology and the policies pursued by the Sudanese regime, using two main theoretical references. The first is Gramscian theory, whose heuristic value to the understanding of Islamism has been confirmed by a number of scholarly contributions (Abdelwahid 2008; Bayat 2007; Butko 2004). The second is the concept of 'totalitarianism'. While Islamism is frequently referred to as a 'totalitarian' ideology, it is suggested here that such a characterization needs to be nuanced through some distinctions if it is to remain an explanatory category without slipping into a value judgement.

Notes for this chapter begin on page 261.

This chapter provides a background on the years of formation and empowerment of the Sudanese Islamic movement, a thorough analysis of the first decade of the Islamist regime and of the internal split that occurred between 1999 and 2001, and finally ends by outlining the evolution brought about in the nature of the regime by the signing of the Comprehensive Peace Agreement (CPA) with the south.[1]

The Islamic Movement and the Traditional Parties in Sudan

The core of the group that planned and executed the 1989 Revolution of National Salvation was formed by the leaders of the so-called Islamic movement (*al-ḥaraka al-islāmiya,* hereinafter *ḥaraka*), whose political incarnation was represented at that time by the National Islamic Front (NIF). The foundation of the NIF – which held its first congress in Khartoum one month after the fall of Jafaʿar Nimeiri in April 1985 – was the last stage in the long history of the movement, born in the mid-1940s as an offshoot of the Egyptian Muslim Brotherhood (*jamaʿat al-ikhwān al-muslimīn,* hereinafter *ikhwān*).[2] The NIF was the brainchild of Hassan Al-Turabi, a charismatic leader and a master of political opportunism who had become secretary general of the movement in 1964. Drawing support from the youth wing of the *ḥaraka,* he had managed to turn what was then an intellectual and student's movement into a full-fledged independent political party. To achieve this, he had to challenge an old guard eager to maintain a close relationship with the Muslim Brotherhood in Egypt and preserve its model of a tight group of committed individuals mainly devoted to education and Islamization from below.[3]

For almost three decades, the movement remained little more than a pressure group, failing to gather significant popular support outside the student milieus. Together with the other modern ideological political force in Sudan – the Sudanese Communist Party (SCP) – it was crushed between the two parties that dominated the scene at that time: the Umma Party (UP) and the so-called unionists.[4] These represented the political expression of the two strongest religious sects of the country, the Ansar – followers of the nineteenth-century Mahdi and his descendants – and the Khatmiyya Sufi brotherhood headed by the Mirghani family.[5] Both had established an interdependent relationship with the state apparatus since the time of the Anglo-Egyptian Condominium and were organically tied – when they did not identify with – a wealthy middle class formed by landowners and traders.

For the Islamists, the opportunity to carve out an autonomous space in political and economic domains came during the military regime of Jafaʿar Nimeiri (1969–85), when the traditional parties were officially banned and their leaders forced into exile. The *ikhwān* had been subjected to heavy repression as well and had joined forces with the sectarian parties to form the National Front, based in Libya. Nevertheless, after the failure in 1976 of a major coup attempt organized by the National Front, the Islamic movement's leadership responded positively to Nimeiri's proposal for a 'National Reconciliation' agreement and joined his government (M. Hamid 1984). The Umma Party and the unionists – although the first initially adhered to the initiative – never accepted being integrated within the regime and continued to stir up opposition against Nimeiri until his ousting by a popular uprising in 1985.

A minority within the Islamic movement did not agree with the choice of joining a regime that had ruthlessly repressed the opposition, was a key ally of the United States in the region and supported Anwar Sadat in his peace efforts towards Israel (Marchal 1995: 7). The dissent culminated in a formal split when veteran Islamist leader Sadiq Abdallah Abdel-Majid decided to form a separate organization retaining the original denomination of 'Muslim Brotherhood'. This weakened the movement but left Al-Turabi in a position of uncontested leadership, enabling him to mould the organization in accordance with his ambitions.

The 'Central Strategy' and the Creation of a 'Historic Block'

The second half of the 1970s witnessed the emergence of what would later become the Islamist ruling class: many militants had gained political experience as student leaders, and others had left the country either to take part in the National Front or to continue their studies in the West. After the National Reconciliation, many came back and were appointed in public institutions or in the newly established Islamic enterprises, mainly banks and insurance companies. Others were either sent for further training in friendly countries such as Iran (Marchal 1995: 24) or encouraged to 'get exposed to the Western culture'[6] by applying for high university degrees in Europe, the United States or Canada. This young generation of cadres was personally loyal to Hassan Al-Turabi, who favoured their rise within the movement's hierarchy (Marchal 1995: 9).

Repeated failures to implement an 'Islamic programme'[7] in cooperation with the sectarian parties, as well as the Islamist elite's growing ambitions, led the movement to devise a 'central strategy' whose stated aim was the taking of power in ten years.[8] The main tenet underlying this plan was that the movement had to become independent by broadening its membership, increasing its political influence and endowing it with the means to be economically self-sufficient.

The 'central strategy' had a horizontal dimension, pursued through the formation of a wide array of satellite organizations: charities, women's associations, societies for the propagation of Islam (the well-known *munazzamāt al-da'wa*) and so forth (Zain Al-Abdin 2008: 10). Women were particularly captivated by the NIF's call for an 'Islamic emancipation' (Hale 1996b), while the Islamist communitarian associations provided recently urbanized individuals with a safe harbour in the anomy of the urban setting, as well as material help for those most in need. The movement also tried to reach the population of the peripheral regions of the country, to which Islamism appealed as a transversal and supratribal ideology (Flint and de Waal 2005: 19). By enlisting the support of those who had been neglected by the centralized nature of the Sudanese state – dominated by the northern riverine tribes, the so-called *awlād al-balad* (sons of the land) – the Islamists hoped to widen their popular basis. In particular, they expected Darfur – imbued with a long tradition of religious fervour – would provide the 'critical mass' needed to challenge the sectarian order (El-Din 2007). Islamist activists in the university campuses were particularly attentive towards students coming from rural areas and were successful in recruiting a lot of them. Many *ikhwān* leaders themselves came from a humble background, and the movement had provided them an opportunity for social mobility in a stagnant society.[9]

On the other hand, the vertical dimension of the 'central strategy' was conceived as a process of 'empowerment' (*tamkīn*) encompassing the political, military and economic spheres. After the National Reconciliation, the appointment of Islamist militants at various levels of the public administration provided the movement with a channel to establish a presence within the state bureaucracy and acquire experience in the management of political power. The parallel infiltration of the army and the security services – while the movement maintained its own 'secret organization' charged with protecting its leaders and providing information – was meant to create a group of loyal officials, something many other political parties could already count on (Taha 1993).

An essential part of the *tamkīn* process concerned the field of economy. Benefitting from the good relationship they maintained with senior figures in the Arab peninsula, Al-Turabi and his acolytes managed to turn Sudan into a laboratory for Islamic banking (E. Ahmed 1997). The availability of credit encouraged many Islamists to engage in profitable import-export activities and attracted new members within the orbit of the movement. Moreover, the Islamist leadership worked to establish close ties with the communities of Sudanese migrants in the Gulf and thus succeeded in intercepting the huge flow of remittances they generated, gaining access to much-needed foreign currency. An 'Islamist middle class' made up of traders – the so-called *tujjār al-jabha* (traders of the Front, meaning the NIF) – bankers, insurers and intermediaries sprang up at this time, challenging the 'big families' of the traditional Sudanese bourgeoisie and, with them, the socioeconomic foundations of the sectarian system.

The 'central strategy' could not have succeeded – as it did, at least partially – without the interplay of a number of factors that were independent from the Islamists' will. In this sense, it is interesting to analyse the process described above as the formation of an Islamist 'historic block'. According to Antonio Gramsci, who developed this concept, the social group that manages to fuse its ideology with the 'material forces' active in a particular historical context, and strives to gather around it a broad alliance encompassing different sectors of society, has a chance to establish itself as a hegemonic 'historic block' (Gramsci 2007: 869; Vacca 2007: 118). Consistent with this definition, the Islamists managed to exploit to their own advantage the combined action of internal social transformations and changes in the regional power balances at move since the late 1970s.

Among the former, we should cite migratory flows (both internal – from rural to urban areas – and external – particularly towards the Gulf countries) (Bernal 1999), the general pauperization of the urban society, the emergence of a class of educated youth and a general increase in the adherence to stricter Islamic norms at the public level, sometimes due to an active engagement by the state (El-Affendi 1991: 131–34).

On the regional level, the post-1973 context was witnessing the rise of the Gulf monarchies – along with their conservative Islamic sociopolitical model – at the expense of Egypt. In 1979, the Iranian Revolution would challenge Saudi ambitions by posing itself as a reference for Islamist militants worldwide (Esposito 1990).[10] In the words of a prominent Sudanese Islamist, 'Definitely Iran was a source of inspiration. The Islamic revolution government in Iran is an obvious contrast with the Saudi Islamic government, it is the model of an Islamic government which came through a revolution.'[11] Nevertheless, the NIF was not in a position to launch a revolutionary movement on the Iranian model, as it still relied almost exclusively on an urban constituency in a country where the majority of the population lived in dispersed rural areas under the persistent influence of Sufi Islam.

Hegemony and Southern Sudan

Since the outlining of the 'central strategy' until the 1989 coup, the Sudanese Islamists engaged themselves in the definition and realization of a hegemonic vision that, once in power, would constitute the core of their political project. 'Hegemony' is defined as a form of exercise of power characterized by a 'combination of force and consent'[12] (Gramsci 2007: 1638). The social group that is determined to affirm its hegemony must first acquire the moral and intellectual *direction* of society and later establish its *dominance* over it through the state's coercive apparatus (Gramsci 2007: 2010–11). Moreover, 'though hegemony is ethical-political, it must be also economic, must necessarily be based on the decisive function exercised by the leading group in the decisive nucleus of economic activity' (Gramsci 2007: 1591).

In this sense, it is possible to characterize the political strategy of the NIF as fully 'hegemonic'. The moral leadership of the society was to be achieved through the spread of a 'high Islam' as opposed to the traditional 'popular Islam' of Sudan, and the aforementioned effort to broaden the popular base of the movement went in this direction.

The results of the elections held one year after the fall of Nimeiri were mixed. On one hand, the NIF gained twenty-three out of twenty-eight 'graduates' constituencies'[13] – meaning that its ideological outlook had become the mainstream thought among the educated class – plus twenty-eight seats in the geographical constituencies, mainly drawing votes from the unionist electoral basin in urban areas (Marchal 1996: 109–10). It must nevertheless be noted that the graduates' votes allowed the Islamists to be overrepresented in the parliament, as they obtained fifty-one seats with a percentage of 18.4 per cent of the overall votes, while, for instance, the Democratic Unionist Party (DUP), with a share of 29.5 per cent of the total, gained sixty-three seats (Woodward 1990: 207). Moreover, the NIF's disappointing performance in Darfur – where it secured only two parliamentary seats – was testament to the fact that despite its efforts, the movement could not dispose of the resources needed to undermine the bonds of religious allegiance and economic patronage that the sectarian order was based on in the rural areas (Gallab 2008). The elections projected the NIF as political force to be reckoned with, but underlined its structural limits in challenging a consolidated party system.

Notwithstanding this objective limit, the growing popularity acquired by the Islamists within the urban milieus convinced them of embodying the leading force in the country, with an inherent right to become the ruling class.[14] This belief eventually justified the conviction that political power – 'dominance' in Gramscian terms – had to be conquered by any means. Moreover, the introduction of *sharīʿa* laws by Nimeiri in 1983 had showed the potential of the state as an agent of Islamization and, more broadly, social change.

During the third parliamentary regime (1986–89), the NIF capitalized on its opposition to Sadiq Al-Mahdi's successive governments – although it participated in two of them – wielding the inability of the sectarian parties to implement *sharīʿa* as proof of their weak Islamic credentials. At the same time, the *ikhwān* staged several popular protests coalescing the growing discontent towards the government's economic policies and its inability to defeat the insurgency in the south.

Armed confrontations in the south had started again in 1983, but unlike the Anyanya rebels who had fought in the first civil war (1955–72), the Sudan People's Liberation Army/Movement (SPLA/M) was led by a charismatic and articulate leader claiming to fight for the liberation of the whole country and not only of the south (Madut-Arop 2006; Khalid and Garang 1992). The 'New Sudan' ideal outlined by John Garang, a former army commander with a Ph.D. from Iowa State University, challenged the dominant northern political discourse – centred on Islam – espousing the values of democracy, secularism and pluralism.

The NIF responded to this challenge by systematizing its political vision in a document called the Sudan Charter and published in 1987, meant to reconcile its call for the establishment of an Islamic state with the need to govern an inherently plural country. In the charter, democracy was meant as a tool to justify the right to establish *sharīʿa* as 'the general source of law' according to 'the will of the democratic majority' (NIF 1987: part 1, para. 2b). Concerning the relation between the state and religion, the charter read: 'As a matter of faith [Muslims] do not espouse secularism (NIF 1987, part 1, paragraph 1.c). Neither do they accept it politically. They see it as a doctrine that is neither neutral nor fair.' (Gallab 2008: 169)[15] Moreover, the NIF proposed the introduction of a federal administration as a key step towards reaching a lasting peace in the south (NIF 1987: part 3).[16] The document didn't mention the need for an Islamization of southern society, but previous NIF publications and declarations by the movement's leadership had indicated that this was seen as the real long-term solution to the problem (Wolf 1990: 79–81; El-Affendi 1990: 378–79).[17] At the same time, a minority within the movement was convinced that, were instability in the south to prevent the constitution of an Islamic state in Khartoum, it would be better to 'let the South go' as an independent entity (El-Affendi 1990: 378).

In November 1988, the DUP leader, Mohamed Othman Ali Al-Mirghani, signed the Sudanese Peace Initiative with John Garang in Addis Ababa, requesting the 'freezing' of *sharīʿa* until the convening of an inclusive constitutional conference. Prime Minister Sadiq Al-Mahdi was forced by the army to endorse the initiative of his main political rival. It was as if the Islamists' worse nightmare threatened to come true: an alliance between the hated sectarians and the secular southerners, which would have left no room for Al-Turabi and his party on the political arena. The deal sacrificed the NIF's main political workhorse – *sharīʿa* – on the altar of peace, while the army intervention was interpreted by the Islamists as a sign of the fact that other political factions were at work within the army. Fearing marginalization or, worst, a leftist-inspired coup, the Islamists decided to strike preemptively. The Shūra Council of the NIF – the party's main collective organ, albeit with a purely consultative role – endorsed the preparation of a military coup d'état by Hassan Al-Turabi and a secret task force of party members, who soon established contacts with Islamist sympathizers within the army and managed to deceive other officials about the real nature of the coup.[18] It was the beginning of the Revolution of National Salvation (*thawra al-inqādh al-waṭanī*), or, as it is commonly known in Sudan, the *inqādh.*

The Foundations of the Revolution

'Your armed forces rose up to implement a project which is national in its direction to rescue Sudan for the sake of preserving its society and safeguarding the unity of its territory and the sake of its soil' (RCC 1989). With these words, the self-proclaimed Revolutionary Command Council (RCC) – a fifteen-member military junta presided over by Brigadier Omar Al-Bashir – addressed the population with a radio message broadcasted on the morning of 30 June 1989.

The Islamist project was 'revolutionary' in the full sense of the term, for it was meant as a comprehensive process of change aimed at altering the fundamental institutions of the state and society (Van Dommelen 1997). The first years of the Inqādh regime resembled – and by many accounts outdid – the initial phase of the Nimeiri regime in terms of violence and repression (Marchal 1995: 6). On the same day of the coup, the military junta ordered the dissolution of all political parties (including the NIF), political associations and civil society organizations. These latter were particularly targeted by the repression, as they had proven capable of overthrowing a military dictatorship in 1964 and 1985.

Hassan Al-Turabi – who had been arrested and jailed as part of the plan – was convinced that leaving the 'dirty work' to the military officials would preserve the Islamists' political credibility and would not affect the enactment of the Islamist project. On the contrary, the arbitrary power left to the coercive apparatus consolidated its influence within the regime to the extent that it became an alternative and independent power centre, something the Islamist intellectual Abdelwahab El-Affendi has called a 'superorganization' (El-Affendi 1995: 44). Individuals animated by an intense hatred towards the ancien régime occupied top positions within the army, the Ministry of Interior and the security services. Eventually, the transition to civil rule took place in 1993, later than initially advocated by Al-Turabi.

The Islamists could then proceed with the restructuring of the political system: the two key concepts in this process were those of *shūra* (consultation) and *wifāq* (consensus). 'Popular committees' (*lajna shaʿabīa*) on the model of the Libyan Jamahiriya were created in every neighbourhood and village, functioning as cells for grassroots political mobilization and providers of basic social services – such as the distribution of rationed staple commodities.[19] In essence, they were a powerful tool for social control in the hands of the Inqādh regime (Lavergne 1997b: 33–35; Kok 1996: 148–56). The committees formed the basis of a complex pyramidal structure called the Congresses System (*niẓām al-mu'tamarāt*), consisting of five levels of 'popular congresses' – from the neighbourhood to the national – and a series of 'sector congresses' such as the women's congress or the youth congress.[20] The Congresses System was purported to realize a 'popular participative democracy', but had little real decision-making power and resembled under many instances the typical structure of a single party within an authoritarian regime (Lowrie 1993: 28).

Unaccomplished Totalitarianism

The characterization of the Islamist regime as 'totalitarian' has been proposed by some Sudanese scholars (ʿAli 2004; Gallab 2001, 2008), emphasizing the all-encompassing role assumed after 1989 by the Sudanese state in its bureaucratic, hierarchic and coercive dimensions. Through the so-called civilizing project (*mashrūʿ al-ḥaḍarī*), the state became the principal agent of social change in an effort to mould a 'new Sudanese Islamic identity' through a 'long term plan to "Islamise" life and fashion all spheres of Muslim activities on true Islamic foundations' (O'Fahey 1997: 60). The 'civilizing project' was meant as an attempt to achieve mass popular mobilization, both through the introduction of the Congresses System and the creation of intermediate bodies such as government-aligned trade unions, women's and youth associations, Islamic NGOs and many others.

The introduction in 1991 of a new penal code based on *sharīʿa* was the cornerstone of a much more ambitious project whose accomplishment was entrusted to the newly established Ministry for Social Planning. The latter was charged with dealing with issues of public morality – such as the wearing of the *ḥijāb* instead of the traditional Sudanese *tōb* – but more importantly was entrusted with co-opting the existing social structures within the new political system. This translated, for instance, into the convening of tribal conferences, as well as the creation of a Council of Remembrance and of Those Who Remember (*majlis al-dhikr wa al-dhākirīn*), gathering representatives from Sufi orders, Koranic schools and Islamic charities (E. Ahmed 2007: 193). Starting with NIF number two Ali Osman Taha, who was the first minister for social planning, those who occupied this office were always key party members, strongly committed to the Islamist cause and often closely tied to the security apparatus. Beyond the centrality of this institution, this confirmed the sinister link between coercion and social change that became one of the trademarks of the regime. Equally significant is the fact that in 2001, after the internal split that provoked the ousting of Hassan Al-Turabi and allegedly put an end to the revolutionary aspirations of the Inqādh regime, the Ministry for Social Planning was suppressed.

The effort to militarize the society by calling for a general conscription into the Popular Defence Forces (PDF) may be inscribed into this context, but needs a deeper analysis given its central role in the development of the Islamist regime. Since its inception, the Inqādh regime posed itself as the defender of national unity, and soon *jihād* in the south became one of the major channels of popular mobilization, particularly among the most radicalized youths. For the majority of those recruited, however, forced conscription into the PDF proved to be an alienating experience of coercive indoctrination and a heavy tribute to pay in terms of physical and mental health. The unintended consequence of this policy was to make the entire Sudanese society aware of the huge human cost of the war, as hundreds of thousands of families lost their own sons on the front (Marchal and Ahmed 2010: 201–2).

Notwithstanding all of the above-mentioned elements – centrality of the state, effort to create a *homo novus,* general mobilization through corporatism and militarism – the Sudanese Islamist regime can be better described as an 'unaccomplished totalitarianism' than a totalitarianism per se. The first reason for this evaluation concerns economic policy, which under totalitarian systems is usually strongly centralized and subject to comprehensive planning under the state's control. Although a minority within the NIF was inclined to promote a state-centred economy and the initial policy statements of the military junta went in this direction, the majority line favoured – despite the very bad relations that Khartoum maintained with the Bretton Woods institutions – a neoliberal economic line, which was enacted starting with the Three-Year Economic Salvation Plan adopted in 1990. However, the state's role was not limited to a regulatory function. The public institutions acted as gatekeepers, allowing only 'friendly' investors to operate in the market. The Inqādh regime also promoted the economic ventures of its apparatuses, namely, the army and the security services. The rise of a regime-linked 'new rich' class, at a time when the government was approving drastic expense cuts by lifting subsidies on staple commodities, was one of the main factors causing a loss of credibility of the Islamist project.

The Sudanese totalitarianism appears 'unaccomplished' even when we analyze it from a political perspective. In fact, the achievements obtained by the government through the enactment of the potentially 'totalitarian' policies described above were very poor. The Congresses System proved to be an intricate and ineffective machinery, prompting the regime to reintroduce a limited multipartite system in 1998.[21] 'Islamic social planning' in general was met with strong resistance by a population that had a long history of reluctance to allow the state to interfere with personal mores and family life. This was paralleled by the progressive failure to mobilize the youth into popular militias after it became clear that the ill-trained PDF were sent to the front lines as cannon fodder.

Another aspect of the Sudanese 'unaccomplished totalitarianism' concerns the relation between the *movement* and the *state*. Totalitarian regimes are usually characterized by a high degree of institutional confusion. This was true of the Sudanese Islamist regime as well. Since 1989, relations between civil and military organs, between state institutions and political bodies, had not been clearly defined, allowing Al-Turabi to exercise a nearly absolute authority.

It has been noted that the lack of an articulated institutional theory is one of the main weaknesses of the Islamist ideology (Roy 1992: 42). The terms in which Abdelwahab El-Affendi has analysed the Sudanese case in this respect are indicative:

> Al-Turabi did not think about institutions, because he thought of himself being the *khalīfa* who led the revolution. Islamists have an aim and a guide, and that's all. Institutions are a check on absolute power, and they tend to be slow in taking decisions: Al-Turabi wanted absolute authority and the revolution couldn't wait for institutions to develop and function effectively. In the end, the lack of civilian institutions worked to Al-Turabi's detriment. He had been fascinated by absolute authority, but he didn't understand that if you govern alone, it's easier for others to remove you.[22]

In her well-known study on totalitarianism, Hannah Arendt has noted that notwithstanding the aforementioned institutional confusion, totalitarian movements 'consciously strive to maintain the essential differences between state and movement and to prevent the "revolutionary" institutions of the movement from being absorbed by the government' (Arendt 1951: 419).

In Sudan, Al-Turabi had decided to dissolve the NIF after the coup in order to dissimulate the real nature of the operation, but shortly after taking power he secretly appointed a new and enlarged council, widely believed to be the real decision-making organ of the regime. The ideal pursued by the Islamist ideologue was that of a 'party-dominated state'. The creation of the Congresses System was meant to abolish the distinction between party and state institutions. Nevertheless, eventually Al-Turabi had to witness the progressive absorption of the movement by the state. This was due to the fact that in order to implement the 'civilizing project', the Islamists needed to dispose of a stronger state in its civil and military components. Senior party officials who had been appointed to top positions within state institutions developed an interest in the preservation of the status quo. These 'Islamist technocrats', as Abdullahi Gallab has called them, 'began to surrender to the rationalization of the state bureaucracy and to distance themselves from the ill-conceived and antagonistic functions of the party' (Gallab 2008: 143). This caused the exhaustion of the revolutionary momentum and accelerated the emergence of factional cleavages within the ruling class.

From the 1995 Addis Ababa Attack to the First 'Islamists' War'

Being the first Sunni Islamist leader to succeed in seizing power, Hassan Al-Turabi aspired to make Sudan an operative centre for dialogue, coordination and cooperation among the world's Islamist movements. He was confirmed in this plan by the outcome of the Gulf War, which created a wave of popular resentment towards Arab secular regimes that Islamic movements were keen to exploit to their own advantage.[23] A few weeks after the end of Operation Desert Storm, Khartoum hosted the first Popular Arab-Islamic Gathering (*al-mu'tamar al-sha'abī al-'arabī al-islāmī*), which saw the presence of more than two hundred delegates from over fifty countries, the majority of whom belonged to Islamist organizations banned in their own countries (Ayalon 1993: 179–80; Marchal and Osman 1997).[24] Although the international reaction to such an 'Islamist international' forced the regime to limit its real operative impact, the opening of the Sudanese frontiers – with the abolition of visas for Arab nationals – made the country a potential breeding ground for terrorist attacks. This risk materialized when, on 25 June 1995, an armed commando attacked the convoy of the Egyptian president Hosni Mubarak in Addis Ababa. A Sudanese man working for an Islamist-affiliated NGO was arrested, while the other three suspects managed to flee and – according to the accusations levelled by Egypt and Ethiopia – took refuge in Sudan (Burr and Collins 2003: 190–91). The assassination attempt manifested the concrete threat posed to international stability by Khartoum's 'revolutionary diplomacy', pushing the United Nations (see UNSC 1996a, 1996b, 1996c) and the United States[25] to approve sanctions against Sudan (Prunier 1998). On the domestic front, the terrorist attack highlighted the disrupting potential of diverted intelligence circles within a context of institutional confusion.

The Addis Ababa attack had a deep effect on the internal dynamics of the Islamist regime. First, the relations between Al-Turabi and the military establishment had always been less smooth than what the NIF leader had planned (Marchal 2004: 8). Army officers – and president Al-Bashir himself – were increasingly unavailable to play the role of front men while Al-Turabi was pulling the strings from behind the curtains. The crisis sparked by the assassination attempt against Hosni Mubarak required a clearer definition of roles and institutions.

Second, generational conflict was once again emerging within the Islamic movement. The generation of Islamist cadres raised under Al-Turabi's wing – now in their forties and fifties – had assumed senior positions in the regime's institutions and was growing impatient with his centralistic attitude. Some also considered Al-Turabi, with his Sufi family background and personal ties to Sadiq Al-Mahdi,[26] to be too imbued with the spirit of the ancien régime to lead the revolution. When in 1992 the Islamist ideologue fell into a coma after an assassination attempt in Ottawa, it seemed that the time had come for his successors to take the lead, but against all expectations he came back even more determined to exercise absolute power. At the same time, the 'old guard' of the Islamic movement – Al-Turabi's peers in terms of seniority – was feeling circumvented by his exclusive relationship with the Islamist popular basis. Some started to resent his ambition to become the new 'sheikh' of Sudanese politics, if not even the 'Sunni Khomeini'.

Finally, six years of rule had created vested interests that had to be protected from the international hostility that the 'revolutionary diplomacy' had attracted. Eventually, an unlikely alliance between the military establishment and the bulk of the 'Islamist technocrats' gathered around Omar Al-Bashir and Ali Osman Taha.[27] Their aim was primarily that of preserving the interests of the ruling class, even though this required the abandonment of the revolutionary character of the Islamist project and a turn towards a more pragmatic stance.

Meanwhile, the international powers were adopting a double strategy towards Khartoum: while the United States supported a regional alliance including Ethiopia, Eritrea and Uganda to back the SPLA/M's military effort, Egypt and the Gulf countries opened channels of communication with Sudan through their intelligence services, proclaiming their support for Al-Turabi's opponents. Both approaches had the effect of accelerating the showdown within the Inqādh regime.

Al-Turabi tried to tighten his control on the regime by assuming, for the first time since 1989, an official institutional office, and in 1996 he was elected speaker of the National Assembly. Quite ingenuously, he thought this position would give him the opportunity to check the executive and introduce a series of reforms meant to gradually open the political arena. The promulgation of the 1998 constitution and the introduction of a limited multipartite system were the first steps in this direction. Al-Turabi's hope was that internal political liberalization would defuse external pressure on the regime. Such attempts, however, failed to break the grip that was gradually tightening around him. In December 1998, ten prominent members of the National Congress Party – with the *placet* of president Al-Bashir – presented to the Shūra Council of the party a memorandum that deprecated the centralistic attitude of the leadership and called for a reorganization of the NCP's institutions aimed at achieving greater transparency.[28] The confrontation escalated and became public, until Al-Bashir decided to dissolve the parliament in December 1999 and finally ordered the arrest of Hassan Al-Turabi in February 2001 (Bellucci 2000).

The Future of the Islamist Hegemony

After slightly more than one decade of 'unaccomplished totalitarianism', the Islamist regime had assumed the features of an ordinary authoritarian government (Linz 2000). Although the official rhetoric still appealed to the revolutionary character of the Inqādh regime and Islamism was professed as the official regime ideology, it was evident that the Khartoum government had turned towards a conservative outlook whose only long-term objective was the preservation of power.

In 2001, the ruling class was facing a situation similar to the one experienced by Jafaʿar Nimeiri after the attempted communist coup in 1971. Having ousted Al-Turabi – and with him, an important component of the political architecture of the regime – Al-Bashir and his acolytes started to consider peace as the right asset to invest in to relaunch their political project. Moreover, the cessation of hostilities with the SPLA/M would allow a stable exploitation of the country's oil reserves. Oil, in turn, would increase the resources available to the government in its effort to gain popular legitimacy through the extension of patronage networks. The combination of these factors with a renewed international engagement in the Sudanese peace process and a growing 'war fatigue' by the two parties resulted in the signing of the Comprehensive Peace Agreement (CPA) in January 2005.

The acceptance of the eventuality of southern secession contained in the CPA marked the definitive abandonment of the hegemonic project conceived by the NIF in the 1980s, when the Islamic state was thought of as capable of integrating the multiple identities of the country. It was also an implicit recognition of the failure by the regime to alter 'the basic exclusionary nature of centralized political rule in Sudan' (Kevane and Gray 1995: 273), further confirmed by the eruption of an armed uprising in Darfur, a region that was meant to play a key role in the original Islamist project.

Islam is still the centrepiece of the regime's rhetoric, but its legitimating function has radically changed. When Hassan Al-Turabi referred to it, he was thinking of a revolutionary force capable of engendering a deep change in the socioeconomic structures of his country and beyond. Nowadays, Islam is invoked to preserve the socioeconomic structures moulded by the regime and to rally the people in defence of an identity that the government claims as threatened by internal and external enemies. This has become particularly salient after the incrimination of Omar Al-Bashir by the International Criminal Court (ICC) in 2008 and even more after the secession of South Sudan in July 2011. Trying to come to terms with the loss of legitimacy deriving from the breakup of the country, the ruling party has reintensified its references to Islam and *sharīʿa* after such rhetoric had somewhat subsided in the years following the peace agreement. Hence, it is alleged that Sudan, freed from its African and Christian burden, can now build an integral 'Muslim state' (Reuters 2011), cease to be considered the stepson of the Islamic *umma* (Islamic worldwide community) and gain full recognition within the Arab-Islamic world.

Up to the time of writing,[29] the regime has been able to survive the 'perfect storm' created by the simultaneous occurrence of the partition of the country and the eruption of the 'Arab Spring'. Most of the NCP's strength comes from the complete lack of credible alternatives – the last of which has been the SPLA/M's 'New Sudan' vision – coupled with the consolidation of a patronage network that ensures the ruling party a solid base of support in the heartland of Sudan, the 'centre' that has historically held sway over the rest of the country. This is the reason why the NCP still keeps in place most of the institutions created to serve the grandiose aims of its early revolutionary times, such as the popular committees. Although nobody talks anymore of *shūra* or 'popular democracy', the committees still remain the ears of the government and, most importantly, the arms through which it delivers services and goods to its constituencies.

The system is nonetheless being put to the test by the strains engendered by South Sudan's secession in 2011. During the decade straddling the signing of the peace agreement, oil rents had created unprecedented social inequalities and further exacerbated the centre-periphery imbalances. The loss of three-quarters of those very rents after 2011 has impoverished the population at large, exacerbating calls for social justice and widening discontent with the government. The maintenance of power by the Inqādh regime's elite will depend upon its ability to manage these cleavages, something it has succeeded in doing in the past with a combination of coercion and co-option.

The NCP also has to face threats from within its ranks. After the demise of Al-Turabi, the Inqādh regime has been ruled as an oligarchy, with competing power centres coalescing around state institutions, personal allegiances and ethnic cleavages. The party possesses enough discipline to keep them from surfacing in public, but unity is guaranteed only by the fear of losing power and by the presence of a situation of permanent crisis. In this sense, the instrumental management of threats – real and supposed, domestic and external – is one of the key tools of rule of the NCP.

On a deeper level, however, it seems that the Islamists are no more capable of keeping together the diverse elements of the 'historic block' upon which they laid the foundations of their power. Many Islamist intellectuals have started criticizing the government for its authoritarian character and for its 'materialistic' orientation. The 'Islamist middle class' formed in the 1970s and the 1980s has witnessed a downfall of its fortunes, while a much less ideologically committed class of younger businessmen has assumed the reins of the economy. Many of them are members of the ruling party, others belong to the 'big families' of the old Sudanese bourgeoisie which have exploited their foreign connections to reenter the market, provided that their activities are politically neutral.

Conclusion

The analysis just conducted outlined the evolution of the Sudanese Islamist project from a revolutionary hegemonic vision to a logic of power conservation, bureaucratic preservation of the status quo (achieved by co-opting existing social structures) and rent seeking through the exploitation of the country's mineral resources. The neoliberal economic policies enacted by the regime projected the Sudanese economy towards the global market, showing not just how an Islamic political system can be compatible with neoliberal globalization, but how the ruling class can benefit from the incorporation in the world economy without this translating into a 'Westernization' – and even less a democratization – of the country's social and political institutions.

In this sense, what is at stake in Sudan is the self-asserted potential of Islamism as a path for modernization in the Arab-Islamic world, or its transformation into another tool for conservative authoritarian rule. The trend identified by Abdou Maliqalim Simone among Islamist militants during the first phases of the Inqādh regime proved to be an early indicator of the path undertaken by the regime in subsequent years. 'There is clear resentment on the part of many of Jabha's [NIF] former supporters ... that the Islamic movement has not really revitalized Islam but rather the state – giving it a new lease as an instrument of alienation' (Simone 1994: 99).

In the aftermath of the Arab uprisings of the last four years and the contested rise to power of Islamist parties in a number of countries, the Inqādh regime will not constitute a paradigm for a modern and democratic Islamic governance. Indeed, it would be wise to regard it as a warning.

Notes

I would like to thank the CEDEJ in Khartoum for the support received during my stays in Sudan.

1. This chapter draws from doctoral research conducted between 2007 and 2010 through a wide bibliographic survey and three fieldwork sessions.
2. A historical account of the development of the Sudanese Islamic movement can be found in Abdelwahid (2008) and El-Affendi (1991). In Arabic, it is also possible to consult the two volumes written by Hassan Makki Mohammad Ahmad (1982, 1990), the official historian of the movement.
3. On the Muslim Brotherhood in Egypt, see R. Mitchell (1993).
4. At the time of decolonization, this political stream supported union with Egypt instead of full independence. The unionists changed their party name a few times and divided into factions several times during their history. Since 1967, the main party representing them is the Democratic Unionist Party (DUP), which has remained an important political actor up to now. For a background on the traditional parties in Sudan, see Warburg (2002).
5. This is the reason why in the literature, as well as by the Sudanese themselves, they are often referred to as 'sectarian parties'.
6. The expression was used by Said Al-Khatib, one of the closest collaborators of Al-Turabi during the 1990s. Author's interview with Said Al-Khatib, Khartoum, 3 February 2011.
7. This is a broad expression that may include a broad set of measures, such as constitutional reforms, the implementation of *sharīʿa* and the Islamization of the economy.
8. Author's interview with Mahjoub 'Urwa, Khartoum, 22 November 2009.
9. A notable exception to this trend was Hassan Al-Turabi, born in eastern Sudan within a prominent religious family.
10. See in particular the chapter authored by John Voll (1990: 283–301). The point here is that the Iranian Revolution was a powerful source of inspiration and encouragement, but given its peculiar Shiite characterization, it could not constitute a political model.
11. Author's interview with Qutbi Al-Mahdi, Khartoum, 27 January 2011.
12. English translations for Gramsci's texts have been taken from the selection from the Prison Notebooks edited by Quintin Hoare and Geoffrey Nowell Smith (1985). The page numbers, however, refer to the original Italian edition (Gramsci 2007).

13. These were constituencies reserved for university students and graduates.
14. Author's interview with Abdel Rahim Omar Muhyy Al-Din, Khartoum, 11 November 2009.
15. The integral text of the Sudan Charter (in its English version) can be found in the appendix to Gallab (2008).
16. It should be noted that in the mid-1960s, the Islamists were among the first northern parties to accept southern calls for the establishment of a federal structure of government (El-Affendi 1990: 374–75).
17. Wolf quotes from a 1985 NIF public paper called *Al-jabhah al-islāmiya, mas'ala janūb al-Sūdān* (The Islamic Front, the Issue of Southern Sudan), while El-Affendi quotes from an internal document circulated clandestinely in 1974 called 'National Unity in the Way of Islam'.
18. The course of these events was confirmed to the author during numerous interviews recorded with NIF cadres between April 2008 and February 2011.
19. On the Libyan political system, see Hajjar (1980).
20. A graphic representation of the Congresses System can be found in Kok (1996: 151).
21. In that year, the National Congress – the highest organ of the political system – became a party to all intents and purposes, with the name of National Congress Party (NCP; *ḥizb al-mu'tamar al-waṭanī*).
22. Author's interview with Abdelwahab Al-Affendi, London, 11 November 2008.
23. Sudan publicly expressed its opposition towards an armed intervention against Saddam Hussein.
24. According to Roland Marchal, this was a project that had already been endorsed during the 1988 NIF Congress (Marchal 1995: 8).
25. The President of the United States of America, Executive Order 13,067 (3 November 1997). It must be noted that Sudan had been included by the US Department of State in its list of state sponsors of terrorism since 1993.
26. The latter, leader of the Umma Party, was Al-Turabi's brother-in-law.
27. Taha had been Al-Turabi's deputy in the NIF for a long time, playing a central operative role in the 1989 coup. At the time of the Mubarak assassination attempt, he was the foreign minister.
28. The so-called Memorandum of Ten can be found in its original Arabic text in the appendix to ʿAli (2004).
29. October 2013.

Chapter 14

Language Policy and Planning in Sudan

From Local Vernaculars to National Languages

Ashraf Abdelhay, Al-Amin Abu-Manga and Catherine Miller

The language situation in Sudan is complex, with more than 120 named languages. This diversity raises many challenges for the promotion and codification of Sudanese languages, including ideological and scientific issues. What are the criteria for defining a specific and autonomous language? Which languages should be selected for codification and for which purposes? The first institutional attempts to codify a number of Sudanese languages occurred during the colonial period and were guided by strong ideological aims: counteracting the spread of Arabic/Islam in the southern part of the country (including South Kordofan). After independence in 1956, a pro-Arabization policy was launched throughout the country as a result of pan-Arabic nationalism among dominant northern political circles. The peace agreements that ended the two long wars in the south (1955–72 and 1983–2005) provided a legal framework for a language policy encouraging cultural and linguistic plurality. This was done first exclusively for the south from 1972 to 1982 (Addis Ababa Agreement of 1972) and then for the whole country since 2005 (the Comprehensive Peace Agreement, also known as the Naivasha Comprehensive Peace Agreement, of 2005).

From 1930 up to the mid-1990s, the promotion and codification of non-Arabic Sudanese languages concerned almost exclusively the southern Sudanese languages and were mainly (but not exclusively) performed by Christian associations. Since the late 1990s, the promotion of Sudanese vernacular languages became the concern of many non-Arabic-speaking

Notes for this chapter begin on page 280.

groups, irrespective of their religious beliefs and their degree of contact with Arabic. This raises new challenges concerning codification choices such as choice of alphabet and choice of standardization. The language situation in Sudan has been mostly conceived in dichotomist terms opposing Arabic (both classical and vernacular, including Juba Arabic spoken in South Sudan) on the one hand to all other non-Arabic languages and English on the other. This conception is still largely dominant. The issue of identity remains the key factor within this struggle, due to the fact that language and ethnicity have been so closely linked to each other, beginning at least since the first attempts to classify Sudanese languages.[1]

Policy towards the promotion of Sudanese vernaculars fits with the present global trend of considering language rights as a key human right.[2] Language rights are therefore officially and theoretically supported by most Sudanese political parties, international institutions and NGOs. This politically correct discourse praising equality of status and rights for all languages does not really take into account the feasibility of such idealistic claims.

The present chapter will analyse some aspects of the various attempts to promote Sudanese languages. It will start by summarizing briefly the historical steps of language codification in Sudan. It will recall the main Sudanese official texts that provided the institutional frame for language planning and will also describe the profiles of the main actors. The bulk of this chapter was written in 2010 and early 2011 and does not cover the changes that occurred following the proclamation of the Republic of South Sudan in July 2011. This important issue needs further research and input from South Sudanese scholars. With this chapter we hope to provide a historical, contextualized analysis of the main formal attempts to promote Sudanese languages (Arabic vernaculars and Juba Arabic excluded) and a framework for further research to assess the ongoing changes in both practice and ideology. By ideology, we mean here the dominant *doxa* that tends to consider language one of the key vectors of identity at the state or national level or the regional/ethnic level.

Linguistic Diversity and Language Boundaries

More than one hundred languages are spoken within Sudan.[3] This linguistic diversity is characterized by two salient features. One is the uneven demographic and geographical distribution of these languages. About 70 per cent of Sudanese languages are found in the western and southern parts of the country (as original home regions), with striking diversity in southern Sudan and the Nuba Mountains. While Sudanese Arabic is supposed to be spoken as a mother tongue by at least fifteen million Sudanese, it is estimated that Dinka, the second main Sudanese language (or macrolanguage), is spoken by less than two million people.[4]

The second salient feature is the instability of the language situation in Sudan due mainly to population movements and urbanization. In the last thirty years, population movements have occurred from all Sudanese regions to the main regional and national urban centres, as well as from one area to another. This has led to greater multilingualism in urban centres as well as the acceleration of a linguistic shift towards Arabic. In addition, more than two million Sudanese are believed to have settled abroad. The result is that the one-to-one correlation between language and ethnicity is no longer valid (Miller 2006). This complex translocality challenges the reductive ideology of ethnolinguistic enumeration, favouring a 'sociolinguistics of mobility' (Blommaert 2010). Yet, the linguistic and ethnic classifications established at the beginning of the twentieth century continue to be considered unquestionable scientific *doxa* by both academic circles and social activists struggling to preserve Sudanese linguistic diversity.

Colonial Policy towards Vernacular Speech

The Rejaf Language Conference and Its Consequences

Identification and classification of Sudanese languages were undertaken systematically beginning in the colonial period (i.e., late nineteenth to mid-twentieth centuries). This process was framed by the dominant European linguistic and racial ideology of that period (Makoni and Pennycook 2005). The focus on non-Arab languages and cultures was mainly inspired by the wish to separate Arab and non-Arab groups and to stop the spread of Arabic and Islam in southern Sudan and the southern Nuba Mountains (Abdelhay 2008, 2010b; Albino 1970; Beshir 1969; Sanderson and Sanderson 1981; Wai 1973). Correlation between language and ethnic groups was considered essential to establish strong ethnic boundaries and avoid acculturation (Abdelhay, Makoni and Makoni 2010).

A key moment in this process of classification and categorization was the Rejaf Language Conference of 1928 (*Report of the Rejaf Language Conference* 1928, henceforth the RLC), which was organized within the general frame of the famous South Policy and Closed District Policy (Closed District Ordinance). The conference was sponsored by the colonial government and attended by missionary representatives from the Congo and Uganda as well as experts from the International Institute of African Languages and Cultures such as Professor Diedrich-Westermann. The aims of the RLC involved (1) discussing the feasibility of adopting a system of group languages for educational purposes, (2) studying the possibility of adopting a unified orthographic system, (3) examining the production of educational textbooks, and (4) designating a classified list of languages and dialects in the south.

The final resolution identified eight group languages (Dinka, Bari, Nuer, Lotuko, Shilluk, Zande, Acholi and Madi) for preparation of textbooks in Roman script in the vernacular elementary schools (RLC 1928: 30). For the other language communities, teaching was to be done either in one of eight selected languages or in colloquial Arabic transcribed in Roman script (RLC 1928: 31). The classification of Sudanese languages, started by Westermann (1911), was pursued by A.N. Tucker and M.A. Bryan (Bryan 1948; Tucker 1934; Tucker and Bryan 1956). The implementation stage of the RLC resolutions faced several difficulties, including lack of consensus over orthographic choices for a single language, and it did not succeed in preventing the spread of Arabic as the main lingua franca of the south.

The RLC, however, did have an important impact for the future. It encouraged missionaries and linguistic experts to research local languages and to write and publish textbooks, grammars and dictionaries contributing to the linguistic knowledge of these languages. Many teaching materials continued to be used up to the 1970s. Most of these readers were based on biblical texts. Translation of the Gospel into Sudanese languages started at this period and continues up to now.

Moreover, the RLC contributed in spreading the idea – if not within the whole southern population, at least among the educated part of it – that vernacular languages could and should become literary languages in order to protect southern ethnic and cultural specificities. This had a strong impact on further positions on the promotion of vernacular languages. After independence and up to the 1980s, the southern political parties were more concerned with the issue of promoting local vernaculars than were other regional parties from northern Sudan.

Colonial Policy towards Vernaculars in Northern Sudan and the Nuba Mountains

The situation was radically different in the north, where a few linguists and civil servants began describing the main northern Sudanese languages, such as Nile Nubian or Beja. There were, however, no plans to teach vernacular languages in Muslim-dominated areas or to produce textbooks for primary education, and no attempt was made to spread the idea of a standardization or codification of local language practices. The result was that, apart from the Nuba Mountains movements discussed next, there were, at independence, no regional northern movements acting to promote vernacular languages.

The Nuba Mountains were regarded as a separate province in 1914 and first assigned to the Sudan United Mission (SUM), an evangelical Protestant mission from New Zealand and Australia (Abdelhay 2010b). The government advised the SUM to provide missionary education on the pattern of southern Sudan and formulated a 'Nuba policy' in order to encourage a Nuba identity. As in southern Sudan, there was an attempt to form 'language groupings' in order to federate isolated communities and to promote the Roman script for writing Arabic. The adopted educational policy for the Nuba Mountains was embedded in the 1930 Memorandum on Educational Policy in the Nuba Pagan Area. But this 'Nuba policy' faced numerous problems, the major one being the fluidity of ethnic boundaries in this region. It was abandoned in 1934, with Arabic written in Arabic script becoming the main language of education.

Interest in Nuba languages led to a number of linguistic descriptions (R. Stevenson 1956–57) and to the publication of readers in different Nuba languages (like Nuba-Moro) as well as biblical translations such as the translation of the New Testament in Moro in 1956 by the American Bible Society. Therefore, the languages of non-Muslim Nuba groups were better described than the languages of Muslim Nuba groups (Quint 2006). But it was only around the 1980s that Nuba regional movements started to put linguistic issues on their political agenda.

Postcolonial Policies from 1956 to 1985

Arabization: 1956–1972

In 1946, the Closed District Policy was abandoned in order to enable national unification and, in 1949, Arabic became the official language of the entire country. Following independence, the linguistic policy of the Sudanese government was characterized by strong Arabization, and the teaching of vernacular languages was altogether stopped in 1964 (Albino 1970; Nyombe 1997; Oduho and Deng 1963; Yokwe 1984).

In 1956, an Egyptian expert, Dr Khalil Mohamed Asakir from Cairo University, was hired by the Sudanese government to supervise the introduction of Arabic in southern Sudanese schools. With the assistance of Yusif Al-Khalifa Abu-Bakr, Dr Asakir began by devising systems for transcribing southern languages using Arabic script, hoping that 'a unification of the alphabet would tend to reduce linguistic diversity and consequently bring South and North socially close together' (Abu-Bakr 1978: 206). The basic idea was that native literacy in Arabic script would facilitate further acquisition of Arabic. Readers in Dinka, Zande, Bari, Moro and Lotuko written in Roman scripts were transliterated into Arabic scripts. This experience did not last long and was quickly abandoned (but reintroduced in 1993, as will be discussed later).

In the north and in western parts of the country, regional movements such as the Beja Congress (1957) or the Nuba Front (1964) were acting for a better distribution of the national wealth, but cultural and linguistic claims remained rather marginal. The only exception was in the Nubian community, where the flooding of the area (following the building of the Aswan Dam in 1969), the displacement of the population and archaeological salvation projects raised Nubian awareness of their cultural heritage, including the writing of the Old Nubian language. Nubian archaeologists and intellectuals started to promote the writing of the modern Nubian languages first in Roman or Arabic script (Badr 1955, n.d.) and then in Nubian scripts following Dr Khalil Mukhtar's initiative in the 1990s.[5] Many Nubian cultural associations were active in Khartoum in the 1960s to the 1980s (Hale 1979).

The Addis Ababa Agreement and the Coming of the SIL in Southern Sudan

In 1972, the Addis Ababa Agreement put an end to the first civil war and recognized the autonomy of southern Sudan. Chapter III, Article 6 of the Regional Self-Government Act stated that 'Arabic shall be the official language for the Sudan and English the principal language for the Southern Sudan, without prejudice to the use of any language or languages which may serve the practical necessity for the efficient and expeditious discharge of executive and administrative functions of the region' (Beshir 1975: 158–177).

An educational conference was organized in Juba in 1974, reendorsing the Rejaf Language Conference recommendations but extending Arabic-language instruction in the south. Henceforth, schools in the south could present their curricula in either Arabic or English. Local languages were classified and grouped into two categories: category A (Bari, Dinka, Kresh, Lotuko, Moru, Ndogo and Nuer) and category B (Acholi, Anuak, Baka, Banda, Didinga, Feroge, Jur-beli, Jur-Luo, Kakwa, Kaliko, Madi, Mundari, Murle, Shilluk, Toposa and Zande). Languages of category A were to be used as means of instruction in rural elementary schools (grades 1–3), whereas those in the second category were targeted for literacy training (Abdelhay 2008: 200).

In 1977, the Summer Institute of Linguistics (SIL) signed an agreement with the Ministry of Education of the Southern Region to set up a programme for implementing the official policy of reintroducing the teaching of local languages (in category A) in rural primary schools. The SIL is an international evangelical institution based in Dallas (Texas, USA) supporting Bible translations into local languages. According to Janet Persson, a long-standing SIL expert on Sudan: 'The Southern Ministry encouraged SIL to assign linguists to other Southern languages where they had a mandate to do linguistic analysis, produce literacy materials and assist the local churches in translating the Bible and any other books they considered important for their communities. 15 languages were added.'[6] In 1978, the Institute of Regional Languages (IRL, supervised by the SIL) was created in Meridi for the training of teachers and the production of readers (in Roman script), starting with the nine selected languages that had already been used in education previously and that therefore had some written materials. From 1977, the SIL started to publish teaching materials in Roman script for the selected languages, including orthographic books, primers, readers and scientific books or papers published in the series Occasional Papers in the Study of Sudanese Languages.[7] The SIL linguists have proved efficient in the description of southern languages, particularly at the phonological level. They participated in the training of a few Sudanese linguists like E. Yokwe, who worked with the SIL on his own mother tongue, Bari, and later published his Ph.D. dissertation in the United States.

The breakout of the second civil war in 1983 interrupted the foundational work for the establishment of language development in southern Sudan. In 1988, the SIL left southern Sudan and moved its main office to Nairobi, Kenya. In 1991, under the Islamic Inqādh government, the SIL's agreement was no longer valid and the SIL had to resort to a new approach (see 3.3.4), continuing its descriptive linguistic work in eastern Africa and Khartoum among southern refugee communities.

In spite of the SIL involvement, the promotion and teaching of southern languages remained limited on the ground in the period 1977–88. In urban areas, ethnic and linguistic diversity seriously constrained the teaching of southern languages. In rural areas, the key targeted areas for the teaching of southern vernaculars, there was a lack of trained teachers and educational infrastructures. Local vernaculars were mainly used as oral languages (together with Juba Arabic) either in churches or in some broadcasting of the Sudan Council of Churches Radio.

Development of Sudanese Linguistics in the North

From 1972 to 1984, institutional interest in Sudanese languages was also growing in Khartoum. In 1972, the Institute of African and Asian Studies (IAAS) was founded and included a linguistic department specializing in the study of African languages. The IAAS started to publish phonological and morphological descriptions of some Sudanese languages, including master's theses, some of them undertaken by SIL linguists like J. Persson (on Jur-Mödö) and E. Kipaltrick (on Bongo). The IAAS also published a series on oral literature (like the one written by Adrob on Beja). Publications were either in English (with Latin transcription for the southern languages) or in Arabic (with Arabic transliteration). Many foreign linguists came to work on Darfuri and Kordofani languages as well as on Nilotic languages, resulting in the publication in Europe and North America of several important volumes on Sudanese African linguistics (either grammars of a single language or historical classifications of language groups). The Nilo-Saharan Association was founded during this period, contributing to the improvement and overall quality of exchanges among researchers.

The period between 1972 and 1988 was characterized by important advances in the knowledge and study of Sudanese languages, both in northern and southern Sudan. In the north, however, the expectations raised by the foundation of the IAAS very quickly became a source of disappointment. Lack of human and material resources as well as a hostile political environment beginning in 1982 hindered active IAAS participation in the promotion of Sudanese languages. In the south, the involvement of political forces appeared to be rather limited, and the region was facing too many economic challenges. As a result, in the mid-1980s, promotion of Sudanese languages remained more virtual than effective. Over the same period, the defence of Sudanese linguistic and cultural diversity became a major point of political debate, and the Sudan People's Liberation Movement's (SPLM) cultural vision started to spread more and more among the non-Arab groups of Sudan (Miller 2003).

Years of War and Resilience: 1984–2005

The years between 1984 and 2005 are characterized by three dynamics at the linguistic and educational levels: (1) the enactment of educational reforms in 1990 by the Islamist regime, which reinforced Arabization and Islamization throughout the country (Berair 2007; Jahallah 2008); (2) an increasing mobilization for the defence of linguistic and cultural diversity among not only southern groups but also northern non-Arab groups, a trend ideologically supported by the SPLM's 'New Sudan' discourse; and (3) the use of Ugandan or Kenyan curricula in southern schools controlled by the SPLM both in southern Sudan and refugee camps in eastern Africa. English was the medium of instruction and vernaculars were not used (Breidlid 2006; Yongo-Bure 2006). Teaching took place under extremely difficult conditions, as southern educational buildings were almost completely destroyed by the war (except in main cities like Juba, Wao and Malakal).

Governmental Policy

Governmental policy was characterized by serious gaps between official resolutions and real social and political practices. A few months after coming to power in September 1989, the Islamic regime organized the National Dialogue Conference for the Problems of Peace. This conference produced a resolution on language and education that recognizes the special position of English in the southern regions and states that 'the government should not take scarcity of financial means as a pretext for barring any indigenous language from being used as a medium of instruction and should adopt the initiatives of ethnic groups wishing to promote their respective tribal languages and use them as media of instruction for their children'.

That was the situation 'on paper' regarding indigenous language rights in 1989. On the ground and in practice, the situation was characterized by the Arabization of higher education (implemented in all Sudanese universities, including those of southern Sudan, as well as for all faculties, including in the applied sciences) and of former private schools, as well as direct and indirect support of the Arabic language and Arab-Islamic culture in all public domains, with a reportedly drastic drop in the previously high standards of English among university graduates (Abu-Manga 2010).

Concerning promotion of the vernacular languages, only two institutional initiatives can be noted: first, in the period from 1991 to 2005 some Sudanese and African languages were used in broadcasting by the National Unity Radio (Radio Omdurman), namely, Hausa, Juba Arabic, Nuer, Dinka and Shilluk. This was essentially to carry the messages and ideology of the regime inside and outside the country (Abu-Manga 1995). Second, in 1993, Yusif Al-Khalifa Abu-Bakr resumed his old 1956 project of writing African languages in Arabic script. Funded by the Islamic Educational Scientific and Cultural Organization (ISESCO), the project was hosted by the International University of Africa in Khartoum and continued up to early 2010. Both initiatives have clear ideological goals: (1) counteracting the SPLM's discourse and attracting non-Arab groups to the regime; (2) trying to disconnect the writing of Sudanese languages from the Roman script (associated with Christianity) in order to maintain a link between Arabic and the other Sudanese languages.

A theoretical acknowledgement of cultural and linguistic diversity was again promulgated in 1997. A constitutional decree came out on 22 November 1997 and created a National Council for Language Planning. In this decree, Arabic was recognized as the 'national language', and the other languages simply as 'local languages'. The cultural diversity and linguistic plurality of Sudan was to be protected and was recognized as part of the cultural personality of Sudan. The right to diversity (although a structured diversity) was also recognized in Article 27 of the 1998 constitution, which stipulated that 'there shall be guaranteed for every community or group of citizens the right to preserve their particular culture, language or religion, and rear children freely within the framework of their particularity, and the same shall not by coercion be effaced'.[8] This Article set up the basis of what would become the 2008 Act of the Council for Promotion and Development of the National Languages.

SIL Activities in Khartoum

Whereas SIL activities were officially stopped in southern Sudan, the organization managed to pursue literacy activities among the southern refugee communities of Khartoum. The Khartoum Diocese of the Episcopal Church of Sudan decided to enlist foreign individuals participating in SIL programmes to work in Khartoum and help the church with Bible translations and literacy classes. The SIL could not work in Khartoum as it had in southern Sudan, however, and adopted a low profile. Instead of bringing several experts it opted for a policy of linguistic development at the grassroots level (Gilley 2006).

A strategy of 'language groups' was initiated in 1993. A language group was formed by a few people of the same ethnic or linguistic group, eager to be trained in order to work on their own language, produce readers and set up literacy classes. Under the Sudan Workshop Program (SWP) the SIL organized training workshops for each community in order to establish orthography and literacy programmes, Bible translation and the transcription of oral traditions. Native speakers and members of the language groups were to decide which dialect of their language they wished to describe, and which orthography they would apply. In 2005, about thirty language groups were working and producing literacy materials (Gilley 2006). The refugees' financial situation, however, was so dramatic that it often restrained the process. Language group members who worked on a voluntary basis often could not find the financial means to publish their readers (the SIL produced the first thirty issues, but the language groups then had to find their own funding in the community among members who, more often than not, could not help). Most groups were unable to produce anything more than a handbook of orthography in their chosen language. Many had difficulty selecting orthographic rules capable of standardization, a problem that eventually led to conflict among subgroups, each one wanting its own dialect/language to become the language group standard (see Manfredi, this volume, for a case description). The overall impression was that, in spite of the SIL's long experience in Sudan, the language groups were unable to build on a shared knowledge base.

However, the impact of SIL activities went deeper than might appear at first glance. If the literacy activity had been conducted under the umbrella of the Sudanese Episcopal Church and was supposedly restricted to Christian refugee groups from the south, the process quickly influenced numerous non-Christian groups, either mixed groups (Muslims and Christians, like several groups from the Nuba Mountains or Northern Bahr Al-Ghazal) or Muslim groups, like the Beja, the Fur, the Ingessana and the Zaghawa. In this way the SIL linguistic ideology spread throughout Sudan irrespective of religious affiliation, the key being that in order to exist, an ethnic group was required to codify and write its own language, a process that might conceivably lead to endless fragmentation.

In spite of a general political climate hostile to Christianity and Christian missionaries in the north at that time, it should be mentioned that the SIL did not work in complete isolation (and in fact was closely watched by the Sudanese security services). Leoma Gilley, the initiator of the SIL workshop programme, succeeded in establishing official links with Sudanese institutions like the University of Khartoum, where she taught African linguistics for a number of years. Some SIL workshop members registered for course work in the IAAS to obtain a diploma in African linguistics. The few Western linguists, who had nothing to do with the church, often worked with Sudanese informants participating in the SIL workshop programme.

Between 1994 and 2005, Khartoum became the meeting point for various individuals (Sudanese church staff, Western or Sudanese linguists, Sudanese intellectuals, social activists, individual members of communities, etc.) who, regardless of religious beliefs or political inclinations, shared a desire to codify and promote Sudanese languages. A concretization of such a process was the holding of the Ninth International Nilo-Saharan Conference organized by the IAAS in Khartoum in 2004, which was attended by several Western and Sudanese linguists.

Internal Resilience

This specific political and social context contributed to another important process, in that work on linguistic codification and transcription was no longer the preserve of experts and academics, but became accessible to a larger circle of activists and lay people whose legitimacy lay with their own native skills and their concern for their linguistic communities. Literacy in vernacular languages, a prior church initiative, became widespread among Muslim groups whose literary language is Arabic.

At this stage, the matter of which script to apply in transcription became increasingly a matter of ideological choice. In the south, Christian and related associations universally opted for Roman scripts. In the Muslim north, non-Arab groups educated in Arabic for centuries (either in Koranic schools or, since the twentieth century, in governmental schools) would logically have preferred to transcribe their languages and produce literary texts using Arabic scripts (like Persian, for example). But the political cleavages between so-called Arabs and non-Arabs became so profound in the last decade of the twentieth century (Sharkey 2008) that most of the regional and ethnic movements, as well as their main activists, opted to mark their cultural and linguistic differences away from Arabic. This neonationalist trend among non-Arab groups is typical of any process of emerging nationalism (Anderson 1991; Hobsbawn and Ranger 1983; Joseph 2004). In this respect, non-Arab Sudanese groups replicated the trend observed all around the world. In the precise case of Sudan, it should also be noted that most linguistic descriptions of Sudanese languages have been written in European languages and transcribed using the Roman or International Phonetic Alphabet (IPA). Very few linguistic descriptions of Sudanese languages (excluding Arabic, of course) have been recorded in Arabic, and African linguistics is rarely associated with Arabic scripts (except for Abu-Bakr's ISESCO experience). While proponents of both scripts present linguistic arguments to defend their choices, it must be recalled that the choice of alphabet for any language of the world is a matter of convention and ultimately a political choice.

During this period of internal resilience, one may note the political and linguistic mobilization of the Sudanese diaspora all around the world (including East Africa, Europe, North America, Australia and even Arab countries), which certainly played an important role in spreading cultural and linguistic awareness both outside and inside Sudan. Through forums, conferences, meetings, publications and now websites, the members of the Sudanese diaspora became particularly active in the strategic defence of Sudanese languages and culture. For example, the first Conference on Beja Linguistics was held in Cairo in September 1999. In 2000, the Dinka Language Institute, Agamlong, was created in Australia.[9] Even though a transnational orientation is evident, the involvement of the Sudanese diaspora has led to numerous uncoordinated actions, which sometimes lack any recognizably regimented linguistic expertise.

The Resolution on Language in the Comprehensive Peace Agreement

A Major Political Step

The 2005 Comprehensive Peace Agreement (CPA) marked the end of the second civil war and included very important linguistic recommendations that, unlike the previous Addis Ababa peace agreement, were not restricted to southern Sudan but were supposed to concern the entire country. The resolution on language included in the CPA and endorsed in the interim constitution of 2005 was organized around five key points:

> 2.8. Language:
>
> 2.8.1. All indigenous languages are national languages which shall be respected, developed and promoted.
>
> 2.8.2. Arabic language is the widely spoken national language in the Sudan.
>
> 2.8.3. Arabic, as a major language at the national level, and English shall be the official working languages of the National Government business and languages of instruction for higher education.
>
> 2.8.4. In addition to Arabic and English, the legislature of any sub-national level of government may adopt any other national language(s) as additional official working language(s) at its level.
>
> 2.8.5. The use of either language at any level of government or education shall not be discriminated against. (CPA 2005: 26–27)

It was further agreed that a council would be established under the presidency to oversee the implementation of the new language policy. The two major facts of the CPA language resolution are: first, the recognition of English as the co-official language (though in practice it remains a second official language); and second, the recognition of all Sudanese languages as national languages that can be eventually used as working languages at the regional level.

These points represented a landmark advance over previous Sudanese linguistic policy, even if practical considerations raise a number of concerns (Abu-Manga 2007; Abdelhay 2010a; Abdelhay, Makoni and Makoni 2010). According to some observers, it appears that nonlinguist decision makers in the northern part of the country adopted a limited view of language policy and were not seriously prepared to discuss these issues, whereas among southern political elites the issues had far greater political currency. This was confirmed by the makeup of the respective delegations for the Nairobi language policy discussions of the Comprehensive Peace Agreement some months before the signature of the CPA: the SPLM was represented by a group of experts that included four trained linguists (Ph.D. holders), whereas the central government was represented by a group of secondary school teachers headed, ironically, by a teacher of mathematics. Similarly, no linguist of any calibre participated on the government's side in the final discussions in Naivasha, while the SPLM's side on this matter was headed by a professor of African languages and linguistics, George Nyombe Bureny, who was then on the faculty of the University of Nairobi in the Department of Linguistics. This disposition was a clear indication that the difficulties inherent in language and culture were well understood by the intellectual and political elites from southern Sudan long before the signing of the CPA. On the other hand, the northern political elites seem to have realized the importance of these issues only later.

The Impact of the CPA in the Pre-2011 South

The first implication of the CPA was the reinforcement of English in all SPLM-held territories, including the Nuba Mountains in the south. English is the working and communication language of the south, and the principal language used in education. The choice of English for educational purposes had been followed by the SPLM for more than twenty years, enabling southern students to pursue higher studies in East African. In 2005 the educational system was in a catastrophic state, with southern Sudan having the lowest access to primary education in the world according to the UN. Rehabilitation projects estimated it would be necessary to construct twenty-five hundred schools per year in the period between 2005 and 2011 (Yongo-Bure 2006).[10] In 2010, and according to southern Sudanese sources, the number of students increased very quickly (Garang 2010a), and numerous institutes have been established with support from the UN and the Norwegian Agency for Development Cooperation, among others (Wright 2006). The use of English at all educational levels raised problems of communication in that there is a general lack of trained teachers, as pointed out by the southern minister of education in July 2010 (Garang 2010b) when he stated that, in many schools, instruction was provided in a local language and that English was taught as a subject. Nevertheless, the implementation of a concrete policy to help the promotion of the 'indigenous national languages' is rather slow in both the north and south.

In 2008–9 the SIL signed a new agreement with the southern Ministry of Education, Science and Technology (MOEST). Two SIL members were assigned to work with the MOEST on reintroducing the teaching of local languages into the primary school system. The minister of education plans to set up an Institute of National Languages (INL), which will presumably be somewhat like the old IRL. Former SIL assistants are expected to participate in this new institute[11]. In 2014, the Department of National Languages within MOEST organized a number of workshops with the SIL advisors in order to develop the guidelines for the further teaching of south Sudanese languages under the supervision of the future INL (Spronk 2014), of 2011, had yet to materialize. The proposal may yet be reworked given the political realities following the outcome of the January 2011 referendum for independence.

Efforts to promote southern languages are more effective via radio media, which have been a regular feature of southern Sudanese information services since 2005. The Sudan Catholic Radio Network (SCRN) began broadcasting in Juba in 2006 and by 2010 had opened stations in Torit, Tonj, Rumbeck, Yei, Malakal and Gidel (southern Nuba Mountains). Other than English and Arabic, SCRN presents broadcasts in the following languages:[12] Bari, Madi, Acholi, Dinka, Lotuko, Didinga, Lango, Madi, Toposa Bongo, Jur, Tira and Otoro. Another radio, Sudan Radio Service (SRS), established in Kenya in 2003 with support from USAID/OTI, relocated to Juba in 2010 and broadcasts many programmes in Sudanese languages. According to its website, 'programming reflects the vibrant communities and cultures in southern Sudan. Regular, weekly programming targets speakers of Dinka, Nuer, Juba-Arabic, Bari, Shilluk, Zande, Moro, Arabic, and English.'[13] Veteran SRS reporter and writer Victor Lugala is reported to have said that 'broadcasting in the mother tongues of South Sudan as well as in the lingua-franca – Juba-Arabic – is the best way to reach his people, since news and stories resonate more when they are heard in the everyday languages of his people. The fact that we are focusing in languages that are well understood by the people makes radio a very good device' (Fick 2011). The status of Juba Arabic, the lingua franca of South Sudan, remains unclear. Although it is not officially categorized as a southern vernacular, it is the mother tongue of many urban dwellers. It has not been granted a national or official status within the 2011 transitional constitution of the Republic of South Sudan.

There are several indications that civil society in South Sudan, and particularly the people and associations coming back from East Africa, are very much concerned by the development of their native languages and cultures. It remains to be seen whether this development will concern mainly oral practices (music, theatre, radio, TV, etc.) or whether the movement will extend to written communications (education, literature, newspaper, Internet, etc.). For the time being, most of the websites for such associations are published in English.

The Impact of the CPA in the North

In the north, several developments took place. At the official level, a presidential decree in February 2009 announced the creation of a Council for

Development and Promotion of the National Languages and appointed a chairman (Professor Al-Amin Abu-Manga) and eight members with balanced regional and ethnolinguistic representation, including three southerners, one from Darfur, one from eastern Sudan, one professor of English and one professor of Arabic linguistics, the latter being Yusif Al-Khalifa Abu-Bakr. The council announced several ambitious goals for the protection and promotion of national languages and cultural heritage.

For the time being, however, the council lacks the financial means to undertake an ambitious programme and its future faces serious uncertainties. The establishment of the council was based on the interim constitution, whose mandate ended in 2011. It is not certain that the council will continue its work with the same vigour and the same support from the northern government now that the country has been partitioned into two independent states.

Most initiatives seem to remain in the civil or religious sectors. Whereas the SIL has stopped its workshop programmes in Khartoum, the Sudanese Episcopal Church in Khartoum maintains its department of literacy and translation for the southern population. Since 2006 the American Bible Society has operated a Moro Literacy Project, offering literacy classes in both Khartoum and the Nuba Mountains (American Bible Society 2009). At the university level, linguistic researchers have experienced new hope with the announcement of new sources of international funding for programmes on Sudanese endangered languages. Most of these programmes have established cooperative relations between Sudanese and SIL linguists and Western universities (such as Edinburgh or Cologne Universities for the Dinka, Shilluk and Nuba languages). These programmes have relied in part on informal networks that were developed during the last decade of the twentieth century, including SIL and IAAS linguists like Leoma Gilley, Eilen Browne and Professor A. Mugadim.

As in the last decade of the twentieth century and the early years of the twenty-first century, a number of language activities have actually been pursued abroad. In Chad, members of the Zaghawa community working with the SIL have proposed a specific writing system for the Beria language, based on a sampling of the markings on camels.[14] This writing system was invented in 1972 by a Sudanese schoolteacher, Adam Tagir (see Norein 2006), adapted by Siddik Adam Issa in 2004 and then designed by SIL volunteers in 2007 (Seonil Yun and Lorna Priest).

Examples of individual, associative or institutional initiatives are numerous and could give the impression of intense activity. However, many initiatives may face a durability problem. As of mid-2010, a number of websites accessed in June 2009 were no longer accessible either outside Sudan (like the site of the Dinka Language Institute in Australia, or the site of the Association for the Promotion of the Beria Language[15], or within Sudan itself. This very issue is the reason why no serious language planning is possible for Sudanese languages without a strong institutional body coordinating the various initiatives.

Conclusion

The description, codification and planning of the preservation of Sudanese languages has a rather long history characterized by few periods of improvement and long periods of decline. Planning for Sudanese language instruction and codification implies two different but interconnected processes.

The first process impacts on human representations of languages. Codifying a language implies per se a process of differentiation. In Sudan this process of linguistic differentiation was intimately connected with the construction of ethnic boundaries in the case of non-Arab languages (but not in the case of Arabic). This means that each ethnic group needs to have its own autonomous language in order to be recognized within the symbolic social order. A striking contradiction is the fact that processes of codification are increasing at a time when actual practices are characterized by language mixing or code switching.

The second process is more ideological and political and reflects the power relationships within Sudan. Relationships between the various languages are more often conceived in terms of competition than coexistence and polarized around Arabic versus non-Arabic languages. This conception has led to well-known authoritarian Arabization policies, which proved to be political and social failures. The idealization of language diversity and language equality without seriously considering functional uses and social practices could just as easily lead to another failure.

The years between 1989 and 2010 witnessed a radical shift in language planning. After a rather fanatic pro-Arabization policy applied to the entire country, the Sudanese government accepted the Comprehensive Peace Agreement, which implied the promotion of all Sudanese languages as national languages. One may wonder to what extent the 2005 CPA-based language policy will impact the maintenance of languages in post-CPA Sudan, particularly on the (conceivably) endangered languages in both the north and the newly independent south. Will the northern government pursue the 2005 CPA-based language policy after the secession of the south?

Compared to previous periods, an important development during the last two decades has been the emergence of a 'civil society' that is involved in the defence of cultural and linguistic plurality. This led to two important steps. First, promotion of vernacular languages is no longer restricted to Christian associations and southern groups but has also spread to most 'non-Arab groups', contributing in this way to the construction of national ethnic boundaries. Second, it means the development of new forms of community-oriented nationalism to challenge state-organized nationalism. At this stage the crucial issue for the Sudanese intellectual elite is to rethink the issue of language demarcation and the very bases of linguistic nationalism.

Notes

1. For a critical approach to the relationship between language and ethnicity continuously advanced by various types of nationalism in Sudan, see, among others, Abdelhay, Makoni and Makoni 2010; Miller 2006; Sharkey 2008.
2. See Article 14 of the Universal Declaration of Linguistic Rights (2006), which states that 'Indigenous peoples have the right to establish and control their educational systems and institutions providing education in their own languages, in a manner appropriate to their cultural methods of teaching and learning'. See http://www.linguistic-declaration.org/index-gb.htm (accessed 19 October 2010).
3. For details on language classification and numbers, see Hurreiz and Bell (1975), Thelwall (1978), Abu-Manga and Abu-Bakr (2006).
4. Data provided by Ethnologue, http://www.ethnologue.com/show_country.asp?name=SD (accessed 25 November 2010).
5. Badr's book (n.d.) transcribes Nubian in both Roman and Arabic script. Khalid Mukhtar, an archaeologist at Cairo University, opted for the use of Old Nubian script to transcribe modern Nubian vernaculars. In 1997–98, he wrote a book that was to be published in Cairo. After his death in 1998, his work was pursued by the Nubian Studies Association in Cairo.
6. Janet Persson, personal email communication, June 2009. The fifteen added languages belong mainly to category B plus Juba Arabic).
7. See http://www.ethnologue.com/show_country_bibl.asp?name=SD (accessed 1 November 2007).
8. See http://www.unesco.org/most/lnsudan.htm (accessed 18 January 2011).
9. See http://home.vicnet.net.au/~agamlong/dlia/index.en.html (the website was first accessed in June 2009; in December 2010, it no longer worked).
10. The 2005 UN report reads: 'Only 2 percent of the population completes primary education and the adult literacy rate is 24 percent. Of the few schools that do exist (there is one school per 1,000 children), only 10 percent are in permanent buildings' (Yongo-Bure 2006).
11. Janet Persson, personal email communication, June 2009.
12. See http://sudancatholicradio.net/ (accessed 29 December 2010).
13. See http://www.evrel.ewf.uni-erlangen.de/pesc/peaceradio-SDN.html (accessed 29 December 2010).
14. See http://scripts.sil.org/ZaghawaBeria/Home (accessed 13 September 2009).
15. http://www.zaghawa.org/ (accessed 7 July 2009).

Chapter 15

'One Tribe, One Language'

Ethnolinguistic Identity and Language Revitalization among the Laggorí in the Nuba Mountains

Stefano Manfredi

This chapter aims to analyse the effects of language revitalization on the ethnolinguistic identity of a minority community living in the Nuba Mountains, the Laggorí. It deals with an intervention aimed at language revitalization by the Summer Institute of Linguistics (SIL) and with the consequent dispute surrounding the affirmation of exclusive ethnic rights over the linguistic variety named Laggorí. Beyond this, the chapter describes the complexity of actors implicated in the process of ethnolinguistic identity building in the Nuba Mountains, drawing particular attention to the role played by Sudanese national language policy and by the system of Native Administration in South Kordofan.

The first part of the chapter introduces the sociohistorical background of the Laggorí. A short survey of bilingualism and language uses follows. After that, I focus on the modalities of language revitalization adopted by the SIL and on their political consequences in terms of tribal reshaping. Last, I analyse the changes that have occurred in the domain of ethnolinguistic identity and language attitudes as a consequence of language revitalization. The chapter argues that the link between language and ethnic identity among the Laggorí has been visibly strengthened by the SIL intervention and by the incoherent implementation of minority languages pursued by the Comprehensive Peace Agreement (CPA).[2]

Notes for this chapter begin on page 300.

Ethnicity, Language and Language Revitalization

Before examining the issue of ethnolinguistic identity and language revitalization among the Laggorí, it is necessary to introduce some of the basic concepts adopted in this chapter. The notion of 'ethnicity', and its relationship with language, is crucial. Broadly speaking, definitions of ethnicity have always been at variance over the role of objective and subjective factors (Liebkind 1999: 140). The first approach assumes that a given ethnic group can be defined according to objective criteria such as a common geographical context and the possession of a single set of customs, religion and language. According to this first perspective, ethnicity is ascribed and invariable and, consequently, people take it for granted. Running counter to this approach, the second approach stresses that ethnicity always depends on a certain degree of subjectivity given that individuals define ethnic membership on the basis of their empirical categorization. On this basis, ethnic identity has been defined as 'a sociopsychological variable which may not be at all conscious but one of which minorities are more often conscious than majorities' (Fishman 1999: 155). Departing from this theoretical dichotomy, one of the most influential models of ethnicity was outlined in *Ethnic Groups and Boundaries* by Fredrik Barth (1969). By focusing on the transactional nature of ethnicity, Barth embraced a predominately social interactionist perspective, arguing that ethnicity depends on two mutually interdependent processes, namely, the internal definition and the external categorization of ethnic boundaries.

The different standpoints in relation to ethnicity are evidently reproduced in interpretations regarding the link between language and ethnic identity. By and large, spoken languages are one of the most salient features of ethnically defined groups simply because people tend to identify with the other speakers of their own language. Consequently, it is generally claimed that ethnic identity is inextricably connected with language (Bourhis 1979). In contrast, some scholars (Appel and Muysken 1987: 15) deny any necessary link between language and ethnicity, arguing that there are more important factors that intervene in the determination of ethnic identity (i.e., racial generalization, political affiliation and class identity). In a sense, both of these interpretations are unsatisfactory as an explanation of the variations underlying the adoption of language as an ethnic marker. For his part, Barth argued that language may be optionally used as a marker of ethnic identity depending on processes of social interactions in conflict or cooperative social contexts. As I will show, the variable relevance of language in shaping the Laggorí ethnicity is perfectly in line with Barth's approach.

An additional aspect of this issue relates to the theoretical grounds of language revitalization. In recent decades, language revitalization has become a significant focus of concern because of the role played by language in expanding minority rights. Language revitalization aims to recover the use of languages that risk extinction because of the declining number of their native speakers. It often implies the development of a standard orthography to be adopted in specific education curricula. The outcomes of language revitalization vary greatly in relation to the motivations underlying the recovering intervention (Grenoble and Whaley 2006: 17–19). In some instances, language revitalization directly emanates from the community's determination to promote its own language. In other cases, revitalization efforts originate from a top-down approach, as an external subject takes the initiative in recovering someone else's language by supposedly acting on the object's behalf. Given the potential link between ethnicity and language, both of these approaches to language revitalization may have strong repercussions on the ethnic identity of linguistic minorities. In this regard, I agree with Costa (2013), who argued that language revitalization is primarily a social phenomenon in which language is invested with particular ideological meaning, thereby redefining the terms of the contact between a minority group and a majority group language. Accordingly, if rights over the recovered language are limited by exclusive ethnic rights, language revitalization may lead to conflict sparked by the issue of access to the language. In this regard, the dispute that followed the standardization of the Laggorí language demonstrates that every revitalization intervention should take into account the power relationships between neighbouring linguistic communities in order to avoid the triggering or the aggravation of ethnolinguistic conflicts.

Sociohistorical Background

The Laggorí and Their Language

The Laggorí language (also referred to as Logorí or Liguri) is classified within the eastern Sudanic subgroup of the Nilo-Saharan family (Bender 2000: 47). Laggorí, together with the Shatt Damam of the southwestern Nuba Mountains, represents the eastern branch of the so-called Daju languages. There is broad agreement on the fact that the Daju moved from their homelands in Wadai (eastern Chad) after the rise of the Tunjur dynasty in the fifteenth century. They subsequently went through a sequence of displacements that led them to Dar Sila and eventually to Dar Fur and Kordofan (Henderson 1931: 51; Hillelson 1932: 59). With regard to the Laggorí, it seems reasonable to think that they originated as an offshoot of the Daju of Logawa, with whom they share oral traditions about their western origins. We do not possess historical documentation describing the arrival of the Laggorí's ancestors in the Nuba Mountains. Nevertheless, when Baggara Arabs penetrated Kordofan at the end of the eighteenth century, they found Laggorí people already living in their current location in the northeast of Kadugli.

Laggorí is generally considered to be a dialect cluster including three different varieties that are respectively referred to as Laggorí, Soborí and Tillew (Tucker and Bryan 1956: 60; Thelwall 1981: 168; Thelwall and Schadeberg 1983: 220; Grimes 2000: 223). This subclassification is based on lexicostatistical comparisons that demonstrate a higher lexical affinity between the Laggorí dialects as compared with other Daju languages (MacDiarmid 1931: 201; Thelwall 1981: 170–71). This means that, in spite of the adoption of different glossonyms, the three dialects are mutually intelligible.[3] In this regard, it is important to underline that a common characteristic of Nuba groups is the use of the ethnonyms applied to them by Baggara Arabs. Unlike Arab groups, which are usually defined according to anthroponyms stemming from patrilineal filiation, the majority of Nuba ethnonyms originated from locality names. For the purposes of this chapter, it is interesting that Nuba toponyms and ethnonyms are also used to refer to languages regardless of the fact that neighbouring communities may speak dialects of the same language (R. Stevenson 1956–57: 98, 101). Thus, different glossonyms may not reflect an effective linguistic differentiation. Moreover, the correspondence between toponyms and ethnonyms demonstrates that in the Nuba Mountains the basic factor in determining ethnic boundaries is not language, but locality (Jakobi 1991: 156–57).

The ethnonym 'Laggorí' is derived from an Arabic distortion of the syntagm *lág k-kòrí,* which literally means 'Kòrí's house'.[4] Arabs originally applied this name to the hill inhabited by the Laggorí (*jebel laggorí*). The term has subsequently expanded its semantic reference, and it is nowadays used to indicate both the Laggorí people and their language. According to my informants, the Laggorí formerly used to refer to themselves as *èggá t-bá,* which literally means 'the people of the house'. This earlier ethnonym clearly denotes kinship solidarity rather than a specific geographical origin. In spite of this, the adoption of the ethnonym 'Laggorí' was decisively encouraged by the British colonial administration, which adopted it in the process of establishing tribal borders in the southwestern Nuba Mountains. The acceptance of the new ethnonym eventually contributed to the shaping of a new autochthonous basis of identification for the Laggorí and to the severing of their historical links with outsider groups such as the Daju.

For the purposes of this chapter, it is also necessary to take into account the reasons for the differentiation between the Laggorí and the Soborí. Laggorí people generally have a negative attitude towards the Soborí and their language. This state of affairs dates from the Turkiyya period (1821–81), when the Laggorí were used to control a slave camp located on the slopes of today's Soborí hill. The Soborí, in fact, are thought to be the descendants of slaves captured from different Nuba groups who intermarried with Laggorí after the end of the system of slavery. According to my Laggorí informants, the ethnonym 'Soborí' is related to the Arabic expression *ṣobor-o,* meaning 'they remained', in reference to the former slaves who settled in that area. In addition to the stigmatization related to their status as former slaves, Laggorí people argue that the mixed origins of the Soborí represent the main cause of the linguistic differentiation between the two groups. In reality, even if it is generally accepted that Laggorí and Soborí constitute two different dialects, the linguistic data for determining the degree of linguistic divergence between the two varieties are still scant. Nevertheless, Laggorí people tend to stress the originality of their language as compared with Soborí and Tillew, and to claim a prominent position within the Laggorí dialect cluster. This state of affairs evidently contributed to the rise of the ethnolinguistic dispute that followed the adoption of the glossonym 'Laggorí' for referring to the language targeted by the SIL revitalization intervention.

Settlement Processes

At the turn of the twentieth century, a significant majority of the Laggorí community was found on the ridges of today's Laggorí hill. A minority group was located on the Tokswana hill, approximately five kilometres north of Laggorí. Most of them practiced a system of intensive hill cultivation with a limited involvement in the rearing of livestock. This situation gradually changed from 1930, when Nuba groups were forced by the British administration to descend from their hills to the surrounding plains (Manger 1994: 18). Even if many Laggorí remained on their hill until as late as Sudanese independence (i.e., 1956), the majority gradually moved to a nearby plateau and formed the village of Laggorí-Umm Bres. This downward movement resulted in a shift from traditional hill cultivation to a more extensive kind of agriculture. The diffusion of cotton in the Nuba Mountains required larger field cultivation for commercial production. As a result, many Laggorí moved to neighbouring localities such as Tarai, Dorot and Daldakó, where they started to enjoy close relations with Baggara Arabs.

The Laggorí have been highly affected by forced urbanization since the beginning of the civil war in 1987. The first massive urbanization expe-

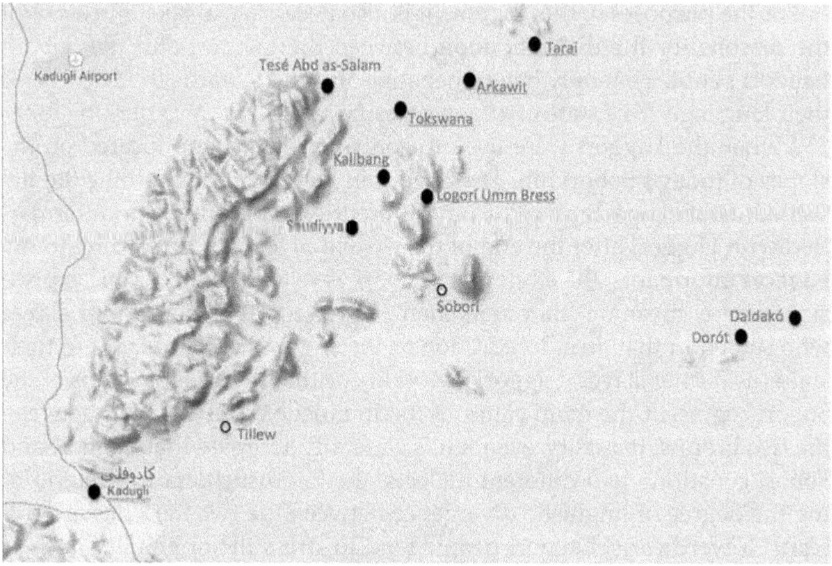

Figure 15.1. Map of Laggorí Settlements
• <u>Kadugli</u>: Localities touched by the fieldwork
• Sa'udiyya: Localities with a presence of ethnically defined Laggorí
○ Tillew: Other localities

rienced by Laggorí people began in 1991, when many of them settled in Kadugli (mainly in the quarter of Ḥajar al-Makk). The outbreak of war also forced many Laggorí to move to northern Sudan. Indeed, a significant proportion of the ethnically defined Laggorí currently reside in Khartoum (mainly in the quarters of Umbadda and in Ḥājj Yūsif) and in other northern Sudanese urban centres (Wadi Ḥalfa, Atbara, Wad Medani and Kosti). It should be recalled that after the signing of the CPA in 2005, internally displaced people, of whom Nuba groups living in northern Sudan represented an important number, were allowed to go back to their homelands. Thus, many Laggorí started to move back to the Nuba Mountains in 2006 to constitute sizeable returnee communities in Arkawit and Kalibang. This situation dramatically changed with the eruption of a new armed conflict after the referendum in 2011.

The Dynamics of Arabization among the Laggorí

Despite the fact that the Laggorí have remained culturally distinct from Arabs, they are characterized by a relatively high degree of Arabization when compared with other Nuba groups. In this regard, it should be stated that the linguistic Arabization of the Laggorí worked independently from their Islamization. The Laggorí started to acquire a form of Arabic from their first contacts with the Baggara Arabs at the beginning of the nineteenth century. However, they did not begin to Islamize until the installation of the Anglo-Egyptian Condominium. The socioeconomic relations with Rawāwga Arabs (a section of the Ḥawāzma tribe) represented the most important cause of the Arabization of the Laggorí. It is well-known that under Turkish rule Baggara Arabs systematically engaged in slave-raiding expeditions in the Nuba Mountains. Nevertheless, Nuba-Baggara relations also depended on economic patterns, namely, on the marked complementarity between the sedentary and the nomadic modes of production.

The Laggorí traditionally rely on rain-fed cultivation of cereals, whereas Baggara Arabs are basically cattle nomads. In their first phase, the economic relations between the Laggorí and Baggara Arabs consisted of the exchange of sorghum for animal products. Similar to the situation described by Haaland (1969) with reference to the Fur, the need for economic differentiation eventually led some Laggorí to become engaged in livestock raising and to establish themselves in Baggara nomads' camps. At the same time, the most economically marginal Rawāwga nomads gradually settled in Tarai and Tokswana and became sedentary farmers alongside the Laggorí people. More recently, the introduction of extensive cotton cropping intensified the links between Nuba groups and Baggara Arabs, mainly because of the interethnic managing of cultivation (Saavedra 1998: 241). With regard to the Laggorí, it is interesting to note that this collaborative mode of production brought about a balanced pattern of bilingualism in which they rapidly incremented the use of Arabic, while Baggara children started to acquire Laggorí as a second language (Manfredi 2013: 466).

The strong economic relations between the Laggorí and Baggara Arabs came to an end with the beginning of the civil war in 1987. The ethnicization of the conflict pursued by both the Inqādh government and the SPLM drove a profound wedge between the Nuba groups and the Arabs. Nonetheless, the interruption of the relations between the Laggorí and Baggara Arabs did not result in a decrease in Arabization. The evidence indicates that, following urbanization, the Laggorí became more exposed to institutional Arabization as a consequence of the spread of formal education.

Establishing Tribal Structures

In this section, I briefly describe the evolution of the Laggorí tribal organization, as it represents an important element for understanding the political consequences of language revitalization. Prior to British colonial rule, the Laggorí did not possess a centralized tribal structure; they were an assembly of self-reliant households that could barely claim to comprise a collective political organization. In 1921, the British introduced a Native Administration policy aimed at installing tribal leaders in the three hierarchically related positions of *nāẓir*,[5] *'omda* (*makk* for certain Nuba groups) and sheikh in order to facilitate tax collecting (A. Ibrahim 1985: 30–31). Administrative devolution to Arab tribes generally conformed to preexisting agnatic structures, whereas the definition of Nuba tribal entities depended on geographical proximity. On this basis, the Laggorí were subdivided into fourteen *mashāīkha* under the leadership of the *makk* of Kadugli. This situation endured until 1969, when under Nimeiri's rule the Native Administration system was abolished.

In 1995, the Inqādh government reintroduced the Native Administration system, and this led to a new tribal configuration for the Laggorí. In consideration of their demographic expansion, the Laggorí formed a new *'omodiya* within the *amāra* of Eastern Kadugli, which also included the Soborí, the Tillew, the Keiga, the Timoró and the Damík. Thus, in line with the British model of Native Administration, Nuba tribal boundaries were not traced according to the criterion of a common ethnolinguistic background inasmuch as they were determined by geographical proximity. Indeed, the administrative boundaries of Nuba groups started to have conventional ethnic connotations only after the end of the second Sudanese civil war. As I will explain, the tribal conferences that anticipated the codification of the regional constitution of South Kordofan established a direct correlation between tribal membership and sociocultural setting. Against this background, access to an ethnically defined language became a strong argument for affirming the aspirations to self-determination of many Nuba groups.

The Sociolinguistic Situation of the Laggorí

The Sample

We do not possess reliable data on the number of Laggorí speakers, although UNESCO (2009) considers Laggorí to be a 'critically endangered language'.[6] In the following section, I do not attempt to quantify the number of Laggorí speakers inasmuch as I draw an overview of the Laggorí sociolinguistic situation based on a statistical survey on bilingualism and language uses. The quantitative data are primarily intended to give information about the present-day linguistic vitality of Laggorí. Previous statistical information[7] will also allow me to examine the degree of linguistic regression diachronically.

The sample, which was conducted using questionnaires, consisted of 587 individuals with annotations on gender, age, ethnic affiliation, residence, literacy, first language, second language and patterns of language use. The sample was selected based on the function of the opposition between urban and rural contexts. This choice was justified by the assumption that urbanization in Sudan often encourages the acquisition of Arabic, whereas rural environments are generally less affected by linguistic normalization. On this basis, I investigated both urbanized Laggorí in Kadugli and rural communities in Laggorí-Umm Bres, Tokswana and Tarai. In addition, I surveyed the two returnee communities of Arkawit and Kalibang. Children under five years of age were not included in the survey. The surveyed sample was organized into five age groups (5–15, 16–30, 31–45, 46–60 and >60 years). With regard to the literacy variable, almost 70 per cent of my sample claimed to be able to read and write in Arabic. This demonstrates that Laggorí have a fairly high degree of literacy compared with other Nuba and Arab groups of the region (H. Bell 1976: 13; Casciarri and Manfredi 2009). Table 15.1 summarizes the composition of the sample according to the gender, age, literacy and residence variables.

Table 15.1. Composition of the Sample Group

		Individuals	%
Gender	Men	307	52.2
	Women	280	48.8
Age	5–15	185	31.5
	16–30	192	32.7
	31–45	135	22.9
	46–60	50	8.6
	>60	25	4.3
Literacy	Literate	415	70.6
	Illiterate	172	29.4
Residence	Urban	243	41.4
	Rural	170	28.9
	Returnee	174	29.6

Note: Respondents numbered 587 in 89 households (a ratio of 6.6 per household).

Bilingualism and Ethnic Membership

Statistical data drawn from questionnaires on bilingualism cannot realistically reflect the sociolinguistic situation of a given community, as they depend on the subjective views of the respondent in determining an ar-

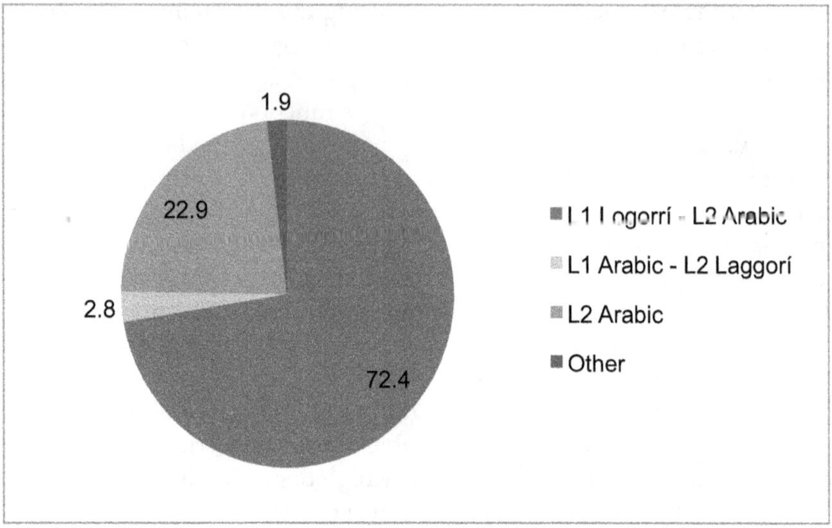

Figure 15.2. Laggorí/Arabic Patterns of Bilingualism

bitrary cutoff point between the first and second languages. Nonetheless, some important trends can be observed.

The Laggorí can be considered a bilingual community in the course of assimilation, where Arabic is passing from the status of a second language to that of the main native language. On the one hand, the overwhelming majority of my sample (425 individuals, 72.4 per cent) claimed to have acquired Laggorí as a first language and to speak Arabic as a second language. On the other hand, there are no longer any Laggorí monolingual speakers. Arabic monolinguals represented almost a quarter of the sample (135 individuals, 22.9 per cent), whereas only 2.8 per cent (17 individuals) declared that they had acquired Laggorí as a second language. Furthermore, despite the fact that the majority of the respondents claimed to be able to speak Laggorí, a tendency towards language abandonment clearly exists. However, the acquisition of Arabic as a first language does not result in the abandoning of the Laggorí ethnic identity. In fact, all of the respondents claimed to be ethnically defined as Laggorí, or more generally as Nuba.

In diachronic terms, we can note that 87.8 per cent of Bell's sample acquired Laggorí as a native language, compared with 7.8 per cent who claimed to have learned Arabic (H. Bell 1976: 3). This means that, independently from the differences between the two surveys, a noticeable decrease in the acquisition of Laggorí has occurred during the last thirty-five years. If we examine the present-day composition of Arabic monolinguals, we can better understand the causes of the regression of the Laggorí language.

Table 15.2. Detailed Information about Arabic Monolinguals

		Individuals	%
Gender	Men	77	57%
	Women	58	43%
Age	5–15	104	77%
	16–30	28	20.80%
	31–45	2	2.20%
	46–60	0	0%
	>60	0	0%
Literacy	Literate	119	88.20%
	Illiterate	16	11.80%
Residence	Urban	75	55.60%
	Rural	16	11.80%
	Returnee	44	32.60%

Note: Arabic monolinguals consisted of 135 respondents.

The most striking point is that almost all of the respondents who are not able to speak Laggorí are less than thirty years old (104 + 28 = 132 individuals, 97.8 per cent). This figure can be easily interpreted in light of the changes that accompanied the beginning of the second Sudanese civil war, the most important of which was forced urbanization. Currently, 55.6 per cent of Arabic monolingual respondents reside in Kadugli, in contrast to only 11.8 per cent who live in rural villages. The trend towards language abandonment by urban groups is also confirmed by data about returnees, who constitute almost one-third of the Arabic monolinguals (44 individuals, 32.6 per cent). Urbanization also induces an increase in literacy that in turn encourages a higher level of exposure to the official language. As a reflection of this trend, only sixteen Arabic monolingual (11.8 per cent) speakers are illiterate. Furthermore, we can observe that language regression is less evident among women (58 individuals, 43 per cent).

An additional remark relates to the respondents who declared that they had acquired a language different from both Laggorí and Arabic. From a general point of view, Laggorí people rarely acquire other local languages mainly because of their endogamous marriage strategies. The few respondents (11 individuals, 1.6 per cent) who declared that they had learned a local language other than Laggorí were children born in two mixed marriages between Laggorí men and outsider women. Five respondents declared that they spoke Dilling and Arabic. More interestingly for the purposes of this study, the remaining six respondents affirmed that they had acquired Soborí as their mother tongue and Laggorí as a second language.

Arabic, for its part, was reported as a third language. This could mean that these respondents recognized a linguistic difference between Soborí and Laggorí to such an extent that they judged them to be two distinct languages. However, if we consider that Laggorí and Soborí are mutually intelligible, the stigmatization of a linguistic distinction between the two varieties may be a more plausible explanation for the use of different glossonyms for referring to similar linguistic varieties.

Language Uses

In this section I focus on the language uses of bilingual respondents who acquired Laggorí as a native language. First, I limited the inquiry to the domestic domain, mainly because the Laggorí always adopt Arabic for their interethnic relations. Second, given that linguistic uses in the domestic domain significantly affect language acquisition, I intended to evaluate the possible gap between the degree of acquisition of Laggorí and its actual use.

As a matter of fact, of a total of 425 respondents who acquired Laggorí as their first language, only 57 individuals (13.5 per cent) claimed to speak it at home. Unlike the acquisition of Arabic as a first language, the gender variable is not relevant for understanding the decrease in the use of Laggorí. In contrast, language uses are highly influenced by both the respondent's place of residence and his or her age.

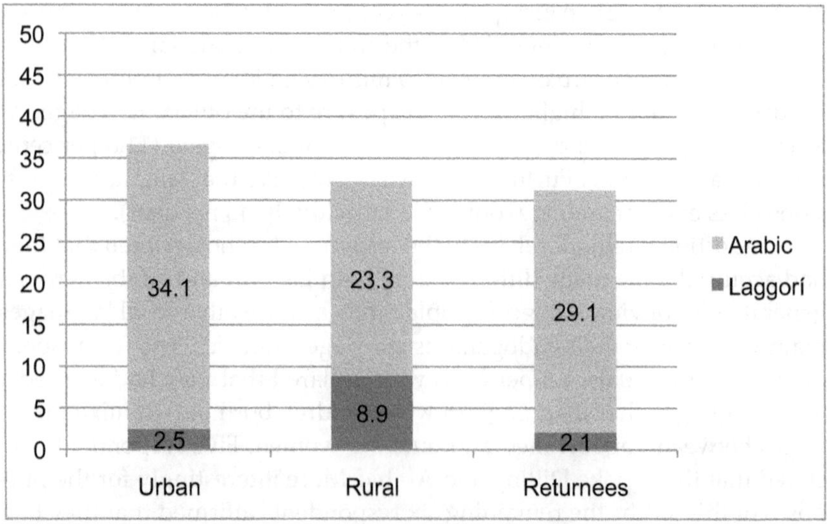

Figure 15.3. Language Uses According to Type of Residence

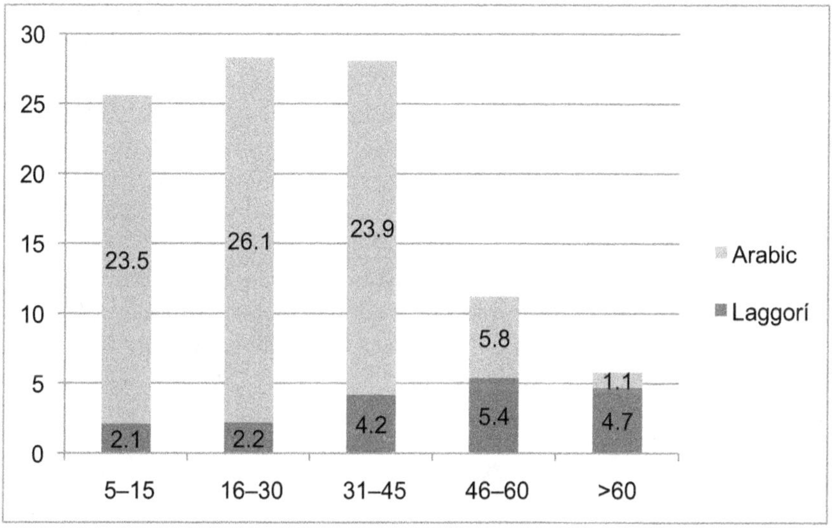

Figure 15.4. Language Uses According to Age

If we consider the residence variable, we find that only a minority of the rural respondents (51 individuals, 8.9 per cent) showed an appreciable use of the Laggorí language. Urban and rural returnee respondents, for their part, virtually spoke only Arabic at home. As regards the age parameter, it is not surprising to find that the largest proportion of the respondents who declared that they speak Laggorí at home were more than forty-five years old. Nevertheless, in light of the larger quantitative representation of the class aged thirty-one to forty-five, a relatively important part of middle-aged respondents still use Laggorí for domestic communication. Respondents under the age of thirty-one, for their part, are characterized by a critically low use of Laggorí. It should be remarked that H. Bell (1976: 9) already stated that there was some evidence that Laggorí was declining in 1976. However, if we consider the relatively high number of Laggorí who still claim to have acquired Laggorí as a first language, it seems that the adoption of Arabic for domestic communication is a relatively new phenomenon that is now posing a serious risk to language transmission.[8]

Language Revitalization and Tribal Reshaping

The SIL Intervention and the Linguistic Dispute with the Sobori

The SIL is one of the largest nonprofit organizations in the field of language development and revitalization. Founded in 1934 in the United

States, the SIL promotes a faith-based approach to language revitalization. Officially, 'the SIL's service is founded on the principle that communities should be able to pursue their social, cultural, political, economic and spiritual goals without sacrificing their God-given ethnolinguistic identity'.[9] Despite the benevolent intent of its initiative in revitalizing minority languages around the world, the SIL's approach to language diversity and language revitalization has been the subject of severe criticism (Calvet 1987; Errington 2004).

In 1993, the Laggorí language was included by the SIL in its Programme of Local Languages Development in Sudan (*barnāmaj li-taṭwīr al-luġāt al-maḥalliya fi al-sūdān*). This project aimed to provide courses in descriptive linguistics to native speakers of almost thirty minority languages spoken in Sudan and to involve them in the development of their own standard languages. At the time, Arabic was the only official language of Sudan; even so, the SIL project was intended to produce didactic materials for teaching minority languages in primary schools. It should be noted that, despite the direct involvement of native speakers, the SIL's intervention also had largely ineffectual aspects. First, the SIL's approach to language revitalization was mediated exclusively through the standardization of written languages. This meant that, contrary to what it is generally considered an indispensable condition for sustainable language development (see Fishman 1991), the SIL did not encourage the oral use of local languages, but rather encouraged their institutional recognition by means of formal education. Second, all of the native speakers involved in the project were internally displaced people residing in Khartoum. Thus, the SIL did not permit the wider linguistic community to share in the modalities of the standardization of their own language.

As regards the Laggorí language, the SIL started to work with four educated native speakers, two of whom were from the Soborí tribe. Thus, at the beginning of the project there was real collaboration between Laggorí and Soborí individuals for the development of a common standard language. This cooperative situation changed in consequence of the formal adoption of the glossonym 'Laggorí' to refer to the new standardized language. In 1997, the Soborí members of the project explicitly asked for a broader label that would reflect the multiplicity of the Laggorí ethnolinguistic communities. The Laggorí, for their part, rejected the appeal and started to organize teacher training workshops on the 'Laggorí' language. In an attempt to hinder a possible institutionalization of an exclusive ethnic label for the standard language, the Soborí members of the project finally called for a response from their tribal leaders.

At that point, the central government took advantage of the mounting ethnolinguistic dispute and imposed a new tribal organization under a politicized and co-opted leadership. In 1998, with the pretext of unifying the Laggorí, Soborí and Tillew languages on the basis of their common linguistic background, the government established the new *amāra* of Umm Mulewwiye.[10] This new tribal entity also included the linguistically unrelated Tesé-Umm Danab, who were at the time engaged in a conflict over land with their Laggorí neighbours. In 2000, the Umm Mulewwiye leaders organized a summit in Khartoum, where they finally decided to prohibit the use of the glossonym 'Laggorí' in reference to the new written language. In response to this decision, the Laggorí members of the project turned to an administrative tribunal in an attempt to validate their choice of the ethnonym. During the case, the SIL played an active role in supporting the 'Laggorí' ethnic label on the basis of British colonial documentation, but the court finally decided to resolve the dispute by the adoption of the earlier glossonym *ŋákà t-ba,* meaning 'the language of the house'.

Following the court decision, the process of language revitalization came to a standstill. By this time, the SIL had already published education textbooks bearing the glossonym 'Laggorí'. Notwithstanding this, the absence of trained teachers precluded the implementation of a bilingual curriculum in the SPLM primary school of Kalibang. This state of affairs has in some ways deadened the ethnolinguistic attrition between the Laggorí and the Soborí. Afterwards, the establishment of an independent Laggorí tribal conference rekindled the debate concerning the affirmation of ethnic rights to the language.

'One Tribe, One Language': The Affirmation of Exclusive Ethnic Rights to the Laggorí Language

Following the signing of the CPA in 2005, Sudan passed from a prohibitive policy of Arabization to a permissive policy of multilingualism. According to the CPA, Arabic and English were the official languages of the former unified Sudan, whereas the other 'indigenous' languages were categorized as national languages (Miller 2009: 28). The CPA also inaugurated a promotion-oriented language policy according to which any Sudanese language might be used at the subnational levels of government and in education (Abdelhay 2008: 226, 2010a: 28). In line with the federal reform of Sudan, regional governments were then supposed to recognize the constitutional status of each 'indigenous' language.

In December 2002, in anticipation of the imminent peace agreements, the Nuba branch of the SPLM organized the All-Nuba Conference in Kawda. This conference was primarily intended to prepare the Nuba communities for the oncoming federal reform of Sudan and to propose new political strategies for local representation. It finally suggested the organization of single tribal conferences to report the different administrative and sociocultural claims of Nuba groups to the Ministry of Regional Affairs of South Kordofan. By this time, several groups were already in possession of a standardized language because of the intervention of external actors such as the SIL. Subsequently, the use of local languages in primary education became a basic demand of many Nuba conferences.

The Laggorí political leaders inaugurated their own tribal conference in May 2005. The establishment of a separate Laggorí conference was primarily aimed at affirming an independent tribal status within the future Native Administration system of South Kordofan. On this basis, the pronouncement of sociocultural claims was part of a larger political endeavour to achieve autonomy and jurisdiction over the tribal organization. With regard to language, the conference explicitly advocated the right to use the 'local language' (*luġa maḥaliya* in Arabic) for traditional ceremonies and primary education. Even if the tribal statute did not directly mention the 'Laggorí' language, the exclusion of Soborí and Tillew from the consultations determined the definitive affirmation of exclusive ethnic rights to the local language. Two months later, the first tribal conference of Umm Mulewwiye was instituted. The conference was basically intended to discredit the autonomous aspirations of the Laggorí and to formalize the existence of the new tribal ensemble. As a result, all of the Laggorí boycotted the Umm Mulewwiye summit, even though the Umm Mulewwiye conference did not ask for specific linguistic rights.

When I finished my fieldwork in January 2009, the drafting of the regional constitution of South Kordofan was still underway. I was not then able to analyse the administrative resolution that followed the proclamation of two contradictory tribal statutes. However, it is clear that during the CPA the absence of common criteria for determining the representation range of the single Nuba conferences favoured the triggering of conflicts between neighbouring communities.

Ethnolinguistic Identity and Language Attitudes

Variation in Ethnolinguistic Identity

The following paragraph is based on the analysis of qualitative interviews that aimed to assess the relationship between language and ethnic identity among the Laggorí. The interviews also investigated language attitudes to better understand the quantitative data concerning Laggorí/Arabic bilingualism. As already remarked, the decline of Laggorí as a native language did not result in a decrease in Laggorí ethnic identity. This state of affairs evidently shows the incongruence between linguistic and ethnic identity.

In spite of this, language has recently become an important factor for the definition of the Laggorí ethnicity.

The Laggorí living in their home territory (i.e., Laggorí-Umm Bres, Tokswana and Tarai) are to an extent aware of the fact that their ethnic identity is directly related to the early establishment of tribal borders imposed by the British. Most of my rural informants, in fact, grounded their Laggorí ethnic membership on the fact that their ancestors resided within the territory assigned to the Laggorí by the British administration. It is true that attachment to a specific territory is a common characteristic of ethnically defined groups, but the Laggorí heavily strengthened this tendency following the 2005 tribal conference in which they reaffirmed their hereditary rights to the tribal territory. Rural middle-aged male informants claimed that the Laggorí ethnic identity is also linked to the individual's patrilineal filiation. Thus, in the face of the former tradition of matrilineality, the acquisition of the Islamic patrilineal inheritance had important consequences for the identity of Laggorí men. In this regard, it is interesting to note that some informants interpreted the ethnonym 'Laggorí' in light of a supposed patrilineal descendent group having reference to a common agnatic ancestor known as Kòrí.

In this overall situation, the adoption of language as a marker of Laggorí ethnicity seems to be a relatively new phenomenon limited to a highly educated segment of the community. Even if the Laggorí always stressed the originality of their language in comparison with Soborí, there was not an exclusive connection between the language and its speaker's identity. Contrary to this general outlook, several educated young and middle-aged informants overtly claimed that if an individual is unable to speak Laggorí, he or she could not be considered a member of the Laggorí. The fact that Arabic monolinguals also affirmed that knowledge of the local language is an indispensable prerequisite of Laggorí ethnic membership suggests that this opinion is somewhat ideological and that it does not correlate to a preexisting link between language and Laggorí ethnic identity.

Furthermore, the role played by language in the definition of Laggorí identity may be influenced by multiple group membership. In more detailed terms, urban informants tended to define themselves as Nuba rather than Laggorí. In this way, they stressed their relationship with other non-Arab groups of the region, deadening their narrower ethnolinguistic identification. Consequently, many Laggorí residing in Kadugli are not motivated to stress the specificity of their linguistic background because they think that the use of local languages may hinder the affirmation of a common Nuba identity. Moreover, two highly educated informants rejected the larger Nuba ethnic membership by affirming that their ethnolinguistic identity must be reconnected to the Daju. Founding their statements on the study of the Daju by Hillelson (1932), they rationally pointed to the inclusion of Laggorí in the Daju languages. Consequently, they believed that the only way to leave behind the Laggorí-Soborí dispute was to promote the use of a supratribal language drawing on the resemblances between the different Daju varieties (including Soborí).

To conclude, the Laggorí language increased its identity-making value mainly in consequence of an ideological understanding of linguistic diversity in postwar Sudan. The need for ethnolinguistic recognition induced the Laggorí to consider their language as a political resource for affirming their aspirations to self-determination. Nevertheless, multiple group memberships still impede the language from being collectively recognized as a marker of Laggorí ethnic identity.

Language Attitudes

Despite the fact that the Laggorí largely adopt Arabic for their domestic communication, most of them display a positive attitude towards their local language and its revitalization. As a matter of fact, the overwhelming majority of my informants stated that it was necessary to preserve the Laggorí language because of its ritual function in traditional ceremonial activities such as the *kambala*.[11] In addition, they stressed that Laggorí can be used as a sort of secret idiom for excluding outsiders from intraethnic communication. Yet Laggorí speakers generally do not contemplate the possibility of expanding the use of their language to everyday communication. Apart from a small number of highly educated persons, my informants did not associate Laggorí with the institutional domains of language use. When I asked about opportunities to learn Laggorí at school, the majority of the informants declared themselves to be well disposed to a bilingual curriculum, but only subject to the primary role of Arabic in education.[12]

It should be recalled that a basic feature of many multicultural societies is that the language of the dominant group is also seen as the most important language (Liebkind 1999: 144). As far as northern Sudan is concerned, the connection between Arabic, Islam and national identity has favoured the acquisition of the national language as the basic means of communication. In this context, failure to speak Arabic may have severe repercussions for the socioeconomic integration of minority communities within the wider Sudanese society. Thus, despite the ethnolinguistic revival, the majority of the Laggorí have maintained a positive attitude towards Arabic. Male middle-aged informants generally adopt the Koranic standpoint on Arabic, remarking on the uniqueness of the language of Islam in contrast to the ephemeral nature of any local language (*ruṭāna* in Sudanese Arabic). In this regard, it is also interesting to note that few people affirmed that they would have preferred the Arabic alphabet rather than the Latin alphabet for the standardization of their language. An opposing viewpoint is that expressed by the most ideologized and educated part of the Laggorí community, which instead has asserted the necessity of limiting the use of Arabic and preserving their language from the integration of Arabic linguistic material. However, this antagonistic attitude towards Arabic that has arisen as an ideological reaction to the policies of Arabization pursued by different Sudanese governments seems not to affect the majority of Laggorí speakers, given that they still integrate many lexical and grammatical borrowings from Arabic into their language (Manfredi 2013).

Conclusion

From the beginning of the second Sudanese civil war in the Nuba Mountains (1987), the Laggorí language went rapidly into decline, losing ground to Arabic due to the forced urbanization of its speakers. In 2009, the majority of the Laggorí still claimed to have acquired their language as native speakers, but most of them had already adopted Arabic for domestic communication. This situation shows an increasing detachment from the Laggorí language mainly as a consequence of the dominant status of Arabic in Sudan. However, the abandoning of the Laggorí language does not directly affect the ethnolinguistic identity of its speakers. In line with other minority groups in the Nuba Mountains, locality represents a foremost component of the Laggorí ethnic identity. Following the acceptance of Islam, patrilineal kinship also became an important factor for the definition of Laggorí ethnicity. The acknowledgement of language as an ethnic marker thus represents a relatively new phenomenon that has been strengthened by external actors. First, the SIL intervention and its subsequent support for the adoption of the glossonym 'Laggorí' not only reinforced the link between the Laggorí language and ethnic identity, but also excluded a linguistically related community from the process of language revitalization. In truth, regardless of the fact that the attempts to limit Laggorí aspirations to self-determination emanated from the central state, the refusal to adopt a broader ethnolinguistic label definitively excluded the Soborí from future access to the standardized language. Second, the new policy of multilingualism in Sudan contributed to the affirmation of a direct association between linguistic, ethnic and tribal boundaries. The temporary political situation of the CPA encouraged a belief that language is a key marker of ethnicity, and that group negotiations over political status would therefore be enhanced by an overt insistence on the use of a local language.

It is clear that the safeguard of the ethnonym 'Laggorí' was functional in supporting an autonomous status within the Native Administration of South Kordofan, rather being aimed at preserving a specific ethnolinguistic heritage. This overall situation eventually resulted in the adoption of the language as a concrete resource through which the community tried to reconstitute itself during a period marked by political change (i.e., the CPA). However, if we consider that even after the SIL intervention Laggorí people still preferred to speak Arabic, the language revitalization seems to have affected Laggorí ethnolinguistic identity and political relations more than it affected the domain of actual language use. This state of affairs clearly shows the failure of the SIL top-down approach to language revitalization, and it proves the risks inherent in recovering languages without taking into account the power relationships between minority linguistic communities.

Notes

I would like to express my gratitude to Suleyman, Faḍl al-Karim and Ibrahim for their crucial support during my fieldwork. I also would like to thank the editors and two anonymous reviewers whose useful comments were included in this study.

1. This chapter is the result of original fieldwork financed by the CEDEJ in Khartoum. The fieldwork was carried out from December 2008 to January 2009. The fieldwork covered several Laggorí communities residing in Kadugli, the administrative capital of South Kordofan, and in several rural settlements (i.e., Laggorí-Umm Bres, Tokswana, Tarai, Kalibang and Arkawit). In light of the recent political changes that have affected this area, it should be remarked that all of the data presented in this study were gathered during the temporary political situation determined by the Comprehensive Peace Agreement (2005–11). Furthermore, the continuation of the armed conflict that started in June 2011 (just two months before South Sudan's declaration of independence) precludes any possible consideration regarding the present-day sociolinguistic and political situation of South Kordofan.
2. At the present time, only the Laggorí and Soborí dialects have a relatively stable number of native speakers. The Tillew dialect, for its part, is nearly extinguished.
3. Kòrí is a male given name traditionally applied to second-born children (Tayara 2006: 10). The expression *lágg kòrí* could be interpreted as an ethnic designation referring to a common agnatic ancestor known as Kòrí. However, the majority of my informants denied this interpretation, claiming that the origin of the word 'Laggorí' arose in interactions during the early contacts with the Baggara Arabs.
4. In the Native Administration system adopted during the CPA, the *amīr* replaced the *nāẓir* in the higher level of tribal organization. The group of people dependent on an

amīr was referred to as an *amāra*. The group of people dependent on an *'omda* was referred to as an *'omodiya*. Last, the group of people dependent on a sheikh was referred to as a *mashāīkha*.

5. UNESCO defines different degrees of linguistic endangerment according to the age of speakers and to the frequency of language use. According to the UNESCO classification, a language is to be considered critically endangered when 'its youngest speakers are grandparents and older, and they speak the language partially or infrequently'. As I will explain, this picture does not apply to the Laggorí sociolinguistic situation nowadays. See http://www.unesco.org/new/en/culture/themes/endangered-languages/language-vitality/ (accessed 6 February 2014).
6. In 1972 the Institute of African and Asian Studies of the University of Khartoum launched the first language survey of Sudan. The data concerning the Laggorí were part of a survey of twenty-nine localities in the Nuba Mountains coordinated by Herman Bell in April 1976. Bell included Laggorí-Umm Bres and Tesé-Abd As-Salam in a single sample of locality reporting data on the Laggorí and Jirru languages. Even if it is useful for understanding the historical dimensions of language regression, Bell's sample was fairly limited because it consisted of 180 informants, only 79 of whom were from Laggorí-Umm Bres.
7. It is interesting to note that for more than forty years, all sociolinguistic surveys of Sudan have indicated that the youngest generations of minority groups were shifting to Arabic. This means that those who acquired Arabic as a first language and were less than twenty-five years of age in 1976 are now over fifty-five years old. In contrast, the present information concerning Laggorí shows that the decisive shift towards Arabic, which was declared in the 1970s, in fact took place almost ten years later.
8. See http://www-01.sil.org/sil/ (accessed 24 January 2013).
9. *Umm mulewiyye* is an Arabic expression that means 'wrapped'. Baggara Arabs applied this term to different Nuba groups to refer to their way of wearing the *sutra*, the traditional skin loincloth. Both the Laggorí and the Soborí are strongly averse to this ethnonym because of its deprecatory connotations.
10. The *kambala* (an Arabic distortion of the word *kámàl*) is the most important agricultural ritual of the Laggorí. It is traditionally celebrated at the end of the sowing season.
11. Arabic is the only language of instruction in northern Sudan. In contrast, it is not contemplated by the 'New Sudan' curriculum adopted in SPLM-controlled areas. Regardless of the fact that Arabic is the wider spoken language in the Nuba Mountains, English is the primary language of instruction in the SPLM schools of South Kordofan. Local languages, for their part, can be taught as an additional subject in primary schools.

Chapter 16

Between Ideological Security and Intellectual Plurality

'Colonialism' and 'Globalization' in Northern Sudanese Educational Discourses

Iris Seri-Hersch

The last two decades have witnessed the proliferation of discourses on globalization, both by critics and apologists, in political, economic and academic forums all over the world. In Arabic-speaking countries, intellectuals and writers have engaged in journalistic and scholarly debates about what is perceived as an unfolding, inevitable process, carrying a wide range of challenges and opportunities (Al-ʿAzm 1996; Yafūt 1998; ʿAbd Al-Muʿṭī 1999; Al-Sādah 1999; Al-Dīn 2000; Hudson 2000; Aḥmad 2002; Al-Sabīl 2004; Marsá Fuentes 2005; Murād 2010). Often considered a periphery in the Arab world on geographical, historical and cultural grounds, Sudan has not remained outside these discussions on *ʿawlama* (the Arabic term for globalization). In particular, northern Sudanese educationists, scholars and state officials have contributed to ongoing discussions about the meaning of globalization and its impact upon Sudanese society and culture.

In his seminal work on colonial studies, Cooper (2005) persuasively demonstrated the importance of distinguishing between two types of categories: 'indigenous' or 'normative' categories, which are used by people throughout history, and 'analytical' categories, which are designed and used by social scientists as tools for academic enquiry. This basic but crucial distinction has been neglected in much of the scholarly literature dealing with notions of identity, modernity and globalization. In line with Cooper's argument, it ought to be stressed that the normative uses of a term, how numerous and fashionable, do not grant it an inherent ana-

Notes for this chapter begin on page 317.

lytical value for social research. This chapter[1] is concerned with globalization neither as a taken-for-granted ongoing process, nor as a heuristic tool that can provide a useful framework for analysing such a process, but primarily as an indigenous category. I shall not discuss the implications of globalization for the educational policies, pedagogies and politics of nation-states, as has been attempted by scholars of education (Apple, Kenway and Singh 2005). I shall rather examine how northern Sudanese intellectuals and policy makers have conceived globalization in the first decade of the twenty-first century, and how they have mobilized it to achieve specific ends. The analysis of recent writings by northern Sudanese educationists and state officials provides strong incentives to study their conceptualizations of globalization (*ʿawlama*) through a comparison with their representations of colonialism/imperialism (*istiʿmār*). Indeed, there are striking similarities at two levels. First, in terms of meaning, the two notions are used to depict historical or current phenomena that share a number of common features. Second, both categories are often mobilized to promote the same kind of historical narrative and/or political ideology, working as powerful (de)legitimizing devices.

Without embarking on a detailed study of the historical appearance and uses of *istiʿmār* and *ʿawlama* in the Arabic-speaking world,[2] it is useful to outline the basic meaning and broad evolution of each of these terms. Derived from the Arabic root *ʿamara* (to populate, to dwell, to live, to flourish), the term *istiʿmār* initially referred to the act of populating a land. This meaning is found in the Koran (11:61): 'Huwa ansha'akum min al-arḍ wa-staʿmarakum fīhā' (It is he who has produced you from the earth and settled you therein). The notion later evolved to designate the settling of an area by foreigners, as did the Latin-derived word 'colonization'. The Arabic *istiʿmār* acquired new political significance in the modern era. In the aftermath of the First World War, it started being used to refer explicitly to the British and French mandates in the Middle East (Bengio 1998: 128). As opposed to 'colonization', its meaning moved closer to the concepts of 'colonialism' and 'imperialism'.[3] The neologism *ʿawlama* emerged in the mid-1990s in Arabic intellectual and political discourses. Derived from the word *ʿālam* (world), it was first used to describe dynamics of economic interdependency between different regions across the globe (Marsá Fuentes 2005: 65). It was then broadened to include political, cultural and technological processes affecting the world as a whole.

Drawing upon documents produced by Sudan's Ministry of General Education, issues of *Dirāsāt Tarbawiyya* (*Educational Studies*)[4] and history textbooks used in Sudanese secondary schools in 2008–9,[5] this chapter investigates the meanings and functions of *istiʿmār* and *ʿawlama* in northern Sudanese educational discourses. Rather than assessing the historical validity of the arguments contained in the source material, the main purpose is to analyse how 'colonialism' and 'globalization' are represented and used to promote particular historical narratives, shape identities and political allegiance, and call for educational reforms.

Although northern Sudanese scholars have framed an anticolonial and/or antiglobalization critique using similar arguments as many intellectuals all over the world, it will be shown that their stance, which is indigenized through Arab and Islamic 'self-references', is often more ambivalent than it seems at first sight. The findings of this chapter can therefore contribute important nuances to the recent scholarship on Sudanese education. The Arabization and Islamization of the curriculum that followed the 1989 military coup have already been examined in a number of works (Breidlid 2005; H. Ibrahim 2008; Förster 2008). Despite or besides these trends, it will be argued, the authoritarian character of the regime and the 'Islamist' orientation of the current ruling elite have not automatically entailed a single, unified, 'pro–National Islamic Front' educational discourse in northern Sudan.

Historical Agency

Let us turn to the shared features of *istiʿmār* and *ʿawlama* in the writings of several northern Sudanese scholars and state officials. These abstract categories are frequently assigned historical agency, namely, the ability to shape past or present realities.[6] For instance, in a history textbook for first-year secondary pupils (aged fifteen), European colonialism literally wipes out the ancient names of African regions and countries (Aḥmad et al. n.d.: 151). At the end of the chapter on European colonialism in Africa, the pupils are asked to explain why and how 'colonialism strove and still strives to maintain nations and peoples in a backward state' (Aḥmad et al. n.d.: 157). Associated with some natural disaster or calamity (*kāritha*), French colonialism sought to annihilate Algeria's Islamic and Arab identity (Aḥmad et al. n.d.: 163). Prepared by the same pedagogic team, the third-year secondary history textbook tends to reify and personify colonialism without naming the historical actors actually involved. In the first half of the twentieth century, 'imperialist forces' shaped the Sudanese economy according to 'their' needs and interests (Aḥmad et al. 2002: 41). Even if they formally achieved political independence, many formerly colonized peoples continue to suffer from the 'numerous misdeeds of colonialism' (Aḥmad et al. 2002: 116).

Such a personification of colonialism also occurs in northern Sudanese research articles. In a paper dealing with the Sudanese school curriculum,

ʿAbd Al-Ghanī Ibrāhīm Muḥammad (NCCER deputy director in 2002) writes that colonialism 'came' and 'had' specific aims, such as taking the country's goods, exploiting its resources and plundering its raw materials. In the educational field, colonialism 'wanted' Sudanese schools to be modelled upon imported schools that focused on 'material sciences' while neglecting 'religious sciences' (Muḥammad 2002: 69). More recently, the head of the NCCER Koran Section argued that colonialism 'considers' the firm bond linking the Arabs to the Islamic faith a great danger. 'It' has sought, therefore, and still seeks, to destroy this connection in order to divide the Arabs (Al-Dāʾim 2008: 14). In the same vein, colonialism 'sees' the Arabic language as a threat to its interests; 'it' has thus attempted to weaken Arabic by encouraging students to use the spoken language (*ʿāmiyya*), introducing foreign languages or supporting writers that do not master Arabic grammar (Al-Dāʾim 2008: 15).

The representation of globalization as an individual agent actively shaping social reality is less frequent. This may be due to its relative newness both as a word and as the reality this word is meant to describe: an ongoing, multifaceted process that people are still trying to characterize and define. In spite of its amorphousness, the notion of globalization is attributed agency, as is the case in an article by a scholar from Omdurman Islamic University. Intending to investigate the impact of globalization upon educational planning in Sudan, ʿIṣām Al-Dīn Birayr Ādam ʿAwaḍ Allah (2006: 55) claims that 'current globalization … seeks to spread the Western capitalist liberal identity' in the world. Here, one agent imposes one monolithic identity upon humanity.

Altering Borders

Istiʿmār and *ʿawlama* are conceived as powerful forces that can, and do, transform past or current realities. What is, then, their actual effect on reality according to northern Sudanese scholars of education and textbook authors? In the writings under scrutiny, both colonialism and globalization deform, alter and redefine territorial borders between social groups.

First-year secondary pupils study the late nineteenth-century partition of Africa among European states, which concluded various treaties to delineate the borders of their colonies and divide the 'booty' (Aḥmad et al. n.d.: 150). European colonialism erased the old names of African lands and modified existing borders, reordering the continent into new spaces: British West Africa, French West Africa and Portuguese Africa. The textbook points to the fact that geographical entities were given names of European conquerors and sovereigns (Leopoldville, Stanleyville, Lake

Victoria, Lake Albert, Rhodesia), highlighting the symbolic aspect of the colonial process of territorial appropriation (Aḥmad et al. n.d.: 151). Similarly, after the Battle of Kararī (2 September 1898), the British renamed the Sudanese territory 'Anglo-Egyptian Sudan', whereas the country was referred to as the 'Egyptian-English Sudan' (*Al-Sūdān al-Miṣrī al-Inglīzī*) on Egyptian maps (Aḥmad et al. 2002: 9).[7] The conquest of Sudan by Anglo-Egyptian forces was part of a larger imperialist scheme whereby the British strove to dominate African territories stretching 'from Alexandria to the Cape of Good Hope' (Aḥmad et al. 2002: 114). The history textbook for third-year secondary pupils lays heavy emphasis on British divisive policies inside Sudan. Seeking to thwart the Arabization and Islamization of the south – viewed as a natural, historical process by the textbook authors – the British established a new border line between the northern and southern parts of the country (approximately along the thirteenth parallel north). From the early 1920s onwards, they barred northern Sudanese and Egyptians from accessing southern Sudan through the Closed District Ordinance and the Passport and Permit Ordinance (Aḥmad et al. 2002: 34).[8] Africa, however, was not the only target of colonial policies of territorial dislocation; in the twentieth century, the Islamic community experienced a process of physical fragmentation (*taftīt jisd al-umma*) resulting in a series of small states separated by colonially created 'artificial boundaries' (Aḥmad et al. 2002: 116).

While colonialism tends to obliterate old boundaries and reshape places and spaces with new borders, creating smaller or larger territorial units, globalization seems to imply a one-way course towards a single, large-scale unit. Current dynamics of economic, political and cultural integration at the world level, which involve increasing flows of people, information, ideas and goods across national boundaries, are transforming humanity into a global society without borders (ʿAwaḍ Allah 2006: 48).[9]

Subordinating the Majority World

Beyond the issue of boundaries, colonialism and globalization involve political and economic forms of subordination that chiefly affect non-Western countries.[10] Sudanese history textbooks bring out the selfish interests of European states as a root cause of modern colonialism. With regards to Africa, the Treaty of Berlin (1885) officialized the organized plunder of the continent, consecrating European interests while totally excluding the 'rights and interests of the weak, colonized peoples' (Aḥmad et al. n.d.: 150). In the Middle East, the European colonizer aimed at humiliating the Muslims, breaking down their power, extending his grip over their countries, looting their wealth and exploiting them (Aḥmad et al. 2008: 59, 101; Aḥmad et al. 2002: 86). The possession of a large number of colonies meant political prestige and glory. Moreover, the control of strategic trade routes, the importation of raw materials to the metropole and the selling of manufactured products to the colonies allowed European states to satisfy their economic needs, which had drastically evolved since the industrial revolution (Aḥmad et al. 2002: 86). What made the unscrupulous use of force by colonial powers possible in the modern era is nothing but the 'Western wisdom' developed by Nicola Machiavelli in the early sixteenth century, according to which 'the end justifies the means' (Aḥmad et al. 2008: 95). The British colonial regime in Sudan involved patterns of political and economic marginalization. Based on religious or tribal mobilizations, Sudanese popular revolts against British rule were brutally suppressed in the early decades of the twentieth century. Large schemes of cotton cultivation were initiated following the development of the textile industry in Britain and the sharp decline of cotton production in Egypt at the turn of the twentieth century. Foreign investments in Sudan produced financial gains for private companies; the great majority of the Sudanese population did not benefit from the colonial economy (Aḥmad et al. 2002: 41–45).

According to one Sudanese scholar of education, globalization has implied increasing Western political supremacy over the world and the parallel weakening of the authority of individual nation-states (ʿAwaḍ Allah 2006: 46). The economic subordination of non-Western, developing countries is even more pregnant: multinational or supranational companies dominate the world system, negatively affecting local economies (ʿAwaḍ Allah 2006: 45, 52). Although Sudan requires skilled manpower to work in the new industries and services that have been brought up by the latest technological revolution, the state has reacted to the pressures of economic globalization by reducing its expenditure on education. Sudanese citizens are faced with the growing privatization of education and its concomitant financial costs (ʿAwaḍ Allah 2006: 53). These global pressures also affect the decision-making powers of poor countries, which cannot enjoy full political and economic sovereignty as long as they do not expand local food production and their self-reliance capacities (Al-Dāʾim 2008: 25).

A Cultural Assault

The association of colonialism, as well as globalization, with aggressive trends of cultural imposition is extremely salient in northern Sudanese pedagogic and scholarly production. According to the first-year secondary history textbook previously analysed, the interests of colonial regimes converged with those of Christian missions in Africa. Struggling against Islam, European missionaries were efficient tools in the hands of colonial powers (Aḥmad et al. n.d.: 154). They exploited local poverty and lack of health facilities to spread Christianity. European colonial states sought not only to impose their religion upon colonized peoples, but also their language and culture. The French are mentioned as a case in point. In North Africa, and especially in Algeria, they tried to wipe out all Islamic and Arab elements of identity, violently repressing local revolts (Aḥmad et al. n.d.: 154, 163). The third-year secondary textbook stresses the civilizational dimension of what is represented as a European assault against the Islamic world. This cultural onslaught included the diffusion of both Christian and secular values and practices. After the First World War, the Allies took advantage of their victory to eliminate the Islamic caliphate (Aḥmad et al. 2002: 82), depriving Muslims of political and religious sovereignty.[11]

The Christian character of British colonialism in Sudan is also very much emphasized. Even before the actual colonial era (1899–1956), the appointment of an 'extremist Christian' as governor-general of the Ottoman-Egyptian Sudan (Charles G. Gordon, 1877–80) hurt the 'religious and national feelings' of the Sudanese (Aḥmad et al. 2008: 22, 58). In the subsequent Mahdist era (1881–98), the Sudanese state was threatened by the 'Christian European peril' (embodied by Britain, Belgium, Italy and France) before being destroyed by the British (Aḥmad et al. 2002: 2). The major objective of British colonial policy was to prevent the cultural fusion of northern and southern Sudan. Arabic names and dress were prohibited in the south, as was the teaching of the Arabic language. Missions were instrumental in 'replacing' Arab and Islamic culture with Christian culture. Given a free hand in the south, missionaries taught local vernaculars in Roman letters, the Bible and the English language. Christianity was also spread by 'foreign merchants', who replaced northern Sudanese traders in the southern provinces (Aḥmad et al. 2002: 34–35, 45, 48).

Cultural dimensions of colonialism also appear in northern Sudanese educational research. The colonial assault on the Arabic language, both in Sudan and in the wider Arabic-speaking world, is a recurrent theme (Al-Sayyid 2005: 24–25; Al-Dāʾim 2008: 15). In the eyes of the former NCCER deputy director, the Western type of education that colonial administrators imported into Sudan was totally disconnected from the Sudanese cultural heritage. An elite of foreign officials directed the production of school curricula according to their own conceptions and beliefs (Muḥammad 2002: 69–70).[12] In an article on the Islamic character of the Sudanese curriculum, Muḥammad Mazmal Al-Bashīr (NCCER director, 2004–7) argues that the long-lasting rule of Western colonialism over the Islamic world has caused Muslim students to adopt secular conceptions of society and culture. The sciences of education, which historically developed in the West, are particularly harmful because they are based on an empirical, material perception of the world. This secular approach favours consumerist culture, research on artificial intelligence and a dangerous belief in the all-powerfulness of the human mind. It dispossesses Sudanese and other Muslim students from their Islamic identity (Al-Bashīr 2006: 3–4).

Like *isti*ʿ*mār*, ʿ*awlama* in the northern Sudanese writings under review always involves some kind of cultural foreignness that is imposed upon indigenous societies. ʿAwaḍ Allah (2006: 45) refers to globalization as the hegemony of American culture in the world, which has forced the reshaping of local economic, political, cultural and social norms in line with American ways. Western culture invades people's minds through an uninterrupted flow of information, ideas and products presented on satellite television. Communication technologies play a central role in this uncontrollable 'cultural and intellectual invasion' (ʿAwaḍ Allah 2006: 52): movies, television shows, music and computer software pose a cultural challenge to Sudanese society and values. The attracting, even seducing, power of mass media is also underlined by Muḥammad (2002: 75), who argues that in current times schools are no longer the only place where knowledge is transmitted and acquired.[13] Mass media supply Sudanese youth with ideas that are 'foreign to Muslim society' and tempt them to abandon their moral values and intellectual heritage.

An Enduring Clash of Civilizations

The northern Sudanese discourses analysed in this chapter present an implicit or explicit anticolonial/antiglobalization critique based on arguments that are shared by many other intellectuals and social scientists all over the world.[14] More specific 'Islamist' claims are raised with regards to the identity of the victims of *isti*ʿ*mār* and/or ʿ*awlama,* and to how these phenomena should be fought against. History textbooks and scholarly works draw a clear-cut distinction between the agents of colonialism/globalization and the people they target. Those who initiate, and benefit from, colonial and/or globalizing processes are systematically 'Western' actors, sometimes specified as Europeans or Americans. Those who suffer from these powerful processes are invariably linked to the 'East' or the Arab Muslim world. Hence, northern Sudanese writers use the monolithic categories that have been associated with European Orientalist thought since Edward Said's (1978) famously polemical essay.[15]

Non-Western colonial expansion and domination is not presented as such, even if considered brutal and oppressive. For instance, the second-year history textbook does not describe the Ottoman-Egyptian occupation of Sudan (1820–85) as a colonial or imperialist venture. It is acknowledged that most governors were 'cruel and oppressive', especially in the field of taxation policy (Aḥmad et al. 2008: 9, 40), and that the Ottoman-Egyptian regime adopted the 'colonial' policy of 'divide and rule' in order to create divisions among Sudanese tribes and religious orders (Aḥmad et al. 2008: 40). However, unlike European states, the Ottoman-Egyptian government is not represented as a colonial power in its very essence. The notion of *istiʿmār* seems to be reserved for European/Western colonial enterprises, in which Christian missionary motives are assigned a significant role. The third-year secondary history textbook reveals the powerful potential of *istiʿmār* as a delegitimizing tool when referring to the French occupation of Egypt (1798–1802) as follows: 'They [the Egyptians] understood that no good can come out of a colonizer' (Aḥmad et al. 2002: 110). The colonizer is inherently bad; in fact, he always uses force and violence to quell 'national revolts'. Non-Muslim colonized societies are equally absent from the textbooks, whose authors claim that European missionaries primarily targeted Muslims rather than pagan people (Aḥmad et al. n.d.: 155).[16]

The textbook offers third-year secondary pupils the picture of a long-lasting struggle between two self-contained entities, Europe and the Arab East. Unwary of historical shortcuts and anachronisms, its authors claim that 'Europe' started coveting the lands of the 'Arab East' (*al-mashriq al-ʿarabī*) at the time of Alexander the Great, in the fourth century BC. Such colonial appetite was renewed in the eleventh to the thirteenth centuries, as the Crusades provided Europe with economic and religious gains. Subsequent geographical discoveries fulfilled similar goals, while being a direct prelude to modern European colonialism (Aḥmad et al. 2002: 86). Spread over more than two thousand years of human history, this chain of interrelated events epitomizes a quasi-eternal conflict between two essentialized entities. In the writings of ʿAwaḍ Allah (2006: 55–56) and Muḥammad (2002: 75), globalization is represented as the latest episode of this historically entrenched confrontation opposing the Muslim and Arab East to the foreign – Christian, secular or liberal – West. We are not far from Samuel Huntington's controversial theory (1996) postulating an inevitable clash of civilizations in the post–Cold War world.[17]

As *istiʿmār* and *ʿawlama* are different expressions, in various historical eras, of basically the same Western aggression against the Arab and Islamic world, resistance against it has been and should continue to be championed by Muslim individuals and societies. The three history textbooks analysed here emphasize the role of Islam – as both a religious faith and a political system – in leading anticolonial struggles in the nineteenth and twentieth centuries. In colonial Africa, Christian missions encountered the strongest movements of resistance in Muslim-populated areas such as Sudan, Senegal, Guinea, Niger, northern Nigeria, Chad and Somalia (Aḥmad et al. n.d.: 154). By the time 'most Muslim countries' had fallen under European colonial domination,[18] Muḥammad Aḥmad Al-Mahdī initiated a successful religious revolution, establishing an independent Islamic state in Sudan (Aḥmad et al. 2008: 39). In the early twentieth century, Sudanese religious and tribal uprisings succeeded in keeping the 'flame of jihad' alive, paving the way for modern Sudanese nationalism (Aḥmad et al. 2002: 15).

In the perspective of several northern Sudanese scholars, Arab and Islamic civilizations provide suitable values and principles to help Sudanese society defend itself against the current threats of globalization. The Islamic religion can efficiently protect Sudanese youth from Western liberal capitalism, secularism and consumerism (Muḥammad 2002: 75; ʿAwaḍ Allah 2006: 55; Al-Bashīr 2006: 16).

Colonialism and Globalization as Discursive Resources

'Colonialism' and 'globalization' fulfil several functions in the northern Sudanese educational sphere. Their role in discursive strategies of legitimization and delegitimization is particularly important. In history textbooks, for instance, the recurring representation of colonialism as a Western, Machiavellian actor devoting all his efforts to annihilate the religion, identity and political sovereignty of the Arab-Islamic world is meant to delegitimize Western culture in the eyes of the pupils and strengthen their feeling of belongingness, and allegiance, to an idealized Arab-Islamic community.[19]

Northern Sudanese intellectuals and state officials have time and again resorted to *istiʿmār* and/or *ʿawlama* in order to denounce, or warn against, real or imagined foreign threats. Explicit or implicit references to neocolonialist phenomena are frequent in publications by state educational agencies. A report on the 'revolution of public education' initiated by Omar Al-Bashir's regime in 1990 highlights the striking contrast between Sudan's huge economic potential and its actual poverty. Although the country has plenty of animal, mineral, oil and land resources, it is argued, Sudanese trade has failed to flourish because of 'colonialist/imperialist monopolizing companies' (Al-Mughrabī 1992: 2–3). The editorial of the first issue of *Manāhij* (*Curricula*)[20] somewhat enigmatically states: 'It [this periodical] comes out as we breathe the winds of liberation from the colonizer's chains, as we breathe the air of freedom' (Al-Markaz al-Qawmī 2008: 3). Without overtly using the term *istiʿmār*, an official of the Ministry of Education has claimed that in the parliamentary era (1985–89), the social and economic crisis was due to 'foreign forces', which shaped Sudanese reality through their embassies in Khartoum; this situation changed under Al-Bashir's government of National Salvation (Al-Sayyid 2005: 29). Underlying a liberation rhetoric, such condemnation of 'colonialist' or 'foreign' forces allows the representation of Sudan, or the Sudanese state, as a victim who needs the support of the citizens in order to overcome external threats. Public attention is classically diverted towards an abstract enemy, allowing local policy makers to downplay their responsibility in managing social and economic crises.

Finally, *ʿawlama* has also been mobilized to justify and advocate specific educational policies. According to ʿAwaḍ Allah (2006), the wide-ranging social, economic and cultural effects of globalization require the modernization of the Sudanese school system, the expansion of educational facilities and a careful planning of all aspects of education that takes into account the shifting demands of the labour market. Al-Bashīr (2006) presents the latest 'revolution' of information and communication technologies and the current explosion of knowledge as threatening factors that call for the further Islamization of school curricula in Sudan and in the broader Muslim world.[21] In Muḥammad's view (2002), Sudanese educationists should Islamize the curriculum while developing the use of modern technologies and self-learning skills at school.

As discursive resources, *istiʿmār* and *ʿawlama* provide northern Sudanese scholars and officials with a securing ideological framework whereby regional and international past and present processes are seen in terms of a sharp opposition between 'us' and 'them'. The issue of borders, which I raised above, is crucial in this respect. Colonialism and globalization can easily be portrayed as menacing forces precisely because they undermine the imagined line between an Arab-Islamic Orient and a European-American West by setting up new boundaries and/or wiping out old ones.[22] Yet a rigorous enquiry into history textbooks and scholarly works by northern Sudanese educationists reveals, beneath what could be seen as a homogeneous and hegemonic ideological discourse, intriguing contradictions and hesitations regarding developments labelled as *istiʿmār* or *ʿawlama.* Even if not recognized or explicitly assumed as such, ambivalent assessments and subtle nuances do appear in the writings under consideration.

The Unacknowledged Complexities of Colonialism

A detailed examination of the secondary history textbooks brings out quite a contradictory picture of colonialism as both an abstract, repulsive phenomenon and as a set of concrete policies whose overall impact was not entirely negative. The subversive potential of education in colonial systems is suggested by the claim that 'modern' educational systems set up by colonial regimes in Africa broadened the horizons of Africans, fuelling nationalist feelings and ultimately contributing to resistance movements against the colonial order itself (Aḥmad et al. n.d.: 155). In Sudan, the British used typically imperialist tactics including fallacious propaganda, hidden agendas and 'divide-and-rule' policies. For instance, in the 1890s, British officers wrote fake petitions to Lord Cromer, begging him – in the name of Sudanese leaders – to deliver the country from Khalifa Abdullahi's tyrannical rule (Aḥmad et al. 2002: 3). Although Britain's official policy was to evacuate Sudan after the Mahdist victory, her real, hidden objective was to invade and colonize the country once Egyptian finances and military had been consolidated (Aḥmad et al. 2002: 2). The colonial South Policy, which succeeded in fostering southern distrust towards the north, was deliberate: the colonizer 'knew' that the southern problem would persist after the country's independence (Aḥmad et al. 2002: 36). Morally blaming the British for their hypocrisy and malicious schemes does not deter the authors, in another part of the textbook, from crediting the British colonial administration with efficient work. Its officials were more 'responsible' and had 'broader horizons' than the civil servants of previous administrations in Sudan (Aḥmad et al. 2002: 9).

In several instances the authors appear to endorse the very hierarchical categorizations advocated by enthusiast proponents of European colonialism as an enlightening, civilizing enterprise. Thus, Africans who enjoyed a Western type of education and learned European languages could realize their ambitions by working in towns, deemed as 'more developed' than traditional village society (Aḥmad et al. n.d.: 153). With regards to the Islamic reformist movements that emerged against European domination in the late nineteenth and early twentieth centuries, they aimed at elevating the spiritual and intellectual standard of the colonized people so as to enable them to get out of their 'backward state' and join the parade of 'advanced nations' (Aḥmad et al. 2002: 87). What does 'advanced nations' here refer to? To the very European countries that are discredited as covetous colonialist states in the same textbook? The authors do not elaborate further, leaving an impression of ambivalence.

Azharī al-Tijānī ʿAwaḍ Al-Sayyid (2005: 24), while denouncing the British policy of isolating southern Sudan from the 'sources of progressive northern culture' and thwarting a long, natural process of Arabization, portrays colonial education as fairly 'progressive' and 'liberal', especially under the British educationists James Currie and Vincent L. Griffiths.[23] The Gordon Memorial College produced educated Sudanese who, thanks to their English education and their exposure to Egyptian publications, got interested in both the Western world and the Arab Middle East (Al-Sayyid 2005: 19–21).

Confused or Ambivalent Attitudes towards Globalization?

Beyond a militant rhetoric against the perceived threats of globalization, educational research by northern Sudanese scholars presents a fascinating variety of – sometimes contradicting – positions and recommendations. Different, conflicting views are found not only among various writers, but also within individual works.

The most interesting case is ʿAwaḍ Allah's study of the impact of globalization on educational planning in Sudan (2006). Several suggestions are offered as to how Sudanese society may best face globalization in the educational sphere. On the one hand, ʿAwaḍ Allah argues that schools should prepare young Sudanese to cope with the expected changes of the twenty-first century by strengthening their Islamic faith and values. The preservation of the 'Arab-Islamic identity' is the surest way to defend oneself against the 'Western capitalist liberal identity' increasingly disseminated by globalization (ʿAwaḍ Allah 2006: 55–56). On the other hand, he advocates the adoption of a new school curriculum, one that has been recently worked out by the 'advanced world' to facilitate pupils' chances of success in the twenty-first century. Besides reading and writing, mathematics, logic, statistics and natural sciences, this curriculum includes reasoning skills, teamwork, information processing, computers, history, international affairs, world geography, the study and understanding of cultural diversity, critical thinking as applied to problem solving, conflict resolution, training in citizenship and environmental studies (ʿAwaḍ Allah 2006: 56). ʿAwaḍ Allah does not specify what he means by 'advanced world', but the curriculum he mentions, with its emphasis on cultural diversity, critical thinking and conflict resolution, strongly recalls curricula that are currently promoted in Western countries. Is the 'advanced world' constituted by the very Western capitalist countries that threaten the Arab-Islamic community through aggressive communication technologies? This unresolved contradiction may be due to the variety of sources the writer relies on to bolster each one of his arguments – respectively, Yamānī (1998) and Imām (2003) on the one side, and Nūfal (1998) on the other. By advocating a defensive position based on the sense of belonging to a particular religious and cultural community, and at the same time calling for the adoption of a curriculum derived from Western educational practice, ʿAwaḍ Allah hints at the diversity of opinions on the globalization issue within the Arabic-speaking world. His apparently incoherent stance may also reveal ambivalent attitudes towards the so-called Western world and the phenomenon of globalization as a mixture of technological revolution, cultural imperialism and economic competition.

In the thinking of Al-Bashīr (2006: 17), the Islamization of Sudanese school programmes can and should go hand in hand with the teaching of the latest scientific and technical innovations. The fact that many of these modern technologies were developed by Western secular scientists endorsing 'materialistic' values does not seem to bother him. Although – or perhaps because – modern information and communication technologies pose a cultural threat to the Islamic world, they need to be appropriated and used by Muslim societies.

Finally, another way to address globalization in relation to educational policy is put forward by ʿAbd Al-Bāqī ʿAbd Al-Ghanī Bābiker (a professor at the Faculty of Education, University of Khartoum, and a former official of the Ministry of Higher Education and Scientific Research), who deals with the question of human rights (2004). He grounds the relevance of this topic in the current global context by emphasizing that human rights have become one of the most important issues in many countries in the world. The growing involvement of the media and world organizations such as UNESCO in promoting human rights and liberties (Bābiker 2004: 84) also denote the current significance of the subject. After reviewing the Sudanese public school curriculum and finding that it includes certain concepts related to human rights, Bābiker urges policy makers to expand education for human rights in several ways: by introducing into the school curriculum all the rights that are mentioned in the Universal Declaration of Human Rights, by issuing a handbook for teachers and by providing them with special training in the field (Bābiker 2004: 99). Rather than a threatening process, globalization is conceived in terms of a rising consciousness and a commitment to human rights – as a set of shared values – on a world scale.

Conclusion: Nonassumed Plurality and the Pervasiveness of Self-Reference

Although there is no single, homogenous northern Sudanese discourse about globalization in the educational sphere, one can identify the recurring perception of an inevitable process that threatens, or at least challenges, Sudan and the wider Arab-Islamic world. In the 2000s, the great majority of scholars and state officials under review have taken for granted that Sudan (in its pre-2011 borders) belongs to what they conceive of as an Arab-Islamic community. Indeed, the textbooks and research articles include very scarce references to the actual cultural, linguistic and religious diversity of Sudanese society.[24] Muḥammad (2002: 75–76) presents a noticeable exception, as he refers to the 'ethnic and cultural heterogeneity' of Sudan and acknowledges the difficulty of designing a national school curriculum that would fit all Sudanese. Yet there is a general tendency not to assume, or even to negate, the cultural plurality of Sudanese society. This has been widely recognized in the recent scholarship on Sudanese education (Breidlid 2005; H. Ibrahim 2008; Förster 2008).

Yet such an ideological posture of nonassumed plurality does not only pertain to the cultural composition of the Sudanese population, but also to the very existence of diverse and conflicting opinions among northern Sudanese intellectuals and policy makers. There seems to be a kind of self-censorship that prevents northern Sudanese scholars from presenting diverging or ambivalent views as such. The set of economic and cultural challenges labelled *ʿawlama* serves as a pretext for prescribing two types of educational reform: (1) the Islamization of the school curriculum (Muḥammad 2002; Al-Bashīr 2006; ʿAwaḍ Allah 2006), which is often apologetically argued for;[25] and (2) the adoption of pedagogic ideas and practices that, although initially developed in Western countries, are not recognized as such, for example, integrated curricula (Al-Bashīr 2006), human rights education (Bābiker 2004) and skills related to critical thinking, cultural diversity and conflict resolution (ʿAwaḍ Allah 2006). These pedagogic items are 'indigenized' – in these cases, Islamized – before being put forwards as useful recommendations for policy makers. Some northern Sudanese scholars rather anachronistically attribute to early Islam or Islamic sacred texts educational conceptions and practices that were elaborated in Europe or North America in modern times[26] (Al-Bashīr 2006: 17; Bābiker 2004: 87, 92). All educational initiatives, therefore, are advocated through an Islamized frame of reference, as though the indigenizing of heterogeneous elements under an 'all-Islamic' umbrella was the only possible way to legitimately call for changes in the Sudanese educational system. The metanarrative underlying this mechanism is one according to which Sudan, assumed to be Arab and Islamic in essence, uses its 'own' indigenous tools to defend itself against the threats of globalizing forces coming from the West.

Constant references to Islam as both a religion and a civilization in Sudanese textbooks and educational research should not be simply considered one 'hegemonic discourse' (Breidlid 2005) or 'hegemonic ideology' (H. Ibrahim 2008), but rather 'self-references' that provide a legitimate and legitimizing framework for advancing a *variety* of historical claims and pedagogic initiatives, some of which seek to meet the perceived challenges of globalization. Hence, the authoritarian, NIF-led Sudanese regime has probably been more successful in imposing and banalizing such a framework than in silencing the multiplicity of northern Sudanese voices in the educational sphere. These voices may well grow increasingly loud now that fierce 'wars of visions' (Deng 1995) and harsh competition for political and economic resources have translated into the reshaping of Sudanese boundaries, fragmenting the country into two separate states since 2011.

Notes

1. Fieldwork for this research was conducted in early 2009, before the referendum and independence of South Sudan in 2011. I warmly thank Dr. Barbara Casciarri (CEDEJ) and Professor Ghislaine Alleaume (IREMAM) for their support, as well as Gamar Adam El Makki (Omdurman/Ed Dueim) and Ihab Ahmed (NCCER – Computer Section) for their kind collaboration and help. All translations from Arabic into English are mine.
2. I know of no such study about *istiʿmār*; for a thorough investigation of the semantic evolution of 'imperialism' between 1840 and 1960, see Koebner and Schmidt (1964). With regards to *ʿawlama*, see Marsá Fuentes (2005).
3. Despite the occupation and/or colonization of large parts of the Arabic-speaking world by France and Britain in the nineteenth century (Algeria in 1830, Aden in 1839, Tunisia in 1881, Egypt in 1882, Sudan in 1899), historical sources do not provide hard evidence that *istiʿmār* was used in the sense of 'colonialism' or 'imperialism' before the early twentieth century. In Egypt, neither ʿAbdallah Al-Nadīm in his magazine *Al-Ustādh* (1893) nor Muṣṭafā Kāmil in his book *Al-masʾala al-sharqiyya* (1898) used *istiʿmār* to refer to the British presence in the country; see Al-Nadīm (1985) and Kāmil Bāshā (1909). In Sudan, the Ottoman-Egyptian occupation (1820–85) was not described in these terms until the emergence of a pro-independence, anti-Egyptian stream of Sudanese nationalism after the First World War. Arab Marxist thinkers coined the loanword *imbiryāliyya* in the 1960s to refer to indirect imperialism as opposed to older forms of direct domination (Rodinson 1972: 486n5; Bengio 1998: 128).
4. A biannual journal published by the National Center for Curriculum and Educational Research (NCCER), Bakht er Ruda, Sudan. Founded in 1996, the NCCER is the direct successor of Sudan's Institute of Education, which was established in the colonial period (1934) as a small teacher training college (Griffiths 1953; Al-Amīn 2007, 2010).
5. See Aḥmad et al. (n.d., 2002, 2008). Specific examples and quotations are taken from the following chapters: 'European Colonialism in Africa', 'Two Examples of National Liberation Movements: Ghana and Algeria' (first year), 'The Invasion of Sudan 1820–1821', 'The Reign of Khedive Ismail 1863–1879', 'The Reasons for the Outbreak and Success of the Mahdist Revolution', 'The Events of the Mahdist Revolution from Aba to the Liberation of Khartoum 1881–1885', 'The Intellectual Foundations and Positions of the Mahdist Revolution', 'The European Renaissance', 'The Geographic Discoveries' (second year), 'Condominium Rule', 'Resistance to Condominium Rule', 'British Policy in Sudan 1899–1955', 'Economic and Social Developments in the Condominium Era', 'The Decline and Collapse of the Ottoman Caliphate', 'Reformist Movements in the Islamic World' and 'Imperialist Greed in the Islamic World' (third year).

6. For a useful survey of the scholarship on agency, see Ahearn (2001). About individual agency in history, see Pomper (1996).
7. Anglo-Egyptian troops conquered Sudan and overthrew the Mahdist state in 1896–99. From 1899 to 1956 Sudan was theoretically ruled by a joint Anglo-Egyptian government known as the Condominium, but actually administered by a British colonial type of regime. For historical works on British colonialism in Sudan, see, for instance, Abd Al-Rahim (1969); Daly (1986, 1991); Grandin (1982); Sharkey (2003).
8. The British officially administrated northern and southern Sudan as separate units from 1930 to 1947. They sought to prevent the Arabization and Islamization of the south, allowing various Christian missions to operate there (Beshir 1968; Sanderson and Sanderson 1981; Collins 1983).
9. There is an interesting evolution in critical positions towards the modification, elimination or creation of borders between communities and states: for almost a century 'colonialism' has been harshly criticized for tracing new political boundaries and establishing artificial states in Africa and the Middle East. Nowadays some of the detractors of colonialism view 'globalization' as a threat precisely because it heralds a world without borders. What seems to be at stake are territorial changes that entail significant redistributions of resources and/or transformations in social identities.
10. Successively or alternately called 'Third World', 'underdeveloped countries', 'developing countries' and, more recently, 'majority world' (Apple, Kenway and Singh 2005: 8).
11. Allied with the German and Austro-Hungarian Empires, the Ottoman Empire collapsed at the end of the war. The Islamic caliphate was officially abolished in 1924, one year after the establishment of the Republic of Turkey.
12. In fact, the educational policies of the last two colonial decades were actively shaped by Sudanese educationists such as ʿAbd Al-Raḥman ʿAlī Ṭaha (vice principal of Bakht er Ruda Institute of Education, 1936–48; minister of education, 1948–54), Sirr Al-Khatm Al-Khalīfa (inspector of education for the southern provinces, 1950–60) and ʿAwaḍ Sātī (assistant director of the Publications Bureau, 1946–53; director of education, 1953–56). See Griffiths (1953), ʿAlī Ṭaha (2004), Al-Amīn (2007) and Seri-Hersch (2012).
13. The actual impact of textbooks as 'weapons of mass instruction' (Förster 2008: 31), thus, should be relativized in light of increased access to alternative sources of knowledge such as radio broadcasts, television programmes, movies, and the World Wide Web.
14. Critics of colonialism and/or globalization from formerly colonized and colonizing countries have framed their claims according to various political ideologies and intellectual currents, including secular nationalism, neo-Marxism, postcolonialism, anti-Americanism and Islamism. This literature is too extensive and diverse to be summed up here, but a few general references may be useful: Liauzu (2007); Reza (2003); Held and McGrew (2007).
15. Said was notably criticized for endorsing the very categories of 'Europe/West' and 'Orient/East' he had so virulently denounced (Richardson 1990; Halliday 1993).
16. European missions actually set up stations in 'pagan' rather than Muslim areas across the African continent. In both Sudan and Nigeria, British missionaries concentrated their activities in the southern, non-Muslim zones.
17. Insofar as colonialism/imperialism and globalization are considered useful categories to analyse specific historical processes, ruptures and continuities between these processes should be thoroughly investigated. Western European imperialism, for instance, has been viewed as an earlier era in globalization (Stearns 2003: 155; Apple, Kenway and Singh 2005: 10), or globalization as the current stage of economic imperialism (Vilas and Pérez 2002: 70). On cultural dimensions of globalization (seen as the major feature of the postcolonial era), see Appadurai (1996).

18. By 1881 parts of Indonesia, India, the port city of Aden, Algeria, and Tunisia had been conquered by European powers (respectively, the Netherlands, Britain and France); Egypt was occupied by the British the following year.
19. Until the scission of Sudan into two states (2011), the history textbooks under review were officially intended for all Sudanese public secondary schools, as well as private and foreign schools (such as Comboni schools) whose curricula had been nationalized – that is, Arabized and Islamized – in 1992 (Lesch 1998: 144). Although the Khartoum regime sought to promote strong feelings of identification with Arab and Islamic culture among all Sudanese (Muslim and non-Muslim, Arabic-speaking and non-Arabic-speaking) children, it seems that government history textbooks were primarily used in northern schools in the 2000s. Many southern schools were destroyed during the civil war (1983–2005); moreover, pedagogic materials for southern pupils were supplied by NGOs, and a 'New Sudan' curriculum was drafted by the SPLM-related Secretariat of Education, drawing upon Ugandan and Kenyan curricula. In the first half of the 2000s, there was uniformity neither in curriculum choice nor in textbook provision across southern Sudan (Sommers 2005).
20. A bimonthly periodical published by the Department of Information and Public Relations at the NCCER.
21. By 'Islamization', Al-Bashīr implies that all pedagogic materials should be directed at strengthening the pupils' religious faith, inculcating Islamic values of justice, freedom, charity and deliberation, building a healthy individual, making no artificial distinction between 'religious' and 'modern' sciences, and promoting a servant-master type of relationship between humans and God (2006: 14–16).
22. The writers under scrutiny overlook the historical fluidity of borders, the development of particularistic nationalist movements on 'artificial' territories such as Iraq or Syria, as well as the plurality of social and cultural identities and identifications within each one of these constructed 'Western' and 'Eastern' entities. See Baram (1990), Bengio (1998), Zisser (2003) and Kumaraswamy (2003).
23. James Currie served as the first director of education in the Anglo-Egyptian Sudan (1900–14), whereas Vincent L. Griffiths was Bakht er Ruda's first principal (1934–50) and the initiator of wide-ranging reforms in Sudanese elementary and intermediate education. See Griffiths (1953), Beshir (1969) and Seri-Hersch (2012).
24. In the last centuries, Islam and the Arabic language have been dominant in northern Sudan and present in the south. Yet the north is also home to Muslim groups that have their own languages and do not identify themselves as 'Arabs', such as the Fur, the Masālīt, the Zaghawa and the Beja; in the south Christianity has coexisted with Islam and various local religions. Moreover, dozens of languages are in use in southern Sudan, including English, different forms of Arabic, Dinka, Nuer, Bari and Zande.
25. Al-Bashīr (2006: 4), for instance, claims that the superiority of Islam over other religions is a scientifically proven fact.
26. On the historical development of the integrated curriculum, see Vars (1991) and Wraga (1997); on human rights education, see Suárez (2007); on conflict resolution as a school subject, see Sweeney and Carruthers (1996).

Epilogue

A New Sudan?

Roland Marchal

All the chapters of this book make a point that political scientists often tend to ignore or downplay: whatever encroachment of the state apparatus and ideology driving a political regime, the society is cultivating an autonomy rooted in social relations and mode of production. One can make a further argument at the core of the debate about changes throughout the Inqādh[1] regime's rule: states have their own dynamics and autonomy that politicians should control if the latter pretend to be more than spokespersons.

This point would be obvious in most cases, but it is not in Sudan's because over the years, academics, journalists and NGO activists have cultivated a much less nuanced appraisal of Sudan politics, as reflected by the Save Darfur Coalition analyzed by Maria Gabrielsen Jumbert in this volume. For instance, it is uncommon to have a pensioned academic calling for arming Sudanese people to overthrow their regime, based on an analysis that seems drawn from an SPLM leaflet instead of from scholarly knowledge (Prunier 2012). As Sudanese politics have polarized much beyond its population, addressing some issues without entering into an ethics debate has become nearly impossible. Should history be assessed through the eyes of the victims? Should history also be interpreted in the terms of the victims? And who are the victims and the perpetrators?[2]

There are no obvious answers to those questions in the hot conversations academics and activists have on Sudan. Answers are even more difficult when we consider the way other regimes in the region are assessed by those promoting the most vibrant democracy for Sudan: Ethiopia's regime won elections by 98.6 per cent, forbade access to humanitarian NGOs throughout the drought in 2007 in its Somali region and banned foreign

Notes for this chapter begin on page 331.

NGOs willing to monitor human rights and governance issues. Meles Zenawi never called his opponents 'insects', only 'terrorists' (but reads *The Economist* every week, a quality Omar Al-Bashir has consistently failed to show). We hardly hear a comparable amount of criticisms directed against Addis Ababa. The same issue came throughout the Darfur crisis, when activists had to make sense of the support provided by Libya's Qadhafi and Chad's Idriss Déby to the Darfur insurgency that claimed to overwhelmingly represent the population. Yet, those two leaders had hardly showed a commitment to the values activists intended to promote.

What has been happening to Sudan deserves a colder analysis than often heard, which does not mean to downplay the magnitude of the coercion or the casualties the current Sudanese regime is responsible for. This is certainly what this volume intends to do. And let us make sure that the parameters used to monitor Sudan politics are the same used when other countries of the region are considered. We still have a long way to go.

In June 1989, National Islamic Front (NIF) members dressed as the military (some were indeed soldiers, others were not) took power in Sudan and embarked on an attempt to set up an Islamic state and enforce a civilizational project that the NIF had defined months before.[3] In a matter of weeks, parties were dissolved, civil society activists put in jail and a long period of coercion imposed on the society. Despite claims that the regime was weak and would be overthrown by an *intifāḍa,* it survived and is still around in 2013, after having been cornered by the international community (1995–96), allowing China to reassert itself on the African continent (1999–2013),[4] signing a peace deal with its southern insurgency (2005), allowing South Sudan to secede (2011) and be in early 2002 near a new war, many of those events taking place while fighting in Darfur was ongoing (2003–13).

This epilogue, written less than two years after South Sudan became independent, would like to reflect on a failed ambition promoted by the Sudanese Islamists. When the National Islamic Front was set up, its leadership articulated a project that very humbly was called civilizational. This project was in many ways congruent with what Theda Skocpol (1979) called a social revolution, that is, a radical change in state institutions and in social structures. It also brought new ambitions related to the role Sudan should play in the world and in accommodating modernity with Islamic law.

The purpose of this reflection is not to assess the consistency of this ideological project, but more the actual challenge of postcolonial state regulations that it created. What this collection of chapters shows is that whether approved or not by the Sudanese population, this regime has been able to bring about transformations into the private and public spheres. These changes did not meet expectations and have significantly altered the management of some public and private goods such as water and land.

The point made here is that the inability of the Islamists to transform the state while transforming the society stuck them in a posture by which the state apparatus became the only way to gain popular support and express hegemony. Because they were a small minority group in the society, the Islamists were captured by the state as much as they took it over. The separation of South Sudan and the ongoing economic crisis in northern Sudan should remind us that changes may be on the agenda, but their actual implementation follows very indirect paths.

A Civilizational Project?

With hindsight, the project articulated by Hassan Al-Turabi was more original than initially thought on several aspects. Those differences with the current Islamist *doxa* became more obvious after 9/11 and proved that Al-Turabi had to be taken more seriously than wished by many of his denigrators. The 'Arab Spring' also offers a new moment of interest to the theorization made by the charismatic Sudanese leader, since in Tunisia, for instance, he is read with attention and sympathy by the cadres of Ennahda. The opportunism of Hassan Al-Turabi is not the subject of this epilogue, and the Sudanese disaffection with him just shows that he went too far in that regard. But it would be wrong to reduce this multifaceted politician to this sole dimension.

The first striking aspect of his project certainly raises interesting questions on whether it was fully understood and endorsed by the National Islamic Front leadership, as the Darfur crisis proved. The problem could be spelled out in a very simple way. Political Islam developed in the course of the nationalist movement in Egypt, and Sudanese sympathizers supported that trend despite the existence of a small, more indigenous group in Sudan that developed the same views, broadly speaking. But Hassan Al-Turabi and his colleagues in the 1960s were increasingly reluctant to follow the mainstream political Islam represented by the Egyptian branch of the Muslim Brotherhood. There were two important justifications for their stance.

The first one was rooted in the colonial history of Sudan and the refusal by most Sudanese Islamists in the 1960s to follow the leadership of an Egyptian organization, a posture that would have been reminiscent of the colonial period. By taking a different path, Hassan Al-Turabi was able to play his own cards both politically and ideologically. He was able to transform the practices of the organization he was chairing, the Islamic Charter Front, and get more involved in mundane politics than at any time before (though not so successfully at first, since the parliamentary elections of 1965 were a disaster for his group) while disconnecting from the educational role the Muslim Brotherhood had ambitioned. He could also promote himself as an independent thinker who could articulate his own views on important subjects.

People interpreted this change of status in the narrow sense of the self-promotion of an egocentric leader. Due to that decision, Wahhabism and Salafism (as understood in 2013) were not claimed as such and did not become the cornerstones of the NIF and the NCP (at least in its earlier phase), simply because the Muslim Brotherhood by the mid-1960s were much closer to Wahhabi thinkers since they had taken refuge in Saudi Arabia and compromised with its regime. Because of his personal heterodoxy on several aspects of the Islamist ideology and his need to differentiate his organization from the Egyptian Muslim Brotherhood, Hassan Al-Turabi was able to draw his own path within the global Islamist movement. He also made sure for a long while that allegiance to schools of thought different from his own (heterodox) was weak in the leadership of the movements he chaired. Islam's scholars will certainly compare this behaviour to similar ways of dealing within Sufi Islamic orders in a less political setting.

An implication of this choice was the ability of the NIF and later of the Inqādh regime to bitterly criticize Gulf monarchies (while still getting support from some of them from time to time). But Hassan Al-Turabi focused most of his criticisms against Saudi Arabia for reasons not dissimilar to those articulated by Osama bin Laden in the early 1990s: a gerontocracy that allowed Western troops to settle in such a Muslim land.

The second justification was that Islam was a global religion and should not be left to Arabs because they spoke the language of the Koran. Again, people often reduced this commitment to the personal ambition of the Sudanese leader. However, Hassan Al-Turabi was serious about this on multiple occasions. The NIF, for instance, claimed a continental ambition and tried to promote policies that would have won Sudan Islamists influence in western Africa, but also in Central Asia and in the Balkans (not to please the West). The hospitality provided to Osama bin Laden from 1992 to 1996 had several motivations, among them this ambition to connect with Islamic militants from other continents and not leave the (Arab) Muslim Brotherhood or the Gulf monarchies to lead the global *umma*.

One may smile today in the face of such an ambition, since this latter was clearly not backed with resources significant enough. One should measure the bitterness of the Sudanese Islamists after having heard the not-so-kind jokes of their invitees at the Arab and Islamic Conference in the aftermath of the international intervention in Iraq in 1992: Khartoum was facing shortages of all sorts and suddenly wanted to appear the world's headquarters of all nationalist and Islamist movements. But this ambition also pushed Khartoum to mobilize new tools such as Islamic international humanitarian NGOs (which faced problems in the region after 1995).

An interesting question is why the NCP leadership at one point became so narrowly polarized on Arab identity while its political ambitions were continental and even global. Whatever Hassan Al-Turabi lectured his own followers, the actual lessons were drawn from the practice of power in Sudan itself. Perhaps the civilizational project was unable to provide a unique vision of what an Islamic state in Sudan should be within a struggle to win support from the global *umma.*

In 2013, the situation seems to have changed radically on many aspects. First, Wahhabism and Salafism have today gained more ground in the NCP and the Sudanese society than at any time before. The marginal importance of Wahhabi politics has been reversed for several reasons, the exclusion of Hassan Al-Turabi from the NCP in December 1999 not being the main one. The coercive norms put in place by the Inqādh regime in the social realm, the importance of diaspora cadres in the NCP and state apparatus in the early 1990s, the need to normalize relations with Gulf countries after the attempted killing of Hosni Mubarak in June 1995 and the subsequent UN sanctions, and the increasingly undermined credibility of Hassan Al-Turabi in the 2000s are among the explanations to be considered. A further argument could be that ideology is no longer relevant and that the crude conservation of power is at the top of the agenda of the current political elites.

A second important aspect is that Islamist movements saw their credibility suffer more from accession to power than resistance to oppressive (and/or secular) rule. The ability of Khartoum to influence African countries has gone down tremendously for obvious reasons. The conditions of the war in the southern part of the country up to 2002, the inability to forge peace afterwards (i.e., make unity desirable) and the long war in Darfur, with tens of thousands of people killed and hundreds of thousands displaced, did not provide any credibility to the civilizational project on the African continent. Sudanese Islamists just demonstrated an amazing degree of confusion on Arab-African identity, which curtailed any prospect of support.

Perhaps more importantly, the Sudanese regime failed to show the advantages for African states to move closer to Khartoum. When Sudan became an oil state, it became so self-centred and busy with its internal wars that it did not do anything related to its African friends (except bribing diplomats when the ICC was discussed in African fora). After 9/11, Khartoum's opposition to *jihād* has not been seen as a defining moment of its project, since the Sudanese regime carried out *jihād* in the south for nearly ten years to eventually sit with the very people it had claimed to eradicate. Many Islamists today feel that Khartoum's opposition to *jihād* and to Al-Qa'ida affiliates is just part of a bargaining plot with sections of the international community.

Internally, the project was not as innovative as many people thought. While interviewing Islamist leaders in the early 1990s, one term came up often in the conversation: discipline (Marchal 1995). There was a sense that things were to be put in order, that, indeed, Sudan was a Muslim country but that confusion was preeminent and therefore should be dealt with accordingly. Although today observers and Sudanese would talk about that period in terms of brutalization of the society, one should keep in mind that the purpose was this disciplinary process reminiscent of state building (Dandeker 1990).

One aspect of Sudanese life that has not been explored in this volume, though it has been in some studies published elsewhere, was the transformation of the private sphere. Urban Sudan was a quite conservative society, and to a large extent the June 1989 regime could not claim that Islam was challenged by secular habits and a Westernization of the private sphere. Yet gender relations were reshaped in drastic ways, and what may appear today as a more relaxed form is built on the repression of the early period of the regime (Hale 1996a).

The Islamist project was also very much in continuity with previous episodes of Islamic state building in the country: the Ottoman conquest and the construction of the first Sudan state (1821–83) and the Mahdiyya (1884–99) (Holt 1999; Grandin 1982). First, it decided to co-opt its own class of religious authorities, as the Ottomans and the Mahdists did. It was a difficult moment because, as so many other Islamist parties in the world, the religious credentials of the Sudanese Islamists were not the most impressive. Second, it was a frontier state and, as in the two previous experiences, increased its presence through war, not by expanding the civilian state apparatus. Third, it developed its resources by mobilizing its agricultural class and expanding it.

By doing so, the Islamists were prisoners of specific interpretations of their history. The co-optation of a new group of religious authorities and their bureaucratization was a clear declaration of their minority status within Sudanese Islam. Unable to be a mass movement, the Islamists mobilized the security apparatus to diffuse their religious prescriptions. What was amazing is that they were using techniques promoted by the

Ottoman Empire to teach their new Sudanese subjects the 'true' Islam, and also were not too different from those promoted by Ja'afar Nimeiri (1969–85). The target was clearly the dominant Sufi Islam, and the regime was successful in its first years in avoiding any public manifestation of those religious groups. Later, new challenges came up, and the coercion of Sufism became more differentiated. But the NIF wanted to solve once and for all the competition for an Islamic constitution that framed the behaviour of the two biggest political parties in Sudan who were the heirs of those events in the nineteenth century.

The notion of the 'frontier state' was explored in various meanings (Marchal and Ahmed 2010). The first one that was vital for the regime was to increase its base for accumulation, since it was sanctioned internationally and bankrupt internally. The huge development of rain-fed agriculture and later of commercial irrigated farming was unsurprising but also framed a narrative that reminded people of the time of prosperity of the 1970s, when Sudan claimed that it would become the 'breadbasket of the Arab world'. While many observers were trying to identify alternative sources of funding (especially from the international Islamic movement), Sudan's rulers were getting back to basics and saved their regime with farming and traditional exports. Paradoxically, this policy, which allowed the regime to get through a long period of financial shortage, was given up when oil revenues increased dramatically after 1999.

The war in the south was the most paradoxical element of this project. Since 1988, the idea that South Sudan could become independent (though not in its 1956 borders) was discussed in NIF circles (El-Affendi 1990). The concept was that Sudan would gain a full Islamic identity and get rid of many controversies related to the situation of non-Muslims in a Muslim land. Oil was a strategic issue, but the Islamists' expertise on the subject was not a strong point, and most thought that oil was anyway at the border with north Sudan: redrawing the borders would not be a difficult exercise. As the development of rain-fed agriculture and the external Islamist aid, war was an organizing moment of the state and an identifying moment of the society (Gallab 2011).

Negotiating the State

The Inqādh regime is the longest-standing regime in postcolonial Sudan, although from its beginning until now many have been predicting its collapse through an *intifāḍa* that has yet to take place. Mentioning stability here does not mean dismissing the massive coercion apparatus that has been built for that purpose and the human cost of this stability.

When the military took over on 30 June 1989, their statement did not differ from those following other coups in an African context: it mentioned the corruption of the elites, the need to save the nation, the possibility of stopping a bloody conflict between brothers and the like. As elsewhere, they put many people in jail and prohibited all political parties, but eventually were unable to get those elites who were undermining the nation sentenced. They paid more attention to all those who were able because of their role in the state apparatus, the civil society or the political parties to become the rallying point of an opposition to the coup.

To a large extent this military façade was not deep enough to hide the strategic Islamist involvement. Few analysts reflected on the moment of the coup, since it appeared mostly connected to the decay of the then parliamentary government and its inaction on all major issues (the war in the south, but also in Darfur, the economic predicament or the humanitarian situation after the disastrous drought of 1988).

This coup was not a revolution, but its masterminds were more ambitious than the usual praetorian supporters. The new rulers took note of the new international dynamics after the collapse of the Berlin Wall. By securing the overthrow of Mengistu Haile Mariam in Ethiopia and Eritrean independence, Khartoum played a card that proved very valuable. Despite adventurist initiatives to develop the presence of militant Islam in its two neighbouring countries, Khartoum used those relations for several purposes until today: fighting the southern insurgency, avoiding continental isolation, preventing an overall successful containment, developing close relations with allies of the West. The same calculus was made with Chad. By supporting Idriss Déby's offensive against Hissène Habré, Khartoum appeared as a good friend of Tripoli and Paris. This friendship was useful in the 1990s and was only reversed at the time of the Darfur crisis.

This model of diplomacy was possible because of the end of the Cold War. By betting on new regimes in the region (both eastwards and westwards) the Islamists considerably blurred the usual lines. Although seen with distrust by Washington, they enjoined a more than cordial relation with France (because of Chad) and Egypt and shared concerns with Ethiopia and Eritrea against their global patron. Relations with Malaysia and China also developed in this new context, often based on older contacts (Marchal 2011).

Nevertheless, the regime had several priorities. The first one was to preventively undo whatever opposition could emerge by arresting people and creating a social sense of fear: the ghost houses and the often unexplained arrests for days, weeks or months distilled terror and made collective actions nearly impossible. The targets were civil servants and military on the one hand, and on the other people in the business realm who had connections with political parties and could be seen as potential funders of political opponents.

This period, which lasted until 1992, is actually the turning point in the regime: it is as important internally as the attempted killing of Hosni Mubarak was externally. This period allowed the regime to get rid of any potential opposition but, more important for the purpose of this text, was the moment the coup makers had to negotiate with the state apparatus and basically lost the direction they were supposed to take for the sake of controlling the state.

A strategic aim was not only to purge the security apparatus of possible dissent but also to get rid of the core business class. As in previous experiences under the Ottoman Empire, the Mahdiyya and the Condominium, the new regime intended to build its own business class and, in order to be successful, needed to get rid of the older one. This aim was understood sometimes as 'catching up' to what was the norm in many North African countries (including Algeria and Libya) and making it easier to fund the security apparatus, since in those countries import-export business was eventually in the hands of the security services. The goal was also to make sure that the traditional parties would never again be provided with the resources to control politics. In that sense, the move made by the Inqādh regime was radical since it meant eradicating the main structuring elements of the political arena. One can say that this process has been successful until today.[5]

However, very clearly, different dynamics came to shape and provoke divisions within the leadership. Some dealt with the attitude of the security apparatus, especially the army seen by all, including the Islamists, as the national institution par excellence. Others had to deal with the ways a minority group could control the civilian state apparatus and move collectively. Some also had to do with ambitions and the sudden fear of being marginalized by losing positions within the state.

The first such dynamic was the attitude towards the military. In Sudanese history, the military performs coups and does not fight wars, and the Islamists knew that reality. In 1988, when the NIF leadership had to define its strategy, few were hostile to the coup because of their distrust of the army and the opposition to disbanding the organization (which implied giving leaders the right to make decisions without having the right to discuss them). This distrust grew quickly after the coup, because the military junta should have given up power in one year's time but stayed in power until 1993 (Marchal 2004; Abdel Salam 2010; International Crisis Group 2011). Relations between Hassan Al-Turabi and President Omar Al-Bashir were always very poor because, in the view of the former, the latter had been created by the media propaganda of the NIF[6] and had little charisma to the extent that he was considered for years the spokesperson of the regime more than its natural leader.[7] But at that time, the junta number two, Zubeyr Mohamed Saleh, was not accommodating and had behind him a coterie of security people plus civilian NIF politicians such as Ali Osman Mohamed Taha, who had been enthusiastically supportive of the coup.

Trained by the Iranian security forces and paranoid about their own safety, the Islamists who were in charge of security policy multiplied the security services in order to avoid any coup. The growth of this sector was not so surprising because the same dynamic had taken place under Jaʿafar Nimeiri, and the new Sudanese regime decided to recruit many of those people who had been fired after the overthrow of the despot in May 1985. But a monster was being created, and no one knew for sure who was in charge.

While tensions were unresolved on that side, new developments took place in the control of the state bureaucracy. The NIF tried first to set up underground cells that would manage ministries, but the system became dysfunctional at an early stage and the decision was made to allocate the main positions within the ministries to NIF members. The end result was that everyone started to evaluate his position according to the function he had within the state. People then started arguing not because of different understandings of the implementation of their civilizational project but because their ministry was poorly considered in the decision-making process. As in other experiences, the party lost its members and the state got fresh civil servants who were concerned with the allocation of power to (and within) their ministry more than the overall political project.

What was remarkable was the inability of experienced Islamists to put at bay the set of practices rooted in the functioning of the state apparatus to define their own way of rebuilding the state and making it work for their political strategy. Hassan Al-Turabi was not the last to make that mistake when he actually felt that leading from behind was no longer enough and wanted to become speaker of the parliament.[8] A consequence of this was the musical chairs game that characterized the selection of all cabinets until now: losing state position was synonymous to political marginalization. This did not contribute to building a stronger constituency for the NCP.

The lack of any way to interact with the population was felt as soon as coercion was successful enough to envision more reforms in the society in 1992. The local committee system that was created in 1989 and 1990 was implemented for two purposes: pleasing Qadhafi, who was generous in his reward for copying his system; and policing urban areas and managing shortages without creating a strong black market or room for opposition to develop. More was needed, and the creation of the NCP tried to fill the vacuum.

The NCP tried to find a solution to different questions. One was to manage the countryside. The Sudanese state is often described as weak and nearly collapsing. Such a normative definition of the state creates a wrong assessment of the situation. For more than two centuries, with many local differences, the state in Sudan can be seen as the conjunction of three different kinds of authorities working conjointly: the tribal chief, the religious authority and the local authority. Empowering the local authority at the expenses of the two others was tried at different moments (especially in the leftist period of Nimeiri, from 1969 to 1971) and failed, notably because the state was unable (and unwilling) to provide enough resources to perform honourably and often lacked the local legitimacy to make its decision respected.

The NCP functioned as a tool to co-opt some local figures and minimize the cost of local administration. By doing so the Islamists were able to contest the control of the countryside by traditional parties. Despite the NCP's success in the 2010 elections, it seems difficult to announce the death of the traditional parties in rural northern Sudan (urban areas are often a more open political arena). Those parties were nearly bankrupt and were unable to cope with the campaign led by the leading party using state means and state money with comfort. Although internationally endorsed, many observers believe that the 2010 elections were significantly rigged both in northern and southern Sudan. In that narrative, the international community made a deal: it would not contest the results (which also gave the SPLM the upper hand in the South) if the Sudanese president, Omar Al-Bashir, 'democratically' elected, would support the independence of the south.

The peak of the crisis between Hassan Al-Turabi and his colleagues came in 1999 when it became clear that the former wanted to use his control on the party to get rid of a generation of Islamists who had been running the state since the 1990s and co-opt a younger one more devoted to him and ready to follow his orders. Hassan Al-Turabi again misunderstood the strength of the state apparatus and thought that ideological superiority would make the difference: he was simply wrong and was purged.

Conclusion

The oil decade in Sudan is today mostly analysed in regard to the peace agreement and the secession of South Sudan. This makes sense, since the creation of a new state in the region is a global event and may reconfigure regional balances concerning the Nile or the influence of Islam. The simple fact that the new Republic of South Sudan decided to open its embassy in Israel in Jerusalem and not Tel Aviv as most countries did is the best testimony of the debt the SPLM has to pay back. The emergence of a new oil economy in East Africa (and the Horn) is also an important moment for clarifications on the role of Ethiopia, Kenya and Uganda in the building of the young state and the reconfiguration of the region.

The course of events at the time of writing in early 2013 is paradoxical in many ways. The sociology of the NCP gives ground to an accommodating scenario, a Thermidorian period of the regime, since many NCP cadres are more bourgeois businessmen than Islamic militants. Yet, peace is not on the agenda, because the independence of South Sudan does not end a conflict that was encompassing many stakes beyond this one. While many observers are eager to blame this regime for the current crisis, one should be careful to not repeat the usual mistakes.

The tragic failure of the Islamists seems to be that they have been unable to propose a new sense of citizenship for their country and, because they are contested, that they have tried to go back to the old coercive methods to silence the society. As some activists used to say, they are more interested in the land than in the people. They may need a new civilizational project.

Notes

1. *Inqādh* is the name commonly given to the regime after June 1989.
2. Questions that are reminiscent of other conflicts such as Darfur or Rwanda.
3. See Giorgio Musso's contribution in this volume.
4. See Irene Panozzo's contribution in this volume.
5. This course of events also took place in Eritrea and Ethiopia, but critics were not as loud as for Sudan, though the way coercion and monopolization worked was quite similar.
6. Omar Al-Bashir was celebrated in the NIF media for having saved northern traders kidnapped by an SPLA squad. In 1989, he was a junior NIF member.
7. This changed after 2003 when Omar Al-Bashir was able to end the tutelage of his vice president, Ali Osman Mohamed Taha, who was sent to Kenya to lead the negotiations with John Garang. The death of Garang in July 2005 meant the strategic weakening of the negotiating team and the upper hand moved to President Al-Bashir, as witnessed when the cabinet of National Unity was established in September 2005.
8. Some people in the NCP even claimed that at one point he wanted to take Omar Al-Bashir's position.

Bibliography

Abbas, A.M. 1980. *White Nile Arabs: Political Leadership and Economic Change.* London: Athlone Press.

Abdal-Kareem, Z.M. 2010. 'Farmers versus Pastoralists: Contested Land Rights and Ethnic Conflicts in Dar Masalit, West Darfur State', master's thesis. Khartoum: University of Khartoum.

Abdalla, M.A. 2008. *Poverty and Inequality in Urban Sudan: Policies, Institutions and Governance.* African Studies Collection 13. Leiden: African Studies Centre.

Abdalla, S.D.H. 2007. *Al-qudra al-takhzīniyya l-il-sudūd 'ala al-Nīl wa rawāfidihī dākhil al-Sudan* [Towards a national strategy of water in the Sudan]. Khartoum: Middle East and African Studies Centre.

ʿAbd Al-Muʿṭī, ʿA.B. (ed.). 1999. *Al-ʿAwlama wa-l-Taḥawwulāt al-Mujtamaʿiyya fī al-Waṭan al-ʿArabī.* Cairo: Maktabat Madbūlī.

Abd Al-Rahim, M. 1969. *Imperialism and Nationalism in the Sudan: A Study in Constitutional and Political Development, 1899–1956.* Oxford: Clarendon Press.

Abdelhay, A. 2008. 'The Politics of Language Planning in the Sudan: The Case of the Naivasha Language Policy', Ph.D. dissertation. Edinburgh: University of Edinburgh.

———. 2010a. 'A Critical Commentary on the Discourse of Language Rights in the Naivasha Language Policy in Sudan Using Habitus as a Method', *International Journal of the Sociology of Language* 206: 21–45.

———. 2010b. 'The Politics of Writing Tribal Identities in the Sudan: The Case of Colonial Nuba Policy', *Journal of Multilingual and Multicultural Development* 31(2): 201–13.

Abdelhay, A., B. Makoni and S. Makoni. 2010. 'The Politics of Linguistic Indigenousness in the Sudan', in J. Spaulding et al. (eds), *Sudan's War and Peace Agreements.* Newcastle upon Tyne: Cambridge Scholars, pp. 17–56.

Abdel Salam, M. 2010. *Haraka al-islamiya al-sudaniya* [The Sudanese Islamic movement]. Cairo.

Abdelwahid, M.A. 2008. *The Rise of the Islamic Movement in Sudan (1945–1989).* Lewiston, N.Y.: Edwin Mellen Press.

Abdul-Jabar, F. and H. Dawod (eds). 2003. *Tribes and Power: Nationalism and Ethnicity in the Middle East.* London: Saqi.

Abdul-Jalil, M.A. 2006. 'The Dynamics of Customary Land Tenure and Natural Resource Management in Darfur', *Land Reform* 2: 8–23.

———. 2009a. 'Intertribal Conflicts in Darfur: Scarcity of Resources or Crisis of Governance?', in M. Leroy (ed.), *Environment and Conflict in Africa: Reflections on Darfur*. Khartoum: University for Peace, Africa Programme, pp. 271–76.

———. 2009b. 'Nomad-Sedentary Relations and the Question of Land Rights in Darfur: From Complementarity to Conflict', in R. Rottenburg (ed.), *Nomadic-Sedentary Relations and Failing State Institutions in Darfur and Kordofan*. Halle: MPI, pp. 1–24.

Abu-Bakr, Y.K. 1978. 'Orthographical Experiments in the Southern Sudan', in R. Thelwall (ed.), *Aspects of Learning in the Sudan*. Coleraine, U.K.: New University of Ulster, pp. 200–10.

Abu-Manga, A.A. 1995. 'Uses of Local Languages in National Unity Radio-Omdurman (Sudan)' [in Arabic], paper presented at the Third Conference on Languages in Sudan, Khartoum. 3–5 December.

———. 2007. 'The Indigenous Languages in the Current Post-Civil War Interim Constitution of the Sudan: The Political and the Practical', paper presented at the Tenth Nilo-Saharan Linguistics Colloquium, Paris, 22–24 August.

———. 2010. 'Challenges to Management of Linguistic Diversity in the Sudan', *International Seminar on India and Africa: Partnership for Capacity Building and Human Resource Development*. New Delhi: J.L. Nehru University.

Abu-Manga, A.A and Y.K. Abu-Bakr. 2006. *Language Situation in Sudan* [in Arabic]. Khartoum: University of Khartoum, Institute of African and Asian Studies.

Achterhuis, H., R. Boelens and M. Zwarteveen. 2012. 'Water Property Relations and Modern Policy Regimes: Neoliberal Utopia and the Disempowerment of Collective Action', in R. Boelens, D. Getches and A. Guevara-Gil (eds), *Out of the Mainstream: Water Rights, Politics and Identity*. London and New York: Earthscan, pp. 27–56.

AfDB/OECD. 2009. 'Sudan', in *African Economic Outlook 2009*. Paris: AfDB/OECD, pp. 715–29.

———. 2010. 'Sudan', in *African Economic Outlook 2010*. Paris: AfDB/OECD. Retrieved 1 September 2010 from http://www.africaneconomicoutlook.org/en/countries/east-africa/sudan/

Agence France-Presse. 2008. 'Four Indian Oil Workers Kidnapped in Abyei', 15 May.

———. 2009. 'Sudan Inaugurates Massive Nile Dam', 3 March.

Ahearn, L.M. 2001. 'Language and Agency', *Annual Review of Anthropology* 30: 109–37.

Aḥmad, A.ʿA.K., et al. n.d. *Al-Taʾrīkh li-l-Ṣaff al-Awwal*. Bakht al-Ruḍā, Sudan: Wizārat al-Tarbiya wa-l-Taʿlīm al-ʿĀmm, Al-Markaz al-Qawmī li-l-Manāhij wa-l-Baḥth al-Tarbawī.

———. 2002. *Al-Taʾrīkh: Al-Ṣaff al-Thālith al-Thānawī*. Bakht al-Ruḍā, Sudan: Muʾassasat al-Tarbiya li-l-Ṭibāʿa wa-l-Nashr.

———. 2008. *Al-Taʾrīkh: Al-Ṣaff al-Thānī al-Thānawī*, 2nd ed. Khartoum: Maṭbaʿat al-Tamaddun al-Maḥdūda.

Ahmad, A.M. 2002. 'Low-Cost Housing Projects in Khartoum with a Special Focus on Housing Patterns', *Habitat International* 26: 139–57.

Ahmad, H.M.M. 1982. *Harakat al-Ikhwan al-Muslimin fi al-Sudan, 1944 M–1969 M*. Khartoum: Institute of African and Asian Studies.

———. 1990. *Al-harakah al-islamiya fi al-Sudan, 1969–1985: Tarikhuha wa khitabuha al-siyasi*. Khartoum: Ma'had al-Buhuth wa al-Dirasat al-Ijtima`iyah, Bayt al-Ma`rifah lil-intaj al-Thaqafi.

Aḥmad, L.M. 2002. *Al-ʿAwlama wa-Risālat al-Jāmiʿa: Ruʾya Mustaqbaliyya*. Cairo: Al-Dār al-Miṣriyya al-Lubnāniyya.

Ahmed, A.M. and A. Al-Battahani. 1995. 'Poverty in Khartoum', *Environment and Urbanisation* 7(2): 195–206.

Ahmed, E. 1997. 'Banques islamiques et sociétés islamiques d'investissement', *Politique africaine* 66: 39–48.

———. 2007. 'Political Islam in Sudan: Islamists and the Challenge of State Power (1989–2004)', in B.F. Soares and R. Otayek (eds), *Islam and Muslim Politics in Africa*. New York: Palgrave Macmillan, pp. 189–208.

Ahmed, M.M. 2008. *Can the Sudan Achieve the MDGs Given Its Past and Present Expenditure Allocation Patterns?* Sudan Report 2. Bergen: Christian Michelsen Institute.

Aït-Hatrit, S. 2007. 'Les rebelles soudanais appellent l'OTAN à intervenir au Darfour', Afrik.com, 17 January. Retrieved 6 July 2010 from http://www.afrik.com/article11048.html.

Al-Amīn, ʿU.A. 2007. *Bakht al-Ruḍā, Sittat ʿUqūd fī Masīrat al-Taʿlīm: 1934 / 1935–1994 / 1995*, 2nd ed. Khartoum: Maṭbaʿat Jāmiʿat al-Kharṭūm.

———. 2010. 'Al-Markaz al-Qawmī li-l-Manāhij wa-l-Baḥth al-Tarbawī Bakht al-Ruḍā: Khalfiyya Taʾrīkhiyya'. Retrieved 13 August 2010 from http://www.nccer.edu.sd/rscmarticle.html?rscmid=10

Al-ʿAzm, Ṣ.J. 1996. *Mā Hiya al-ʿAwlama?* Tunis: Al-Munaẓẓama al-ʿArabiyya li-l-Tarbiya wa-l-Thaqāfa wa-l-ʿUlūm.

Al-Bashīr, M.M. 2006. 'Al-Tawjīh al-Islāmī li-Muḥtawā al-Manhaj', *Dirāsāt Tarbawiyya* 14: 2–18.

Al-Battahani, A., et al. 1998. *Urban Problems in Khartoum*. Khartoum: Oxfam.

Albino, O. 1970. *The Sudan: A Southern Viewpoint*. London: Oxford University Press.

Al-Dāʾim, Ṭ.M.N. 2008. 'Al-Tarbiya al-Waṭaniyya fī al-Islām', *Dirāsāt Tarbawiyya* 17: 2–32.

Alden, C. 2007. *China in Africa*. London and New York: Zed Books.

Al-Dīn, Ḥ.K.B. 2000. *Al-Waṭaniyya fī ʿĀlam bi-lā Hawiyya: Taḥaddiyāt al-ʿAwlama*. Cairo: Dār al-Maʿārif.

Ali, A.A. 2008. 'Sudan-China Relations: Still on a High pitch', *Sudan Tribune*, 29 April. Retrieved 4 September 2010 from http://www.sudantribune.com.

ʿAli, H.I. 2004. *Suqut al-mashruʿ al-hadari* [Failure of the civilization project]. Khartoum: Markaz al-Dirasat al-Sudaniya.

ʿAlī Ṭaha, F.ʿA.R. 2004. *ʿAbd al-Raḥman ʿAlī Ṭaha, 1901–1969: Bayna al-Taʿlīm wa-l-Siyāsa wa-Arbajī*. Khartoum: Dār Jāmiʿat al-Kharṭūm li-l-Nashr.

AllAfrica. 2004. 'Sudan: Darfur Is World's Greatest Humanitarian Disaster, Says UN Official', 22 March.

Al-Markaz al-Qawmī li-l-Manāhij wa-l-Baḥth al-Tarbawī Bakht al-Ruḍā. 2008. 'Bakht al-Ruḍā 74 ʿĀman min al-Badhl wa-l-ʿAṭāʾ wa-l-Ṣumūd', *Manāhij: Dawriyya Akhbāriyya Taṣduruha Idārat al-ʿAlāqāt al-ʿĀmma* 1(1): 1–10.

Al-Mufti, A. 2010. *Minuted Facts about the Negotiations of the Cooperative Framework Agreement (CFA) Among the Nile Basin Countries: February 1995–15 February 2010*. Khartoum: Khartoum International Centre for Human Rights.

Al-Mughrabī, Y.ʿA.A. 1992. *Al-Siyāsa al-Tarbawiyya wa-l-Taʿlīmiyya fī al-Sūdān (Thawrat al-Taʿlīm al-ʿĀmm 1991)*. Khartoum: Majlis al-Ittiḥād Dawrat al-Kharṭūm.

Al-Nadīm, ʿA. 1985. *Al-Aʿdād al-Kāmila li-Majallat al-Ustādh*. Cairo: Dār Kutubkhāna.

Al-Sabīl, ʿA.ʿA.ʿA. 2004. *Al-Tarbiya wa-l-Taʿlīm fī al-Waṭan al-ʿArabī ʿalā Mashārif al-Qarn al-Ḥādī wa-l-ʿIshrīn*. Riyadh: Dār al-Marīkh.

Al-Sādah, H.ʿA. 1999. 'Al-ʿAwlama wa-l-Taʿlīm fī Dawlat al-Baḥrayn', paper presented at the Mustaqbal al-Tarbiya al-ʿArabiyya fī Ẓill al-ʿAwlama: Al-Taḥaddiyāt wa-l-Furaṣ symposium, University of Bahrain, Bahrain, 2–3 March.

Al-Sayyid, A.T.ʿA. 2005. *Taṭawwur al-Taʿlīm fī al-Sūdān*. Al-Markaz al-Qawmī li-l-Intāj al-Iʿlāmī, Salsalat Iṣdārāt al-Waʿd al-Ḥaqq, Iṣdāra Raqm 16. Beirut: Dār al-Fikr.

Al-Watan. 2009a. 'About the Compensation and the Requisition of Abu Se'id *Sagia'*, 23 January.

———. 2009b. 'The Sit-In Organized by the Landowners of Abu Se'id in the Construction Site of Medinat al-Noor', 3 February.

American Bible Society. 2009. 'Changing Lives through Literacy', March. Retrieved on January 2011 from http://record.americanbible.org/content/around-world/changing-lives-through-literacy.

Amin, S. 1995. 'Les conditions globales d'un développement durable', *Alternatives Sud* 2(4): 115–34.

Amnesty International. 2007. 'Sudan: Arms Continuing to Fuel Serious Human Rights Violations in Darfur', 8 May. Retrieved 10 September 2010 from http://www.amnesty.org.

Amun, P. 2008. 'Organisational Report, Presented to the 2nd National Convention of the Sudan People Liberation Movement by SPLM Secretary-General Pa'gan Amun Okiech', 16 May, Juba. Retrieved 4 September 2010 from http://www.splmtoday.com.

Anand, N. 2011. 'Pressure: The PoliTechnics of Water Supply in Mumbai', *Cultural Anthropology* 26(4): 542–64.

Anderson, B. 1991. *Imagined Communities: Reflections on the Origin and Spread of Nationalism*. London: Verso.

Appadurai, A. 1996. *Modernity at Large: Cultural Dimensions of Globalization*. Minneapolis: University of Minnesota Press.

Appel, R. and P. Muysken 1987. *Language Contact and Bilingualism*. London: Arnold.

Apple, M., J. Kenway and M. Singh (eds). 2005. *Globalizing Education: Policies, Pedagogies, and Politics*. New York: Peter Lang.

Arango, L. 2009. 'L'eau derrière le tuyau : de l'homogénéité apparente, la diversification effective et le partage dans le changement. Etude socio-anthropologique de la gestion de l'eau dans le quartier populaire de Deim, Khartoum – Soudan', master's thesis. Saint Denis: Université Paris 8.

Arendt, H. 1951. *The Origins of Totalitarianism*. New York: Harcourt.

Arthur, A.J.V. 1980. 'Slum Clearance in Khartoum', in V. Pons (eds), *Urbanization and Urban Life in the Sudan*. Hull: University of Hull, pp. 523–39.

Askouri, A. 2007. 'China's Investment in Sudan: Displacing Villages and Destroying Communities', in F. Manji and S. Marks (eds), *African Perspectives on China in Africa*. Nairobi and Oxford: Fahamu, Networks for Social Justice, pp. 71–86.

———. 2008. 'Civil Society Initiative in Africa', in D.G. Guerrero and F. Manji (eds), *China's New Role in Africa and the South: A Search for a New Perspective*. Nairobi and Oxford: Fahamu, Networks for Social Justice, pp. 151–56.

Assal, M. 2004. *Displaced Persons in Khartoum and Post-war Scenarios*. Cairo: Population Council.

———. 2006a. 'Sudan: Identity and Conflict Over Natural Resources', *Development* 49(3): 101–5.

———. 2006b. *Whose Rights Count? National and International Responses to the Rights of IDPs in the Sudan*. Brighton, U.K.: Development Research Centre on Migration, Globalization and Poverty, University of Sussex.

———. 2008. 'Rights and Decisions to Return: Internally Displaced Persons in Post-war Sudan', in K. Grabska and L. Mehta (eds), *Forced Displacement: Whose Needs Are Right?* London: Palgrave Macmillan, pp. 139–58.

———. 2009. 'The Relationship between Nomadic and Sedentary Peoples in the Context of State Policies and Internationalization', *Nomadic Peoples* (13)1: 145–62.

———. 2011. 'From the Country to the Town', in J. Ryle et al. (eds.), *The Sudan Handbook*. Oxford: James Currey, pp. 63–69.

Associated Press. 2007. 'China Not Supplying Arms for Use in Violence-Wracked Darfur: FM', 8 May.

Ayalon, A. (ed.). 1993. *Middle East Contemporary Survey*. Boulder, C.O.: Westview Press.

Ayelew, D. and S. Dercon. 2007. *Property Rights in a Very Poor Country: Tenure Insecurity and Investment in Ethiopia*. Policy Research Working Paper 4363. Washington, D.C.: World Bank.

ʿAwaḍ Allah, ʿI.D.B.Ā. 2006. 'Al-ʿAwlama wa-Atharuhā fī al-Takhṭīṭ al-Tarbawī bi-l-Sūdān', *Dirāsāt Tarbawiyya* 13: 43–76.

Bābiker, ʿA.B.ʿA.G. 2004. 'Ḥuqūq al-Insān fī Manāhij al-Taʿlīm al-ʿĀmm maʿa Tarkīz ʿalā Tajribat al-Sūdān', *Dirāsāt Tarbawiyya* 10: 84–101.

Babiker, B. 2003. *Khartoum: Past, Present and the Prospects for the Future*. Working paper, University of Durham. Retrieved 17 August 2013 from http://dro.dur.ac.uk/89/1/Babiker.pdf?DDD35

Babiker, M. 2009. 'Pastoral Land Rights and Peace Building in North Kordofan: Policy and Legislative Challenges', *Nomadic Peoples* 13(1): 134–53.

Badr, M.M. 1955. *Study in Nubian Language*. Cairo: Egypt Publishing House.

———. n.d. *Nobiin nog gery: Iqra bi-1-lugha nubiyya*. Khartoum.

Badri, B. 2002. 'Rural Water Consumption in Sudan: An Entitlement Approach', Ph.D. dissertation. Liverpool: University of Liverpool, Department of Geography.

Baillard, I. and P. Haenni. 1997. 'Libéralité prétorienne et État minimum au Soudan : l'effort civique entre la poudre et les travaux publics', *Egypte/Monde Arabe* 32: 71–96.

Bakker, K. 2007. 'The "Commons" versus the "Commodity": Alter-globalization, Anti-privatization and the Human Right to Water in the Global South', *Antipode* 39(3): 430–55.

———. 2008. 'The Ambiguity of the Community: Debating Alternatives to Private-Sector Provision of Urban Water Supply', *Water Alternatives* 1(2): 236–52.

Banks, M. 1996. *Ethnicity: Anthropological Constructions*. London: Routledge.

Bannaga, M. 1987. 'Family and Community Life in a Housing Estate: El-Sha'abiya, Khartoum North', in M. Salih and M. Salih (eds), *Family Life in Sudan*. Khartoum: University of Khartoum Press, pp. 91–104.

Bannaga, S.D. 1992. *Unauthorised and Squatter Settlements in Khartoum: History, Magnitude and Treatment*. Khartoum: Ministry of Engineering Affairs.

———. 1996. *Mawa, Unauthorized and Squatter Settlements in Khartoum*. Zurich: Habitat Group, School of Architecture.

———. 2000. *Al Shorouk, the Organization of Villages in the State of Khartoum*. Zurich: Habitat Group, School of Architecture.

———. 2002. *Peace and the Displaced in Sudan*. Zurich: Habitat Group, School of Architecture.

———. 2010. 'The Development of Khartoum Urban Structure and Agenda 21', paper presented at the City Day Seminar, University of Khartoum, 10 November.

Baram, A. 1990. 'Territorial Nationalism in the Middle East', *Middle Eastern Studies* 26(4): 425–48.

Barnett, J. 2000. 'Destabilising the Environment-Conflict Thesis', *Review of International Studies* 26(2): 271–88.

Barnett, T. 1977. *The Gezira Scheme: An Illusion of Development*. London: Frank Cass.

Baroin, C. 2003. 'L'hydraulique pastorale : un bienfait pour les éleveurs du Sahel?', *Afrique contemporaine* 1(205): 205–24.

Baron, C. 2007. 'De l'eau sacrée à l'eau marchandise : représentations de l'eau en Afrique', in H. Aubry (ed.), *Imaginaires de l'eau, imaginaire du monde : 10 regards sur l'eau et sa symbolique dans les sociétés humaines*. Paris: La Dispute, pp. 109–37.

Barth, F. 1969. 'Introduction', in F. Barth (ed.), *Ethnic Groups and Boundaries: The Social Organization of Culture*. Bergen: Universitets Forlaget, pp. 9–38.

Barthel, P.A. 2010. 'Arab Mega-Projects', *Built Environment* 36(2): 133–45.

Bayart, F. 2000. 'Africa in the World: A History of Extraversion', *African Affairs* 99: 217–67.

Bayat, A. 2007. *Making Islam Democratic: Social Movements and the Post-Islamist Turn*. Stanford, C.A.: Stanford University Press.

BBC News. 2004. 'Mass Rape Atrocity in West Sudan', 19 March.

Beckedorf, A.S. 2012. *Political Waters: Governmental Water Management and Neoliberal Reforms in Khartoum (Sudan)*. Berlin: Lit Verlag.

Bédoucha, G. 1987. *'L'eau, amie du puissant' : une communauté oasienne du Sud tunisien*. Paris: Editions des Archives contemporains.

———. 2003. 'Discordances momentanées : analyse comparative', *Techniques et Cultures* 40: 1–14.

Bell, E. 2001. *Water for Production: An Overview of the Main Issues and Collection of Supporting Resources*. Report prepared for the Royal Danish Ministry of Foreign Affairs (Danida).

Bell, H. 1976. *Language Survey Questionnaire Manual*. Khartoum: Institute of African and Asian Studies.

Bellucci, S. 2000. 'Islam and Democracy: The 1999 Palace Coup in Sudan', *Middle East Policy* 7(3): 168–75.

Bender, L. 2000. 'Nilo-Saharan', in B. Heine and D. Nurse (eds), *African Languages: An Introduction*. Cambridge: Cambridge University Press, pp. 43–73.

Bengio, O. 1998. *Saddam's Word: Political Discourse in Iraq*. New York: Oxford University Press.

Berair, A.S. 2007. 'Linguistic Politics in Sudan: Issues of Power, Ideology and Cultural Difference', Ph.D. dissertation. Khartoum: University of Khartoum, Institute of African and Asian Studies.

Bernal, V. 1999. 'Migration, Modernity and Islam in Rural Sudan', *Middle East Report* 29(211): 26–28.

Beshir, M.O. 1968. *The Southern Sudan: Background to Conflict*. London: C. Hurst.

———. 1969. *Educational Development in the Sudan, 1898 to 1956*. Oxford: Clarendon Press.

Blayton, J. 2009. 'Human Rights Reporting on Darfur: A Genre that Redefines Tragedy (1)', *Making Sense of Darfur* (SSRC blog), 21 August. Retrieved 6 May 2010 from http://blogs.ssrc.org/darfur/2009/08/21/human-rights-reporting-on-darfur-a-genre-that-redefines-tragedy-1/

Blommaert, J. 2010. *The Sociolinguistics of Globalization*. Cambridge: Cambridge University Press.

Bob, C. 2005. *The Marketing of Rebellion: Insurgents, Media, and International Activism*. Cambridge: Cambridge University Press.

Boelens, R., D. Getches and A. Guevara-Gil. 2012. 'Water Struggles and the Politics of Identity', in R. Boelens, D. Getches and A. Guevara-Gil (eds), *Out of the Mainstream: Water Rights, Politics and Identity*. London and New York: Earthscan, pp. 3–26.

Bonte, P. 1981. 'Marxist Theory and Anthropological Analyisis: The Study of Nomadic Pastoral Societies', in J.S. Kahn and J.R. Llobera (eds), *The Anthropology of Precapitalist Societies*. London: Macmillan Press, pp. 22–57.

Bonte, P., E. Conte and P. Dresch (eds). 2001. *Emirs et présidents : figures de la parenté et du politique dans le monde arabe*. Paris: Editions du CNRS.

Bonte, P., E. Conte and A.W. Ould Cheikh. 1991. *Al-Ansâb la quête des origines*. Paris: Editions de la Maison des Sciences de l'Homme.

Booker, S. and A.L. Colgan. 2004. 'Genocide in Darfur', *The Nation*, 12 July. Retrieved 6 May 2010 from http://www.thenation.com/article/genocide-darfur.

Bosshard, P. and N. Hildyard. 2005. *A Critical Junction for Peace, Democracy and the Environment: Sudan and the Merowe/Hamadab Dam Project*. Report from a visit to Sudan and a fact-finding mission to the Merowe Dam project, 22 February–1 March 2005, International Rivers Network and The Corner House. Retrieved 15 October 2010 from http://www.internationalrivers.org/files/050428merowe.pdf.

Boswell, A. 2010. 'China Pledges to Boost Southern Sudan Ties after January Vote on Secession', *Bloomberg*, 14 October. Retrieved 14 October 2010 from http://www.bloomberg.com.

Bourhis, R.Y. 1979. 'Language in Ethnic Interaction: A Social Psychological Approach', in H. Giles and B. Saint-Jacques (eds), *Language and Ethnic Relations*. Oxford: Pergamon Press, pp. 117–42.

Brautigam, D. 2009. *The Dragon's Gift: The Real Story of China in Africa*. Oxford: Oxford University Press.

Breidlid, A. 2005. 'Education in the Sudan: The Privileging of an Islamic Discourse', *Compare: A Journal of Comparative Education* 35(3): 247–63.

———. 2006. 'Educational Discourses in the Sudan: Conflict or Coexistence?', *Proceedings of the 7th International Sudan Studies Conference,* Bergen (Norway), 6–8 April (CD-ROM). Bergen: University of Bergen.

Broadman, H. G., et al. 2007. *Africa's Silk Road: China and India's New Economic Frontier.* Washington, D.C.: World Bank.

Bryan, M.A. 1948. *Distribution of the Nilotic and Nilo-Hamitic Languages of Africa.* London: Oxford University Press.

Buhaug, H. 2010. 'Climate Not To Blame for African Civil Wars', *Proceedings of the National Academy of Sciences* 107(138): 16477–82.

Burke, B.E. 2001. 'Hardin Revisited: A Critical Look at Perceptions and the Logics of the Commons', *Human Ecology* 29(4): 449–76.

Burke, C. 2007. 'Evaluating China's Involvement in Sudan's Merowe Dam Project', *The China Monitor* 17. Retrieved 4 June 2010 from http://www.ccs.org.za.

Burr, M. and R.O. Collins. 2003. *Revolutionary Sudan: Hasan al-Turabi and the Islamist State, 1989–2000.* Leiden: Brill.

Butko, T.J. 2004. 'Revelation or Revolution: A Gramscian Approach to the Rise of Political Islam', *British Journal of Middle Eastern Studies* 31(1): 41–62.

Calvet, L. 1987. 'Politique linguistique et impérialisme : l'Institut linguistique d'été', in L. Calvet (ed.), *La guerre des langues et les politiques linguistiques.* Paris: Payot, pp. 205–17.

Cascão, A.M. 2008. 'Ethiopia: Challenges to Egyptian Hegemony in the Nile Basin', *Water Policy* 10(2): 13–28.

———. 2009. 'Changing Power Relations in the Nile River Basin: Unilateralism vs. Cooperation?', *Water Alternatives* 2(2): 245–68.

Casciarri, B. 1997. 'Les pasteurs Ahâmda du Soudan central : usages de la parenté arabe dans l'histoire d'une recomposition territoriale, politique et identitaire', Ph.D. dissertation. Paris: EHESS.

———. 2002. 'Local Trends and Perceptions of Processes of Commoditisation in Central Sudan: The Response of the Ahâmda Pastoral System to State Pressures and Capitalist Dynamics', *Nomadic Peoples* 6(2): 32–50.

———. 2008. 'Du partage au clivage : marchandisation de l'eau et des rapports sociaux dans un village du Maroc présaharien (Tiraf, Vallée du Dra)', in E. Bauman et al. (eds), *Anthropologues et économistes face à la globalisation.* Paris: L'Harmattan, pp. 87–127.

———. 2009a. 'Between Market Logics and Communal Practices: Pastoral Nomad Groups and Globalization in Contemporary Sudan', *Nomadic Peoples* 13(1): 69–91.

———. 2009b. 'Hommes, troupeaux et capitaux : le phénomène tribal au Soudan à l'heure de la globalisation', in P. Bonte and Y. Ben Hounet (eds), 'La tribu à l'heure de la globalisation', special issue, *Etudes Rurales* 184: 47–64.

———. 2011. 'La desocializacion del agua en las comunidades del Sur en tiempos de globalizacion capitalista: Del sureste de Marueccos al Sudan central', in H. Ayeb (ed.), *El agua en el mundo arabe: Percepcion global y realidades locales.* Madrid: Casa Arabe, pp. 107–39.

———. 2013. 'Systèmes socio-techniques, savoirs locaux et idéologies de l'intervention : deux exemples de gestion de l'eau chez les pasteurs du Soudan et du Maroc', *Autrepart* 65: 169–90.

———. 2014. 'A Central Marginality: The "Invisibilization" of Urban Pastoralists in Khartoum State', in J. Gerzel, R. Rottenbourg and S. Calkins (eds), *Disrupting Territories: Land, Commodification and Conflict in Rural Sudan*. London: James Currey.

Casciarri, B. and A.M. Ahmed. 2009. 'Pastoralists Under Pressure in Present-Day Sudan: An Introduction', *Nomadic Peoples* 13(1): 10–22.

Casciarri, B. and S. Manfredi 2009. 'Dynamics of Adaptation to Conflict and to Political and Economical Changes Among the Hawazma Pastoralists (Baggara) of Southern Kordofan: an Insight Through Process of Education', *16th IUAES Congress, 27–31 July 2009, Kunming*. Kunming: University of Yunnan.

Casciarri, B. and M. Van Aken. 2013. 'Anthropologie et eau(x) : affaires globales, eaux locales et flux de cultures', in B. Casciarri and M. Van Aken (eds), 'Anthropologie et eau(x)', special issue, *Journal des anthropologues* 132–33: 15–44.

Castles, S. 2005. 'The Political Economy of Forced Migration in the New Global Order', *Séminaire du Centre d'etude des relations internationales, Projet transversal migrations et relations internationales, 2 december 2005, Paris*. Paris: CERI.

Central Bank of Sudan. 2006. *Foreign Trade Statistical Digest, Annual 2006*. Khartoum: Statistics Directorate, Central Bank of Sudan. Retrieved 10 September 2010 from http://www.cbos.gov.sd.

———. 2008. *Foreign Trade Statistical Digest, Annual 2008*. Khartoum: Statistics Directorate, Central Bank of Sudan. Retrieved 11 September 2010 from http://www.cbos.gov.sd.

———. 2009. *Foreign Trade Statistical Digest, Annual 2009*. Khartoum: Statistics Directorate, Central Bank of Sudan. Retrieved 11 September 2010 from http://www.cbos.gov.sd.

———. 2012. *Foreign Trade Statistical Digest, Annual 2012*. Khartoum: Statistics Directorate, Central Bank of Sudan. Retrieved 4 April 2013 from http://www.cbos.gov.sd.

Central Bureau of Statistics (CBS). 2006. *Sudan Household Health Survey (SHHS)*. Khartoum: Central Bureau of Statistics.

———. 2009. *Preliminary Results of the 5th Population Census for Sudan*. Khartoum: Central Bureau of Statistics.

Chivallon, C. 2002. 'La diaspora noire des Amériques, réflexions sur le modèle de l'*hybridité* de Paul Gilroy', *L'Homme* 161: 51–73.

Choplin, A. and A. Franck 2010. 'A Glimpse of Dubai in Khartoum and Nouakchott: Prestige Urban Project on the Margins of the Arab World', *Built Environment* 36(2): 192–205.

Clifford, J. 1992. 'Travelling Cultures', in L. Grossberg, C. Nelson and P.A. Treichler (eds), *Cultural Studies*. New York: Routledge, pp. 96–116.

Collins, R.O. 1990. *The Waters of the Nile: Hydropolitics and the Jonglei Canal 1900–1988*. Oxford: Oxford University Press.

———. 1983. *Shadows in the Grass: Britain in the Southern Sudan, 1918–1956*. New Haven, C.T.: Yale University Press.

Comaroff, J. and J.L. Comaroff. 2000. 'Millennial Capitalism: First Thoughts on a Second Coming', *Public Culture* 12(2): 241–343.

Committee of Anti Dal-Kajbar Dams. 2011. *The Sudanese Government Plan of Demographic Engineering of Nubia & the Chinese & Egyptian Connection to It: A Letter of Protest & Resistance*. Khartoum.

Comprehensive Peace Agreement (CPA). 2005. *The Comprehensive Peace Agreement between the Government of the Republic of Sudan and the Sudan's People's Liberation Movement/Sudan People's Liberation Army*. Retrieved 24 August 2010 from http://www.sd.undp.org/doc/CPA.pdf.

Cooper, F. 2005. 'Concepts in Question', in *Colonialism in Question: Theory, Knowledge, History*. Berkeley: University of California Press, pp. 57–149.

Costa, J. 2013. 'Language Endangerment and Revitalization as Elements of Regimes of Truth: Shifting Terminology to Shift Perspective', *Journal of Multilingual and Multicultural Development* 34(4): 317–31.

Cotula, L., et al. 2009. *Land Grab or Development Opportunity? Agricultural Investment and International Land Deals in Africa*. London and Rome: IIED/FAO/IFAD.

Council of the European Union. 2008. *Climate Change and International Security, Report from the Commission and the Secretary-General/High Representative to the European Council, 7249/08*. Brussels: Council of the European Union.

Crossette, B. 1995. 'Severe Water Crisis Ahead for Poorest Nations in New Two Decades', *New York Times*, 10 August.

Cunningham, H. 1999. *Environmental Science: a Global Concern*. Sydney (Australia): MacGraw-Hill Higher Education.

Dak, J.G. 2008. 'China to Increase Investments in Southern Sudan – Diplomat', *Sudan Tribune*, 22 September. Retrieved 27 September 2010 from http://www.sudantribune.com.

Daly, M.W. 1986. *Empire on the Nile: The Anglo-Egyptian Sudan, 1898–1934*. Cambridge: Cambridge University Press.

———. 1991. *Imperial Sudan: The Anglo-Egyptian Condominium, 1934–1956*. Cambridge: Cambridge University Press.

Dams Implementation Unit (DIU). n.d. *Merowe Dam Project*. Retrieved 13 September 2010 from http://www.merowedam.gov.sd/en.

———. 2008. *Mashrū' sadd Kajbar: Ma'lūmāt muwjaza – mashrū' i'ādat binā' al-ḥadāra bi-i'ādat al-tawṭīn*. Khartoum: DIU.

———. 2009. *Roseires Heightening Project*. Retrieved 13 September 2010 from http://diu.gov.sd/roseires/en.

———. 2010. *Merowe Dam Project: A Battle of Dignity and Independence of Decision*. Khartoum: DIU.

———. 2011. *Said about the Merowe Dam Project*. Khartoum: DIU. Retrieved on 15 February 2014 from http://www.merowedam.gov.sd/en/testimonials.html.

Dandeker, C. 1990. *Surveillance, Power and Modernity*. Oxford: Polity Press.

David, L. and L. Halbert. 2010. 'Logiques financières globales et fabrique de la ville', in P. Jacquet et al. (eds), *Regards sur la Terre 2010. Villes: Changer de trajectoire*. Paris: Presses de Sciences Po, pp. 90–108.

Davies, M., et al. 2008. *How China Delivers Development Assistance to Africa*. Stellenbosch: Centre for Chinese Studies, University of Stellenbosch. Retrieved 4 April 2009 from http://www.ccs.org.za.

de Geoffroy, A. 2005. 'IDPs and Urban Planning', *Forced Migration Review* 24: 38–39.

———. 2009. 'Aux marges de la ville, les populations déplacées par la force : enjeux, acteurs et politiques – étude comparée des cas de Bogotá (Colombie) et de Khartoum (Soudan)', Ph.D. dissertation. Saint Denis: Université Paris 8.

Deng, F.M. 1995. *War of Visions: Conflict of Identities in the Sudan.* Washington, D.C.: Brookings Institution.

Denis, E. 2005. 'De quelques dimensions de Khartoum et de l'urbanisation au Soudan', *Lettre de l'Observatoire Urbaine du Caire Contemporain* 6–7: 19–29.

———. 2006. 'Khartoum : ville refuge et métropole rentière', *Cahier du GREMAMO* 18: 87–127.

Deressa, T.T. and R. Hassan. 2009. 'Economic Impact of Climate Change on Crop Production in Ethiopia: Evidence from Cross-Section Measures', *Journal of African Economies* 18(4): 529–54.

de Waal, A. 2005. 'Who Are the Darfurians? Arab and African Identities, Violence and External Engagement', *African Affairs* 104(415): 181–205.

———. 2007. 'Sudan: The Turbulent State', in A. de Waal (ed.), *War in Darfur and the Search for Peace.* Cambridge and London: Global Equity Initiative, Harvard University/Justice Africa, pp. 1–38.

———. 2010. 'Sudan's Choices: Scenarios Beyond the CPA', in Heinrich Böll Foundation (ed.), *Sudan: No Easy Way Ahead.* Berlin: HBF, pp. 9–30.

de Waal, A. and A.H. Abdel Salam. 2004. 'Islamism, State Power and Jihad in Sudan', in A. de Waal (ed.), *Islamism and Its Enemies in the Horn of Africa.* London: Hurst, pp. 71–113.

Dinar, S. 2007. 'Water Wars? Conflict, Cooperation and Negotiation over Transboundary Water', in V. Grover (ed.), *Water: A Source of Conflict or Cooperation?* Enfield, N.H.: Science, pp. 21–38.

Duffield, M. 1997. 'NGO Relief in War Zones: Towards an Analysis of the New Aid Paradigm', *Third World Quarterly* 18(3): 527–42.

———. 2001. *Global Governance and the New Wars: The Merging of Development and Security.* London and New York: Zed Books.

Edelman, M. and A. Haugerud. 2005. 'Introduction: The Anthropology of Development and Globalization', in M. Edelman and A. Haugerud (eds), *The Anthropology of Development and Globalization: From Classical Political Economy to Contemporary Neoliberalism.* Oxford: Blackwell, pp. 1–74.

El-Affendi, A. 1990. 'Discovering the South: Sudanese Dilemmas for Islam in Africa', *African Affairs* 89(356): 371–89.

———. 1991. *Turabi's Revolution: Islam and Power in Sudan.* London: Grey Seal.

———. 1995. *Al-thawra wa-al-islah al-siyasi fi al-Sudan* [Revolution and political reform in Sudan]. London: Muntada ibn Rushd.

El-Amin, K. 2004. 'Eastern Sudan Indigenous Conflict Prevention, Management and Resolution Mechanisms: Effectiveness, Continuity and Change', *African Security Review* 13(2): 7–22.

El-Din, A.K. 2007. 'Islam and Islamism in Darfur', in A. de Waal (ed.), *War in Darfur and the Search for Peace.* Cambridge and London: Global Equity Initiative, Harvard University/Justice Africa, pp. 92–112.

Elhiraika, A.B. and S.A. Ahmed. 1998. *Agricultural Credit under Economic Liberalization and Islamization in Sudan.* Nairobi: Africa Economic Research Consortium.

El Mahdi, S. 1979. *Introduction to the Land Law of the Sudan*. Khartoum: University of Khartoum Press.

El-Sammani, M.O. and A.A. Salih. 2006. *Nomads' Settlement in Sudan: Experiences, Lessons and Future Action*. Reduction of Resource Based Conflict Project. Khartoum: UNDP-Sudan Country Office.

Elsheshtawy, Y. 2006. 'From Dubai to Cairo: Competing Global Cities, Models, and Shifting Centers of Influence?', in P. Ammar and D. Singermann (eds), *Cairo Cosmopolitan: Politics, Culture, and Space in the New Middle East*. Cairo: American University in Cairo Press, pp. 235–50.

Embassy of India in Khartoum. n.d. *India and Sudan Partners in Development*. Retrieved 15 September 2010 from http://www.indembsdn.com/eng/india_sdn_partners.html.

Eriksen, T.H. 2002. *Ethnicity and Nationalism: Anthropological Perspectives*. London: Pluto Press.

Errington, J. 2004. 'Getting Language Rights: The Rhetorics of Language Endangerment and Loss', *American Anthropologist* 105(4): 723–32.

Esposito, J.L. (ed.). 1990. *The Iranian Revolution: Its Global Impact*. Miami: Florida International University Press.

Ethiopian Ministry of Finance and Economic Development. 2010. *Growth and Transformation Plan 2010/11–2014/15*. Addis Ababa: MoFED.

European Coalition on Oil in Sudan. 2010. *Unpaid Debt: The Legacy of Lundin, Petronas and OMV in Block 5A, Sudan 1997–2003*. Utrecht: European Coalition on Oil in Sudan. Retrieved 20 September 2010 from http://www.ecosonline.org.

Fellowship for African Relief (FAR), et al. 2005. 'Khartoum State Rapid Assessment Report: Report of the Results of an Interagency Rapid Assessment Undertaken November–December 2004'. Unpublished document.

Farah, I., A. Hussein and J. Lind. 2002. 'Deegaan, Politics and War in Somalia', in J. Lind and K. Sturman (eds), *Scarcity and Surfeit: The Ecology of Africa's Conflicts*. Nairobi: Institute for Security Studies, pp. 321–56.

Fawzi, S.E.D. 1953. *The Khartoum Deims: Some Housing Problems, Based on a Survey of Men's Opinion Conducted in July 1953 in the New Deims*. Khartoum: University of Khartoum.

———. 1980. 'Old and New Deims in Khartoum', in V. Pons (eds), *Urbanization and Urban Life in the Sudan*. Hull, U.K.: University of Hull, pp. 514–22.

Fenton, S. 2010. *Ethnicity*. Oxford: Polity Press.

Fick, Maggie. 2011. '"Speaking to the People": Sudan Radio Service Is Now Live from Juba', *Maggie Fick* (blog), 2 January. Retrieved 29 December 2010 from http://maggiefick.com/2011/01/02/speaking-to-the-people-sudan-radio-service-is-now-live-from-juba/

Finnemore, M. and K. Sikkink. 1998. 'International Norm Dynamics and Political Change', *International Organization* 52(4): 887–917.

Fishman, J. 1991. *Reversing Language Shift: Theory and Practice of Assistance to Threatened Languages*. Clevedon, U.K.: Multilingual Matters.

———. 1999. 'Sociolinguistics', in J. Fishman (ed.), *The Handbook of Language and Ethnic Identity*. Oxford: Oxford University Press, pp. 153–63.

Flint, J. and A. de Waal. 2008. *Darfur: A Short History of a Long War*. New York: Zed Books.

Förster, J. 2008. 'Die Reform der sudanesischen Schulbücher unter ʿUmar al-Bashir: Analyse der Schulbuchreihe *al-insān wa-l-kawn*', master's thesis. Berlin: Frei Universität.

Foucault, M. 1982. 'The Subject and Power', in H. Dreyfus and P. Rainbow (eds), *Michel Foucault: Beyond Structuralism and Hermeneutics.* Chicago: University of Chicago Press, pp. 208–26.

Founou-Tchouigoua, B. 1996. 'Africa Confronted with the Ravages of Neo-liberalism', *Africa Development* 21(2–3): 5–24.

Franck, A. 2007. 'Produire pour la ville, produire la ville : étude de l'intégration des activités agricoles et des agriculteurs dans l'agglomération du grand Khartoum', Ph.D. dissertation. Paris: University Paris X Nanterre.

Friedman, J. 2000. 'Concretizing the Continuity Argument in Global System Analysis', in R. Denemark et al. (eds), *World System History: The Science of Long Term Change.* London: Routledge, pp. 133–52.

Gabrielsen, M. 2007. 'La sécurité humaine et l'internationalisation des conflits intra-étatiques : le cas du conflit au Sud-Soudan', *Human Security Journal* 3: 29–42.

———. 2009. 'Mobilisation des opinions publiques autour de la crise au Darfour', in B. Casciarri (ed.), *Cycle de conférences du CEDEJ Khartoum au Centre culturel français 2007–2008.* Khartoum: Dar Azza, pp. 38–55.

Gabrielsen Jumbert, M. 2010. 'The Internationalization of the Sudanese Conflicts: From South Sudan to Darfur – Agenda-Setting, Mobilization and Qualifications', Ph.D. dissertation. Paris: Institute of Political Studies.

Gabrielsen Jumbert, M. and D. Lanz. 2013. 'Globalised Rebellion: The Darfur Insurgents and the World', *Journal of Modern African Studies* 51(2): 193–217.

Gadkarim, H.A. 2010. *Oil, Peace and Development: The Sudan Impasse.* Sudan Working Papers 2. Bergen: Christian Michelsen Institute.

Gallab, A. 2001. 'The Insecure Rendezvous between Islam and Totalitarianism: The Failure of the Islamist State in the Sudan', *Arab Studies Quarterly* 23(2): 87–109.

———. 2008. *The First Islamist Republic: Development and Disintegration of Islamism in the Sudan.* Aldershot and Burlington, U.K.: Ashgate.

———. 2011. *A Civil Society Deferred: The Tertiary Grip of Violence in the Sudan.* Gainesville: University of Florida Press.

Garang, Ngor Arol. 2010a. 'Over 3 Million People Get Free Primary Education in South Sudan', *Sudan Tribune,* 19 May. Retrieved 1 December 2010 from http://www.sudantribune.com/spip.php?article35132

———. 2010b. 'South Sudan Education Ministry to Address Language Barrier among Officials', *Sudan Tribune,* 29 July. Retrieved 1 December 2010 from http://www.sudantribune.com/spip.php?page=imprimable&id_article=35812

Geere, J.L., P.R. Hunter and P. Jaglas. 2010. 'Domestic Water Carrying and Its Implications for Health: A Review and Mixed Methods Pilot Study in Limpopo Province, South Africa', *Environmental Health 9: 52–65.*

Gilley, L. 2006. 'Linguistic Development at the Grassroots Level in Sudan 1993–2004', *Proceedings of the 7th International Sudan Studies Conference, Bergen (Norway), 6–8 April* (CD-ROM). Bergen: University of Bergen.

Gilroy, P. 1993. *The Black Atlantic: Modernity and Double Consciousness.* London: Verso.

Gledhill, J. 2005. '"Disappearing the Poor?" A Critique of the New Wisdoms of Social Democracy in an Age of Globalization", in M. Edelman and A. Haugerud (eds), *The Anthropology of Development and Globalization: From Classical Political Economy to Contemporary Neoliberalism*. Oxford: Blackwell, pp. 382–90.

Gleditsch, N.P., H. Hegre and H.P. Wollebaek Toset. 2007. 'Conflicts in Shared River Basins', in V. Grover (ed.), *Water: A Source of Conflict or Cooperation?* Enfield, N.H.: Science, pp. 39–66.

———. 2012. 'Whither the Weather? Climate Change and Conflict', *Journal of Peace Research* 49(1): 3–9.

Goertz, G. 1994. *Contexts of International Politics*. Cambridge: Cambridge University Press.

Goldstein, A., et al. 2006. *The Rise of China and India: What's In It for Africa?* Paris: Development Centre Studies, OECD.

Gordon, C.N. 1986. 'Recent Developments in the Land Law of the Sudan: A Legislative Analysis', *Journal of African Law* 30(2): 143–74.

Gramsci, A. 2007. *Quaderni dal carcere*. Torino: Einaudi.

Grandin, N. 1982. *Le Soudan nilotique et l'administration britannique (1898–1956) : éléments d'interprétation sociohistorique d'une expérience coloniale*. Leiden: Brill.

Grenoble, L. and L. Whaley 2006. *Saving Languages: An Introduction to Language Revitalization*. Cambridge: Cambridge University Press.

Griffiths, V.L. 1953. *An Experiment in Education: An Account of the Attempts to Improve the Lower Stages of Boys' Education in the Moslem Anglo-Egyptian Sudan, 1930–1950*. London: Longmans, Green.

Grimes, B. 2000. *Ethnologue: Languages of the World*, vol. 1. Dallas: SIL.

Gudina, M. 2011. 'Elections and Democratization in Ethiopia, 1991–2010', *Journal of Eastern African Studies* 5(4): 664–80.

Haaland, G. 1969. 'Economic Determinants in Ethnic Processes', in F. Barth (ed.), *Ethnic Groups and Boundaries: The Social Organization of Culture*. Bergen: Universitets Forlaget, pp. 58–73.

Hag Mussa, B.O. (ed.). 2010. *Traditional Tuti*. Khartoum: Sinan Printing Press.

Hajjar, S.G. 1980. 'The Jamahiriya Experiment in Libya: Qadhafi and Rousseau', *Journal of Modern African Studies* 18(2): 181–200.

Hale, S. 1979. 'The Changing Ethnic Identity of Nubians in an Urban Milieu, Khartoum, Sudan', Ph.D. dissertation. Los Angeles: University of California.

———. 1996a. *Gender Politics in Sudan: Islamism, Socialism, and the State*. Boulder, C.O.: Westview Press.

———. 1996b. '"The New Muslim Woman": Sudan's National Islamic Front and the Invention of Identity', *The Muslim World* 86(2): 176–99.

Hall, D. and Lobina, E. 2007. 'Profitability and the Poor: Corporate Strategies, Innovation and Sustainability', *Geoforum* 38: 772–85.

Halliday, F. 1993. '"Orientalism" and Its Critics', *British Journal of Middle Eastern Studies* 20(2): 145–63.

Hamdi, A.R. 2005. *Mustaqbal al-istithmar fil-fitra al-intiqaliya*. Paper presented to the economic forum of the National Congress Party, Khartoum.

Hamid, G.M. 1996. *Population Displacement in the Sudan: Patterns, Responses, Coping Strategies*. New York: Centre for Migration Studies.

———. 2000a. *Localizing the Local: Reflections on the Experience of Local Authorities in Sudan*. Retrieved 12 March 2013 from http://www.mafhoum.com/press4/117S27.pdf.

———. 2000b. 'Local Level Authorities and Local Action in Greater Khartoum, Sudan', *The Arab World Geographer* 3(4): 230–48.

Hamid, M.B. 1984. *The Politics of National Reconciliation in the Sudan: The Numayri Regime and the National Front Opposition*. Washington, D.C.: Georgetown University/Center for Contemporary Arab Studies.

Harir, S. 1994. '"Arab Belt" versus "African Belt": Ethno-tribal Conflict in Darfur and the Regional Political Factors,' in S. Harir and T. Tvedt (eds), *Short-Cut to Decay: The Case of Sudan*. Uppsala: Nordiska Afrikainstitutet, pp. 144–85.

Harneit-Sievers, A., S. Marks and S. Naidu (eds). 2010. *Chinese and African Perspectives on China and Africa*. Kampala: Pambazuka Press.

Hashim, M.J. 2009. 'The Dams of Northern Sudan and the Policy of Demographic Engineering', paper presented at the International Sudan Studies Conference, Pretoria, 25–28 November.

He, W. 2010. 'The Darfur Issue and China's Role', in A. Harneit-Sievers, S. Marks and S. Naidu (eds), *Chinese and African Perspectives on China and Africa*. Kampala: Pambazuka Press, pp. 176–93.

Held, D. and A. McGrew. 2007. *Globalization/Anti-Globalization: Beyond the Great Divide*. Cambridge: Polity.

Henderson, K. 1931. 'Origin of the Dagu', *Sudan Notes and Records* 14: 151–52.

Hillelson, S. 1932. 'Notes on the Dago with Special Reference to the Dago Settlement in Western Kordofan', *Sudan Notes and Records* 7: 59–73.

Hoare, Q. and G. Nowell Smith (eds). 1985. *Selections from the Prison Notebooks of Antonio Gramsci*. New York: International.

Hobsbawm, E. and T. Ranger (eds). 1983. *The Invention of Tradition*. Cambridge: Cambridge University Press.

Holt, P. (with M. Daly). 1999. *A History of the Sudan from the Coming of Islam to the Present Day*. London: Longman.

Howell, P.P., M. Lock and S. Cobb (eds). 1988. *The Jonglei Canal: Impact and Opportunity*. Cambridge: Cambridge University Press.

Hudson, M.C. 2000. 'A "Pan-Arab Virtual Think Thank": Enriching the Arab Information Environment', *Middle East Journal* 54(3): 362–77.

Huntington, S.P. 1996. *The Clash of Civilizations and the Remaking of World Order*. New York: Simon and Schuster.

Hurreiz, S.H. and H. Bell (eds). 1975. *Directions in Sudanese Linguistics and Folklore*. Khartoum: University of Khartoum Press.

Hutchinson, J. and A.D. Smith. 1996. *Ethnicity*. Oxford: Oxford University Press.

Ibrahim, A. 1985. *The Dilemma of British Rule in the Nuba Mountains 1898–1947*. Khartoum: University of Khartoum Press.

Ibrahim, H.A. 2008. *Sudan, A Nation in Turmoil: Is Education to Blame? An Analysis of Basic Schools Curriculum*. Saarbrücken: Vdm Verlag.

Ibrahim, M.O. and H.R.J. Davies, 1991. 'Tuti Island: A Rural System in an Urban Locality', in M.E. Abu Sin and H.R.J. Davies (eds), *The Future of Sudan's Capital Region: A Study in Development and Change*. Khartoum: University of Khartoum Press, pp. 115–19.

Ibrahim, S. 2004. 'A Traditional Mechanism for Resolution of Disputes between Misiriyae Tribe and Ngok-Dinka' [in Arabic], *Almootmar Bulletin* 1(3): 4–5.

Ille, E. 2013. 'Literacy, Translation, Practices: Groundwater Location Under Stress in South Kordofan (Republic of Sudan)', *Journal des anthropologues* 132–33: 219–42.

Imām, Z.B. 2003. *Al-Takhṭīṭ al-Istrātījī wa-l-Taʿlīm al-ʿĀlī fī al-Waṭan al-ʿArabī – Dirāsa Taḥlīliyya fī al-Naẓariyya al-Tarbawiyya al-Muʿāṣira*. Khartoum: Sharikat Maṭābiʿ al-ʿUmala.

Intergovernmental Panel on Climate Change (IPCC). 2007. *Impacts, Adaptation, and Vulnerability: Contribution of Working Group II to the Third Assessment Report of the IPCC*. Cambridge: Cambridge University Press.

Internal Displacement Monitoring Centre (IDMC). 2006. *Sudan: Slow IDP Return to the South while Darfur Crisis Continues Unabated*. Geneva: IDMC. Retrieved from http://www.internal-displacement.org (Sudan country page).

———. 2010. Sudan: Rising Inter-tribal Violence in the South and Renewed Clashes in Darfur Cause New Waves of Displacement. Geneva: IDMC. Retrieved 15 November 2014 from http://www.internal-displacement.org/assets/library/Africa/Sudan/pdf/Sudan-May-2010.pdf.

International Crisis Group. 2008. *China's Thirst for Oil*. Asia Report 153. Seoul and Brussels: International Crisis Group. Retrieved 9 January 2009 from http://www.crisisgroup.org.

———. 2011. *Divisions in Sudan's Ruling Party and the Threat to the Country's Stability*. Africa Report 174. Brussels: International Crisis Group. Retrieved 28 May 2012 from http://www.crisisgroup.org/~/media/Files/africa/horn-of-africa/sudan/174%20Divisions%20in%20Sudans%20Ruling%20Party%20and%20the%20Threat%20to%20the%20Countrys%20Future%20Stability%202.pdf.

International Food Policy Research Institute (IFPRI). 2006. *Empowering the Rural Poor Under Volatile Policy Environments in the Near East and North Africa Region: Case Study Sudan*. Khartoum and Rome: IFPRI/IFAD.

International Monetary Fund (IMF). 2010. *Sudan, Country Report No. 10/256*. Washington, D.C.: IMF.

International Water Management Institute (IWMI). 2008. *Institutional Settings and Livelihood Strategies in the Blue Nile Basin: Implications for Upstream/Downstream Linkages*. Working Paper 132. Addis Ababa: IWMI.

Ivens, S. 2008. 'Does Increased Water Access Empower Women?' *Development* 51: 63–67.

Jabri, V. 1996. *Discourses on Violence: Conflict Analysis Reconsidered*. Manchester: Manchester University Press.

Jacobsen, K. 2008. *Internal Displacement to Urban Areas: The Tufts-IDMC Profiling Study, Case 1 Khartoum, Sudan*. Somerville, M.A.: Feinstein International Centre, Tufts University (in collaboration with Internal Displacement Monitoring Centre, Geneva).

Jaglin, S. 2005. *Services d'eau en Afrique sub-saharienne : la fragmentation urbaine en question*. Paris: Editions du CNRS.

Jahallah, K.M. 2008. 'Language Policies in Sudan with Special Reference to the Period of Inqadh Regime 1989–2004' [in Arabic], in O. Abdelfattah and S. Salama (eds), *Proceedings of the International Conference on Language and Politics in Africa*. Cairo: Center for Research on African Studies.

Jakobi, A. 1991. 'Ethnonyms and Language Names as Indicators of Group Identities: A Case Study from the Nuba Mountains', *Proceedings of the Second International Sudan Studies Conference: Sudan, Environment and People.* Durham, N.C.: University of Durham Press, pp. 155–65.

James, W. 2007. *War and Survival in Sudan's Frontierlands: Voices from the Blue Nile.* Oxford: Oxford University Press.

Jassens, S. and Thill, Z. 2013. 'Water in Azraq (Jordan): A Fluid Link between State and Society', *Journal des anthropologues* 132–33: 317–38.

Johnson, D. 2003. *The Root Causes of Sudan's Civil Wars.* Oxford: James Currey.

Joseph, J.E. 2004. *Language and Identity: National, Ethnic, Religious.* New York: Palgrave Macmillan.

Kälin, W. 2008. 'Renewed Effort Needed to Help the Displaced', *Irish Times,* 30 October. Retrieved 12 May 2011 from http://www.irishtimes.com/newspaper/opinion.

Kāmil Bāshā, M. 1909. *Al-Masʾala al-Sharqiyya,* 2nd ed, Part 1. Cairo: Maṭbaʿat al-Liwāʾ. Retrieved 2 August 2010 from http://www.archive.org/stream/mustafakamilbash07mustuoft#page/n835/mode/2up.

Kevane, M. and L. Gray. 1995. 'Local Politics in the Time of Turabi's Revolution: Gender, Class and Ethnicity in Western Sudan', *Africa: Journal of the International African Institute* 65(2): 271–96.

Khalid, M. and J. Garang. 1992. *The Call for Democracy in Sudan.* London: Kegan Paul.

Koebner, R. and H.D. Schmidt. 1964. *Imperialism: The Study and Significance of a Political Word, 1840–1960.* Cambridge: Cambridge University Press.

Kok, P.N. 1996. *Governance and Conflict in the Sudan, 1985–1995: Analysis, Evaluation and Documentation.* Hamburg: Deutsches Orient-Institut.

Komey, G.K. 2008. 'The Denied Land Rights of the Indigenous Peoples and Their Endangered Livelihood and Survival: The Case of the Nuba of the Sudan', *Ethnic and Racial Studies* 31(5): 991–1008.

Krätli, S., O.H. El-Dirani and H. Young. 2013. *Standing Wealth: Pastoralist Livestock Production and Local Livelihoods in Sudan.* Nairobi: UNEP.

Kumaraswamy, P.R. 2003. 'Problems of Studying Minorities in the Middle East', *Alternatives: Turkish Journal of International Relations* 2(2): 244–64. Retrieved 12 August 2010 from http://www.alternativesjournal.net/volume2/number2/kumar.pdf.

Large, D. 2007. 'China and Sudan', *Development* 50(3): 57–62.

———. 2008. *Sudan's Foreign Relations with Asia: China and the Politics of 'Looking East'.* ISS Paper 158. Pretoria: Institute for Security Studies. Retrieved 5 March 2008 from http://www.iss.co.za.

———. 2009. 'China's Sudan Engagement: Changing Northern and Southern Political Trajectories in Peace and War', in J.C. Strauss and M. Saavedra (eds), *China and Africa: Emerging Patterns in Globalization and Development.* The China Quarterly Special Issues, New Series 9. Cambridge: Cambridge University Press, pp. 60–76.

———. 2010. 'China's Emerging Two-Sudan's Diplomacy', *The China Monitor* 55. Retrieved 9 October 2010 from http://www.ccs.org.za.

Larkin, B.D. 1973. *China and Africa, 1949–1970: The Foreign Policy of the People's Republic of China.* Berkeley: University of California Press.

Lavergne, M. 1997a. 'La violence d'Etat comme mode de régulation de la croissance urbaine : le cas de Khartoum', *Espaces, Populations et Sociétés* 15(1): 49–64.

———. 1997b. 'Le nouveau système politique soudanais ou la démocratie en trompe-l'oeil', *Politique Africaine* 66: 23–38.

Lehouerou, F. 2004. *Migrants forcés éthiopiens et érythréens en Egypte et au Soudan.* Paris: L'Harmattan.

Lesch, A.M. 1998. *The Sudan: Contested National Identities.* Bloomington: Indiana University Press and Oxford: James Currey.

Lévy, B.H. 2007. 'Choses vues au Darfour', *Le Monde,* 12 March.

Liauzu, C. 2007. *Histoire de l'anticolonialisme en France du XVIe siècle à nos jours.* Paris: Armand Colin.

Liebkind, K. 1999. 'Social Psychology', in J. A. Fishman (ed.), *The Handbook of Language and Ethnic Identity.* Oxford: Oxford University Press, pp. 140–51.

Linton, J. 2012. 'The Human Right to What? Water, Rights, Humans, and the Relation of Things', in F. Sultana and A. Loftus (eds), *The Right to Water: Politics, Governance and Social Struggles.* London and New York: Earthscan, pp. 45–60.

Linz, J.J. 2000. *Totalitarian and Authoritarian Regimes.* Boulder, C.O.: Lynne Rienner.

Liu, G. 2008. 'Darfur and Sino-African Relations', transcript, 22 February, Chatham House. Retrieved 20 April 2008 from http://www.chathamhouse.org.uk.

Lobban, R. 1982. 'Class and Kinship in Sudanese Urban Communities', *Journal of the International African Institute* 52(2): 51–76.

Lowrie, A.L. 1993. *Islam, Democracy, the State and the West: A Round Table with Dr. Hasan Turabi, May 10, 1992.* Tampa, F.L.: World & Islam Studies Enterprise.

MacDiarmid, P. 1931. 'The Languages of the Nuba Mountains', *Sudan Notes and Records* 3: 197–216.

MacFarlane, N.S. 2002. *Intervention in Contemporary World Politics.* London: International Institute for Strategic Studies, Oxford University Press.

Madut-Arop, A. 2006. *Sudan's Painful Road to Peace: A Full Story of the Founding and Development of SPLM/SPLA.* Charleston, S.C.: BookSurge.

Maglad, N.E.A. 2008. *Scoping Study on Chinese Relations with Sudan.* Nairobi: African Economic Research Consortium, AERC. Retrieved 15 March 2009 from http://www.aercafrica.org/documents/china_africa_relations/Sudan.pdf.

Makoni, S. and A. Pennycook. 2005. 'Disinventing and (Re)constituting Languages', *Critical Inquiry in Languages Studies* 2(3): 137–56.

Malone, B. 2010. 'Ethiopian PM Warns Egypt of Nile War'. Reuters, 23 November. Retrieved from http://uk.reuters.com/article/2010/11/23/uk-ethiopia-egypt-meles-idUKTRE6AM3IS20101123

Mamdani, M. 2007. 'The Politics of Naming: Genocide, Civil War, Insurgency', *London Review of Books,* 8 March. Retrieved 9 June 2010 from http://www.lrb.co.uk/v29/n05/mamd01_.html.

Manfredi, S. 2013. 'Arabic Borrowings in Laggorí (Eastern Daju)', in T. Schadeberg and R. Blench (eds), *Nuba Mountain Language Studies.* Cologne: Rüdiger Köppe Verlag, pp. 463–84.

Manger, L. 1994. *From the Mountains to the Plains: The Integration of the Lofofa Nuba into Sudanese Society.* Uppsala: Nordiska Afrikainstitutet.

———. 2005. 'Understanding Resource Management in the Western Sudan: A Critical Look at New Institutional Economics', in Q. Gausset, M.A. Whyte and T.B. Thomsen (eds), *Beyond Territory and Scarcity: Exploring Conflicts over Natural Resource Management*. Nordiska Afrikainstitutet, pp. 135–48.

Manji, F. 2008. 'The Depoliticisation of Poverty', in R. Warah (ed.), *Missionaries, Mercenaries and Misfits: An Anthology*. Milton Keynes, U.K.: Authorhouse, pp. 173–89.

Marchal, R. 1995. 'Eléments d'une sociologie du Front National Islamique soudanais', *Les Etudes du CERI* 5. Retrieved 28 May 2012 from http://www.ceri-sciences-po.org/publica/etude/etude5.pdf.

———. 1996. 'Soudan : vers une recomposition du champ politique?', *Revue du monde musulman et de la Méditerranée* 81: 93–117.

———. 2004. 'Soudan : d'un conflit à l'autre', *Les Etudes du CERI* 107–8. Retrieved 28 May 2012 from http://www.ceri-sciences-po.org/publica/etude/etude107.pdf.

———. 2008. 'La Chine et l'Afrique : des retrouvailles aux faux-semblants', in C. Jaffrelot (ed.), *L'enjeu mondial : les pays émergents*. Paris: Presses de Sciences Po, pp. 235–47.

———. 2011. 'Malaysia-Sudan: From Islamist Students to Rentier Bourgeois', in D. Large and L. Patey (eds), *Sudan looks East: China, India and the Politics of Asian Alternatives*. Oxford: James Currey, pp. 102–19.

Marchal, R. and E. Ahmed. 2010. 'Multiple Uses of Neoliberalism: War, New Boundaries and the Reorganisation of the Government in Sudan', in F. Gutiérrez and G. Schönwälder (eds), *Utopia or Dystopia? Economic Liberalization and Political Violence*. London: Pluto Press, pp. 173–208.

Marchal, R and O. Osman. 1997. 'Les ambitions internationales du Soudan islamiste', *Politique Africaine* 66: 74–87.

Marsá Fuentes, J. 2005. 'La globalización en el mundo árabe a través del discurso de sus intelectuales', Ph.D. dissertation. Granada: Universidad de Granada. Retrieved 2 August 2010 from http://digibug.ugr.es/handle/10481/649

Mayom, M. 2010. 'Indian, Korean and Indonesian Ambassadors on Investment Trip to S. Sudan', *Sudan Tribune*, 15 January. Retrieved 26 September 2010 from http://www.sudantribune.com.

Mazo, J. 2010. *Climate Conflict*. London: International Institute for Strategic Studies.

Melber, H. and R. Southall. 2009. 'Introduction: A New Scramble for Africa?', in R. Southall and H. Melber (eds), *A New Scramble for Africa? Imperialism, Investment and Development*. Scottsville, South Africa: University of KwaZulu-Natal Press, pp. xix–xxvii.

Middle East Online. 2008. 'Khartoum Investors Eye Tuti Island', 24 March. Retrieved 14 November 2012 from http://www.middle-east-online.com/english/?id=25011.

Miller, C. 2003. 'Linguistic Policies and the Issue of Ethno-linguistic Minorities in the Middle East', in A. Usuki and H. Kato (eds), *Islam in the Middle Eastern Studies: Muslims and Minorities*. JCAS Symposium Series 7. Osaka: Japan Center for Area Studies, pp. 149–74.

———. 2006. 'Languages, Identity and Ideologies: A New Era for Sudan?', *Proceedings of the 7th International Sudan Studies Conference, Bergen (Norway), 6–8 April*. Bergen: University of Bergen. Retrieved 14 February 2015 from http://halshs.archives-ouvertes.fr/halshs-00150438/fr/

———. 2009. 'La situation linguistique au Soudan : évolution et enjeux', in B. Casciarri (ed.), *Cycle de conférences du CEDEJ Khartoum au Centre culturel français 2007–2008*. Khartoum: Dar Azza, pp. 12–37.

Mitchell, R.P. 1993. *The Society of the Muslim Brothers*. New York and Oxford: Oxford University Press.

Mitchell, T. 1989. *Colonising Egypt*. Cairo: AUC Press.

Mohamed, A.A. and Badri, B.Y. 2005. *Inter-communal Conflicts in Sudan: Causes, Resolution Mechanisms and Transformation – a Case Study of the Darfur Region*. Omdurman: Ahfad University for Women.

Mohamed, A.A., et al. 2003. *Al-tanmiya muftah al-salām fi Darfúr* [Development: The key for peace building in Darfur]. Khartoum: Friedrich Ebert Stiftung and Centre for Peace Studies, Juba University.

Mohamed, S.M. 2000. *Al-Sudān: Hurub al-mwārid wa al-huiya* [Identity and resource-based conflicts in Sudan]. Khartoum: Dar Azza.

Mohamed Salih, M.A. 1990a. 'Agropastoralist Response to Agricultural Policies: The Predicament of the Baggara, Western Sudan', in M. Bovin and L. Manger (eds), *Adaptive Strategies in African Arid Lands*. Uppsala: Nordiska Afrikainstitutet, pp. 59–75.

———. 1990b. 'Government Policy and Pastoral Development in the Sudan', *Nomadic Peoples* 25–26: 65–78.

Moriarty, P. and J. Butterworth. 2003. *The Productive Use of Domestic Water Supplies: How Water Supplies Can Play a Wider Role in Livelihood Improvement and Poverty Reduction*. Thematic Overview Paper. The Hague: IRC International Water and Sanitation Centre.

Mosse, D. 1997. 'The Symbolic Making of a Common Property Resource: History, Ecology and Locality in a Tank-Irrigated Landscape in South India', *Development and Change* 28: 467–504.

———. 2003. *The Rule of Water: Statecraft, Ecology and Collective Action in South India*. Oxford: Oxford University Press.

———. 2008. 'Epilogue: The Cultural Politics of Water – a Comparative Perspective', *Journal of Southern African Studies* 34(4): 939–48.

Muḥammad, ʿA.G.I. 2002. 'Manāhij al-Taʿlīm fī al-Sūdān bayna Taʿdīlāt al-Māḍī wa-Taḥaddiyāt al-Mustaqbal', *Dirāsāt Tarbawiyya* 5: 68–78.

Murād, B.M. 2010. 'Al-ʿAwlama wa-Ṣirāʿ al-Ḥaḍārāt', *Majallat al-Waʿī al-Islāmī* 530. Retrieved 1 March 2010 from http://alwaei.com/topics/view/article_new.php?sdd=569&issue=460

National Islamic Front (NIF). 1987. *Sudan Charter: National Unity and Diversity*. Khartoum: National Islamic Front.

Nègre, M. 2004. *ONG et autoritarisme au Soudan : l'eau en question*. Cairo: CEDEJ.

Njiru, C. and M. Albu. 2004. 'Improving Access to Water through Support to Small Water-Providing Enterprises', *Small Enterprise Development* 15(2): 30–37.

Nonini, D.M. 2007. *The Global Idea of 'The Commons'*. New York: Berghahn Books.

Norein, O.S. 2006. 'Phonology of Zaghawa Language in Sudan', in A.A. Abu-Manga, L. Gilley and A. Storch (eds), *Insights into Nilo-Saharan Language, History and Culture: Proceedings of the 9th Nilo-Saharan Linguistic Colloquium*. Cologne: Rüdiger Koppe.

Nūfal, M.N. 1998. *Iʿdād al-Talāmīdh li-l-Qarn al-Ḥādī wa-l-ʿIshrīn.* Damascus: Al-Munaẓẓama al-ʿArabiyya li-l-Tarbiya wa-l-Thaqāfa wa-l-ʿUlūm.

Nyombe, B.G.V. 1997. 'Survival or Extinction: The Fate of the Local Languages of Southern Sudan', *International Journal of the Sociology of Language* 125: 99–130.

Oduho, J. and W. Deng. 1963. *The Problem of the Southern Sudan.* Oxford: Oxford University Press.

O'Fahey, R.S. 1980. *State and Society in Dār Fūr.* New York: St. Martin's Press.

———. 1997. '"Defining the Community": The National Islamic Front, Its Opponents and the Sharia Issue', *Islam et sociétés au sud du Sahara* 11: 55–65.

Ohtsuka, K. 1996. 'Water, Land and Labor in Irrigation Agriculture along the Nile: Cases from Northern Sudan', in S. Sato and E. Kurimoto (eds), *Essays in Northern African Studies.* Senri Ethnological Studies 43. Tokyo: National Museum of Ethnology, pp. 59–75.

Olutayo, A.O. and A.O. Omobowale. 2007. 'Capitalism, Globalization and the Underdevelopment Process in Africa: History in Perpetuity', *Africa Development,* 32(2): 97–112.

Organisation Mondiale Contre la Torture (OMCT). 2007. *Sudan: Ongoing Violence Against Communities Resisting Dam Construction in the Northern Nile Valley.* Geneva: OMCT.

Ould-Mey, M. 1994. 'Global Adjustment: Implication for Peripheral States', *Third World Quarterly* 15(2): 319–36.

Oxfam International. 2009. *Beyond Band Aids: Tackling Disasters in Ethiopia 25 Years after Famine.* Briefing Paper. London: OI.

Panozzo, I. 2009. 'Le safari de la China en Afrique : opportunité ou danger?', in B. Casciarri (ed.), *Cycle des conferences du CEDEJ Khartoum au Centre culturel français 2007–2008* Khartoum: Dar Azza, pp. 74–95.

Pantulliano, S. 2010. 'Oil, Land and Conflict: The Decline of Misseriyya Pastoralism in the Sudan', *Review of African Political Economy* 37(123): 7–23.

Pantulliano, S., O. Egemi, et al. 2009. *Put Out to Pasture: War, Oil and the Decline of Misseriyya Humr Pastoralism in the Sudan.* London: Overseas Development Institute.

Pantulliano, S., M. Assal, et al. 2011. *City Limits: Urbanization and Vulnerability in Khartoum.* London: Overseas Development Institute.

Permanent Court of Arbitration (PCA). 2009. 'PCA Press Release: Abyei Arbitration', 22 July, The Hague.

Pérouse de Montclos, M.A. 2001. *Migrations forcées et urbanisation : le cas de Khartoum.* Paris: CEPED.

Perrot, S. and D. Malaquais. 2009. 'Afrique, la globalisation par les Suds', *Politique africaine* 113: 5–27.

Petterson, D., et al. 2005. 'Abyei Boundaries Commission Report', 14 July, IGAD. Retrieved 9 August 2008 from http://www.sudanarchive.net.

Polanyi, K. 1944. *The Great Transformation: The Origins of Our Time.* New York: Farrar & Heinart.

——— (with G. Dalton). 1968. *Primitive, Archaic and Modern Economics.* New York: Anchor Books.

Pomper, P. 1996. 'Historians and Individual Agency', *History and Theory* 35(3): 281–308.

Porto, J.G. 2002. 'Contemporary Conflict Analysis in Perspective', in J. Lind and K. Sturman (eds), *Scarcity and Surfeit: The Ecology of Africa's Conflicts*. Nairobi: African Centre for Technology Studies and Institute for Security Studies, pp. 1–50.

Power, S. 2002. *'A Problem from Hell': America and the Age of Genocide*. New York: Basic Books.

———. 2004. 'Remember Rwanda, but Take Action in Sudan', *New York Times*, 6 April.

Prunier, G. 1998. 'Les Frères Musulmans Soudanais : une nouvelle diplomatie révolutionnaire', in O. Kane and J.L. Triaud (eds), *Islam et Islamismes au sud du Sahara*. Paris: Khartala, pp. 5–16.

———. 2005. *Darfur: The Ambiguous Genocide*. Ithaca, N.Y.: Cornell University Press.

———. 2012. 'In Sudan, Give War a Chance', *New York Times*, 7 May.

Quint, N. 2006. 'Do You Speak Kordofanian?', *Proceedings of the 7th International Sudan Studies Conference, Bergen (Norway), 6–8 April* (CD-ROM). Bergen: University of Bergen.

Rabāh, N.A. 1998. 'Dor al-hukuma al-markaziya wa al-idāra al-ahaliya fi fad al-nizāt al-gabaliya fi darfúr' [The role of central government and Native Administration in tribal conflict resolution in Darfur], Ph.D. dissertation. Khartoum: University of Khartoum.

Ravaillon, M. 2008. *Are There Lessons for Africa from China's Success against Poverty?* Policy Research Working Paper 4463. Washington D.C.: World Bank. Retrieved 20 September 2010 from http://econ.worldbank.com.

Report of the Rejaf Language Conference. 1928. London: Sudan Government.

Reuters. 2007. 'Hu Visits Sudan and Presses on Darfur', 2 February.

———. 2008. 'Kidnappers Kill 5 Chinese Hostages in Sudan', 27 October.

———. 2009a. 'Saudi Firm in $400 Million Farming Investment in Africa', 15 April.

———. 2009b. 'Saudi Hail Starts Farm Investment Abroad in Sudan', 16 February.

———. 2011. 'Bashir Says Sudan Will Adopt Islamic Constitution', 13 October. Retrieved 8 January 2014 from http://www.reuters.com/article/2011/10/13/ozatp-sudan-constitution-idAFJOE79C00F20111013

Revolutionary Command Council (RCC). 1989. *Revolutionary Command Council for National Salvation Policy Statement*. Khartoum: Revolutionary Command Council.

Reza, F. (ed.). 2003. *Anti-imperialism: A Guide for the Movement*. London: Bookmarks.

Richards, P. 2005. *No Peace, No War: An Anthropology of Contemporary Armed Conflicts*. Athens: Ohio University Press.

Richardson, M. 1990. 'Enough Said: Reflections on Orientalism', *Anthropology Today* 6(4): 16–19.

Rodinson, M. 1972. *Marxisme et monde musulman*. Paris: Éditions du Seuil.

Rottenburg, R.D. (ed.). 2008. *Nomadic-Sedentary Relations and Failing State Institutions in Darfur and Kordofan (Sudan)*. Halle (Salle): Orientwissenschaftliches Zentrum.

Roy, O. 1992. *L'échec de l'Islam politique*. Paris: Editions du Seuil.

Ryle, J. and J. Willis. 2011. 'Introduction: Many Sudans', in J. Ryle et al. (eds), *The Sudan Handbook*. Oxford: James Currey, pp. 1–9.

Saavedra, M. 1998. 'Ethnicity, Resources and the Central State: Politics in the Nuba Mountains, 1950 to the 1990s', in E. Stiansen and M. Kevane (eds), *Kordofan Invaded: Peripheral Incorporation and Social Transformation in Islamic Africa*. Amsterdam: Brill, pp. 223–53.

Saeed, *A. 2009.* 'Abyei Area at the Crossroads: An Enterprise of Unity, an Eyeball of Disunity?', in H. Abdel-Ati and G.D. El-Tayeb (eds), *Peace in Sudan: So Near … So Far? Proceedings of the National Civic Forum Dialogue Sessions 2007–2008*. Khartoum: National Civic Forum, pp. 82–92.

———. 2010. *Challenges Facing Sudan after the Referendum Day 2011. Persistent and Emerging Conflict in the North-South Borderline States*. Report prepared for the Christian Michelsen Institute. Bergen: Christian Michelsen Institute.

Said, E. 1978. *Orientalism*. New York: Pantheon Books.

Salah, B.M. and S.M. Abbas. 1991. 'Water Supply in Greater Khartoum', in M.E. Abu Sin and H.R.J. Davies (eds), *The Future of Sudan's Capital Region: A Study in Development and Change*. Khartoum: University of Khartoum Press, pp. 65–76.

Sanderson, L. and N. Sanderson. 1981. *Education, Religion and Politics in Southern Sudan 1899–1964*. London: Ithaca Press; Khartoum: University of Khartoum Press.

Satgar, V. 2009. 'Global Capitalism and the Neoliberalisation of Africa', in R. Southall and H. Melber (eds), *A New Scramble for Africa? Imperialism, Investment and Development*. Scottsville, South Africa: University of KwaZulu-Natal Press, pp. 35–55.

Sautman, B. and Y. Hairong. 2009. 'African Perspectives on China-Africa Links', in J.C. Strauss and M. Saavedra (eds), *China and Africa: Emerging Patterns in Globalization and Development*. The China Quarterly Special Issues, New Series 9. Cambridge: Cambridge University Press, pp. 178–209.

Schlee, G. 2010. *How Enemies Are Made: Towards a Theory of Ethnic and Religious Conflicts*. Oxford and New York: Berghahn Books.

Schmidinger, T. 2009. 'Another Darfur in the North? Kajbar Dam, Dal Dam and the Destruction of Nubia', paper presented at the International Sudan Studies Conference, Pretoria, 25–28 November.

Schouten, A.J. and P.B. Moriarty. 2003. *Community Water, Community Management: From System to Service in Rural Areas*. Report 64. London: ITDG Publications.

Scott, J.C. 1987. *Weapons of the Weak: Everyday Forms of Peasant Resistance*. New Haven, C.T.: Yale University Press.

Sengupta, S. 2004. 'Leader of Darfur Rebels Resorts to Damage Control', *New York Times*, 5 December. Retrieved 9 July 2010 from http://www.nytimes.com/2004/12/05/international/africa/05sudan.html?scp=5&sq=Darfur%20SLA&st=cse.

Seri-Hersch, I. 2012. 'Histoire scolaire, impérialisme(s) et décolonisation(s) : le cas du Soudan anglo-égyptien (1945–1958)', Ph.D. dissertation. Aix-en-Provence: Aix-Marseille Université.

Sharkey, H.J. 2003. *Living with Colonialism: Nationalism and Culture in the Anglo-Egyptian Sudan*. Berkeley: University of California Press.

———. 2008. 'Arab Identity and Ideology in the Sudan: The Politics of Language, Ethnicity and Race', *African Affairs* 107(426): 21–43.

Shazali, S.D., et al. 2006. *Share the Land or Part the Nation: The Pastoral Land Tenure System in Sudan.* Reduction of Resource Based Conflicts Project. Khartoum: UNDP-Sudan Country Office.

Shepherd, A., M. Norris and J. Watson. 1987. *Water Planning in Arid Sudan.* London: Ithaca Press.

Skocpol, T. 1979. *States and Social Revolutions.* Cambridge: Cambridge University Press.

Sikainga, A.A. 1996. *Slaves into Workers: Emancipation and Labor in Colonial Sudan.* Austin: University of Texas Press.

Simone, T.A.M. 1994. *In Whose Image? Political Islam and Urban Practises in Sudan.* Chicago: University of Chicago Press.

Sisk, T.D. 1996. *Power Sharing and International Mediation in Ethnic Conflicts.* Washington D.C.: US Institute of Peace Press.

Small Arms Survey. 2012. *The Conflict in Blue Nile.* Geneva: Small Arms Survey. Retrieved from http://www.smallarmssurveysudan.org/fileadmin/docs/facts-figures/sudan/blue-nile/HSBA-Blue-Nile.pdf.

Sommers, M. 2005. *Islands of Education: Schooling, Civil War and the Southern Sudanese (1983–2004).* Paris: International Institute for Educational Planning. Retrieved 17 December 2013 from http://www.unesco.org/iiep/PDF/pubs/sudan.pdf.

Sorbo, G. 1985. *Tenants and Nomads in Eastern Sudan: A Study of Economic Adaptations in New Halfa Scheme.* Uppsala: Nordiska Afrikainstitutet.

Southall, R. & H. Melber (eds). 2009. *A New Scramble for Africa? Imperialism, Investment and Development.* Scottsville, South Africa: University of KwaZulu-Natal Press.

Spronk, T. 2014. 'Addressing the challenges of language choices in the implementation of mother-tongue based bilingual education in South Sudan', *Multilingual Education* 2014, 4(16): 1–10. Retrieved 13 November 2014 from http://www.multilingual-education.com/content/pdf/s13616-014-0016-z.pdf.

Stearns, P.N. 2003. 'Treating Globalization in History Surveys', *The History Teacher* 36(2): 153–60.

Stevenson, A. 2009. 'India Builds on Sudanese Oil Interests', *Financial Times,* 9 December. Retrieved 15 October 2010 from http://www.ft.com.

Stevenson, R.C. 1956–57. 'A Survey of the Phonetics and Grammatical Structure of the Nuba Mountain Languages, with Particular Reference to Otoro, Katcha and Nyimang', *Afrika und Übersee* 40: 73–84, 93–115; 41: 27–65, 117–52, 171–96.

Straus, S. 2005. 'Darfur and the Genocide Debate', *Foreign Affairs* 84(1): 123–33.

Strauss, J.C. and M. Saavedra (eds). 2009. *China and Africa: Emerging Patterns in Globalization and Development.* The China Quarterly Special Issues, New Series 9. Cambridge: Cambridge University Press.

Suárez, D. 2007. 'Education Professionals and the Construction of Human Rights Education', *Comparative Education Review* 51(1): 48–70.

Sudan National Multi-Donor Trust Fund (MDTF). 2010. *Turning the Corner: 2009 Annual Report.* Information update on Sudan (vol. 2), report 56480. Washington D.C.: World Bank. Retrieved 29 August 2010 from http://www-wds.worldbank.org.

Sudan Tribune. 2005. 'Hamdab Dam: Row over Water Wells between Chinese and Residents', 29 November.
———. 2006. 'Merowe Dam Affected Areas Exploded into Violence and Burning', 12 April.
———. 2008a. 'China Grants Sudan US$ 3 m for North-South Unity', 30 November.
———. 2008b. 'Sudan and China Signed Eight Economic Agreements', 10 June.
———. 2009a. 'China and Kenya Discuss New Corridor for Southern Sudan Oil', 15 October.
———. 2009b. 'Sudan Will Put Its Agricultural Resources at Africa's Disposal', 2 July.
———. 2010a. 'Chinese Firm Given Land Deal in Sudan', 17 March.
———. 2010b. 'SPLM Gives Assurances on Chinese Oil Investment in South Sudan', 15 October.
———. 2010c. 'Toyota Proposes Kenya-Juba Pipeline Bypassing Port Sudan', 3 March.
———. 2011a. 'Sudanese Will Start Feeling the Sting of Austerity Plan Approved by Parliament', 5 January.
———. 2011b. 'VP Taha Cut Short His Visit to Sudan's Blue Nile State', 22 February.
Sullivan, C.A. and J.R. Meigh. 2003. 'Considering the Water Poverty Index in the Context of Poverty Alleviation', *Water Policy* 5: 513–28.
Sweeney, B. and W.L. Carruthers. 1996. 'Conflict Resolution: History, Philosophy, Theory, and Educational Applications', *School Counselor* 43(5): 326–44.
Swyngedouw, E. 2004. *Social Power and the Urbanization of Water: Flows of Power.* Oxford: Oxford University Press.
Taha, H. 1993. *Al-Ikhwan wa-al-'askar: Qissat al-Jabhah al-Islamiya wa-al-sulta fi al-Sudan* [The Brothers and the military: Story of the Islamic Front and power in Sudan]. Cairo: Markaz al-Hadarah al-'Arabiyah lil-I'lam wa-al-Nashr.
Tayara, S. 2006. *Linguistic Study and Analysis of the Logori Language.* Khartoum: Sudan Workshop Programme.
Teodoru, C., A. Wuest and B. Wehrli. 2006. *Independent Review of the Environmental Impacts Assessment for the Merowe Dam Project.* Kastanienbaum (Swiss): EAWAG.
Thelwall, R. (ed.). 1978. *Aspects of Language in the Sudan.* Coleraine, U.K.: New University of Ulster.
———. 1981. 'Lexicostatistical Sub-Grouping and Reconstruction of Daju', in T. Schadeberg and L. Bender (eds), *Proceedings of the 1st Nilo-Saharan Colloquium.* Amsterdam: Foris, pp. 167–84.
Thelwall, R. and T. Schadeberg. 1983. 'The Linguistic Settlement of the Nuba Mountains', *Sprache und Geschichte in Afrika* 5: 219–31.
Tubiana, J. 2007. 'Darfur: A War of Land?', in A. de Waal (ed.), *War in Darfur and the Search for Peace.* Cambridge and London: Global Equity Initiative, Harvard University/Justice Africa, pp. 68–91.
Tucker, A.N. 1934. 'The Language Situation in the Southern Sudan', *Africa* 8: 28–39.
Tucker, A.N. and M.A. Bryan. 1956. *The Non-Bantu Languages of North-East Africa.* London: Oxford University Press.
Turton, D. 2003. *Conceptualising Forced Migration.* Refugee Studies Centre Working Paper 12. Khartoum: Refugee Studies Centre.

Ulin, R.C. 1991. 'Critical Anthropology Twenty Years Later: Modernism and Postmodernism in Anthropology', *Critique of Anthropology* 11(1): 63–89.

United Nations, 1998. *The Guiding Principles on Internal Displacement.* New York: United Nations Secretary-General on the Human Rights of Internally Displaced Persons. Retrieved 15 November 2012 from http://daccess-dds-ny.un.org/doc/UNDOC/GEN/G98/104/93/PDF/G9810493.pdf?OpenElement.

United Nations, 2007. 'UN Expert Urges Sudan to Respect Human Rights of Communities Affected by Hydro-electric Dam Projects', press release, 27 August, Geneva. Retrieved 15 November 2012 from http://www.unhchr.ch.

United Nations Children's Fund (UNICEF). 2009. *Water, Sanitation and Hygiene: North Kordofan Fact Sheet.* Water, Sanitation and Hygiene Section of the UNICEF, North Sudan Area Program. Khartoum: UNICEF Office.

United Nations Development Programme (UNDP). 2006. *Human Development Report 2006: Beyond Scarcity: Power, Poverty and the Global Water Crisis.* New York: UNDP.

United Nations Educational, Scientific and Cultural Organization (UNESCO) 2009. *Atlas of the World's Languages in Danger.* Retrieved from http://www.unesco.org/culture/languages-atlas/

United Nations Security Council (UNSC). 1996a. 'Resolution 1044 (1996) [Letter dated 9 January 1996 from the Permanent Representative of Ethiopia to the United Nations addressed to the President of the Security Council concerning the extradition of the suspects wanted in the assassination attempt on the life of the President of the Arab Republic of Egypt in Addis Ababa, Ethiopia, on 26 June 1995 (S/1996/10)]', S/RES/1044, 3627th meeting, 31 January 1996. Retrieved 12 February 2014 from http://www.treasury.gov/resource-center/sanctions/Documents/1044.pdf.

———. 1996b.. 'Resolution 1054 (1996) [Letter dated 9 January 1996 from the Permanent Representative of Ethiopia to the United Nations addressed to the President of the Security Council concerning the extradition of the suspects wanted in the assassination attempt on the life of the President of the Arab Republic of Egypt in Addis Ababa, Ethiopia, on 26 June 1995 (S/1996/10)]', S/RES/1054, 3660th meeting, 26 April 1996. Retrieved 12 February 2014 from http://daccess-dds-ny.un.org/doc/UNDOC/GEN/N96/107/86/PDF/N9610786.pdf?OpenElement.

———. 1996c. 'Resolution 1070 (1996) [Letter dated 9 January 1996 from the Permanent Representative of Ethiopia to the United Nations addressed to the President of the Security Council concerning the extradition of the suspects wanted in the assassination attempt on the life of the President of the Arab Republic of Egypt in Addis Ababa, Ethiopia, on 26 June 1995 (S/1996/10)]', S/RES/1070, 3690th meeting, 16 August 1996. Retrieved 12 February 2014 from http://daccess-dds-ny.un.org/doc/UNDOC/GEN/N96/214/20/PDF/N9621420.pdf?OpenElement.

———. 2009. *Report of the Panel of Experts Established Pursuant to Resolution 1591 (2005) Concerning the Sudan, S/2009/562, 29 October 2009.* Retrieved 15 May 2010 from http://www.un.org/ga/search/view_doc.asp?symbol=S/2009/562&Submit=Search&Lang=E.

United Nations and partners. 2006. 'Work Plan for Sudan 2007 (vol. 1)', 4 December. Retrieved 5 February 2014 from http://www.unochq.org/cap/appeals/united-nations-and-partners-2007-work-plan-sudan.

UN News Centre. 2004. 'Sudan: Envoy Warns of Ethnic Cleansing as Security Council Calls for Ceasefire', 2 April.

Vacca, G. (ed.). 2007. *Nel mondo grande e terribile: Antologia degli scritti 1914–1935.* Torino: Einaudi.

Van Aken, M. 2011. 'Riego y desorden tecno-lógico: La disputa por el agua, el conocimiento y la técnica de la agroindustria en el valle del Jordán (Jordania)', in H. Ayeb (ed.), *El agua en el mundo Árabe: Percepciones globales y realidades locales.* Madrid: Casa Árabe, pp. 59–86.

Van Dommelen, J. 1997. 'Soudan : mouvement islamique et société', in *Afrique politique 1997: Revendications populaires et recompositions politiques.* Paris: Khartala, pp. 129–39.

Vars, G.F. 1991. 'Integrated Curriculum in Historical Perspective', *Educational Leadership* 49(2): 14–15.

Verhoeven, H. 2011a. *Black Gold for Blue Gold? Oil and Hydro Energy Policy in the Horn of Africa and the Limits to Regional Integration for Sudan and Ethiopia.* London: Royal Institute for International Affairs/Chatham House.

———. 2011b. 'Climate Change, Conflict and Development in Sudan: Neo-Malthusian Global Narratives and Local Power Struggles', *Development and Change* 42(3): 679–707.

———. 2011c. '"Dams Are Development": The Al-Ingaz Regime, China and the (Hydro)Political Game around the Sudanese Nile', in D. Large and L.A. Patey (eds), *Asia's Foreign Relations with Sudan.* Oxford: James Currey, pp. 120–38.

———. 2012. 'Sudan and Its Agricultural Revival: A Regional Breadbasket at Last or Another Mirage in the Desert?', in T. Allan et al. (eds), *Handbook of Land and Water Grabs.* London: Routledge, pp. 41–54.

———. 2013a. 'The Politics of African Energy Development: Ethiopia's Hydro-agricultural State-Building Strategy and Clashing Paradigms of Water Security', *The Philosophical Transactions of the Royal Society A* 371(2002). Retrieved 15 November 2014 from http://rsta.royalsocietypublishing.org/content/371/2002/20120411.short.

———. 2013b. '*The Rise and Fall of Sudan's Al-Ingaz Revolution: The Transition from Militarised Islamism to Economic Salvation and the Comprehensive Peace Agreement*', *Civil Wars* 15(2): 118–40.

———. 2014 'Gardens of Edens or Hearts of Darkness? The Genealogy of Discourses on Environmental Insecurity and Climate Wars in Africa', *Geopolitics* 19(4): 784–805.

Vilas, C.M. and C. Pérez. 2002. 'Globalization as Imperialism', *Latin American Perspectives* 29(6): 70–79.

Voll, J.O. 1990. 'Islamization in the Sudan and the Iranian Revolution', in J.L. Esposito (ed.). *The Iranian Revolution: Its Global Impact.* Miami: Florida International University Press, pp. 283–301.

Wai, D. (ed.). 1973. *The Southern Sudan: The Problem of National Integration.* London: Frank Cass.

Wallace-Wells, B. 2009. 'Darfuristan', *Rolling Stone,* 11 December. Retrieved 6 May 2010 from http://www.rollingstone.com/politics/story/31343773/darfuristan.

Wallerstein, I. 2002. 'La mondialisation n'est pas nouvelle', postface, in *Le capitalisme historique,* 2nd ed. Paris: La Découverte.

Warburg, G. 2002. *Sudan: Islam, Sectarianism, and Politics since the Mahdiyya.* Madison: University of Wisconsin Press.

Waterbury, J. 1979. *Hydropolitics of the Nile Valley.* Syracuse, N.Y.: Syracuse University Press.

———. 1983. *The Egypt of Nasser and Sadat: The Political Economy of Two Regimes.* Princeton, N.J.: Princeton University Press.

Water Page. 1996. 'Africa Sector Review Report.' Retrieved 15 November 2012 from http://www.africanwater.org/council.htm#_Toc372958947.

Webb, P. and M. Iskandarani. 1998. *Water Insecurity and the Poor: Issues and Research Needs.* ZEF, Discussion Papers on Development Policy 2. Bonn: Center for Development Research.

Wesselink, E. and E. Weller. 2006. 'Oil and Violence in Sudan Drilling, Poverty and Death in Upper Nile State', *Multinational Monitor* 27(3) (online). Retrieved 15 November 2014 from http://www.multinationalmonitor.org/mm2006/052006/wesselink.html.

Westermann, D. 1911. *Die Sudansprachen: Eine sprachvergleichende Studie.* Hamburg: L. Friederichsen.

Wheeler, N.J. 2000. *Saving Strangers: Humanitarian Intervention in International Society.* Oxford and New York: Oxford University Press.

Wittfogel, K.A. 1957. *Oriental Despotism.* New Haven, C.T.: Yale University Press.

Wolf, S. 1990. 'The Muslim Brotherhood in the Sudan', master's thesis. Hamburg: University of Hamburg.

Woodward, P. 1990. *Sudan, 1898–1989: The Unstable State.* Boulder, C.O.: Lynne Rienner; London: Lester Crook.

Worall, G.A. 1958. 'Soils and Land Use in the Vicinity of the Three Towns', *Sudan Notes and Records* 39: 2–15.

World Bank. 2006. 'World Bank Sanctions Lahmeyer International for Corrupt Activities in Bank-Financed Projects', November. Retrieved 15 November 2014 from http://web.worldbank.org/WBSITE/EXTERNAL/NEWS/0,,contentMDK:21116129~pagePK:64257043~piPK:437376~theSitePK:4607,00.html.

———. 2008. *Country Assistance Strategy for the Federal Democratic Republic of Ethiopia. Report No 43051-ET.* Addis Ababa: World Bank.

———. 2009. *Sudan: The Road Toward a Sustainable and Broad-Based Growth.* Washington, D.C.: World Bank.

———. 2012. *Interim Strategy Note for the Arab Republic of Egypt: Report No 66433-EG.* Cairo: World Bank.

Wraga, W.G. 1997. 'Patterns of Interdisciplinary Curriculum Organization and Professional Knowledge of the Curriculum Field', *Journal of Curriculum and Supervision* 12(12): 98–117.

Wright, Sharon. 2006. 'Evaluation Report: Teacher Education in Southern Sudan Supported by NCA', 31 March, Norwegian Church Aid. Retrieved 1 December 2010 from http://www.norad.no/en/Tools+and+publications/Publications/Publication+Page?key=117408

Xinhua. 2007. 'Merowe Dam: Pearl of the Nile in Sudan', 23 December.

Yafūt, S. 1998. 'Hawiyyatunā al-Thaqāfiyya wa-l-ʿAwlama: Naḥwa Tanāwul Naqdī', *Majallat Fikr wa-Naqd* 11. Retrieved 1 March 2010 from http://www.fikrwanakd.aljabriabed.net/n11_3fikryafut.htm.

Yamānī, M.ʿA. 1998. 'ʿAṣr al-Maʿlūmāt wa-l-Maʿārif wa-l-Taʿlīm', *Majallat al-Maʿrifa* 35: 61–67 (Riyadh: Wizārat al-Maʿārif).

Yath, A. 1995. 'On the Expulsion of Rural Immigrants from Greater Khartoum: The Example of the Dinka', *Geojournal* 36(1): 93–101.

Yokwe, E.M. 1984. 'Arabicisation and Language Policy in the Sudan', *Studies in the Linguistic Sciences* 14(2): 149–70.

Yongo-Bure, B. 2006. 'Education for Sustainable Development in Southern Sudan', *Proceedings of the 7th International Sudan Studies Conference, Bergen (Norway), 6–8 April* (CD-ROM). Bergen: University of Bergen.

———. 2007. *Economic Development of Southern Sudan*. Lanham, M.D.: University Press of America.

Zain Al-Abdin, A.T. 2008. 'Islamic Movement in Sudan: From Muslim Brotherhood to the Ruling National Congress', *Islamic Political Parties, Movements, Conflict and Democracy, January 21–22, 2008*. The Hague: Institute of Social Studies.

Zeitoun, M. and J. Warner. 2006. 'Hydro-hegemony: A Framework for Analysis for Transboundary Water Conflicts', *Water Policy* 8(5): 435–60.

Zisser, E. 2003. 'The Mediterranenan Idea in Syria and Lebanon: Between Territorial Nationalism and Pan-Arabism', *Mediterranean Historical Review* 18(1): 76–90.

Zug, S. 2013. 'Between Capital Exchange and Moral Entitlements: Integrating Morality in Bourdieu's Theory of Practice to Understand Water Gifts in Khartoum, Sudan', Ph.D. dissertation. Fribourg: University of Fribourg.

Contributors

Zahir M. Abdal-Kareem is a Ph.D. researcher at the Max Planck Institute for Social Anthropology and at the Martin Luther University in Halle, Germany. He is also a researcher at the International Max Planck School on Retaliation, Mediation and Punishment (REMEP) and a lecturer at the Department of Sociology and Social Anthropology, Faculty of Economic and Social Studies, at the University of Khartoum. His Ph.D. project deals with 'Identification and Conflict in Gedaref State, Eastern Sudan: Resource Contestation, Livelihood Transformation and Ethnic Polarization'. His research interests include integration and conflict, ethnicity, and mechanisms of conflict resolution in Sudan with a particular focus on Darfur and Eastern regions.

Ashraf Abdelhay holds a B.A. (honours) in linguistics from the University of Khartoum and an M.Sc. and Ph.D. in applied linguistics from the University of Edinburgh. His research interests lie in the area of language planning and policy, focusing on the links between language, ideology and power relations. He was an ESRC postdoctoral fellow at the Department of Middle Eastern Studies, University of Cambridge (2009–10). He is currently a postdoctoral associate at Clare Hall College, University of Cambridge.

Musa A. Abdul-Jalil is an associate professor in the Department of Sociology and Social Anthropology at the University of Khartoum, Sudan. His research and publications have focused mainly on Darfur and covered the areas of ethnicity, migration, local-level politics, legal anthropology, customary land tenure and traditional mechanisms for conflict management. His recently published works include 'Power-Sharing and Ethnic Mobilization: The Role of Schoolteachers in Conflict Management in North Darfur', in S.M. Hassan and C.E. Ray (eds), *Darfur and the Crisis of Governance* *in Sudan: A Critical Reader,* New York: Cornell University Press and the Prince Claus Fund Library (2009).

Al-Amin Abu-Manga holds a Ph.D. in African languages and linguistics from the University of Marburg, Germany. He has been the head of the Department of Sudanese and African Languages, Institute of African and Asian Studies, at the University of Khartoum for several years and is the former director of the Institute of African and Asian Studies. He is presently the chairman of the Council for the Development and Promotion of the National Languages. He has worked extensively on language contact (between Arabic, Fulfulde and Hausa) and on the settlement of West Africans in Sudan. He has published nine books as author or coauthor and seven others as editor, as well as more than forty articles.

Luisa Arango is a Ph.D. candidate in anthropology at the University of Paris 8, France. Her research issues focus on the interaction between social networks and water management particularly in urban milieus, with special attention paid to the relationships between local populations and the state and to the dynamics related to water commoditization. She did fieldwork in Colombia (Caribbean islands and the city of Cartagena) and in Sudan (Greater Khartoum, Deim and Tuti Island) and develops a comparative anthropological approach to issues of resource access and management.

Munzoul A.M. Assal is professor of social anthropology and director of the Graduates Affairs Administration at the University of Khartoum. Prior to joining the Anthropology Department in Khartoum he was a research fellow at the Department of Social Anthropology, University of Bergen, Norway, where he obtained his Ph.D. His research focuses on refugees, internally displaced persons and urban issues. His major publications include *Diaspora within and without Africa: Heterogeneity, Homogeneity, Variation* (coedited with Leif Manger, 2006); *Sticky Labels or Rich Ambiguities? Diaspora and Challenges of Homemaking for Somalis and Sudanese in Norway* (2004); and forthcoming *Fifty Years of Anthropology in Sudan: Past, Present and Future* (coedited with Musa Abdul-Jalil, 2015).

Barbara Casciarri holds a Ph.D. in ethnology and social anthropology from the Ecole des Hautes Etudes en Sciences Sociales (EHESS) in Paris, France. She did fieldwork focusing on economic and political anthropology issues among pastoral Arab-speaking groups of Sudan (1989–2014) and on the relationship between Berber-speaking pastoralists and Arab-speaking farmers in southeastern Morocco (2000–6). She was the coordinator of the CEDEJ in Khartoum between 2006 and 2009. Since 2004 she is associate professor at the Department of Sociology, University of Paris 8, France, and researcher at the LAVUE – UMR 7218. She edited, with A.M. Ahmed, a special issue of *Nomadic Peoples,* volume 13, number 1 (2009), 'Pastoralists Under Pressure in Present-Day Sudan', and, with M. Van Aken, a special issue of *Journal des anthropologues,* volume 132–33 (2013), 'Anthropology and Water(s)'. She was the scientific coordinator of two ANR projects in Sudan, WAMAKHAIR (2008–12) and ANDROMAQUE (2011–14), and since 2009 she is responsible for the scientific agreement between the Faculty of Economic and Social Studies, University of Khartoum, and University of Paris 8.

Agnès de Geoffroy holds a Ph.D. in geopolitics from the University of Paris 8, France, and is associated researcher at the Centre de Recherches et Analyses Géopolitiques (CRAG) at the same university. Between 2010 and 2013 she coordinated the activities of the CEDEJ in Khartoum. Her main research topics deal with forced displacement issues in relation to urbanization dynamics, and her fieldwork focuses mainly on Sudan and Colombia. As a consultant for humanitarian aid organizations and development agencies, she did several missions in Afghanistan, Cambodia, the Central African Republic, Somalia and Chad.

Alice Franck is associate professor of geography at Paris 1 Panthéon-Sorbonne University. After a Ph.D. research on urban agriculture in Greater Khartoum, Sudan, her research looks at urban landed dynamics and agricultural land in particular. Within the recent context of the Sudanese capital city's urban development, analysing land property conflicts is one of the core points of her research. Since 2014 she is the coordinator of the CEDEJ in Khartoum.

Maria Gabrielsen Jumbert holds a Ph.D. in international relations from the Institute of Political Studies (Sciences Po) in Paris, France. She is a senior researcher at the Peace Research Institute Oslo (PRIO) in Oslo, Norway, and teaches at the Institute of Political Studies in Lille, France, where she is attached to the master's programme in conflict analysis and peace building.

François Ireton is a socioeconomist and researcher at the French National Center of Scientific Research (CNRS), working in the Centre Jacques Berque, Rabat, Morocco. He spent many years in Egypt and Sudan, doing research on topics like agricultural transformations, peasantry differentiation and rural poverty. He is a member of the editorial board of *Revue Tiers Monde* and coordinates a seminar entitled 'Issues on Social Policies and Reforms in MENA' at the EHESS, Paris. He has coedited the books *Dynamiques de la pauvreté en Afrique du Nord et au Moyen Orient* (Paris: Karthala, 2005) and *L'Egypte au présent. Inventaire d'une société avant révolution* (Paris: Actes Sud, 2011).

Elsamawal Khalil Makki is assistant professor and dean at the REED School (Rural Extension Education and Development), Ahfad University for Women, Omdurman, Sudan. He is involved in several scientific international collaborations (France, Germany, Switzerland) and in the training of scholars, especially in a gendered approach to development issues in urban and rural Sudan.

Stefano Manfredi is a CNRS junior researcher at the SEDYL-CELIA in Villejuif, France. He obtained an M.A. in African linguistics in 2005 with a work focusing on Juba Arabic (fieldwork among Sudanese community in Cairo) and a Ph.D. in African linguistics in 2010 with a thesis on Kordofanian Baggara Arabic. His main fields of interest are the description and the comparison of Arabic dialects and Arabic-based pidgins and creoles, contact linguistics and sociolinguistics in Sudan and South Sudan.

Roland Marchal is a CNRS researcher at the CERI-Sciences Po in Paris, France. His research focuses on the economy of conflicts in sub-Saharan Africa and the Horn, the politics of the great powers in the African continent and new actors in Africa (China, India, Brazil, Korea).

Catherine Miller holds a Ph.D. in Arabic sociolinguistics from the University of Sorbonne, Paris, France. She is a senior researcher within the CNRS and is presently linked with the Institute of Research and Studies on Muslim and Arab words (IREMAM) University of Aix-Marseille. She has worked for several years in Sudan. Her research interests cover language change, language contact, ethnic identity and language policy. She has published five books as coauthor or editor and more than fifty articles on Sudan, Egypt and, presently, Morocco.

Giorgio Musso is a postdoctoral researcher of African history and institutions at the University of Genoa, Italy, Department of Political Sciences, and teaches a course on Politics and Society in Africa at the Collège Universitaire de Sciences Po, Campus Moyen-Orient/Méditerranée, Menton, France. In 2013, he has been elected in the board of directors of the Italian Society for Middle Eastern Studies (SeSaMO). He obtained a Ph.D. in democracy and human rights at the University of Genoa in 2010 with a dissertation on the history of the Sudanese Islamist movement, which is being revised by the author to become a publication soon. He has conducted extensive fieldwork in Sudan and collaborates actively with the CEDEJ in Khartoum and several international academic institutions.

Irene Panozzo is a political adviser to the European Union Special Representative for the Horn of Africa and is based in Juba. Prior to this, she was lecturer at the University of Trieste, Italy, and 2011 Leverhulme visiting fellow at the University of Durham, U.K. She holds a Ph.D. in history, institutions and international relations of non-European countries from the University of Pisa, Italy. Her research work focuses on the history of global North-South relationships. She published two books on Sudan (2000, 2005) and coauthored the volume *China's 'Safari' in Africa* (2007). She has cooperated with Italian and foreign research centres (Centro Studi Politica Internazionale-CeSPI, Society for International Development, CEDEJ Khartoum), on issues related to Sudan. The views expressed in her article in this volume are her own's.

Abdalbasit Saeed is a sociocultural anthropologist. He graduated from the Faculty of Economic and Social Studies in 1971 and obtained an M.A. in 1978 from the Institute of African and Asian Studies at the University of Khartoum. He earned a Ph.D. in 1982 in sociocultural anthropology from the Faculty of Liberal Arts, University of Connecticut. He is currently engaged as the African coordinator for a German-African joint research project, Sustainable Use of Natural Resources and Peace in Pastoralist Regions in Africa (SUNARPA). As an independent consultant, he was engaged in various interdisciplinary teams of national and international experts for studying pastoral and other rural groups' development issues in Sennar, Blue Nile, White Nile, North Kordofan and South Kordofan.

Iris Seri-Hersch holds a Ph.D. (2012) in Middle Eastern and African history from Aix-Marseille Université, France. From 2012 to 2014 she was a Swiss National Science Foundation postdoctoral fellow. Since 2014 she is an Assistant Professor at the Department of Middle East Studies, Aix-Marseille Université. She specializes in the modern history of Sudan and Palestine/Israel. Her research interests include circulations and empires, education, oral history and social memory, and historiographical practices in and about the modern Middle East. She has published academic articles on Mahdist Sudan, education in colonial Sudan and the British Empire, Sudan Studies, and the history and memory of the Arab Israeli village of Jisr al-Zarqa.

Harry Verhoeven is a postdoctoral fellow at the Department of Politics and International Relations, University of Oxford, and a junior research fellow at Wolfson College. He is also the Convenor of the Oxford University China-Africa Network (OUCAN). He is the author of *Water, Civilisation and Power in Sudan: The Political Economy of Military-Islamist State-Building* (Cambridge University Press, 2015). He holds prior degrees from Gent University and the London School of Economics and Political Science and completed his doctorate at St Cross College, University of Oxford. From January 2015, he will be based in Qatar as an Assistant-Professor in Comparative Politics and International Relations at the School of Foreign Service of Georgetown University.

Index

www.ingramcontent.com/pod-product-compliance
Lightning Source LLC
Chambersburg PA
CBHW070901030426
42336CB00014BA/2274